FUNDAMENTAL RIGHTS IN THE EU

This collection joins the new and expanding scholarship on the protection of fundamental rights in Europe and reflects on the relationship between the Court of Justice of the European Union (CJEU) and the European Court of Human Rights (ECtHR). The book questions whether the changes introduced by the Lisbon Treaty align the CJEU to the ECtHR's interpretation and methods, triggering different processes of institutionalisation within a coherent European system. These issues are explored through a contextual analysis of areas of law such as equality rights in employment law, citizenship and migration, internet law and access to justice. This volume includes perspectives from the scholarly community as well as practitioners, judges and European policy makers. It also examines the state of accession of the EU to the European Convention on Human Rights (ECHR) and considers the legal implications of the interactions of the two courts for the protection of the fundamental rights of EU citizens and individuals legally residing in Europe.

The volume is essential reading for practitioners, judges, European policy makers and members of the scholarly community working in this area of law.

Volume 53 in the Series Modern Studies in European Law

Modern Studies in European Law
Recent titles in this series:

The Legitimacy of Family Rights in Strasbourg Case Law:
Living Instrument or Extinguished Sovereignty?
Carmen Draghici

Strengthening the Rule of Law in Europe:
From a Common Concept to Mechanisms of Implementation
Edited by Werner Schroeder

The Pluralist Character of the European Economic Constitution
Clemens Kaupa

Exceptions from EU Free Movement Law
Edited by Panos Koutrakos, Niamh Nic Shuibhne and Phil Syrpis

Reconceptualising European Equality Law: A Comparative Institutional Analysis
Johanna Croon-Gestefeld

Marketing and Advertising Law in a Process of Harmonization
Edited by Ulf Bernitz and Caroline Heide-Jörgensen

The Fundamental Right to Data Protection:
Normative Value in the Context of Counter-Terrorism Surveillance
Maria Tzanou

Republican Europe
Anna Kocharov

Family Reunification in the EU
Chiara Berneri

EU Liability and International Economic Law
Armin Steinbach

The EU and Nanotechnologies: A Critical Analysis
Tanja Ehnert

Human Rights Between Law and Politics:
The Margin of Appreciation in Post-National Contexts
Edited by Petr Agha

The European Union and Social Security Law
Jaan Paju

The Rule of Law in the European Union: The Internal Dimension
Theodore Konstadinides

For the complete list of titles in this series, see
'Modern Studies in European Law' link at
www.bloomsburyprofessional.com/uk/series/modern-studies-in-european-law

Fundamental Rights in the EU

A Matter for Two Courts

Edited by
Sonia Morano-Foadi
and
Lucy Vickers

•HART•
PUBLISHING
OXFORD AND PORTLAND, OREGON
2017

Hart Publishing
An imprint of Bloomsbury Publishing Plc

Hart Publishing Ltd
Kemp House
Chawley Park
Cumnor Hill
Oxford OX2 9PH
UK

Bloomsbury Publishing Plc
50 Bedford Square
London
WC1B 3DP
UK

www.hartpub.co.uk
www.bloomsbury.com

Published in North America (US and Canada) by
Hart Publishing
c/o International Specialized Book Services
920 NE 58th Avenue, Suite 300
Portland, OR 97213-3786
USA

www.isbs.com

First published in hardback, 2015
Paperback edition, 2017

British Library Cataloguing-in-Publication Data
A catalogue record for this book is available from the British Library.

ISBN: PB: 978-1-50991-547-7
HB: 978-1-84946-707-0

Typeset by Compuscript Ltd, Shannon
Printed and bound in Great Britain by
Lightning Source UK Ltd

Table of Contents

PART II

Biographies

Stelios Andreadakis

Stelios Andreadakis (LLM, PhD) is a Lecturer in Law in the School of Law of the University of Leicester. Prior to his appointment at Leicester, Stelios has worked as a lecturer (2008–2011) and senior lecturer (2011–2013) at Oxford Brookes University. He has also worked as a Teaching Assistant and a Research Assistant in a number of projects at the University of Leicester, while pursuing his PhD studies at the same institution. Dr Andreadakis completed his undergraduate studies at the School of Legal Studies of the Kapodestreian University of Athens in Greece, obtaining his degree in 2004. He then moved to the UK, where he studied for the LLM degree in International Commercial Law at the University of Leicester. Dr Andreadakis is a qualified lawyer, non-practising member of the Bar Association of Athens since 2004 and a member of the Higher Education Academy since 2009. Dr Andreadakis' main research interests are in the areas of corporate law and EU law. He is particularly interested in corporate governance, exploring aspects of regulation of companies, corporate theories, the operation of financial markets and the role of scandals in the introduction of new legislation. Stelios is currently working on a British Academy-funded project on the accession of the EU to the European Convention on Human Rights, exploring the process of the negotiation process, the role of the judiciary and policy-makers as well as the future of European integration.

Lorna Gillies

Lorna Gillies is a Senior Lecturer in Law at the School of Law, University of Leicester. Lorna's principal research interests focus on the pragmatic aspects of commercial international private law/conflict of laws and the theoretical influence of the EU on the reform and development of international private law. She has research expertise in jurisdiction and choice of law aspects of electronic commerce (Ashgate, 2008) and has published in the *Journal of Private International Law*, *International and Comparative Law Quarterly* and the *Yearbook of Private International Law*. Her early work was referenced by Advocate General Trstenjak in Cases C-585/08 (*Pammer*) and C-144/09 (*Hotel Alpenhof*) (18 May 2010).

Niilo Jääskinen

Niilo Jääskinen wasborn in 1958. He studied for his Doctor of Laws at the University of Helsinki. Niilo has held the following positions: Lecturer at the University of Helsinki (1980–1986); Legal Secretary and acting judge at the District Court, Rovaniemi (1983–1984); Legal Adviser (1987–1989), and subsequently Head of the European Law Section (1990–1995) at the Ministry of Justice; Legal Adviser at the Ministry of Foreign Affairs (1989–1990); Adviser, and Clerk for European Affairs, of the Grand Committee of the Finnish Parliament (1995–2000); acting judge (July 2000 to December 2002), then judge (January 2003 to September 2009) at the Supreme Administrative Court. In addition, Niilo was responsible for legal and institutional questions during the negotiations for the accession of the Republic of Finland to the EU. Since 7 October 2009, he has served as Advocate General at the Court of Justice.

Titia Loenen

Titia Loenen (PhD) is Professor of Human rights and Diversity at Leiden University. She holds degrees in history and law from this same university. Her research covers human rights, equality theory and international, European and Dutch non-discrimination law. She is now focusing on gender and cultural and religious pluralism. Titia takes an international and comparative perspective. Her recent work includes research on the interaction and overlap between human rights protection in this area under the European Convention of Human Rights and EU law.

Sonia Morano-Foadi

Sonia Morano-Foadi is Reader in Law at the School of Law, Oxford Brookes University where she also teaches EU law and immigration and asylum. She holds a *Laurea cum Laude* in Law and a *Specializzazione* in EU law awarded by the University of Bari, Italy. She was Lecturer in Law at the School of Law of the University of Leeds. Her research focuses on the relationship between citizenship, migration and fundamental rights in the context of an enlarging EU. It looks at EU citizens and third-country nationals' (TCNs) migrant workers and family members. She has been working in the field of EU citizenship and migration for around 15 years and has published high quality international standard papers, articles and book chapters. She is co-editor of the book *Integration for Third-Country Nationals: The Equality Challenge* (Edward Elgar Publishing, November 2012).

Jörg Polakiewicz

Jörg Polakiewicz has been the Director of Legal Advice and Public International Law (*Jurisconsult*) of the Council of Europe since 1 October 2013. Between 2010 and 2013, he was head of the human rights development department in the Council of Europe, overseeing the Council's intergovernmental and cooperation work related to human rights, including reform of the European Court of Human Rights, accession of the EU to the European Convention on Human Rights, and capacity-building activities in Eastern and Central Europe.

Between 2008 and 2010, he was head of the law reform department, covering judicial cooperation and standard-setting in criminal, civil and public law. During this period he served as secretary to the committee set up under the Budapest Convention on Cybercrime (T-CY) and oversaw the launching of the modernisation of data protection Convention 108.

Jörg joined the Council of Europe in 1993, working on constitutional reform in Eastern and Central Europe (with the European Commission for Democracy through Law—Venice Commission), and subsequently in the Council of Europe's legal service and human rights law and policy division.

He is also a Professor at the Europa-Institut of the University of the Saarland in Saarbrücken. From 1986 to 1993, he was a research fellow at the Max Planck Institute for Comparative Public and International Law in Heidelberg. In addition to writing numerous articles on international, European and constitutional law, he is co-editor of *Fundamental Rights in Europe* (Oxford University Press, 2001), author of *Treaty-making in the Council of Europe* (Council of Europe Publishing, 1999) and *The Obligations of States arising from the Judgments of the European Court of Human Rights* (Springer) which was published in German in 1993.

Oreste Pollicino

Oreste Pollicino is an Associate Professor at the Department of Law of Bocconi University in Milan where he gained his PhD in constitutional law in 2004. His areas of research expertise include European and comparative constitutional law, media law and internet law. He is the editor of the *International Journal of Communications Law and Policy*, as well as an editorial committee member of the Observatory of European and Comparative Private Law on conformity to fundamental laws in Europe. He is also the founder and managing director of two Italian blogs (diritticomparati.it and medialaws.eu) and has authored four monographs and numerous essays in the areas of comparative law, European constitutional law and media law. He is at the moment under contract with Hart Publishing to write a monograph entitled 'Protection of Fundamental Rights in the Internet and Judicial Interaction; a Comparative Constitutional Perspective'.

Dragoljub Popović

Dragoljub Popović was born on 25 July 1951 in Belgrade, Serbia. He completed his law studies and Master of Laws at the University of Belgrade from 1970 to 1974 and from 1974 to 1976, respectively. He then practised law in two commercial enterprises from 1976 to 1980. In 1984, Popović gained his law doctorate at the University of Belgrade, and then obtained his Third cycle degree in Comparative Law at the International Faculty of Comparative Law, Brussels, Belgium, the following year.

Dragoljub became a Lecturer of Legal and Constitutional History and Comparative Law at the Law School of Belgrade University from 1980 to 1998 (Professor, from 1995). He then practised as an Attorney at Law in a legal office in Belgrade from 1998 to 2001. Popović then returned to academia in 2001 as a visiting Professor at the Institute of Federalism of the University of

Fribourg, Switzerland. Notably, Popović was appointed Ambassador of Serbia and Montenegro to Switzerland, from 2001 to 2004. From 2004 to 2005, he was a Professor of Constitutional Law and Comparative Law at the Law School of the Union University of Belgrade, and is still affiliated to the University, teaching human rights law in a joint programme with Washington and Lee University from Lexington (Virginia) as of 2010.

Since 26 January 2005, Dragoljub has served as a judge of the European Court of Human Rights. He was also President of the Serbian Association of Constitutionalists from 2005 to 2007.

Kristi Raba

Kristi Raba (BA, LLM) studied law at Tartu Univerisity in Estonia and at Vrije Universiteit Brussel in Belgium. She has worked for the Ministry of Justice of Estonia in the EU law department. In 2000 the Ministry posted Kristi to work in Brussels for the accession negotiations of Estonia to the EU, in the fields of judicial cooperation in civil and criminal matters, judicial reform and company law. Since 2004 she has worked for the General Secretariat of the Council. She first dealt with negotiations in the field of judicial cooperation in civil and commercial matters. She then worked on e-Justice and the setting up of the European e-Justice portal. Currently, she works in the Fundamental Rights and Data Protection unit and deals with the Council Working Party on Fundmental Rights, Citizens' Rights and Free Movement of Persons.

Samantha Velluti

Samantha Velluti (LLB, LLM, PhD) is Reader in EU Law at Lincoln Law School, UK. Previously, she was Lecturer in Law at the School of Law of the University of Manchester and the University of Liverpool.

Dr Velluti has researched extensively in European governance with a particular focus on the relationship between new governance, law and constitutionalism, including the role of the Court of Justice of the EU, in the policy areas of EU sex equality, employment, immigration and asylum. Her current research interests are in the promotion of human rights and International Labour Organization (ILO) standards in the EU's Common Commercial Policy.

Her publications in the field of asylum and human rights include a volume entitled *Reforming the Common European Asylum System—Legislative Developments and Judicial Activism of the European Courts*, published by Springer.

Lucy Vickers

Lucy Vickers is Professor of Law at Oxford Brookes University. Her main research area is the protection of human rights within the workplace, with a focus on freedom of speech and religious freedom. She is the author of *Freedom of Speech and Employment* (Oxford University Press, 2002), *Religious Freedom,*

Religious Discrimination and the Workplace, (Hart Publishing, 2008), and a report for the European Commission on Religion and Belief Discrimination in Employment—The EU Law (2007).

Wolfgang Weiß

Wolfgang Weiß was born in 1966 and studied law and economics at the University of Bayreuth, Germany, where he also received his doctorate in law and his habilitation. He holds a Chair in Public Law, European Law and Public International Law at the German University of Administrative Sciences in Speyer. He is also affiliated with Oxford Brookes University as an Honorary Research Fellow, where he was a Reader and Professor previously. Wolfgang's main research areas are EU constitutional and administrative law, World Trade Organization (WTO) law, public international law and German public law.

Robert Wintemute

Robert Wintemute is a Professor of Human Rights Law at King's College London, where he also teaches anti-discrimination law and EU law. He is originally from Calgary, Alberta, Canada. He studied law at McGill University, practised bankruptcy law in New York City, and completed his DPhil in human rights law at the University of Oxford. He is the author of *Sexual Orientation and Human Rights* (Oxford University Press, 1997), the editor of *Legal Recognition of Same-Sex Partnerships* (Hart Publishing, 2001), and the co-editor of *Confronting Homophobia in Europe* (Hart Publishing, 2012). Since 2000, he has participated in cases of discrimination against lesbian and gay parents or prospective parents, and against same-sex couples claiming the same rights as unmarried or married different-sex couples, in the European Court of Human Rights, the Court of Justice of the EU, the Inter-American Court of Human Rights, and the Supreme Courts of Argentina, Colombia and Massachusetts.

Prologue

The EU's Accession to the European Convention on Human Rights—A Matter of Coherence and Consistency

JÖRG POLAKIEWICZ*

THE LISBON TREATY, with its two complementary achievements of a legally-binding EU Charter of Fundamental Rights and a commitment by the EU to accede to the ECHR, marked a major step forward towards a stronger and more coherent system of fundamental rights protection. However, while the Charter deployed its legal effects immediately upon entry into force of the Lisbon Treaty on 1 December 2009, EU accession is still far from being completed.

Despite being an obligation under Article 6 (2) TEU, the merits and rationale for EU accession have been the object of much debate. After protracted negotiations, which lasted more than three years, the draft accession agreement was referred to the CJEU. It was encouraging to witness that during the pleadings on 5 and 6 May 2014, the representatives of the three EU institutions, as well as all intervening member states, argued that the draft accession agreement was in conformity with the requirements of EU law. Advocate General Kokott's comprehensive view of 13 June 2014 considered the agreement to be compatible on condition that some—mostly technical—adjustments are made. However, the CJEU concluded on 18 December 2014 that the accession agreement was not compatible with EU law.[1] While some amendments, required by the CJEU, are rather technical in nature and may be acceptable, others concern central issues such as the need to coordinate the EU Charter with the ECHR, EU legislation in the area of justice and home affairs (JHA) or the EU's common foreign and security policy (CFSP).

* Professor at the *Europainstitut* of the University of Saarbrücken and Director of Legal Advice and Public International Law (Legal Adviser), Council of Europe. This contribution was written in a strictly personal capacity and does not necessarily reflect the official position of the Council of Europe.

[1] CJEU, Opinion 2/13 (Full Court) (18 December 2014).

THE NEED FOR COHERENCE AND CONSISTENCY IN FUNDAMENTAL RIGHTS PROTECTION

EU accession to the ECHR will enhance consistency in the protection of human rights all over Europe, fostering a harmonious development of the relevant case-law of the ECtHR and the CJEU. Citizens and judicial authorities are confronted with different legally-binding texts to be applied simultaneously, to some extent with different standards, structures, terminology and qualifications:

— their own domestic law, including, in most cases, the national constitution's fundamental rights catalogue;
— the ECHR and its protocols;
— the EU law, in particular the EU Charter of Fundamental Rights.

How to best describe the resulting complexity? At the opening of the judicial year on 31 January 2014 in Strasbourg, the President of the German Federal Constitutional Court, Andreas Voßkuhle, compared the delicate balance between the various institutions to a mobile—a kinetic sculpture consisting of an ensemble of balanced parts that move but are connected by strings or wire.[2] Another metaphor uses the musical counterpoint, the relationship between voices that are interdependent harmonically and yet are independent in rhythm and contour.[3] In any case, the idea of a Kelsian-type hierarchical pyramid is generally rejected.

Clarity about the applicable standards and their coherence is crucial, in particular for domestic courts and other judicial authorities that play a central role, not only as 'Union courts of ordinary jurisdiction', but also as 'Convention courts of ordinary jurisdiction'. There is certainly a high degree of consensus among European and national constitutional and supreme courts. To give just one example, on 19 February 2013, the ECtHR and the German Federal Constitutional Court recognised simultaneously, albeit with a different reasoning, adoption rights of same-sex couples. At the same time, the large degree of overlap between the various legal instruments may occasionally generate competition, sometimes even tensions, between their respective ultimate interpreters. Different approaches can be mutually enriching as long as the various actors base their interaction on a set of shared principles.

The EU Charter already contains safeguards to ensure that its rights should be interpreted consistently with the ECHR. Article 52 (3) seeks to ensure the necessary consistency between the Charter and the ECHR by establishing the rule that, insofar as the rights in the Charter correspond to rights guaranteed under the ECHR, the meaning and scope of those rights, including authorised limitations,

[2] A Voßkuhle 'Pyramid or Mobile?'—Human Rights Protection by the European Constitutional Courts' Opening of the Judicial Year 2014 at the European Court of Human Rights Strasbourg, 31 January 2014, available at http://www.echr.coe.int/Documents/Speech_20140131_Vosskuhle_ENG.pdf.

[3] MP Maduro 'Contrapunctual Law: Europe's Constitutional Pluralism in Action' in N Walker (ed) *Sovereignty in Transition* (Oxford, Hart, 2003) 501–37.

should be the same as those laid down by the ECHR. Article 53 provides that nothing in the Charter may be interpreted as restricting or adversely affecting the human rights and fundamental freedoms recognised in international agreements, such as, in particular, the ECHR, and national constitutions.

In Opinion 2/13, the CJEU confirms its previous case-law insisting that 'the unity, primacy and effectiveness of EU law' must not be affected by EU accession. The CJEU extends to the ECHR its long-standing principle that the primacy of EU law prevents member states from having higher or even different human rights standards where EU law has fully harmonised the matters concerned. In 2013, in *Melloni*, the CJEU had ruled that once the EU has adopted a common fundamental rights standard, EU member states are no longer entitled to apply higher standards, even when provided for in national constitutions.[4] According to the CJEU, as Article 53 ECHR allows Contracting Parties to the ECHR to apply higher standards of protection than those guaranteed by the ECHR,

> that provision should be coordinated with Article 53 of the Charter ... so that the power granted to member states by Article 53 of the ECHR is limited—with respect to the rights recognised by the Charter that correspond to those guaranteed by the ECHR—to that which is necessary to ensure that the level of protection provided for by the Charter and the primacy, unity and effectiveness of EU law are not compromised.[5]

Human rights are based on universal values transcending the various domestic legal orders. In Europe, that idea has found expression in the ECHR and in the setting-up of the ECtHR as an independent international supervisory body. The ECHR and Union law are based on the same values and principles. More fundamentally, the very utility of using the 'high' and 'low', maximal and minimal, nomenclature can be questioned in the context of human rights protection.[6] Human rights entail choices as to the appropriate balance between the interests of individuals against those of other individuals or the community. The quantification of levels of protection based on generally worded provisions of fundamental rights catalogues often proves difficult. Ronald Dworkin observed pertinently that 'it is very difficult to think of liberty as a commodity.'[7]

A 'race to the top', seeking ever higher standards makes little sense in cases of competing human-rights interests which must be reconciled, such as freedom of expression versus privacy or the right to property versus the right to strike. In such multipolar relations, extending the protection of one right or attaching more weight to it, will inevitably have the consequence of restricting the right of others.

[4] C-399/11 *Stefano Melloni v Ministerio Fiscal* (26 February 2013). See also C-206/13 *Cruciano Siragusa v Regione Sicilia—Soprintendenza Beni Culturali e Ambientali di Palermo* (6 March 2013).

[5] CJEU (n 1) para 189.

[6] JHH Weiler 'Fundamental Rights and Fundamental Boundaries: On Standards and Values in the Protection of Human Rights' (1995), reprinted in JHH Weiler *The Constitution of Europe: do the New Clothes Have an Emperor? and other essays on European integration* (Cambridge, Cambridge University Press, 1999) 107–16.

[7] R Dworkin *Taking Rights Seriously* (Cambridge, MA, Harvard University Press 1977) 270.

Where competing rights are at stake, the aim should be to strike a balance, trying to reconcile competing rights, so that the limitation on the one right is equal to the limitation on the other, taking into account the circumstances of each case.

A major goal pursued by accession is to close existing gaps in judicial protection by giving European citizens the same protection vis-a-vis acts of the Union as they presently enjoy vis-a-vis all EU member states. In that context, the CJEU's objection regarding JHA's matters appears problematic. The CJEU argues that the ECtHR's external scrutiny would be incompatible with the obligation of mutual trust between EU member states and accession thus liable to upset the underlying balance of the EU and to undermine the autonomy of EU law.[8] This reasoning seems questionable even from a purely EU law perspective.[9] While the 'values' of the EU include human rights and the rule of law, there is no mention of the primacy of EU law, of mutual trust in JHA matters, or of preventing any international court from exercising jurisdiction over EU-related matters. Under the EU treaties, mutual recognition is merely a 'principle' to be used to facilitate judicial cooperation among EU member states. It should not be weighed against, or, even worse, used to escape compliance with legal obligations to respect fundamental rights under EU primary law.

Respect for fundamental rights constitutes a key component of the area of freedom, security and justice, as explicitly foreseen by Article 67 (1) TFEU. It is noteworthy that the EU's own Fundamental Rights Agency advocates the use of fundamental rights-based refusal grounds in EU legislation providing for mutual recognition.[10] More significantly, in a recent JHA legal instrument, Directive 2014/41/EU on the European Investigation Order, non-compliance with fundamental rights was explicitly provided for as a refusal ground.

In the *NS* case, the CJEU itself was prepared to give precedence to fundamental rights over the obligations of member states to comply with the provisions of the Dublin II Regulation regarding the return of asylum seekers to their first country of entry into the EU. The CJEU recognised that member states must not return asylum seekers when systemic deficiencies in the asylum procedure and in the reception conditions of the country to which they would be returned result in a real risk of asylum seekers being subjected to inhuman or degrading treatment within the meaning of Article 4 of the Charter.[11] As the ECtHR Grand chamber judgment in *MSS v Greece and Belgium* 11 months earlier,[12] the CJEU found that there existed such systemic flaws in Greece.

[8] CJEU (n 1) para 194.

[9] See J Polakiewicz 'EU law and the ECHR: Will the European Union's accession square the circle?' (2013) 592 *European Human Rights Law Review* 602–05.

[10] Opinion of the European Union Agency for Fundamental Rights on the draft Directive regarding the European Investigation Order (February 2011) http://fra.europa.eu/sites/default/files/fra_uploads/1490-FRA-Opinion-EIO-Directive-15022011.pdf.

[11] Joined cases C-411/10 and C-493/10 *NS* (21 December 2011) para 94.

[12] Application no 30696/09, judgment of 21 January 2011.

For national constitutional and supreme courts, it is normal practice to review whether the unfettered application of ordinary legislation violates fundamental rights in individual cases. The UK Supreme Court, for example, held that surrender under a European Arrest Warrant may be refused if it constitutes a disproportionate interference with the mother and her children's rights under Article 8 ECHR. Depending on the circumstances of the case, the best interests of the child may, in a particular case, outweigh the very high public interest in surrender, in particular if the alleged offences are not particularly serious compared to the damage that would be caused to the children.[13] Why should this principle not apply in the EU's legal order?

EU member states are not immune from being found in violation of even the core human rights such as Article 3 ECHR, the prohibition of torture and inhuman and degrading treatment and punishment. A recent illustration of the different approaches of the two European courts is the ECtHR's *Tarakhel* judgment,[14] whose individualised assessment of the applicants' situation contrasts with the CJEU's defence of the Dublin system in the *Abdullahi* judgment.[15] These judgments show at the same time that even without accession JHA issues are already before the ECtHR. The challenge to the conception of mutual trust in JHA matters could hardly become more severe than it already is. Rather on the contrary, accession and a strong co-respondent mechanism provide the possibility for comprehensive external scrutiny of the JHA system as a whole, with the active participation of protagonists from both the supranational and the national levels, thereby enhancing both trust in the various mutual recognition systems and human rights protection for the individuals concerned. Exempting JHA matters from the scope of external control would be a curtailment of existing ECHR jurisdiction in one of the core areas where effective fundamental rights protection is most important.[16]

RECENT CJEU CASE LAW: TOWARDS A MERELY RESIDUAL ROLE OF THE ECHR?

In the past, the CJEU had explicitly recognised 'the special significance' of the ECHR as interpreted by the ECtHR.[17] Following the entry into force of the EU Charter, the use of human rights law in general and ECHR case law in particular has become more occasional and selective.

[13] *F-K v Polish Judicial Authority* [2012] UKSC 25; for extradition cases see *Norris v Government of the United States of America* (No 2) [2010] UKSC 9; *ZH (Tanzania) v Secretary of State for the Home Department* [2011] UKSC 4.

[14] *Tarakhel v Switzerland*, Application no 29217/12, judgment of 4 November 2014.

[15] Case C-394/12 *Shamso Abdullahi v Bundesasylamt* (10 December 2013).

[16] S Peers 'The CJEU and the EU's accession to the ECHR: a clear and present danger to human rights protection' Blog on EU Law Analysis, available at http://eulawanalysis.blogspot.fr/2014/12/the-cjeu-and-eus-accession-to-echr.html, accessed on 15 January 2015.

[17] Case C–305/05 *Ordre des barreaux francophones et germanophone and Others* [2007] ECR I–5305, para 29 and case-law cited, notably Case C-29/69 Stauder [1969] ECR 419; Case C-274/99 *Connolly v Commission* [2001] ECR I-1611; Joined Cases C-402/05 P and C-415/05 P *Kadi v Council* [2008] ECR I-6351, para 283.

In 2012, Professor Gráinne de Búrca conducted an analysis of all cases in which the CJEU and General Court—previously the Court of First Instance—had referred to the Charter since it has had binding effect.[18] During the period in question (December 2009 until 31 December 2012), the CJEU referred to the EU Charter in at least 122 cases. Out of those 122 cases, the CJEU referred to the ECHR in only 18 cases (with 10 of these involving mention or discussion of ECHR case law, the other 8 merely mentioning an ECHR provision). In none of the 122 cases was any other source of human rights jurisprudence or interpretation referred to, with the exception of a mention in a group of cases of the Refugee Convention and in one case of the Convention on the Rights of the Child. The Advocate General referred to the ECHR in 34 of these 122 cases and to the case law of the Strasbourg Court in 19 of the 122 cases, almost twice as many times as the Court. Professor Gráinne de Búrca also noted a trend towards dispensing with the need for an Advocate General's Opinion in 24 of the 122 cases. The General Court made references to the EU Charter in at least 37 cases. In 15 of these, the Court referred to a provision of the ECHR, and in 6 to case law of the ECtHR.

The research conducted by Professor Gráinne de Búrca confirms a trend in the CJEU's case law to interpret the provisions of the Charter in isolation from the jurisprudence emerging from other human rights instruments. The CJEU draws only sporadically on international human rights sources, insisting that it remains the final and authoritative arbiter of their meaning and impact within the EU. The emerging pattern seems to suggest a kind of division of labour, with the ECHR having only residual application where EU law applies. The mere existence of two different texts to be interpreted by two distinct Courts operating in very different contexts is not conducive to legal certainty. It might ultimately lead to the existence of two sets of human or fundamental rights standards in a Europe where membership in the EU and the Council of Europe increasingly overlaps.

Referring to the EU Charter, the then President of the European Court of Human Rights, Luzius Wildhaber, had declared on 7 March 2000 before the Committee of Ministers of the Council of Europe that the main concern was

> to avoid a situation in which there are alternative, competing and potentially conflicting systems of human rights protection both within the Union and in the greater Europe. The duplication of protection systems runs the risk of weakening the overall protection offered and undermining legal certainty in this field.

The Committee of Ministers, on which all EU countries are represented, accepted this position unreservedly.[19] This is precisely why the Laeken Declaration (2001) and the subsequent EU Convention (2001–2003) and Intergovernmental Conferences (2003 and 2007) had established a *junktim* between the incorporation of the EU Charter into the Treaties and accession of the EU to the ECHR.

[18] G De Búrca 'After the EU Charter of Fundamental Rights: The Court of Justice as a Human Rights Adjudicator?' (2013) 20 *Maastricht Journal of European and Comparative Law* 168 et seq.

[19] See Committee of Ministers' reply to Parliamentary Assembly Recommendation 1439 (2000), adopted on 31 May 2000 at the 711th meeting of the Ministers' Deputies 21 HRLJ 188 (2000).

THE AUTONOMY OF EU LAW

In Opinion 2/13, the CJEU justifies its most important objections by reference to the autonomy of the EU's legal system. It is precisely respect for this autonomy and the role of the CJEU that have been advocated by the EU throughout the accession negotiations. The negotiators have taken those concerns seriously and have not spared any efforts in striking a fair balance between the respect for the autonomy of EU law and effective external scrutiny by the ECtHR, the declared objective of the whole exercise.

The concern that the ECtHR should not pronounce on the division of competences between the Union and its member states has surfaced on several occasions during the negotiations. It explains, for example, some of the complex wording used in respect of the co-respondent mechanism. The introduction of this mechanism is necessary because the legal systems of the EU and its member states do not merely overlap, they are intrinsically intertwined. Directly applicable Union law is primarily implemented, applied and enforced by national authorities.

With the accession of the EU, the unique situation arises that the Contracting Party enacting a legal act and the Contracting Party implementing that act may not be the same. It is necessary to provide for 'mechanisms necessary to ensure that … individual applications are correctly addressed to Member States and/or the Union, as appropriate.'[20] The co-respondent mechanism enables the EU to defend the compatibility with the ECHR of the arraigned legislative act. Any judgments in which a violation of ECHR rights has been found, will legally bind the co-respondents jointly and in solidarity, thus avoiding gaps in participation, accountability and enforceability.

The concern to prevent the ECtHR from pronouncing on the distribution of competences between the EU and its member states found expression in the rule that the EU cannot be forced to join the proceedings as a co-respondent. Article 3 (2) of the draft accession agreement states that the EU 'may become a co-respondent if it appears that such allegation calls into question the compatibility with the Convention of a provision of EU law.' This will typically be the case where an EU law provision leaves no discretion to a member state as to its implementation at the national level. The draft accession agreement specifies that the ECtHR may invite the EU to become co-respondent and the application of the mechanism will in any case require a decision by the ECtHR. The latter will, however, exercise only a plausibility control when assessing whether the conditions for the co-respondent mechanism are fulfilled (see Article 3 (5) of the draft accession agreement).

Where the finding of a violation arises, Article 3 (7) of the draft accession agreement foresees, in principle, joint responsibility of the respondent and the co-respondent. In this way, the ECtHR will not decide on the apportionment of responsibility as between the respondent and co-respondent, a decision which

[20] Article 1 (b) of Protocol No 8 to the Treaty on the Functioning of the European Union therefore required the accession agreement.

could require a rather detailed analysis of EU law and its application as well as of the division of competences between the EU and its member states, in particular when the breach derives from an omission.

Questions of attribution and responsibility are particularly complex in the context of the EU's common foreign and security policy (CFSP). Uniquely situated between intergovernmentalism and supranationality, this policy field enjoys a special status within EU law. With the exception of targeted sanctions (Article 275 (2) TFEU), the CJEU has no competence in this area. The draft accession agreement, on the other hand, does not exclude it from the jurisdiction of the ECtHR. In Opinion 2/13, the CJEU requires amendments that would curtail the role of the ECtHR to rule on acts adopted in the context of the CFSP (or amendments to EU treaties extending the CJEU's jurisdiction to this policy field). This point goes to the very heart of the compromise reached in the current version of the draft accession agreement. Creating an exception for CFSP matters in the draft accession agreement is difficult to reconcile with the idea of comprehensive and effective supervision by the ECtHR and the principle that the EU should accede to the ECHR on an equal footing with the other Contracting Parties.

When it comes to judicial protection, it must be recalled that legislative measures taken in the CFSP framework will only exceptionally affect the rights of individuals personally, directly and immediately in such a way that they can claim to be 'victims' of ECHR violation within the meaning of Article 34 ECHR. Concrete measures involving the use of force or detentions will typically be taken by the member states and consequently be subject to judicial review before national courts and ultimately, now, before the ECtHR. The attribution of responsibility in this context was one of the central issues in the negotiations. In its current practice, the ECtHR determines the responsibility for extraterritorial acts in the light of ECHR criteria, in particular the notion of effective control over territory and individuals (see among others *Al-Skeini*, *Al-Jedda*, *Behrami*, *Issa*, *Ilaşcu*, *Saramati* cases).[21]

However, in none of the cases so far decided by the ECtHR, has there been a specific rule on attribution of such acts or measures to either the international organisation concerned or its members. The draft accession agreement contains such a rule in Article 1 (4) providing that if an organ of a member state causes a breach of an ECHR obligation when implementing EU law, including with regard to matters related to the CFSP, the act will be attributed to that state. This rule is qualified in two respects. Firstly, it does not preclude the EU from being responsible as a co-respondent for an alleged violation of the ECHR. Secondly, acts, measures and omissions of the EU institutions, bodies, offices or agencies, or of persons acting on their behalf remain attributable to the EU in whichever context they occur, including with regard to matters related to the CFSP. Accepting an

[21] For full references of these cases see the ECtHR's factsheet 'Extra-territorial jurisdiction of States Parties to the European Convention on Human Rights', available at http://www.echr.coe.int/Documents/FS_Extra-territorial_jurisdiction_ENG.pdf (last accessed on 15 January 2015).

independent judicial control based on human rights will be a major achievement providing the Union's action with added legitimacy. Europeans, with their long tradition in human rights protection, are well placed to set an example for the international community.

THE CJEU'S MONOPOLY OF ULTIMATE INTERPRETATION OF EU LAW

In the debate on EU accession to the ECHR, it has been suggested that setting up a sequence of appeals from the CJEU to the ECtHR would leave the CJEU subordinate to a Council of Europe body. This argument overlooks the fact that the Strasbourg Court is no higher court than, for instance, the UK's Supreme Court or Germany's Federal Constitutional Court. It is simply a 'more specialised' court, responsible under the ECHR for '[ensuring] the observance of the engagements undertaken by the High Contracting Parties in the Convention and the Protocols thereto' (Article 19 ECHR). No one can claim that the German Federal Constitutional Court or the British Supreme Court neglect fundamental rights in their rulings. Like the CJEU, they have an excellent record and reputation. Nevertheless, the existence of European supervision, operating outside the national systems whose legal measures it examines, gives citizens a guarantee that their rights will be effectively protected.

Even after accession, the EU institutions, including the CJEU and the General Court, will be primarily responsible for ensuring that the rights enshrined in the ECHR are respected. The ECtHR would not be able to annul legislative acts or other measures taken by the EU, nor would it annul the CJEU's judgments. Its jurisdiction would be limited to cases raising issues involving the protection of fundamental and human rights. As for the other Contracting Parties, supervision by the ECtHR will remain subsidiary in character—a fact reflected, in particular, in the recognition of margins of appreciation.

From the intergovernmental conferences on the future of the ECtHR, held in İzmir (2011) and Brighton (2012), a clear message emerged inviting the ECtHR to show self-restraint over issues best dealt with by national courts and tribunals and democratically elected legislatures in the member states. The ECtHR should resist the 'spider's web temptation', the temptation of pretending to build, on the basis of the ECHR, a complete legal system where the national legal orders and, in the future, the EU's supranational legal order could feel 'trapped' or 'cornered'.[22] The subsidiarity principle and the margin of appreciation doctrine will in future be included in the Convention's preamble.[23]

[22] P Cruz Villalón 'Rights in Europe—The Crowded House' King's College London—Working Paper 01/2012, available at http://www.kcl.ac.uk/law/research/centres/european/research/CELWPEL-012012FINAL.pdf (accessed on 15 Janua 2015) 9–10.

[23] Article 1 of Protocol No 15 amending the Convention for the Protection of Human Rights and Fundamental Freedoms.

Sometimes described as being 'slippery and elusive as an eel', the margin of appreciation doctrine has been consistently applied by the ECtHR for more than 40 years. And yet, the ECtHR faces a continuous challenge to come up with meaningful tests for Convention compatibility, in particular as regards the proportionality of restrictions and the weighing of competing rights against each other. Such tests are taken up by national constitutional and supreme courts not because of hierarchical superiority but because of their persuasive authority.

The ECHR is an international instrument providing for the effective protection of a given number of rights, not a legal order in the same sense as that of the member states or the EU. A major challenge for the ECtHR is to define minimum standards while respecting the plurality of national and supranational fundamental rights provisions. When developing the ECHR standards further, the ECtHR increases the level of acceptance by demonstrating respect for national diversity. Such an approach is particularly warranted in cases raising sensitive moral or ethical issues on which no European consensus has been reached.

While it is certain that the ECtHR will continue to allow margins of appreciation also in respect of the EU and its supranational legal order, some—including a former ECtHR judge—have suggested that the ECtHR might endorse a wider margin of appreciation where the EU is concerned than the one given in relation to individual states, since an EU legal act already represents the product of harmonising European cooperation between 28 EU member states, (ie a majority of member states of the Council of Europe) and the legal act's human rights compliance will usually have been verified beforehand as well as by the other European Courts in Luxembourg.[24] Existing ECtHR case law provides ample evidence that it uses the margin of appreciation doctrine in such a way as to not unduly encroach upon the objectives of European integration (for example in *Michaud v France*).[25]

It is, however, significant that during the negotiations on EU accession, there has been no attempt to codify the so-called *Bosphorus* presumption in whatever form in the accession agreement. Recognising that the EU guarantees a level of fundamental rights protection equivalent to that of the ECHR, the ECtHR held in *Bosphorus* that ECHR compliance can be presumed when a state merely implements EU law, unless, in the circumstances of a particular case, it can be demonstrated that the protection of ECHR rights was 'manifestly deficient'.[26] This presumption acknowledges the fact that the EU is currently not bound by the ECHR. In the event of accession, it loses not only its raison d'être, it would also result in a double standard incompatible with the idea of equal footing. Why should the CJEU be allowed to hide behind the *Bosphorus* veil when all the national constitutional and supreme courts are subject to the full control of the ECtHR?

[24] L Garlicki 'The Relationship between the European Court of Justice and the European Court of Human Rights: The Strasbourg Perspective' in J Iliopoulos-Strangas & H Bauer (eds) *La nouvelle Union européenne* (Athens, Sakkoulas; Berlin, Berliner Wissenschafts-Verlag; Bruxelles, Bruylant, 2006) 127.

[25] *Michaud v France*, Application no 12323/11, judgment of 6 December 2012.

[26] *Bosphorus Hava Yollari Turizm ve Ticaret Anonim Şirketi v Ireland*, Application no 45036/98, Grand Chamber judgment of 30 June 2005.

CONCLUDING REMARKS

The European project will only remain credible if it rests on mutual respect and trust, good will and cooperation. For a mobile to work, the different parts of the system, not only the two European courts, but also the constitutional and supreme courts, have to go about their task with sensitivity in order to preserve the overall balance. All this requires not only sincere dialogue and willingness to engage substantially and transparently with the arguments used by 'other' courts, but also the recognition of certain common (minimum) standards which transcend both national and supranational legal orders.

I remain convinced that EU accession to the ECHR will eventually put in place the missing link in Europe's system of fundamental rights protection, guaranteeing consistency between the approaches of the EU and the Council of Europe. Only the combination of making the EU Charter legally binding and acceding to the ECHR can ultimately ensure effective protection for individuals, legal certainty and coherence in fundamental rights protection all over Europe.

1

Introduction—A Matter for Two Courts: The Fundamental Rights Question for the EU

SONIA MORANO-FOADI AND LUCY VICKERS

THE EU IS one of the oldest and most successful projects of economic integration at the regional level. However, its legal system has grown well beyond the boundaries set by the original treaties, both in terms of competences and supremacy over national laws.

The EU governing institutions have gradually and steadily increased their reach over time. In particular, the doctrine of supremacy and direct effect developed by the Court of Justice of the European Union (CJEU) have created a supranational entity where private litigants can invoke EU rules to challenge national laws conflicting with Union law. Both implicit or explicit extensions of the competences set out in the original treaties, have modified the architecture of the Union.[1] Thus, elements of supranationality have 'spilled over' into areas such as for example asylum and immigration that were, until recently, firmly managed through intergovernmental mechanisms. Moreover, parallel processes of policymaking, the so-called soft law tools, ie the Open Method of Coordination (OMC), voluntary exchange of good practices across the Member States, and involvement of the civil society, industrial and social partners in standard setting have been instilling elements of *Europeanisation* in areas traditionally controlled at national level.[2]

Although this increase in supranationality has been in evidence for some time, most recently it has been argued that the EU has entered a new era of integration inaugurated by the Lisbon Treaty and based on human rights.[3] The post-Lisbon era

[1] S Morano-Foadi, 'Fundamental Rights in Europe: "Constitutional" Dialogue between the Court of Justice of the EU and the European Court of Human Rights' (2013) 5(1) *Oñati Journal of Emergent Socio-Legal Studies* 64, at 64–88, at http://www.sortuz.org/content/pdfs2013/4%20Morano%20-%20human%20rights.pdf.

[2] S Morano-Foadi and F Duina, 'The Institutionalisation of Regional Trade Agreements Worldwide: New Dynamics and Future Perspectives' (2011) 17 *European Law Journal* 5, at 561–67.

[3] S Morano-Foadi and S Andreadakis, 'Reflection on the Architecture of the EU after the Treaty of Lisbon: The European Judicial Approach to Fundamental Rights' (2011) 17 *European Law Journal* 595, at 599.

is characterised by two developmental stages. The first stage is influenced by, on the one hand, the Charter of Fundamental Rights (the Charter) having a binding nature, as set out by Article 6(1) Treaty on European Union (TEU); and, on the other hand, by the extension of the CJEU's jurisdiction in areas such as asylum, immigration, judicial cooperation in civil affairs and criminal matters. The second stage might witness the EU's accession to the European Convention on Human Rights (ECHR), as the legal basis for accession is included in the Treaty.[4] This process is now on hold as the CJEU has declared, in its recent ruling, that the Accession Agreement is incompatible with EU law.[5]

Nonetheless, despite this setback in the process of accession, the two courts retain significant potential for dealing in a mutually compatible manner with the range of issues over which they both share concern. Thus, via the Charter, the CJEU retains a concern with human rights. Although the Charter states that it does not broaden the competences of the EU, its binding effect and the increase in human rights claims in the CJEU post-Lisbon case law, clearly offer the opportunity for a shift of the EU towards integration based on rights. The Court, in its role as 'a hero who has greatly advanced the cause of integration',[6] and in general, the EU institutions could contribute to this process.

As for the Council of Europe, in the fundamental rights realm, an institutional overlap between the EU and the Council of Europe can be seen. The original scope of the Council of Europe, an international organisation regulated by international law, has expanded covering political and civil rights included in the ECHR and economic and social rights contemplated in the Social Charter. The work of the European Court of Human Rights (ECtHR) in interpreting the Convention and having a final word in Europe on the violation of human rights raised by individuals against the States, undoubtedly introduces a significant supranational element to the nation state's dimension. As well as increasing the integration of the two European legal frameworks by joining the EU and Council of Europe's projects, and thus accepting *Europeanisation*, the implementation of the Lisbon Treaty also offered an impact on nation states, in particular by challenging their traditional autonomy and integrity. The new architecture of Europe has meant that there are now multiple agents at national and European levels claiming legal authority within the same geographical area. This raises questions around the *judiciary institutionalisation* itself and the *legitimacy and supremacy* of the competing autonomous legal systems.

This volume collates papers presented at two conferences,[7] which brought together scholars, judges and policymakers coming from different European

[4] See Art 6(2) TEU.

[5] Opinion of the Court (Full Court) of 18 December 2014 pursuant to Article 218(11) TFEU on the compatibility of the draft agreement with the EU and FEU Treaties, available at http://curia.europa.eu/juris/liste.jsf?num=C-2/13

[6] K Alter and S Meunier-Aitsahalia, 'Judicial Politics in the European Community' (1994) 26 *Comparative Political Studies* 535–61, 535–36.

[7] The first conference entitled 'Fundamental Rights in Europe: A Matter For Two Courts' held in Oxford on Friday 18 January 2013. As a follow-up activity a second dissemination event was held

countries to discuss the legal framework for the protection of fundamental rights in Europe and reflect on the relationship between the CJEU in Luxembourg and the ECtHR in Strasbourg. It examined the state of accession of the EU to the ECHR and considered the legal implications of the accession for the protection of the fundamental rights of EU citizens and legally residing individuals in Europe. This topic was explored, focusing on equality rights in employment law, citizenship and migration, fundamental freedom and access to justice.

The chapters in this collection address the above pressing challenges, and question whether the changes introduced by the Lisbon Treaty will affect institutional dynamics within the two European Courts similar in nature and extent to those found in the jurisprudence of the CJEU. They explore whether the changes will align the CJEU to the ECtHR's interpretation and methods triggering different processes of institutionalisation within a coherent European system.

The chapters also raise concerns in relation to the working of the Lisbon Treaty in paving the way for a dialectic adjustment to the EU human rights regime oscillating between continuity and change. They analyse the variety of judicial approaches used by the European Courts in specific human rights fields to predict the future rights regime in Europe.

In order to understand the background to the likely changes that would be required following accession, the EU's accession conditions to the ECHR are explored and an attempt made to trace the likely trajectory Europe is taking to strengthen human rights protection. Moreover, some of the chapters question how the EU itself is evolving in this new environment. These are more than academic questions as they point to dynamics that are bound to shape economic, political, and social realities affecting life in Europe.

The authors in this volume address a number of important and exciting themes and arguments. In particular the interaction between the two Courts in Europe; the fundamental rights quest in relation to equality in employment law; migration and citizenship, computer law, access to justice, judicial cooperation in civil and commercial matters and projections about whether the EU's accession to the ECHR is likely to happen. The following questions are considered in turn.

I. THE INTERACTIONS BETWEEN THE TWO COURTS IN EUROPE

In line with some institutionalist theorists' view,[8] the interactions between existing legislative and judicial bodies within the EU and the network of actors at both national and supranational levels generate more institutionalisation.[9] Hence, the

in Strasbourg on Friday 13 June 2014, at the seat of the Council of Europe. Some of the chapters in this volume also reflect on the findings emerging in a project funded by the British Academy (Small Research Grants (SRG) 2011 Round).

[8] See, for instance, JL Campbell, *Institutional Change and Globalization* (Princeton, Princeton University Press, 2004).

[9] Morano-Foadi and Duina, 'The Institutionalisation of Regional Trade Agreements Worldwide' (n 2) at 562.

role of the two European Courts in shaping the architecture of Europe in the protection of fundamental rights is pivotal.

Member States through the Lisbon Treaty were committed in an unprecedented way to uphold respect for human rights, while implementing EU law, through the binding effect of the Charter. Yet, the actual interpretation of the Charter by the CJEU seems heavily influenced by the jurisprudence of the ECHR. Although the Convention lies outside of the domain of the EU, Article 52 of the Charter makes it necessary to respect it. The EU's future accession to the ECHR aims to close the circle, as the EU would be subject to the external scrutiny of the ECtHR. However, the recent Opinion of the CJEU has made the EU's accession to the ECHR a more remote possibility as it is not currently possible on the basis of the current draft Agreement. However, even without imminent accession, the interplay between the Courts and the use of the Convention is likely to continue and guide EU jurisprudence, constituting the minimum standard of protection in Europe. At EU level, in the absence of accession, a more extensive protection might be guaranteed by the application of the Charter.

The chapters attempt to assess the path taken by each of the two Courts to guarantee an effective protection of rights in Europe. Weiss argues that whilst the ECtHR was already a human rights court by virtue of its intensified proportionality control, the CJEU has tentatively taken first steps on this path but it is still tempted to continue traditional interpretive approaches due to its structural characteristics. The CJEU's recent ruling signals a period of crisis in relation to accession. The CJEU appears to have cautiously considered the implication in relation to autonomy of EU law by disregarding the fundamental values upon which the Union was founded.

In her contribution, Raba argues that conflicts between the Strasbourg Court and the Luxembourg Court concerning the implementation of ECHR cannot in principle be ruled out. Member States are bound to respect the ECHR as interpreted by the Strasbourg Court and at the same time have to observe Union law as interpreted by the Luxembourg Court. Thus, she concludes that a more complete recognition and protection of human rights for people in Europe will be achieved, when it occurs, via the EU accession to the ECHR. She also provides some insight in relation to the CJEU's ruling and the actual status of the negotiations, calling for a pragmatic approach to consider the CJEU opinion in the light of broader questions of EU post-Lisbon fundamental rights architecture.

In a similar vein, Polakiewicz in his prologue underlines the importance and urgency of accession, now temporarily on hold, to obtain legal certainty and enhance consistency in the application of human rights, fostering a harmonious development of the relevant case law of the ECtHR and the CJEU.

Based on empirical findings, Andreadakis argues that the two Courts have adopted a totally different approach towards accession and thus any post-accession relationship will represent one of the most controversial issues to be resolved in any future Accession Agreement. He provides a critical review of the whole process following the CJEU's Opinion of December 2015.

II. THE FUNDAMENTAL RIGHTS QUEST: EQUALITY IN EMPLOYMENT LAW, COMPUTER LAW, CITIZENSHIP AND MIGRATION, ACCESS TO JUSTICE AND JUDICIAL COOPERATION IN CIVIL MATTERS

In his chapter Wintemute attempts to answer the question of which European Court is procedurally 'fitter' to handle novel rights cases with a focus on sexual orientation or gender identity discrimination. He argues that, despite the fact that the CJEU has produced many valuable and influential human rights judgments, especially in the area of sex discrimination law, its tendency is to be substantively cautious. This, combined with the rigidity in its procedures, reduces its procedural 'fitness', and makes it a risky choice of forum for a novel human rights issue. However, Wintemute concludes that the CJEU could become substantively 'braver' if takes seriously Article 52(3) of the Charter conferring a more extensive protection. He then suggests some recommendations to assist the Court to become procedurally 'fitter'.

Following a similar line of argument, Loenen and Vickers argue in the context of the regulation of religious expression in the public sphere and its balance with other equality rights, that if the CJEU accepts a wide margin of appreciation in the level of protection afforded to these human rights, moving to a position equivalent to the ECtHR, then there is the risk that some majorities will not hesitate to use this flexibility and deference to limit the human rights of minority groups.

In balancing economic interests and social policy choices, as suggested by Weiss, the CJEU appears much more rigorous with regard to Member States' measures impeding the exercise of fundamental freedoms, rather than when reviewing the legality of EU institutions' acts. In pre-Lisbon cases, a strong bias in favour of promoting European integration and of preferring EU fundamental freedoms over EU fundamental rights is evident. Even in post-Lisbon cases, the CJEU, when reviewing the proportionality of EU acts, in many cases first of all restates the traditional judicial approach of underscoring the leeway of the EU legislature and of confining itself to a review of whether that measure was not manifestly inappropriate to reach the aim.

As affirmed by Pollicino, the new area of internet law provides the platform to challenge the two Courts' approaches of balancing contrasting fundamental rights, such as, for example, copyright and freedom of expression.

In the context of migration, Morano-Foadi offers a contextual analysis of the various categories of non-EU nationals legally resident within the EU, reflecting on the convergent approaches adopted by the two Courts in migration law cases dealing with a fundamental rights issue. Velluti reflects on the extent to which European Courts are attempting to reduce the present gap between fundamental rights and legal remedies to ensure better protection of asylum-seekers.

Interesting convergences arise in the final pair of chapters which consider the role of both Courts as human rights adjudicators. Gillies notes the development of an increasingly particularised EU jurisprudential framework for the autonomous interpretation of EU private international laws. In his chapter on the recent judgments of the Grand Chamber on access to justice, Popović considers the expansion of the ECHR's protection under Article 6, both by way of giving greater precision to the requirements of the application of Article 6(1) of the Convention and by extending the protection of Article 6 to certain additional classes of cases.

III. THE FUTURE OF FUNDAMENTAL RIGHTS PROTECTION IN EUROPE: THE EU's ACCESSION TO THE ECHR

A number of questions recur throughout the chapters in this volume, relating to the future of fundamental rights in Europe. Perhaps the most important insight about the future rights' framework emerging from the chapters in the volume will depend on the role taken by the Courts and in particular by the CJEU. Convergences, divergences and common trends between the two Courts in safeguarding fundamental rights represent the conundrum of the future.

The shift from the CJEU's conservative approach, even prior to accession, towards a more progressive and creative jurisprudence will advance integration. This swing, together with the EU's accession, when and if it occurs, will represent further evidence of the EU's move away from the Free Trade Area. This is also confirmed by the role of the Charter within the EU legal system. As suggested by Jääskinen, we can now rely upon the Charter as an instrument that continues a certain tradition in fundamental and human rights law, and which at the same time combines the different currents of protection of rights into a legally binding, unified single instrument.

By contrast, opting for a pluralistic vision of Europe where the two complex and multifaceted European entities grow without particular attention to each other, having a separate scope and adopting diverging tools, will slow down the integration process moving towards a more intergovernmentalist view of Europe. For the time being, this seems to be the case as the accession process now appears to be stalled. The CJEU's ruling has questioned issues which lie at the heart of the EU legal system, even though it is likely that the two Courts will still look at each other's case law. Consequently, the approach now being taken by the CJEU arguably ignores certain broad patterns that are already discernible.

The first pattern considers the fact that the EU, as all organisations, exhibits a tendency to expand, whether in its formal architecture and mandates or in its everyday, informal practices and reach. Thus, this expansion has already witnessed more rights-based protection. Also the Council of Europe has made a small movement towards supranationality for the purposes of achieving greater protection of human rights. This is visible in the work of the ECtHR in interpreting the Convention and having a final word in Europe, which undoubtedly introduces a significant supranational element to the national dimension.

A second pattern concerns the difference between formal arrangements and *de facto* operational realities. There is often a split between Member States' or institutional objectives and procedures and practical achievements, due to the change of policy priorities or administrative and financial constraints. Chapters in this volume have invoked solutions addressing specific human rights fields, suggesting a number of significant recommendations to officials, judiciary and member states alike.

This leads to the third pattern. It is quite clear that deeper protection of human rights depends on political and institutional will. In relation to the draft Accession Agreement, as Raba argues, despite the long-term slow pace of negotiation and the fact that the EU political agenda has been 'high jacked' by more pressing issues, impressive progress had been made in the last three years. Nonetheless the CJEU's ruling has temporarily stopped the process. Further legal and political obstacles need to be overcome before accession becomes a reality. In this process it is important not to lose sight of the ultimate purpose of EU accession to the ECHR, that is to enhance fundamental rights protection for the individual.

We hope the chapters in this volume will offer useful insights contributing to the debate on the future architecture of Europe.

Part I

2

The Place of the EU Charter within the Tradition of Fundamental and Human Rights

DR NIILO JÄÄSKINEN*

I. INTRODUCTION

ONE OF THE most important subjects of the German presidency of the first semester of 1999 was the idea of drawing up of a 'bill of rights' or a 'catalogue of fundamental rights' for the European Union (EU). This was to be achieved by a Convention representing the EU institutions, the Member States' governments and the national parliaments. Later on, the Cologne and Tampere European Councils defined the mandate of the Convention, which started its work in December 1999. The Convention published its first draft for the Charter of Fundamental Rights of the European Union (the Charter) in July 2000.

In Finland, the attitude towards an EU bill of rights was at best lukewarm. Its necessity was questioned, there were fears that it represented a first step towards a federal constitution of Europe, and many saw it as an attempt to prevent the accession of the EU to the Convention for the Protection of Human Rights and Fundamental Freedoms (ECHR), which was the preferred option for Finland. However, the Finnish Parliament stated in 1999 something that seems very important even today. Namely, that if an EU bill of rights were adopted, it could and should not be limited to rights protected by the ECHR, the latter being an instrument which was five decades old. Therefore, the EU catalogue of fundamental rights should be comprehensive and modern, and also protect fundamental social rights, rights to participation in decision-making, the right to good administration and the protection of the environment, and the rights of minorities. In July 2000 the European Affairs Committee of the Parliament found that all these

* AG, Court of Justice of the European Union, Luxembourg. The author thanks Dr Pekka Aalto and Mr Joshua Andresen for their invaluable help in the preparation of this chapter. The usual disclaimer applies.

objectives, with the exception of the rights of minorities, were achieved in the light of the draft Charter presented by the Convention.[1]

Indeed, the Charter, proclaimed in 2000 and amended in 2007,[2] can be considered to be the most comprehensive and modern instrument for the protection of fundamental rights not only in Europe, but perhaps also globally in terms of the scope of the rights protected and the level of protection it supplies.

Too often academic discussion on the Charter is focused on the legal technicalities relating to its scope of application and interpretation under Articles 51 to 53, now clarified by the *Åkerberg/Fransson* and *Melloni* judgments of the Court of Justice of the European Union (CJEU),[3] or that the Charter is merely understood as a recast of the ECHR for EU purposes. Such ideas, even if fully legitimate, may miss the point. The Charter is most valuable as a restatement of a comprehensive and modern view of the most fundamental values shared by Europeans.

Therefore, the aim of this chapter is to share some reflections on the Charter as an instrument that continues a certain tradition in fundamental and human rights law, namely that based on the idea of indivisibility of protection, and which at the same time combines the different currents of protection of rights into a unified single instrument, and which has been legally binding since December 2009.[4]

II. THE DIFFERENT SOURCES OF THE LAW OF FUNDAMENTAL AND HUMAN RIGHTS

In modern constitutional and international law the protection of fundamental and human rights plays a primary role. After the Second World War a plethora of national, regional and global instruments and systems of protection have emerged. The interplay between these systems has also blurred the conceptual distinction between these two categories of rights. The constitutional protection of fundamental rights is less and less restricted to a country's own citizens and now includes all residents, or even all human beings.[5] Hence, the difference between the categories of rights, that is fundamental rights protected by the national law,

[1] Opinion 4/2000 of the Grand Committee of the Finnish Parliament of 17 November 2000 on the Government's Communication (E 31/1999 vp) of 11 July 1999 on the European Union Charter of Fundamental Rights. For a succinct account of the process in Finland, see L Nieminen, 'Impulse aus der finnischen Verfassungstradition für den europäischen Grundrechtsschutz' in KJ Tettinger and K Stern (eds), *Kölner Gemeinschaftskommentar zur Europäischen Grundrechte-Charta* (München, Verlag CH Beck, 2006) 1.

[2] The Charter was solemnly proclaimed by the European Parliament, the Council of Ministers and the European Commission on 7 December 2000 and adapted on 12 December 2007.

[3] Case C-617/10 *Åkerberg Fransson*, 26 February 2013, para 29 and Case C-399/11 *Melloni*, 26 February 2013, para 60.

[4] According to the Lisbon Treaty, which entered in to force on 1 December 2009, the Charter has now the same legal value as the founding treaties.

[5] See A Rosas, 'The Charter and Universal Human Rights Instruments' in S Peers, T Hervey, J Kenner, and A Ward (eds), *The EU Charter of Fundamental Rights: A Commentary* (Oxford, Hart Publishing, 2014) 1685–1701, 1685.

and human rights protected by international instruments, relates more to the nature and source of the obligations of states than to the substance of the rights as such.

This said, from the point of view of the history of ideas, both categories represent a combination of different strains. Based on the research of Professor Antero Jyränki, a non-exhaustive list would consist of the following: (i) the instruments protecting privileges of certain social classes or groups. The English Magna Carta (1215) is the most famous but not the first or unique example of such instruments that were not uncommon in pre-modern Europe;[6] (ii) the extension of certain rights, inspired by the natural law philosophy and the Enlightenment, to all (white able-bodied male) citizens (of a certain wealth or income). Examples of this were the British Bill of Rights (1689) and US Bills of Rights (1791) and the Universal declaration of the rights of man and citizen of the Revolutionary France (1789), all concentrating on the *Lockean* trinity of life, liberty and property;[7] (iii) the idea of a hierarchy of laws, originating in the medieval notion of fundamental laws, the *leges fundamentales*, and developing into the modern notion of constitution in nineteenth and twentieth century legal science;[8] (iv) the idea of protection of fundamental rights either as a political task of the representatives of the people and/or by courts through judicial review.[9]

On this basis, a pivotal narrative of legal protection of fundamental rights has developed that has become our intellectual starting point. According to this view, fundamental rights define an autonomous sphere for the abstract individual—be he called the 'citizen' or the 'man'—which is protected against the intervention of the state by virtue of a legal instrument having a higher status than that of ordinary laws. However, this approach, which reflects political liberalism, was challenged as early as the nineteenth century by social liberal and socialist currents, which claimed that the protection of an individual abstracted of his or her social, economic, ethnic qualities and conditions, was inadequate and sometimes unjust. This critique was advanced on two fronts.

The first was to insist on the redefinition of the 'individual' who forms the object of protection.[10] Astonishingly, it is often forgotten that equal constitutional

[6] See A Jyränki, 'Leonista Nizzaan: Eurooppalaisen perusoikeusajattelun historiallisia linjoja' [From Leon to Nizza: Historical Lines of European fundamental rights thinking] in L Nieminen (ed), *Perusoikeudet EU: ssa* (Helsinki, Kauppakaari, 2001), where Professor Jyränki further develops the constitutional themes in his magnum opus; see A Jyränki, *Lakien laki* [The Law of Laws] (Helsinki, Lakimiesliiton Kustannus, 1989).

[7] See J Locke, *Second Treatise of Government* (1690), at www.gutenberg.org.

[8] See H Mohnhaupt, 'Öffentliches Recht in Gestalt der Leges Fundamentales im mittelalterlichen Alten Reich' (2011) 21 *Journal of Constitutional History* 25; and RH Helmholz, *Fundamental Human Rights in Medieval Law*, Fulton Lectures (Chicago, University of Chicago, 2001).

[9] On the development of the competition between parliamentary and judicial models of constitutional control, see A Jyränki, *Valta ja vapaus: valtiosääntöoikeuden yleisiä kysymyksiä* [Power and Freedom: General Questions of Constitutional Law], 3rd edn (Helsinki, Talentum, 2003), 376–81.

[10] See, for example, S Hänninen, 'Social Constitution in Historical Perspective: Hugo Sinzheimer in the Weimar Context' in K Tuori and S Sankari (eds), *The Many Constitutions of Europe* (Aldershot, Ashgate, 2010), 235–39.

protection of the rights of individuals was only fully reached after the 1960s for women,[11] members of racial minorities, disabled people, and still remains imperfect in the case of such categories as certain ethnic minorities, or minority sexual orientations. For example, until the 1970s or 1980s children born out of wedlock were legally discriminated against in most European countries.[12]

Secondly, the value of the rights protected for many individual was challenged. This point was made in an ingenious way by the nineteenth century French writer Anatole France who observed how '[t]he law, in its majestic equality, forbids the rich and the poor alike to sleep under bridges, to beg in the streets, and to steal bread'.[13] In other words, the protection of fundamental rights was considered to be inadequate for less favoured social classes and groups, whose liberty rights and political rights were often insufficiently protected in practice, and for whom rights relating to health, working life, social protection and education were more urgent.

The idea that the constitution should protect concrete individuals and meet the satisfaction of their elementary needs as an objective of the polity was first enshrined in Germany in the constitution of the Weimar Republic (1919) which defined a set of 'second generation' rights protected as fundamental rights, in addition to classic liberties and political rights.[14] At the international level the establishment of the International Labour Organization (1919) started a similar tendency. Thus, whereas the function of the first-generation fundamental rights was to protect against the state becoming too active, the function of the second-generation rights was to ensure that the state does not remain too passive. It was this opposition between the active and passive state, reflected in the philosophical distinction between the negative and positive concept of freedom[15] that was to define the debate after the Second World War, which had, of course, been the theatre of most massive infringements of fundamental and human rights of individuals in any sense of the concept.

[11] For instance, Convention on the Elimination of All Forms of Discrimination against Women (adopted on 18 December 1979, entered into force on 3 September 1981) 1249 UNTS 13, has been ratified by 188 states.

[12] This is true despite the fact that Art 25(2) of the Universal Declaration of Human Rights (adopted on 10 December 1948 (UNGA Res 217 A(III) (UDHR)) states that '[a]ll children whether born in or out of wedlock shall enjoy the same social protection'. This principle was confirmed in The European Convention of 15 October 1975 on the Legal Status of Children born out of Wedlock. A seminal European Court of Human Rights judgment in this regard was *Marckx v Belgium* App no 6833/74, Series A no 31 (ECtHR, 13 June 1979), finding the Belgian law that did not extend equal rights to children born out of wedlock violated Art 8 on private and family life and Art 14 on non-discrimination.

[13] A France, *Le Lys Rouge* (1894).

[14] S Hänninen, 'Social Constitution in Historical Perspective' and AE Dick Howard, 'Another "Springtime of Nations"? Rights in Central and Eastern Europe' in RK Ramazani and Robert Fatton (eds), *The Future of Liberal Democracy: Thomas Jefferson and the Contempory World* (Palgrave, 2004) 133. Howard notes that the Weimar Constitution of 1919 included second-generation rights in 'more general terms' than did the Mexican Constitution of 1917.

[15] The distinction between negative and positive liberty, which was most famously elaborated by Isaiah Berlin in 1958, has a history that goes back at least to Immanuel Kant. See I Berlin, *Two Concepts of Liberty* (Oxford, Oxford University Press, 1958); I Carter, 'Positive and Negative Liberty' in *Stanford Encyclopedia of Philosophy* (Stanford, Stanford University, 2012).

III. COMPREHENSIVE VERSUS SECTORIAL PROTECTION OF FUNDAMENTAL RIGHTS

In the aftermath of the Second World War two international regimes of human rights protection emerged. The United Nations Universal Declaration of Human Rights,[16] albeit not legally binding and justiciable, defined in a comprehensive manner a list of universal human rights, which contained not only political and civil rights but also many social, cultural and economic rights. The Declaration represented the ideology of indivisibility of human rights, which considers the different categories of protected rights as necessary, interdependent and mutually supportive.

However, later on, this comprehensive approach was not followed. Under the auspices of the United Nations (UN), political and civil rights,[17] on the one hand, and economic, cultural and social rights,[18] on the other, were articulated under different conventions in 1966. Moreover, a number of specific conventions, relating inter alia to the rights of women and children, were adopted within the UN regime.[19]

In Western Europe, the Council of Europe Member States adopted in 1950 the ECHR, and later on, put into practice the first international system providing effective judicial protection for individuals against their own states. With the exception of the right to education, the ECHR covers only so-called first-generation rights, and usually entails only negative obligations for its contracting states. Hence, within the Council of Europe, a separate system for the protection of social rights emerged in the form of the European Social Charter (1961), with a control system separate from the European Court of Human Rights (ECtHR).[20]

The division between comprehensive and sectorial approaches was also visible in the constitutions adopted in Europe after the Second World War. The Italian Constitution (1947), and the draft French Constitution (1945), rejected in a referendum, resembled the Weimar Constitution in their comprehensive approach to fundamental rights, whereas the Basic Law of Germany (1949) adopted a more traditional approach and included only classical political and civil rights in its chapter on fundamental rights. It was only later that West-European constitutions

[16] Universal Declaration of Human Rights was adopted on 10 December 1948, with the notable abstentions of the Soviet Bloc countries, South Africa, and Saudi Arabia.

[17] International Covenant on Civil and Political Rights (adopted on 16 December 1966, entered into force on 23 March 1976) 999 UNTS 171.

[18] International Covenant on Economic, Social and Cultural Rights (adopted on 16 December 1966, entered into force on 3 January 1976) 993 UNTS 3.

[19] See, eg, Convention on the Rights of the Child (adopted on 20 November 1989, entered into force on 2 September 1990) 1577 UNTS 3, and the Convention on the Elimination of all Forms of Discrimination against Women, adopted by the UN General Assembly on 18 December 1979 and entering into force on 3 September 1981.

[20] States parties submit annual reports on compliance and implementation of the provisions of the European Social Charter, various trade unions and non-governmental organisations (NGOs) can submit complaints of state party non-compliance, and the European Committee of Social Rights monitors compliance and makes non-binding rulings on the merits of complaints.

widened the scope of protected fundamental rights. This started in 1970s with the new democracies of Spain, Portugal and Greece, and was followed later, for example, by the Netherlands, Belgium, Finland and Switzerland.[21]

Since the Second World War, the view in Europe concerning the rights the individual should be able to enforce against the state has developed considerably. First, all developed countries are welfare states, albeit with considerable differences regarding the scope of their systems, the content of their principles and the levels of protection, and West-European countries have played the most significant role in this development. Secondly, our conceptions of personal liberty, equality and solidarity have radically widened since the 1950s.

To illustrate this point in very concrete terms let me take some examples from Finland in the early 1960s. In Finland at that time, as in most western countries, books or newspapers could be prohibited because of blasphemous or pornographic content. Many disabled persons were not allowed to marry, no contraception was admitted for unmarried women and abortion was illegal. Privacy was not recognised as a right. Psychiatric patients did not enjoy any defined rights. Children born outside wedlock did not legally have fathers. Alcoholics, persons considered idle or women of questionable reputation could be put under administrative detention. Women were not legally equal with men in relation to many family law issues such as guardianship or attribution of surname. Neither law nor practice required equal pay for equal work, and work contracts could be terminated at notice without giving any reasons. Roma children could be taken by the state without any true justification. Certain categories of persons could be sterilised or castrated without their consent. In short, it is astonishing how repressive and unequal our societies were just a short time ago.

To conclude, when the drafting of the Charter became topical, the European populations had value codes that were at the same time more complex and more pluralistic than those of the preceding generations. It is against this background that the Cologne European Council stated in July 1999 that the future Charter should contain the fundamental rights and freedoms as well as basic procedural rights guaranteed by the ECHR and derived from the constitutional traditions common to the Member States. Moreover, the European Council called that account should also be taken of economic and social rights as contained in the European Social Charter and the Community Charter of the Fundamental Social Rights of Workers (1989),[22] insofar as they do not merely establish objectives for action by the Union.[23]

[21] See Jyränki, *Valta ja vapaus* (n 9) 23–29, and The protection of the right to Social Security in European Constitutions, Compendium of provisions of European Constitutions, Comparative tables, prepared by Lola Tonini Alabiso, online edition (International Labour Organization, 2012), at http://www.ilo.org/wcmsp5/groups/public/---ed_norm/---normes/documents/publication/wcms_191459.pdf.

[22] Adopted on 9 December 1989 by a declaration of all Member States, with the exception of the United Kingdom.

[23] Cologne European Council 3 and 4 June 1999, Conclusions of the Presidency, Annex IV, at http://www.europarl.europa.eu/summits/kol2_en.htm#an4.

IV. THE CHARTER AS A COMPREHENSIVE AND PLURALISTIC INSTRUMENT

The pedigree of the provisions of the Charter can be traced to three main sources. These are the ECHR, the European Social Charter together with the Community Charter of the Fundamental Social Rights of Workers, and EU law, the latter comprising the treaties, secondary legislation and the case law of the CJEU. Moreover, some individual provisions are derived from other international human rights instruments: Article 1 of the Charter on human dignity stems from the UN Universal Declaration of Human Rights, Article 24 of the Charter from the UN Convention on the Rights of the Child, Article 18 of the Charter from the Geneva Refugee law convention[24] and Articles 3 and 8 of the Charter from Council of Europe sectorial instruments relating respectively to bioethics[25] and data protection.[26]

In substance, the Charter protects classical first-generation rights relating to civil liberties, political rights and judicial protection, many second-generation economic, cultural and social rights and some third-generation rights such as data protection, consumer protection, and protection of environment. However, as already mentioned, no fourth generation of rights protecting minorities or groups have been included in the Charter. Indeed, one Finnish professor of constitutional law has observed that optically the Charter most closely resembles the South-European constitutions adopted after the end of dictatorships in the 1970s and 1980s,[27] while fully understanding that the last point hardly amounts to a recommendation in the eyes of all audiences. The last part of this chapter will be devoted to explaining why the comprehensive and pluralistic approach adopted by the drafters of the Charter is considered to be a positive development.

First, this chapter shares the position of the German Constitutional Court, according to which a catalogue of fundamental rights strives to define the basic values of a polity, and thereby controls and guides the legislative, executive and judicial functions of a state.[28] In the case of the Charter, its main function is to regulate the activities of the EU and its institutions. As in any developed system of fundamental rights, the main effects of the Charter relate to its status as an instrument (i) limiting and controlling the ways the EU legislator strives to achieve the

[24] Convention Relating to the Status of Refugees (adopted on 28 July 1951, entered into force on 22 April 1954) 189 UNTS 137.

[25] Convention for the Protection of Human Rights and Dignity of the Human Being with regard to the Application of Biology and Medicine: Convention on Human Rights and Biomedicine (4 April 1997) and Convention for the Protection of Individuals with regard to Automatic Processing of Personal Data (28 January 1981).

[26] For further discussion, see JC Piris, *The Lisbon Treaty* (Cambridge, Cambridge University Press, 2010), 152–53.

[27] See A Jyränki, *Valta ja vapaus* (n 9) 529.

[28] See R Alexy, *A Theory of Constitutional Rights* (Oxford, Oxford University Press, 2002), 352 citing the German Federal Constitutional Court, BVerfGE 39, 1 (41).

objectives of the founding treaties,[29] and (ii) guiding the interpretation of the other sources of EU law.[30] Moreover, the Charter is applicable to Member States' activities in so far as they implement EU law.[31]

Given that a catalogue of fundamental rights should strive to define the basic values of a polity, the pluralistic and comprehensive approach of the Charter reflects the value codes of the European populations which are more liberal, social and equality-oriented than, for example, in the United States or Russia. In Europe, we truly appreciate the first-generation political freedoms and civil and economic liberties. However, we also think that all children need to be protected and educated, that a reasonable safety net is necessary against such risks as unemployment, sickness, disability and old age. Moreover, the Europeans appreciate fairness, equality and solidarity, insist on having certain elementary rights as employees, and want the environment to be protected. In other words, any legal theory derived from Whig liberalism or libertarianism, whatever its intellectual attractiveness, does not correspond with the values shared by the European populations at large.

Second, the above list of values demonstrates clearly that our value systems, and a catalogue of fundamental rights reflecting them, necessarily entail tensions and even conflicts between different courses of action, both at the level of politics and at the level of judicial application. An openly pluralistic bill of rights makes the conflicts more visible and thus makes balancing the conflicting rights and values that is inevitable in the application of any system of fundamental rights more easily manageable.

For example, Article 24 of the Charter, which requires that a child be protected as a subject of fundamental rights in her own right, is a necessary balancing provision in relation to Article 7 of the Charter on respect of family life. At least in the Nordic countries, it is often claimed that in the application of Article 8 ECHR, a provision corresponding to Article 7 of the Charter, the children's interests are too often subjected to those of their parents. The ruling of the CJEU in Case C-400/10 *McB v LE*[32] demonstrates the importance of treating children as individuals whose interests cannot be equated with those of either parent. In that case the Court concluded as follows: 'Article 24 of the Charter must be interpreted as not precluding a situation where, for the purposes of applying [the so-called Brussels II Regulation on parental responsibility[33]], rights of custody are granted, as a general rule, exclusively to the mother and a natural father possesses rights of custody

[29] Embodied, for example, in Charter Arts 51(1) on Scope, 52(1) on Scope of Guaranteed Rights, 53 on Level of Protection, 54 on Prohibition of Abuse of Rights, and 44 on the Right to Petition.

[30] Embodied, for example, in Charter Arts 52(2) and 52(3) on Scope of Guaranteed Rights.

[31] Art 51(1) of the Charter.

[32] 5 October 2010.

[33] Council Regulation (EC) No 2201/2003 of 27 November 2003 concerning jurisdiction and the recognition and enforcement of judgments in matrimonial matters and the matters of parental responsibility, repealing Regulation (EC) No 1347/2000 (OJ [2003] L338/1).

only as the result of a court judgment. Such a requirement enables the national court with jurisdiction to take a decision on custody of the child, and on rights of access to that child, while taking into account all the relevant facts … The taking into account of those facts is apt to protect the child's best interests, in accordance with Article 24(2) of the Charter'.[34]

Third, a comprehensive list of fundamental rights adequately reflects the variety of the human condition. This chapter also endorses the philosophical view of political liberalism that puts autonomy or personal liberty at the centre of our values. That said, we are not abstract individuals but persons with bodies, biological, physical and psychological constitutions, born to circumstances we have not chosen. Hence, our capacity for autonomy or liberty is different, not only interpersonally, but also depending on our age, environment and luck. For many individuals, any enjoyment of first-generation rights may depend of the enjoyment of second-generation rights such as the right to education or the right to adequate health services. The philosopher John Rawls defined justice as fairness by referring to institutions we would choose under the veil of ignorance not knowing who we were to become and what kind of properties and capacities we would possess.[35] Therefore taking into account all the different circumstances an individual may encounter is relevant to the question of what rights count as fundamental. In other words, fundamental rights must be relevant also for those with a disability or a chronic illness, or belonging to a national, ethnic or sexual minority or otherwise disadvantaged group which requires that protection goes beyond life, liberty and property.[36]

Finally, it is necessary to make a few remarks on the question of the concept of a fundamental or a human right. Its true nature is somewhat confused by the image of fundamental rights as an instrument in the hands of a morally enlightened supreme court for promoting political or social justice by quashing unjust legislation.[37]

This narrative forgets that, with a few exceptions such as the prohibition of torture, fundamental rights are not absolute rights. This means that they have limits both as to their scope of application and force in relation to conflicting rights and interests; you cannot freely bear an AK-47 assault rifle at the Convention of the Republican Party of the USA. Therefore, fundamental rights should not be

[34] *McB* (n 32), para 62.

[35] See J Rawls, *A Theory of Justice* (Harvard, Harvard University Press, 1971). Philosophically it is debatable whether persons deciding under the veil of ignorance would have any reasons for preferring a certain concept of justice. However, for constitutional law I find Rawls' metaphor important because it emphasises the need to take into account the variety of human condition in the definition and application of fundamental right protection.

[36] For further discussion, see my contribution 'Fundamental Social Rights in the Charter—Are They Rights? Are They Fundamental?' in S Peers et al, *The EU Charter of Fundamental Rights: A Commentary* (n 5) 1703–14.

[37] In my opinion superficial application of some ideas of Ronald Dworkin's legal philosophy has contributed to this confusion.

understood as sacred cows outside of the scope of democratic debate and ethical controversy, but rather as something that develops in the course of political and ethical debate and judicial decision-making. The Charter does not close the development of EU fundamental rights law, but rather defines the parameters of its future development.[38]

[38] This view is confirmed by Art 52(1) of the Charter, Scope of guaranteed rights: 'Any limitation on the exercise of the rights and freedoms recognised by this Charter must be provided for by law and respect the essence of those rights and freedoms. Subject to the principle of proportionality, limitations may be made only if they are necessary and genuinely meet objectives of general interest recognised by the Union or the need to protect the rights and freedoms of others'.

3

Closing the Gaps in the Protection of Fundamental Rights in Europe: Accession of the EU to the ECHR

KRISTI RABA*

I INTRODUCTION

THE AIM OF this chapter is to discuss the significance, procedure and prerequisites for accession to the Convention for the Protection of Human Rights and Fundamental Freedoms (ECHR) from the European Union (EU) perspective, and to record the state of play. In that context this chapter will also touch upon Opinion 2/13 of the Court of Justice of the European Union (CJEU) on the incompatibility of the negotiated text with EU law.

Roughly a year after closing the negotiations provisionally at negotiators' level on the text of the Agreement on the Accession of the European Union (draft Accession Agreement) to the ECHR,[1] on 5–6 May 2014, the CJEU held an oral hearing on the case Opinion 2/13 (the 'CJEU Opinion').[2] The purpose of the request to the CJEU, submitted by the European Commission in July 2013 in accordance with Article 218(11) of the Treaty on the Functioning of the European Union (TFEU), was to establish whether the draft Accession Agreement was compatible with the EU Treaties from EU law perspective. The long anticipated CJEU Opinion was delivered on 18 December 2014[3] and declared that the Accession Agreement was incompatible with EU law.

At this stage it is too early to draw far-reaching conclusions about the consequences of the negative opinion on the EU accession to the ECHR. The political

* Official at the General Secretariat of the Council of the European Union. The views expressed are the author's own and do not in any way reflect the Council's views. The chapter is based on an intervention made at the Oxford Brookes University on 18 January 2013.

[1] The agreement was reached at the fifth negotiation meeting on 3–5 April 2013 between the CDDH ad hoc negotiation group and the EU. The report of the session is available at http://www.coe.int/t/dghl/standardsetting/hrpolicy/Accession/Meeting_reports/Web_47_1(2013)R05_EN.pdf.

[2] See Opinion 2/13 Request for an opinion submitted by the European Commission pursuant to Article 218(11) TFEU, 4 July 2013, [2013] OJ C260/32.

[3] Opinion 2/13 ECLI:EU:C:2014:2475.

and legal implications need to be thoroughly analysed before the best course of action can be chosen.

This chapter does not analyse all the intricacies of the CJEU Opinion. It intends merely to reflect on the legal and political complexities of the negotiations process so far and especially in light of the latest developments.

II. EU's ACCESSION TO THE ECHR

A. Placing Accession in its Context

Against the backdrop of the recent agreement on the text and the CJEU Opinion, it would be useful to be reminded of the significance of EU accession to the ECHR on a broader scale in order not to lose sight of the overall purpose.[4]

Already in 1969, the CJEU confirmed that the respect for fundamental rights formed an integral part of the general principles of law, the observance of which CJEU ensures.[5] In doing so the CJEU drew inspiration from common constitutional traditions of the Member States as well as from international treaties for the protection of human rights. In this context the role of ECHR in the system of protection of fundamental rights in Europe is pivotal.

As the CJEU stated in its Opinion 2/94, accession of the EU to the ECHR would be 'of constitutional significance'[6] and therefore such a change of constitutional significance would require an explicit legal basis.

From the Council of Europe's viewpoint, Protocol 14 allowed for the accession of non-state parties.[7]

From the EU's perspective, the Lisbon Treaty changed the EU's fundamental rights' landscape. The Treaty on European Union (TEU) recognises in its Article 6(1) the Charter of Fundamental Rights of the European Union (the 'Charter') as having the same legal value as the Treaties. However, the Charter only applies to the EU institutions and to the Member States when these implement EU law. The TEU recognises other sources of fundamental rights by stating in Article 6(3) that fundamental rights, as guaranteed by the ECHR and as they result from the constitutional traditions common to the Member States, constitute general principles of EU law.

The Charter further clarifies in its Article 52(3) that in so far as it contains rights which correspond to rights guaranteed by the ECHR, the meaning and

[4] See also JP Jacqué, 'The Accession of the European Union to the European Convention on Human Rights and Fundamental Freedoms' (2011) 48 *CML Rev* 995–1023.

[5] Case C-29/69 *Stauder* [1969] ECR 419; Case C-11/70 *Internationale Handelsgesellschaft* [1970] ECR 1125; Case C-4/73 *Nold* [1974] ECR 491.

[6] Opinion 2/94, Opinion pursuant to Article 228(6) of the EC Treaty [1996] ECR 1759.

[7] See http://conventions.coe.int/Treaty/EN/Treaties/Html/194.htm, entered into force on 1 June 2010.

scope of those rights shall be the same as those laid down by the ECHR and that this provision shall not prevent EU law providing more extensive protection.

Recent years have seen an increase in Charter-related case law both at EU Member States' tribunal level as well as at the CJEU level.[8] However, the case law also proves that the complexity of this multi-layered system of protection of fundamental rights is not evident and easy to comprehend. Accession to the ECHR has been known to constitute the last step of the post-Lisbon interlocked system of fundamental rights.[9]

Since the Lisbon Treaty there is effectively an explicit legal basis—Article 6(2) TEU—for the EU to accede to the ECHR, and not only an explicit legal basis but a legal obligation as such.[10] Article 6(2) TEU states in clear imperative language that the EU 'shall accede' to the ECHR.

The EU's accession to the ECHR would mark a historic step towards closing gaps in the system of fundamental rights protection in Europe. As touched upon above, the Lisbon Treaty simultaneously recognises multiple sources of fundamental rights and also recognises the ECHR as a source of EU law, without clarifying the relationship between these different layers.[11]

Since all EU Member States are already parties to the ECHR, from the perspective of the rights protected the change is not so fundamental, however, there are several elements why the significance cannot be underestimated.

First and foremost, EU accession to the ECHR would mean enhanced accountability and credibility both internally and externally. As such this is a major symbolic and practical step for the EU. The EU would subject itself to external control exercised by the European Court of Human Rights (Strasbourg Court or ECtHR) in light of the rights guaranteed by the ECHR and triggered by an individual application. This means that any person claiming to be a victim of a violation of the ECHR by an institution or body of the EU is able to bring a complaint against the EU under the same conditions as those applying to complaints brought against Member States.

At present, a citizen is deprived of the possibility to go to the Strasbourg Court once powers transferred to the EU are at stake, which means that the EU cannot

[8] See, for example, the report from the Commission to the European Parliament, the Council, the European Economic and Social Committee and the Committee of the Regions, 2013 Report on the Application of the EU Charter of Fundamental Rights, Brussels, 14.4.2014, COM(2014) 224 final.

[9] P Gragl, 'A Giant Leap for European Human Rights? The Final Agreement on the European Union's Accession to the European Convention on Human Rights' (2014) 51 *CML Rev* 13–58, 14–15.

[10] Significance of the Lisbon Treaty is also emphasised in Defeis, 'Human Rights, the European Union, and the Treaty Route: from Maastricht to Lisbon' (2011–12) 35 *Fordham International Law Journal* 1207. For further discussion on this point, see Morano-Foadi and Andreadakis, 'Reflections on the Architecture of the EU after the Treaty of Lisbon: the European Judicial Approach to Fundamental Rights' in a special issue edited by Morano Foadi and Duina, 'The Institutionalisation of Regional Trade Agreements Worldwide: New Dynamics and Future Perspectives' (2011) 17(5) *European Law Journal* 595.

[11] On the role of the ECHR in the EU system of protection of fundamental rights post-Lisbon, see W Weiss, 'Human Rights in the EU: Rethinking the Role of the European Convention on Human Rights After Lisbon' (2001) 7 *European Constitutional Law Review* 64–95.

be brought to the Strasbourg Court. In this context the EU's accession to the ECHR will lead towards increased coherence and effectiveness.

Since the Member States of the EU have transferred substantial competences to the EU, including in rights-sensitive areas such as justice and home affairs, EU accession becomes even more relevant. Being bound by the ECHR would impose restrictions on the EU in the exercise of its competences. However, these restrictions are intrinsic in the nature of fundamental rights which aim to protect the individual.

On a broader scale the EU's legal order would be represented within the Strasbourg control system which has already been dealing with cases linked to EU law. Accession would open the way for the Strasbourg Court to attribute acts adopted by EU institutions directly to the EU instead of attributing them to the Member State(s).[12]

Last but not least, accession will create an institutional link between the two Courts.[13] At present in view of the multiple sources of fundamental rights at the EU level, conflicts between the Strasbourg Court and the CJEU concerning the implementation of the ECHR cannot in principle be excluded. EU Member States are bound to respect the ECHR as interpreted by the Strasbourg Court and also have to observe EU law as interpreted by CJEU.[14] This situation is further complicated by the CJEU Opinion that places the Charter at the heart of the EU legal structure. The CJEU states in clear and unequivocal terms that the interpretation of the fundamental rights recognised by the Charter should be ensured within the framework of the structure and objectives of the EU,[15] whereas no decision by the ECHR bodies may have the effect of binding the EU and its institutions to a particular interpretation of EU law in an exercise of their internal powers.[16]

The draft Accession Agreement attempted to overcome possible conflicts via the so-called prior involvement mechanism that would ideally lead to increased judicial dialogue,[17] more harmonious development of the case law of the two Courts and to mutual enrichment.[18] In light of the CJEU Opinion, the functioning of this

[12] See *Bosphorus v Ireland* App no 45036/98 (ECtHR, 30 June 2005, 2005-VI) and *Matthews v UK* App no 24833/94 (ECtHR, 18 February 1999, 1999-I).

[13] See also paragraph 164 of the Advocate General view in Opinion 2/13.

[14] S Morano-Foadi and S Andreadakis, Report on the Protection of Fundamental Rights in Europe—A Reflection on the Relationship between the Court of Justice of the European Union and the European Court of Human Rights post Lisbon, July 2014, available at http://www.coe.int/en/web/dlapil/news-dlapil.

[15] See paragraphs 169 and 170 of Opinion 2/13 (n 3).

[16] See paragraph 184 of Opinion 2/13 (n 3).

[17] S Morano-Foadi, 'Fundamental Rights in Europe: "Constitutional" Dialogue between the Court of Justice of the EU and the European Court of Human Rights' (2013) 5(1) *Oñati Journal of Emergent Socio-Legal Studies* 64–88, available at http://www.sortuz.org/content/pdfs2013/4%20Morano%20-%20human%20rights.pdf.

[18] On cooperation between the two Courts and the ensuing mutual enrichments, see N Bratza, 'The European Convention on Human Rights and the Charter of Fundamental Rights of the European Union: A Process of Mutual Enrichment' in A Rosas (ed), *The Court of Justice and the Construction of Europe: Analyses and Perspectives on Sixty Years of Case-law* (The Hague, The Netherlands, TMC Asser Press, 2013) 167–81.

mechanism as it is currently laid down in the draft Accession Agreement would have to be reassessed.

B. Pre-requisites of Accession from the EU Perspective

From the outset it was considered important to keep the procedural and substantive features of the current ECHR system the same to the greatest extent possible. This was one of the guiding principles throughout the negotiations. The EU is to submit to the substantive obligations of the Convention and the control machinery it establishes, and to participate in that control machinery, on an equal footing with the other contracting parties. Therefore the draft Accession Agreement confines itself to making only the amendments that are strictly necessary to allow for the accession of the EU.

In a way it is a balancing act. On the one hand, the existing system should not be changed too much; on the other hand, the whole Council of Europe system is designed by States and for States that are members of the Council of Europe. The EU is joining as a non-state party so this already changes the existing system by default.[19]

From the perspective of the EU there are clear pre-requisites and principles for accession to ECHR deriving from EU primary law as set out in Article 6(2) TEU and in Protocol No 8 of the Lisbon Treaty relating to Article 6(2) that had to be followed throughout the negotiations.

Firstly, the EU's accession to the Convention is not to affect the EU's competences (Article 6(2) TEU, second sentence, and Article 2 of Protocol No 8 of the Lisbon Treaty, first sentence). In essence this means that the EU should be liable for ECHR violations only to the extent that its system of competences would have allowed for the adoption of the act or measure at issue.

Secondly, the EU's accession to the Convention is not to affect the powers of the EU's institutions (Article 2 of Protocol No 8 of the Lisbon Treaty, first sentence). No new powers should be conferred on the institutions and bodies of the EU as a result of the accession.

Thirdly, the Accession Agreement must reflect the need to preserve the specific characteristics of the EU and EU law, in particular with regard to the specific arrangements for the EU's possible participation in the control bodies of the ECHR (Article 1(a) of Protocol No 8 of the Lisbon Treaty) and to the mechanisms

[19] For more on the differences between the Strasbourg system and the perspectives of the EU, see:
D Ritleng, 'The Accession of the European Union to the European Convention on Human Rights and Fundamental Freedoms: A Threat to the Specific Characteristics of the European Union and Union Law?', Working paper 2012:1, University of Uppsala, at http://uu.diva-portal.org/smash/record.jsf?pid=diva2:526830;
T Lock, 'Walking on a Tightrope: the Draft ECHR Agreement and the Autonomy of the EU Legal Order' (2011) 48 *CML Rev* 1025–54.

necessary to ensure that proceedings by non–Member States and individual applications are correctly addressed to Member States and/or the EU as appropriate (Article 1(b) of Protocol No 8 of the Lisbon Treaty).[20]

Central to the need to preserve the specific characteristics of the EU and EU law is the principle of autonomy.[21] Not surprisingly, autonomy of EU law is also a key element of the CJEU Opinion. Throughout the negotiations the EU insisted that after EU accession neither the Strasbourg Court nor the Committee of Ministers, in the exercise of their jurisdiction under the ECHR, should be called upon to interpret EU law or to rule on the respective competences of the EU and the Member States, and that for these purposes appropriate guarantees need to be laid down in the accession instruments. Exactly for the purpose of taking into account the specificities of the EU and the EU law the draft Accession Agreement devises new procedural mechanisms such as the co-respondent mechanism and the prior involvement of the CJEU, which will be briefly discussed further below.

Apart from these exceptions to accommodate the EU's specific nature, the EU as the 48th party acceding should be allowed to participate in the Strasbourg Court as well as in other Council of Europe proceedings to the extent their activities are linked to the ECHR on an equal footing[22] with other contracting parties. This means that the EU should have its own judge and to participate in Council of Europe bodies (Committee of Ministers and the Parliamentary Assembly) as regards ECHR-related functions with a right to vote.

Fourthly, the EU's accession to the Convention is not to affect the situation of Member States in relation to the Convention (Article 2 of Protocol No 8 of the Lisbon Treaty, second sentence). This refers to Member States' reservations and derogations as well as different participation in different Protocols.

Fifthly, the Accession Agreement is not to affect Article 344 of the TFEU (Article 3 of Protocol No 8 of the Lisbon Treaty). Under EU law only the CJEU is competent to ensure compliance with the law in the application and interpretation of the Treaties and also to resolve disputes concerning the interpretation and application of EU Treaties.[23]

The EU thus entered the negotiations with clear pre-requisites based on its primary law.

[20] On accession, see also S Andreadakis, 'Problems and Challenges of the EU's Accession to the ECHR', ch 4 in this volume.

[21] See Opinion 1/91 Draft agreement between the European Community and the countries of the European Free Trade Association relating to the creation of the European Economic Area [1991] ECR I-6079 and Opinion 1/09 European and Community Patent Court [2011] ECR I-01137.

[22] See also F Tulkens, 'L'adhésion de l'Union européenne à la Convention des droits de l'homme. Pour et vers une organisation harmonieuse' (2011) 1 *Revue Trimestrielle De Droit Européen* 27.

[23] See Art 19(1) TEU and Art 344 TFEU.

C. Procedure and State of Negotiations

As to procedure, from the EU perspective Article 218 TFEU applies. The constitutional nature of ECHR accession for the EU is reflected in the heavy and elaborate procedural provisions laid down in EU primary law.

The Council of the EU would need unanimity for the Accession Agreement and the consent of the European Parliament. In addition, ratification by the Member States is needed for the entry into force since the decision concluding this agreement shall enter into force after it has been approved by the Member States in accordance with their respective constitutional requirements.

From the Council of Europe's perspective, the Accession Agreement would need to be endorsed by the Committee of Ministers after the Parliamentary Assembly and the Strasbourg Court have given their opinions on it. It will ultimately have to be ratified by all the member countries of the Council of Europe.

As the first step, the Member States of the EU had to agree on the negotiating mandate. In March 2010, the European Commission proposed a recommendation for a Council decision to authorise the Commission to negotiate the Accession Agreement. The Council Decision authorising the Commission to negotiate the Accession Agreement and setting out the negotiating directives was adopted very quickly (on 4 June 2010), considering the usual length of decision-making proceedings.[24]

Thereby, the Commission was nominated the EU negotiator and a Council preparatory body, bringing together the representatives of all Member States—the Working Party on Fundamental Rights, Citizens' Rights and Free Movement of Persons (FREMP)—was appointed as the special committee within the meaning of Article 218(4) TFEU.

Upon the adoption of the above-mentioned decision, the Council made a declaration that is likely to prove very significant in the final phases leading to accession. The declaration states that in parallel with the accession negotiations, it would discuss binding internal rules laying down modalities for the various aspects relating to the EU's accession to the ECHR. These rules should, in accordance with the declaration, be adopted before the conclusion of the Accession Agreement.

It should also be mentioned that as an exception to the usual EU decision-making process, a CJEU representative was participating as an observer in the adoption of the negotiating directives as well as subsequent meetings pertinent to the CJEU domain of interest.[25] Observers are not formal participants in negotiations but are nevertheless allowed to take the floor and submit written comments to make their views known.

[24] Council document 10817/10, available at http://register.consilium.europa.eu/doc/srv?l=EN&f=ST%2010817%202010%20EXT%202.

[25] Council document 13714/10, available at http://register.consilium.europa.eu/doc/srv?l=EN&f=ST%2013714%202010%20INIT.

In the initial phase of negotiations as from June 2010, the Commission, as the EU negotiator, conducted negotiations on behalf of the EU in a group of 14 experts (CDDH-UE 7+7) within the framework of the Steering Committee for Human Rights (CDDH) for the elaboration of a draft Accession Agreement. The experts, seven from EU countries and seven from non-EU countries, were appointed in their personal capacity and not as representatives of their governments.[26]

In June 2011, following intensive discussions and a total of eight negotiating meetings, CDDH-UE 7+7 group finalised the draft Accession Agreement and submitted it to the consideration of the high contracting parties and the EU.[27]

In October 2011, after an initial period of reflection, it appeared that the EU Member States could not unanimously accept the text thus negotiated.[28] The negotiations in Strasbourg came to a standstill, whereas rigorous discussions, with monthly meetings, resumed in Brussels in the FREMP working group in an effort to find a solution to the deadlock.

Finally in April 2012 the EU ministers in the framework of the Justice and Home Affairs (JHA) Council examined the outcome of these intense discussions and adopted certain guidelines[29] on the basis of which the EU negotiator could ask to resume negotiations in Strasbourg.

Accordingly, the second round of negotiations in a different format, commenced in June 2012.

On 13 June 2012, the Committee of Ministers gave a new mandate[30] to the CDDH to pursue negotiations with the EU in an ad hoc group '47+1', with a view to finalising the legal instruments setting out the modalities of accession.

From the EU perspective the changes proposed[31] aimed at better reflecting the specific legal nature of the EU, at clarifying certain aspects of the co-respondent mechanism, and also touched upon the participation of the EU in the Committee of Ministers of the Council of Europe.[32]

[26] See the CDDH report of the 7th meeting, 15–18 June 2010, CDDH(2010)10, available at http://www.coe.int/t/dghl/standardsetting/cddh/Meeting%20reports%20committee/70th_en.pdf.

[27] For an analysis of the draft of June 2011, prepared in the 7+7 format, see X Groussot, T Lock, L Pech, 'EU Accession to the European Convention on Human Rights: a Legal Assessment of the Draft Accession Agreement of 14th October 2011' (2011) 218 *Fondation Robert Schuman, European issues*, 7 November 2011, and T Lock, 'End of an Epic? The Draft Agreement on the EU's Accession to the ECHR' (2012) 31 *Yearbook of European Law* 162–97.

[28] See the report to the Committee of Ministers on the elaboration of legal instruments for the accession of the European Union to the European Convention on Human Rights, CDDH (2011) 09, at http://www.coe.int/t/dghl/standardsetting/hrpolicy/Accession/Meeting_reports/CDDH_2011_009_en.pdf.

[29] Council document 8915/12 RESTREINT UE.

[30] Decisions of the 1145th meeting of the Ministers' Deputies (13 June 2012), at http://www.coe.int/t/dghl/standardsetting/hrpolicy/Accession/Working_documents/47_1(2012)01_CM_Decision_BIL.pdf.

[31] Report of the first negotiation meeting between the CDDH and the European Commission on the accession of the European Union to the European Convention on Human Rights, 21 June 2012, Strasbourg, at http://www.coe.int/t/dghl/standardsetting/hrpolicy/Accession/Meeting_reports/47_1(2012)R01Erev2.pdf.

[32] These concerns will briefly be discussed in Section III.

Understandably, reopening the negotiations meant opening the whole package with all countries coming up with their own points to re-negotiate, going as far as questioning the core legal aspects that had already been agreed on, such as the prior involvement of the CJEU and the EU having a voting right in the Council of Europe organs for ECHR-related matters. Since the Commission was authorised to negotiate on behalf of the EU of 28 Member States, in practice this meant that the Member States did not participate actively in the discussions. This, in turn, purported the non-EU countries to coordinate amongst themselves, culminating in a paper submitted by 16 non-EU countries,[33] highlighting the issues on which in their view re-negotiation was necessary, even if the concerns of individual countries were more nuanced.[34]

Most countries (EU and non-EU) emphasised at the last negotiating meeting that internal procedures would have to be completed in all countries before the final adoption of the instruments.[35]

From the perspective of EU law, the EU has not as of yet expressed its consent to be bound by the draft Accession Agreement. The draft Accession Agreement remains thus an envisaged agreement within the meaning of Article 218(11) TFEU. In accordance with Article 218(11) TFEU it is possible to transmit the text to the CJEU to seek its opinion on the compatibility of the draft Accession Agreement with EU Treaties. The purpose of such a possibility to request an opinion is to forestall complications that would arise if the CJEU found after the conclusion of an agreement that such an agreement was, by reason of its content or of the procedure adopted for its conclusions, incompatible with EU law.[36] Such a situation could provoke serious difficulties internally as well as for international relations.

Accordingly the Commission as the EU negotiator sent a request to the CJEU on 4 July 2013. The hearing in the case—Opinion 2/13—was held on 5–6 May 2014 and the Opinion was delivered on 18 December 2014. In accordance with Article 218(11) TFEU, where such an opinion is adverse the envisaged agreement has to be either amended or the treaties need to be revised.

[33] Common paper of Andorra, Armenia, Azerbaijan, Bosnia-Herzegovina, Iceland, Liechtenstein, Monaco, Montenegro, Norway, Serbia, Switzerland, Russian Federation, Turkey and Ukraine on major concerns regarding the draft revised Agreement on the Accession of the European Union to the European Convention on Human Rights, at http://www.coe.int/t/dghl/standardsetting/hrpolicy/Accession/Working_documents_en.asp. During the meeting Georgia and Moldova associated themselves to the paper.

[34] Report of the fourth negotiation meeting between the CDDH and the European Commission on the accession of the European Union to the European Convention on Human Rights, 17–19 January 2013, Strasbourg, at http://www.coe.int/t/dghl/standardsetting/hrpolicy/Accession/Meeting_reports/Web_47_1(2013)R04_EN_final.pdf, para 2.

[35] Report of the fifth negotiation meeting between the CDDH and the European Commission on the accession of the European Union to the European Convention on Human Rights, 3–5 April 2013, Strasbourg, at http://www.coe.int/t/dghl/standardsetting/hrpolicy/Accession/Meeting_reports/Web_47_1(2013)R05_EN.pdf, para 16.

[36] See Opinion 2/94, ECLI:EU:C:1996:140, paragraph 3; Opinion 1/08, ECLI:EU:C:2009:739, paragraph 107 and Opinion 1/09, ECLI:EU:C:2011:123, paragraph 47.

At this stage it is not clear how the procedure will continue henceforth. This depends how the difficulties highlighted by the CJEU Opinion will be resolved.

In procedural terms and hypothetically speaking, once there is a new version of the draft Accession Agreement or an amended version of the Treaties, presumably the CJEU would be consulted again, a procedure that could take 9 to 18 months as a minimum. In the hypothetical situation that the second opinion would be positive, thereafter the Commission would make its formal proposal or proposals both for EU internal rules, whatever form these may take, and for the Council decision for the conclusion of the Accession Agreement. The negotiations between EU Member States about the internal rules are likely to be subject to unanimity and it is unclear at this stage how long these would take. From a procedural point of view, the European Parliament would formally only be involved from the moment the formal proposal is submitted and the European Parliament is known for taking the procedure whereby its consent is required very seriously, especially in the area of fundamental rights. All in all, there are many variables in the process that make it impossible to predict at this stage, how long the process would take and also what the road to the final destination will ultimately look like.

D. Substance of the CJEU Opinion

The CJEU Opinion took a very strict approach to the accession pre-requisites as laid down in the Treaties and in Protocol 8. In a nutshell the CJEU Opinion boils down to the autonomy of EU law and the CJEU's exclusive jurisdiction. The CJEU emphasised in strong terms that the EU's specific natured legal order with its own constitutional framework, founding principles, institutional structure and a full set of legal rules has consequences as regards the procedure for and conditions of accession to the ECHR.[37] While placing the fundamental rights recognised by the Charter at the heart of the EU legal structure, the CJEU emphasised that the autonomy enjoyed by EU law in relation to the laws of the Member States and in relation to international law requires that the interpretation of fundamental rights *has to be ensured within the framework of the structure and objectives of the EU.*[38] The CJEU also stated in clear terms that any action by the bodies given decision-making powers by the ECHR (this means primarily the Committee of Ministers and the ECtHR) *must not have the effect of binding the EU and its institutions, in the exercise of their internal powers, to a particular interpretation of the rules of EU law.*[39]

It was clear during the hearing that the CJEU would not take the legal implications of accession lightly and intended to engage in an in-depth examination of

[37] Paragraph 158, Opinion 2/13 (n 3).
[38] Paragraph 170, Opinion 2/13 (n 3).
[39] Paragraph 184, Opinion 2/13 (n 3).

the draft Accession Agreement. Therefore no stakeholder took the CJEU outcome for granted. Nevertheless, the thoroughly negative Opinion with its elaborate points sent shockwaves through both the EU and the Council of Europe's legal communities as many hadn't anticipated this kind of outcome.[40]

It is notable that the Union negotiator, the Legal Services of the Council and the European Parliament, as well as 24 of the 28 Member States that intervened in the procedure, all supported the conclusion that the draft Accession Agreement was in fact compatible with EU Treaties. In a similar vein Advocate General Kokott, in the view delivered in Opinion 2/13 on 13 June 2014, concluded, albeit with some substantive qualifications, that the draft Accession Agreement was compatible with EU law.

All in all, the CJEU Opinion contains ten different elements divided into five areas where the draft Accession Agreement falls short of the requirements of EU primary law.

The first area related to the special nature of the EU and EU law. While assessing the draft Accession Agreement from the perspective of the specific characteristics and the autonomy of EU law, the CJEU found fault in three points.[41]

Firstly, it considered that Article 53 of the ECHR[42] needed to be coordinated with Article 53 of the Charter[43] to ensure that the power granted to Member States by Article 53 of the ECHR is limited—with regard to the rights recognised by the Charter that correspond to those guaranteed by the ECHR—to that which is necessary to ensure that the level of protection provided for by the Charter and the primacy, unity and effectiveness of EU law are not compromised.

[40] See for example:
T Lock, 'Oops! We did it again—the CJEU's Opinion on EU Accession to the ECHR,' VerfBlog, 2014/12/18, available at http://www.verfassungsblog.de/en/oops-das-gutachten-des-eugh-zum-emrk-beitritt-der-eu/; S Douglas-Scott, 'Opinion 2/13 on EU accession to the ECHR: a Christmas bombshell from the European Court of Justice,' VerfBlog, 2014/12/24, available at http://www.verfassungsblog.de/en/opinion-213-eu-accession-echr-christmas-bombshell-european-court-justice/; W Michl, 'Thou shalt have no other courts before me,' VerfBlog, 2014/12/23, available at http://www.verfassungsblog.de/en/thou-shalt-no-courts/; and A Łazowski, R Wessel, 'The European Court of Justice blocks the EU's accession to the ECHR,' CEPS commentary, available at http://www.ceps.eu/node/9942.

[41] Paragraphs 179–200, Opinion 2/13 (n 3).

[42] ECHR, Article 53 reads as follows (Safeguard for existing human rights): Nothing in this Convention shall be construed as limiting or derogating from any of the human rights and fundamental freedoms which may be ensured under the laws of any High Contracting Party or under any other agreement to which it is a party.

[43] Charter Article 53 (Level of protection): Nothing in this Charter shall be interpreted as restricting or adversely affecting human rights and fundamental freedoms as recognised, in their respective fields of application, by Union law and international law and by international agreements to which the Union or all the Member States are party, including the European Convention for the Protection of Human Rights and Fundamental Freedoms, and by the Member States' constitutions.

Secondly, it highlighted the principle of mutual trust between EU Member States and considered that, in so far as the ECHR would require a Member State to check that another Member State has observed fundamental rights where EU law imposes an obligation of mutual trust, accession would be liable to upset the underlying balance of the EU and undermine the autonomy of EU law.

Thirdly, in the view of the CJEU, by failing to make any provision in respect of the relationship between the mechanism established by the new Protocol 16 of the ECHR and the preliminary ruling procedure provided for in Article 267 TFEU, the draft Accession Agreement is likely to adversely affect the autonomy and effectiveness of the preliminary reference procedure.[44]

Next and as the second area, the CJEU embarked on Article 344 TFEU and on the exclusive jurisdiction of the CJEU. The CJEU concluded that the draft Accession Agreement lacked an express exclusion of the ECtHR's jurisdiction under Article 33 of the ECHR over disputes between Member States or between Member States and the EU in relation to the application of the ECHR within the material scope of EU law.

Thirdly and fourthly, the CJEU also analysed the core elements of the draft Accession Agreement—the co-respondent mechanism and the prior involvement of the CJEU and found incompatibilities with both these. These will be touched upon further below.

The fifth and final area of the CJEU criticism concerned judicial review in Common Foreign and Security Policy (CFSP) matters that is also discussed below.

III. KEY ELEMENTS OF THE ACCESSION AGREEMENT OF 5 APRIL 2013

A. Main Features of the 2013 Draft Accession Agreement

The reference to the draft Accession Agreement encompasses all draft instruments[45] consisting of a draft Agreement on the Accession of the European Union to the ECHR, a draft declaration by the Union, a draft Rule to be added to the Rules of the Committee of Ministers of the Council of Europe for the supervision and execution of judgements and of the terms of friendly settlements in cases to which the EU is a party, a draft model of a Memorandum of Understanding and a draft explanatory report to the Accession Agreement, all together forming a package necessary for the EU's accession to the ECHR.

[44] Protocol 16 establishes a mechanism which permits the highest courts and tribunals in the Member States to request the ECtHR to give advisory opinions on questions of principle relating to the interpretation or application of the rights and freedoms guaranteed by the ECHR or the protocols thereto. The CJEU found that the mechanism established by that protocol could affect the autonomy and effectiveness of the preliminary reference procedure where the issue concerns rights guaranteed by the Charter.

[45] The latest texts are available at http://www.coe.int/t/dghl/standardsetting/hrpolicy/Accession/Meeting_reports/47_1(2013)008rev2_EN.pdf.

By Article 1(1) of the draft Accession Agreement, the EU accedes *ipso iure* to the Convention, to the first Protocol, and to Protocol No 6. This approach of the 'least common denominator'[46] is consistent with the primary law requirements as regards Member States positions. Article 10(4) of the draft Accession Agreement specifies that the EU will become a party to these instruments at the date of entry into force of the Accession Agreement.

Article 1(2) of the draft Accession Agreement amends Article 59(2) of the Convention: a new subparagraph 2(a) will expressly refer to accession by the EU to the protocols, which is to be governed, *mutatis mutandis*, by the accession provisions in each protocol. Paragraph 17 of the explanatory report makes it clear that subsequent accession by the EU to the protocols other than the first Protocol and Protocol No 6 will require the deposit of separate accession instruments.

In substance the draft of April 2013 is quite similar to the draft of June 2011.[47]

From the EU's viewpoint the issues that were raised, discussed in great detail and that purported the reopening of negotiations, included:

- technical clarifications relating to the nature of the EU as a non-state entity;
- attribution of acts to the Member States and the EU, in particular as regards the Common Foreign and Security Policy (CFSP);
- amendments regarding the participation of the EU in the Committee of Ministers of the Council of Europe.

The first set of changes, relating to the nature of the EU as a non-state entity, were perceived as more technical changes, even if these gave rise to considerable discussions. The discussions on the attribution clause and the voting rights were more complex and time-consuming. A significant amount of time was also devoted to clarifying the functioning of the most important procedural innovations introduced by the draft Accession Agreement that had previously been agreed on: the co-respondent mechanism and the prior involvement of the CJEU.

For many EU as well as non-EU countries the June 2011 draft represented a good draft, and a balanced compromise. There was reluctance to depart from it. One could also sense some 'fatigue' on behalf of the non-EU countries about the specific nature of the EU and its legal system. This is an element that is likely to be very relevant in the next phase, should the EU choose to re-open the negotiations following the negative Opinion of the CJEU. The political cost of reopening negotiations by the EU once again in order to add more EU specific provisions in the ECHR and in the draft Accession Agreement seems impossibly high at this stage.

The second round of negotiations was by no means easy, as recorded in the meeting reports.[48] It was consistently emphasised that adaptations to ECHR

[46] P Gragl, *The Accession of the European Union to the European Convention on Human Rights* (Oxford, Hart Publishing, 2013) 94.

[47] Final version of the draft legal instruments on the Accession of the European Union to the European Convention on Human Rights, CDDH-UE 2011(16), at http://www.coe.int/t/dghl/standardsetting/hrpolicy/Accession/Working_documents/CDDH-UE_2011_16_final_en.pdf.

[48] Meeting reports available at http://www.coe.int/t/dghl/standardsetting/hrpolicy/Accession/Meeting_reports_en.asp.

system should be limited to what was strictly necessary for EU accession and that the Accession Agreement should not bring about procedural privileges or exceptions for one of the contracting parties.

As a result the draft Accession Agreement in itself is quite open-ended and general, especially when it comes to the functioning of the co-respondent mechanism and the prior involvement of the CJEU. However, in a situation where the autonomy of EU law needed to be preserved, while accomplishing the EU's accession to the ECHR within the existing Treaty framework, the only possible way at the time seemed to be to keep the draft Accession Agreement rather general. The logic of this approach was that the general rules of the Accession Agreement would be supplemented by binding EU legal rules, governing the participation of the EU and its Member States in proceedings before the Strasbourg Court in situations where EU law is called into question.[49] In particular, details of the functioning of the co-respondent mechanism were supposed to be regulated internally together with aspects relating to the prior involvement of the CJEU. This approach was purported also by the dynamics of the negotiations where the EU's negotiating partners on the Council of Europe side were reluctant to modify the ECHR and to add too many special provisions to accommodate the EU.

In the next section a brief overview will be given of the main features of the renegotiated draft Accession Agreement: the two procedural mechanisms as well as the attribution clause with a reference to the CJEU Opinion on these elements, and the outcome of the voting rights discussions in the second round of negotiations.

B. Attribution Clause

The purpose of the attribution clause[50] was to make clear that the acts, measures and omissions of Member States remain attributable only to the Member States even if they were acts of implementation of EU law.

In addition to the general attribution clause, the EU sought to have a specific attribution clause relating to the CFSP which would make sure that the Strasbourg Court would not attribute to the EU an act which would not be attributable to the EU under its own legal system, resulting in asymmetry in jurisdiction.

[49] See Section E for internal rules.

[50] Art 1(4) of the draft Accession Agreement reads: For the purposes of the Convention, of the Protocols thereto and of this Agreement, an act, measure or omission of organs of a Member State of the European Union or of persons acting on its behalf shall be attributed to that State, even if such act, measure or omission occurs when the State implements the law of the European Union, including decisions taken under the Treaty on the European Union (hereinafter referred to as 'the TEU') and under the Treaty on the Functioning of the European Union (hereinafter referred to as the 'TFEU'). This shall not preclude the European Union from being responsible as a co-respondent for a violation resulting from such an act, measure or omission, in accordance with Article 36, paragraph 4, of the Convention and Article 3 of this Agreement. Available at http://www.coe.int/t/dghl/standardsetting/hrpolicy/Accession/Meeting_reports/47_1(2013)008rev2_EN.pdf.

Under Article 275 of the TFEU, the CJEU has no jurisdiction with respect to the provisions relating to the CFSP, nor with respect to acts adopted on the basis of those provisions. The only exception is to review the legality of decisions providing for restrictive measures against natural or legal persons.[51]

The more specific attribution rule proposed by the EU to deal with issues related to CFSP in accordance with Article 275 TFEU was seen by some third countries[52] as a carve-out of a politically sensitive area and a restriction from the jurisdiction of Strasbourg Court. On the contrary, the general attribution rule was acceptable to third countries.

In accordance with this general attribution rule, an act, measure or omission of organs or agents of a Member State of the EU shall be attributable only to that state, even if such an act, measure or omission occurs when the state implements the law of the EU. This should be seen differently from the responsibility under the co-respondent mechanism. It can be perfectly feasible that the EU and the Member States take responsibility for a violation even if the act is attributed to only one of them.

In the final round of negotiations, a clarification was added that the reference to the law of the Union in Article 1(4) of the draft Accession Agreement included Council decisions under the TEU (meaning also CFSP decisions).

Accordingly, acts, measures or omissions of organs or agents of a Member State would be only attributable to that Member State, even when implementing a CFSP decision. The EU could become a co-respondent in such cases and with co-respondents being jointly responsible for the violation, it would then be for the EU internal rules to lay down how to handle this internally.

The Advocate General and the CJEU in its Opinion did not agree with the negotiated solution and the interpretative explanations provided in the Explanatory Memorandum. The CJEU stated that it had not yet had the opportunity to define the extent of its jurisdiction in CFSP matters. For the purposes of assessing the compatibility of the draft Accession Agreement with the Treaties the CJEU considered that it was sufficient to declare that certain acts adopted in the context of CFSP fall outside the ambit of judicial review by CJEU. The CJEU went on to consider that the negotiated solution would allow for the ECtHR to rule on the compatibility with the ECHR of certain acts, actions or omissions whose legality the CJEU cannot review in light of fundamental rights. Such a situation would, in the CJEU's Opinion, entrust the judicial review of those acts, actions and omissions on the part of the EU exclusively to a non-EU body, albeit that such a review would be limited to compliance with the rights guaranteed by the ECHR. In the CJEU's view this solution fails to have regard to the specific characteristics of EU law.

[51] On this point, see J Polakiewicz, Foreword in this volume.

[52] See para 7 of the meeting report of the third negotiating session, 7–9 November 2012, at http://www.coe.int/t/dghl/standardsetting/hrpolicy/Accession/Meeting_reports/47_1(2012)R03_EN_final.pdf.

C. EU Participation in the Committee of Ministers

The thorniest issue in the second round of negotiations was the question of voting rights. Until now in the Council of Europe context there was no need to distinguish between the functions of the Committee of Ministers under the ECHR and its other functions as an organ of the Council of Europe.

The ECHR explicitly confers a number of functions upon the Committee of Ministers of the Council of Europe, the main one being the supervision of the execution of the Strasbourg Court's judgments under Article 46 of the ECHR and of the terms of friendly settlements under Article 39 of the ECHR.

The Committee of Ministers is also entitled to request advisory opinions from the ECHR on certain legal questions concerning the interpretation of the ECHR and the Protocols (Article 47 ECHR) and to reduce, at the request of the Strasbourg plenary Court, the number of judges of the Chambers (Article 26, paragraph 2 ECHR).

The Committee of Ministers also carries out other functions in relation to the ECHR such as the adoption of protocols and other documents relating to the ECHR.

The current practice within the Council of Europe has been to grant voting rights in the Committee of Ministers to member countries of the Council of Europe only. In accordance with the principle of equal footing it was agreed that the EU, which is not a member of the Council of Europe, would have a voting right in the Committee of Ministers when the latter exercised ECHR-based functions, once the EU becomes a party to the ECHR.

However, this would mean that the EU and its Member States would have 29 votes out of 48.

Understandably this majority raised concerns amongst the non-EU countries of the Council of Europe, in particular as regards decisions that could be potentially 'disadvantageous' to the EU. The fear was that the EU and its Member States would coordinate their votes, for example, in situations where the Committee of Ministers was monitoring the execution of judgments by the Union or one of its Member States.

Several options were considered in the context of negotiations, seeking to limit that risk. For example, the June 2011 draft contained a specific rule for cases where the Committee of Ministers supervised the fulfilment of obligations either by the EU alone, or by the EU and one or more of its Member States jointly. To make sure, the Committee of Ministers effectively exercised its functions in those circumstances by calculating majorities on the basis of the votes of non-EU Member States. However, after an initial period of reflection this was not acceptable to the EU.

Upon reopening the negotiations, some countries questioned whether the EU should have a voting right at all for the 'statutory' functions of the Committee of Ministers, considering this to be contrary to the way the Committee of Ministers worked. In the view of these countries, EU participation in the Committee of

Ministers should be restricted to those functions which the ECHR explicitly attributes to it.[53]

Therefore it was necessary to devise a solution that would take into account the concerns of the EU as well as third countries.

What followed were lengthy discussions with some novel options on the negotiating table. For example, the EU proposed a gentlemen's agreement and a panel mediation procedure, which were not accepted by the non-EU partners. Different levels of majorities and minorities were discussed.[54]

The prevailing solution is a rather complex system combining different hyper-majorities and hyper-minorities for different types of decisions and with a consultation mechanism for functions not explicitly foreseen in the ECHR.[55]

A majority of four-fifths of the representatives casting a vote and a majority of two-thirds of the representatives entitled to sit on the Committee are required for the adoption of final resolutions (supervision of judgments and friendly settlements).

As regards referrals to the Strasbourg Court for interpretation of a judgment and infringement proceedings, the solution proposed is that a 'hyper-minority' of one quarter of the members entitled to sit on the Committee of Ministers shall be required to consider as adopted a decision under such rules.

In relation to procedural decisions and decisions requesting information, a hyper-minority of one fifth of the representatives entitled to sit on the Committee of Ministers shall be required.

In addition, the draft Accession Agreement will add a new paragraph to Article 54 of the ECHR providing an explicit legal basis for the Committee of Ministers to adopt protocols to the ECHR.

As already mentioned this was the most contentious issue in the second round of negotiations. The solution achieved strikes a good balance between the EU's interests and the interests of non-EU countries. Considering the amount of different options that were examined during negotiations, it is difficult to imagine further solutions that would fulfil the same objective as well as this one. For this reason, the area of voting rights would probably not benefit from a possible renegotiation.

D. Co-respondent Mechanism

One of the specific characteristics of the EU and its legal order is that as a general rule it is the Member States who apply EU law. In the same way, judicial protection with regard to acts or omissions on the part of a Member State is provided

[53] See para 12 of the second meeting report, 17–19 September 2012, at http://www.coe.int/t/dghl/standardsetting/hrpolicy/Accession/Meeting_reports/47_1(2012)R02final_EN.pdf.

[54] ibid, para 14.

[55] See the final report CDDH 47+1(2013)008 for further details, at: http://www.coe.int/t/dghl/standardsetting/hrpolicy/Accession/Meeting_reports/47_1(2013)008_final_report_EN.pdf.

by the courts of that Member State, even when the act or omission is applying a provision of EU law (see Article 19(1) TEU, second subparagraph). Under the EU Treaties, the EU courts have jurisdiction to provide judicial protection to individuals only in respect of acts or omissions on the part of the institutions, bodies, offices or agencies of the EU.[56]

With the accession of the EU to the ECHR there will be a unique system that a legal act could be enacted by one high contracting party and implemented by another.[57] This concerns, in particular, acts adopted by EU institutions (secondary law, for example Directives) that may need further implementation at Member State level. It can also concern EU primary law, i.e. provisions of the Treaties, implemented by EU institutions, agencies, bodies and offices; whereas it is the Member States that are the masters of the Treaties and the institutions, even if involved in the Treaty amendment process, are not able to revise Treaties on their own.

This specificity of EU law had to be taken into account in the course of negotiations in order to avoid gaps in the system. From the perspective of the applicant it could be difficult to ascertain whether it was the EU or the Member State that infringed his/her fundamental rights but the application could be declared inadmissible if the choice of the defendant was incorrect.

Where a violation of the ECHR alleged before the Strasbourg Court—in relation to an act or omission on the part of a Member State—rests on a provision of EU law, it is the EU that is responsible for the provision on which the alleged violation rests. In normal circumstances, however, the EU would not be a party to such proceedings before the Strasbourg Court. For this reason specific procedural rules had to be enacted. The same applies to the Member States collectively, where a violation of the ECHR alleged before the Strasbourg Court in relation to an act or omission on the part of an institution, body, office or agency of the EU rests on a provision of general application laid down directly in the Treaties. In either situation the contracting party that enacted the provision would not be able to take part in the legal debate before the Strasbourg Court, and would not be bound by the obligations to take general measures imposed, as the case may be, by Article 46(1) of the ECHR. Those obligations are binding only on the contracting party that committed the act or omission that is alleged to violate the ECHR, namely the Member State that applied a provision of EU law, or the EU if it has applied a provision laid down directly in the Treaties.

A situation of that kind would be neither in the interests of the EU, nor in the interests of the Member States, nor in the interests of the proper operation of the ECHR control machinery.

[56] TFEU, Arts 263, 265, 267, 268 and 270.

[57] For an analysis of the co-respondent mechanism as in the June 2011 Accession Agreement, see Lock, 'End of an Epic?' (n 23) and G Gaja, 'The "Co-Respondent Mechanisms" According to the Draft Agreement for the Accession of the EU to the ECHR' (2012) 2 *European Society of International Law Reflections*, at http://www.esil-sedi.eu/node/266.

It was therefore negotiated that the draft Accession Agreement laid down specific procedural rules allowing the EU to be a party to the proceedings before the Strasbourg Court in respect of an alleged violation of the ECHR—in relation to an act or omission on the part of a Member State—that rests on a provision of EU law. Conversely, these rules allow for the Member States, taken together, to be parties to proceedings before the Strasbourg Court in respect of an alleged violation of the ECHR—in relation to an act or omission on the part of an institution, body, office or agency of the EU—that rests on a provision of general application laid down directly in the Treaties. That, in substance, is the content of the obligation under Article 1(b) of Protocol No 8 of the Lisbon Treaty, according to which the Accession Agreement must provide for 'the mechanisms necessary to ensure that proceedings by non-Member States and individual applications are correctly addressed to Member States and/or the EU as appropriate'.

Accordingly, Article 3 of the draft Accession Agreement sets out the co-respondent mechanism, which allows the EU to join the proceedings in cases in which the applicant has directed the application only against one or more Member States and it appears that such an allegation calls into question the compatibility with the ECHR rights at issue of a provision of EU law.

It also allows the EU Member States to join the proceedings as co-respondents in cases where the applicant has directed the application only against the EU, if it appears that such allegation calls into question the compatibility with the ECHR rights at issue of a provision of EU primary law.

The new Article 36(4) of the ECHR, added by Article 3(1) of the draft Accession Agreement, states that a co-respondent is a party to the case.

As a party to the case, a co-respondent enjoys full procedural rights to conduct an effective defence of the provision whose compatibility with the ECHR is called into question by the alleged violation of the ECHR.

The co-respondent mechanism should be clearly distinguished from third-party interventions[58] and from cases with multiple respondents. A co-respondent is not confined to the limited rights of a third-party intervener under Article 36(2) ECHR , who is entitled only to submit written comments or to take part in hearings before the Strasbourg Court.

More specifically, as explained in paragraphs 60, 61 and 63 of the explanatory report, friendly settlements under Article 39 ECHR require the agreement of the respondent and of the co-respondent; unilateral declarations acknowledging a violation for which the respondent and the co-respondent are both responsible

[58] In particular, in the negotiations there were discussions about whether the co-respondent mechanism should be extended to situations in which an application directed against a non-EU state puts into question the compatibility with the ECHR of an international agreement between that state and the EU (eg the European Economic Area (EEA) Agreement). This issue will now be dealt with in a separate memorandum of understanding, the model text of which is a part of the package agreed since it was considered that in this instance it would be more appropriate for the EU to intervene as a third party.

require the agreement of both of them; and a co-respondent may request the referral of a case to the Grand Chamber under Article 43 ECHR.

In addition, if the Strasbourg Court judgment finds that the violation at issue has indeed taken place, and thus also calls into question the provision of EU law in question, the co-respondent will have an obligation under Article 46(1) of the ECHR to remedy the violation so as to abide by the judgment. In particular, where the provision is laid down in a legal act enacted by one or more institutions, the EU will be obliged to repeal or amend that act.

The co-respondent mechanism is not a procedural privilege for the EU but rather a further way to avoid gaps in the protection system. It is a unique mechanism, put in place for the EU, because of the unique system of competencies between the EU and its Member States. It is a mechanism for shared responsibility, allowing the party who at the end would bear responsibility for removing the violation to participate in the proceedings before the Strasbourg Court from the outset.[59]

Some concerns have been expressed as to the voluntary nature of the co-respondent mechanism and negotiating partners sought reassurances in the course of negotiations that when the conditions are met the EU would become a co-respondent.[60] Accordingly the EU agreed to make a declaration that it would request to become a co-respondent to the proceedings or accept an invitation from the Strasbourg Court to that effect where the conditions set out in Article 3(2) of the Accession Agreement are met.[61] The idea was to further specify this in the legally binding EU internal rules.

The whole co-respondent mechanism was devised under the assumption that further provisions would be laid down in EU internal rules. Accordingly the draft Accession Agreement is rather short on the co-respondent mechanism. Subsequently the EU would define internally how the co-respondent mechanism would function within the EU, adjusted to the existing system of EU competencies. The internal rules would need to define the conditions for triggering of the co-respondent mechanism, participation of the Member States and the EU in the proceedings as well as enforcement of judgments between the co-respondents.

The CJEU Opinion found three aspects of the co-respondent mechanism not in conformity with the requirement of preserving the specific characteristics of EU law.

Firstly, the draft Accession Agreement foresees that a Contracting Party would become a co-respondent either by accepting an invitation from the ECtHR or by decision of the ECtHR upon the request of that Contracting Party. While the CJEU had no problem with triggering the co-respondent mechanism by the

[59] CDDH-UE (2011) 16, para 33.

[60] For instance, para 12 of the fourth report, at http://www.coe.int/t/dghl/standardsetting/hrpolicy/Accession/Meeting_reports/Web_47_1(2013)R04_EN_final.pdf. See also Gragl, 'A Giant Leap for European Human Rights? (n 9) at 37.

[61] See Appendix II in the final report, at http://www.coe.int/t/dghl/standardsetting/hrpolicy/Accession/Meeting_reports/47_1(2013)008rev2_EN.pdf.

Contracting Party accepting the EctHR's invitation, as regards the second option the CJEU considered that the plausibility review that the ECtHR is to carry out when deciding on the request from the Contracting Party would be liable to interfere with the division of powers between the EU and its Member States.

Secondly, the draft Accession Agreement foresees in Article 3(7) that if a violation would be established, the respondent and co-respondent would be jointly responsible for that violation, unless the ECtHR decides on the basis of reasons given by the respondent and the co-respondent that only one of them is to be held responsible for the violation. The logic behind that provision, once again, was to lay down more detailed rules for allocating responsibility between the EU and its Member State(s) in the EU internal rules. In the view of the CJEU that provision does not preclude a Member State from being held responsible, together with the EU, for the violation of a provision of the ECHR in respect of which that Member State may have made a reservation in accordance with Article 57 of the ECHR.

Last but not least, the CJEU did not agree that the ECtHR could decide on the apportionment of responsibility between the EU and its Member States, albeit on the basis of the reasons given by the co-respondents. This would imply that the ECtHR assesses EU rules governing the division of powers and this would adversely affect autonomy of EU law.

E. Prior Involvement of the CJEU

Already in 2010, the CJEU prepared a discussion paper on certain aspects of the accession of the EU to ECHR. The paper stated that in order to observe the principle of subsidiarity inherent in the ECHR and at the same time to ensure the proper functioning of the system of judicial protection of the EU, a mechanism must be available to ensure that before the Strasbourg Court rules on the compatibility of an EU act with the ECHR, the CJEU should examine the question of the validity of that EU act.

This was followed by the Joint Communication from the Presidents of the Strasbourg Court and the CJEU on 24 January 2011,[62] considering that a procedure should be put in place, in connection with the accession of the EU to the ECHR. That procedure should be flexible and should ensure that the CJEU conducts an internal review before the Strasbourg Court carries out an external review.

Consider a situation where the Strasbourg Court was able to establish a violation in respect of which the EU was a co-respondent to the proceedings. If in such a case the CJEU had not yet considered the validity of the act in light of the fundamental rights, as guaranteed in the EU, and if there was no way in which

[62] Both documents are available on the website of the CJEU under Institution/Various documents at http://curia.europa.eu/jcms/jcms/P 64268/.

the CJEU could make such an assessment, then the CJEU's prerogative to declare an act of the EU invalid might be voided of substance. This situation should be avoided since the CJEU is in fact in the best position to assess the compliance of EU acts with fundamental rights, against the background of complexities and uniqueness of EU law.[63]

Therefore in order to preserve the prerogatives of the CJEU and the specific characteristics of the system of judicial protection in the EU, the negotiations proceeded so as to give the CJEU an opportunity to consider the compatibility of a provision of EU law with the rights guaranteed by the ECHR. This should happen before the Strasbourg Court rules on the substance of the allegation, and thus indirectly on the compatibility of the provision with the fundamental right which it is alleged has been violated.

This mechanism is closely linked to the co-respondent mechanism, since prior involvement of the CJEU only arises in cases where the EU is a co-respondent. In light of that, it is difficult to understand the CJEU Opinion where it expresses concerns that a request for a (non-binding) advisory opinion made pursuant to the new Protocol 16 could trigger the prior involvement of the CJEU.[64] This is one of the questions that needs to be clarified in the next phase.

The draft Accession Agreement is not very detailed on the prior involvement mechanism. The purpose was yet again to lay down more details in the EU internal rules. It has been debated that making the mechanism work internally would require Treaty change.[65] This was also argued by one Member State in the proceedings in the CJEU.[66]

The Advocate General in the Opinion 2/13 admitted that the prior involvement procedure was not among judicial procedures expressly provided for in the EU Treaties but considered that the prior involvement procedure did not constitute a new competence for the CJEU. Rather it was a new means of exercising the existing judicial powers that would not have the effect of changing the essence of the function of the Court provided for in the Treaties.[67] The CJEU seemed to agree with that view since it did not contest the establishment of the new procedure as currently set out in the draft Accession Agreement. However, the CJEU did raise two other issues about the mechanism that need to be tackled subsequently.

Firstly, in the view of the CJEU the prior involvement mechanism should be set up in a way as to ensure that, in any case pending before the ECtHR, the EU is fully and systematically informed so that only the competent EU institution

[63] R Baratta, 'Accession of the EU to the ECHR: the Rationale for the ECJ's Prior Involvement Mechanism' (2013) 50 *CML Rev* 1305–32, 1319.

[64] Paragraph 198, Opinion 2/13.

[65] For more on this, see Lock, 'Walking on a Tightrope' (n 16) and D Ritleng, 'The Accession of the European Union to the European Convention on Human Rights and Fundamental Freedoms: A Threat to the Specific Characteristics of the European Union and Union Law?', Working paper 2012:1, University, Uppsala, at http://uu.diva-portal.org/smash/record.jsf?pid=diva2:526830.

[66] Paragraph 138 of Opinion 2/13.

[67] Paragraphs 64–67 of the Advocate General View in Case 2/13.

is able to assess whether the CJEU has already given a ruling on the issue and, if it has not, to arrange for the prior involvement procedure to be initiated. This assessment should not be done by the ECtHR as the draft Accession Agreement had initially foreseen, since in the view of the CJEU this would amount to conferring on ECtHR jurisdiction to interpret the case-law of the CJEU.

Secondly, the CJEU also questioned limiting the scope of the prior involvement procedure only to questions of validity and considered that interpretation of secondary law in the light of the rights guaranteed by the ECHR should also be allowed. These questions would have to be explored further.

Apart from the issues that the CJEU has raised, it is clear that the EU also needs to regulate internally questions such as the conduct of proceedings, who could submit the request, procedure before the CJEU, scope of the CJEU assessment, actors entitled to participate in proceedings, time-limits and consequences of the CJEU decision for proceedings before the Strasbourg Court.

F. The Relationship between the Draft Accession Agreement and the EU Internal Rules

This chapter has repeatedly referred to the EU internal rules in the sections above. As matters currently stand these internal rules do not exist yet. It is not even clear yet what form these would take or their exact content. In light of the CJEU Opinion, even the small number of elements that had already been discussed informally between the Member States are no longer of much relevance. For the purposes of this chapter all references to internal rules should be interpreted loosely as norms that need to be laid down in an EU instrument at a certain point to make accession work internally within the EU system of competences.

As mentioned above, upon the adoption of the negotiating mandate the Council made a declaration. The declaration states that in parallel with the accession negotiations, the Council would discuss binding internal rules laying down modalities for the various aspects relating to the EU accession to the ECHR.[68] These rules should, in accordance with the declaration, be adopted before the conclusion of the Accession Agreement. In essence this means that for EU Member States the Accession Agreement should be read together with the EU internal rules on this; in order to have a full picture of how the fundamental rights protection would function post-accession from the perspective of the EU as well as Member States. This was also the compromise in order not to overburden the Strasbourg instruments with too many EU-specific rules.

Even if there is a lot of uncertainty about the internal rules, it is clear that besides the accession instruments the EU also needs to define internally how, for example, the co-respondent mechanism and the prior involvement of the CJEU

[68] Council document 16573/12, available at http://register.consilium.europa.eu/doc/srv?l=EN&f=ST%2016573%202012%20INIT.

would function within the EU, since these mechanisms need to be adjusted to the existing system of EU competencies.

The Commission has exclusive right of legislative initiative and since at this stage there is no Commission proposal yet, it is not possible to discuss the internal rules in detail. The exact formulation and the choice of a legal instrument still remain to be discussed once the Commission comes forward with a formal proposal. At this stage it is not yet clear what legal instrument or instruments the Commission would propose and on which legal basis.

One could speculate about whether the internal rules should be contained in a directly applicable Regulation based on Article 352 TFEU or incorporated as part of the proposal for a Council decision concluding the Accession Agreement, thus based on Article 218 TFEU and Article 6(2) TEU. One could also examine whether another legal basis in the Treaties could be relevant. This is not clear yet. As matters currently stand there is no general fundamental rights competence in the EU Treaties.[69] Since the Commission has an exclusive right of initiative, until there is a Commission proposal, it is not possible to discuss in detail the form and drafting of these rules.

In light of the CJEU Opinion it remains to be seen what the content of these internal rules should be. The CJEU in its Opinion, despite the Commission and certain Member States raising elements of internal rules in the court proceedings, refused to go into it. The CJEU stated that since the internal rules had not been adopted, their content was hypothetical and by reason of them being EU internal law (in the future) they could not form the object of the Opinion.

It seems that as a minimum the internal rules would need to define modalities for the functioning of the co-respondent mechanism and the prior involvement of the CJEU, rules for the participation of the Member States and the EU in the proceedings, enforcement of judgments, appointment of the EU judge,[70] representation of the EU in proceedings and determining positions to be presented in the proceedings on behalf of the EU.[71]

The Advocate General in the Opinion 2/13 has made some suggestions on formulating the prior involvement procedure at EU level and has suggested that the Statute of the CJEU should be amended for that purpose.[72]

[69] See also paragraph 46 of the view of the Advocate General in case Opinion 2/13.

[70] See also A Drzemczewski, 'L'élection du juge de l'Union européenne à la Cour européenne des droits de l'homme' (2013) 95 *Revue Trimestrielle des Droits de l'Homme* 551.

J-M Sauvé, 'Le rôle du comité 255 dans la sélection du juge de l'Union' in Rosas (ed), *The Court of Justice and the Construction of Europe* (n 15) 99–119.

[71] In an action brought on 10 February 2014 the Council brought a case against the Commission (Case C-73/14 *Council of the European Union v European Commission* [2014] OJ C93/21). This case raises some fundamental issues relating to Union external representation, institutional balance and sincere cooperation. See http://curia.europa.eu/juris/document/document.jsf?docid=149168&mode=req&pageIndex=1&dir=&occ=first&part=1&text=law%2Bof%2Bthe%2Bsea&doclang=EN&cid=54582#ctx1.

[72] Paragraph 74 of AG view in Opinion 2/13.

The internal rules, which, considering the available legal bases, would most likely need to be agreed on by unanimity, and raise complex legal issues, as shown above. At this stage there are no definite answers, as seen above, but there are many questions to which answers will have to be found and by unanimity amongst the 28 EU Member States for that matter. Even if the unanimity required should not serve as an excuse to delay the clear and mandatory objective enshrined in the Treaties,[73] it is inevitable that unanimity sets its constraints for the negotiations. It is a simple fact that unanimity in an EU consisting of 28 Member States means that any single Member State can block adoption. For this reason the process has been and will be consensus-building to get everyone on board which naturally takes more time.

IV. WHAT NEXT FOR EU ACCESSION TO THE ECHR?

This chapter has tried to explain the legal and political complexities in relation to accession. For someone not following the negotiations from close by, the pace of progress amongst the 28 EU Member States can seem painstakingly slow at times and seems to be further complicated, if not halted, by the negative CJEU Opinion. The immediate consequence of the CJEU Opinion is that the EU accession to the ECHR cannot go ahead. There are now further major legal and political hurdles that need to be tackled before accession is to become a reality.

The agreement at negotiators' level was a significant step but the CJEU Opinion questions the essence of some of the concepts that were the delicate outcome of very burdensome negotiations. It is clear that a reflection period and further in-depth analysis are needed about how to proceed in the light of the CJEU Opinion. The difficult dilemma lies in taking a step backwards and assessing the CJEU's conclusions while trying not to lose political momentum.

Academics have been quick to suggest possible ways forward, ranging from hammering out a new deal, preparing declarative statements and changing the Treaties, to freezing the accession process indefinitely.[74] It is clear that some of the

[73] Report from the Commission to the European Parliament, the Council, the European Economic and Social Committee and the Committee of the Regions—2012 Report on the Application of the EU Charter of Fundamental Rights, Council document 9297/13.

[74] See for example S Peers, 'The CJEU and the EU's accession to the ECHR: a clear and present danger to human rights protection', available at http://eulawanalysis.blogspot.co.uk/2014/12/the-cjeu-and-eus-accession-to-echr.html; T Lock, 'Oops! We did it again—the CJEU's Opinion on EU Accession to the ECHR', VerfBlog, 2014/12/18, available at http://www.verfassungsblog.de/en/oops-das-gutachten-des-eugh-zum-emrk-beitritt-der-eu; S Douglas-Scott, 'Opinion 2/13 on EU accession to the ECHR: a Christmas bombshell from the European Court of Justice', VerfBlog, 2014/12/24, available at http://www.verfassungsblog.de/en/opinion-213-eu-accession-echr-christmas-bombshell-european-court-justice; W Michl, 'Thou shalt have no other courts before me,' VerfBlog, 2014/12/23, available at http://www.verfassungsblog.de/en/thou-shalt-no-courts.

CJEU objections correspond to the intentions of the negotiating parties so that some of the points could possibly be dealt with by clarifications or declarations. It could also be argued that some of the points relate more to the EU's internal *cuisine* and it remains to be seen how these could be 'externalised' in order to appease the CJEU. Different solutions could be possible for different points of the CJEU's criticism.

Article 218(11) TFEU is clear in the sense that the EU accession process is now brought to a halt and cannot continue unless the Accession Agreement is changed or the Treaties modified. Modifying the Treaties is a path that is quite unlikely in the current political climate within the EU. Reopening negotiations on the other hand is unlikely to be appreciated by the EU's negotiating partners in Strasbourg, as discussed above. Whether we like it or not, the EU is not the only driving force in this process. It is not clear what would be the impact of reopening negotiations on other key areas that were not the subject of the CJEU criticism but that are nevertheless very significant for the overall compromise, such as voting rights. Reopening negotiations would mean that all bets are off and discussions are likely to start from a scratch and could lead to solutions very different from the existing ones that took months, if not years, of careful crafting. It is also uncertain at this stage how the EU's negotiating partners would react to possible EU-specific provisions or even clarifications in sensitive areas such as the CFSP and the Area of Freedom, Security and Justice as would appear to be necessary from the first reading of the CJEU Opinion. It is clear that every point made by the CJEU should be analysed.

The legal and political ramifications of the Lisbon Treaty leave little choice other than to proceed with EU accession to the ECHR. For this reason we should look past the surprise and disbelief at the outcome of the CJEU Opinion and the ensuing speculations. It would be useful to take a pragmatic approach in order to assess how to accommodate the CJEU criticism in the current legal and political circumstances. All in all, there are many variables in the process that make it impossible to predict at this stage how long the process would take and also what the road to the final destination will ultimately look like. One should not forget that in terms of closing the gap in the protection of human rights at European level, it took more than 30 years to get to this point and now in the past three years impressive progress has been made. As pointed out by the civil society representatives, it should be at the forefront that 'the teleological purpose of EU accession to ECHR is to ensure that the people of Europe enjoy more complete recognition and protection of their human rights'.[75] This is possibly an excellent thought to keep in mind while assessing how the CJEU Opinion fits into the wider questions of EU's post-Lisbon fundamental rights protection architecture.

[75] Submission of Amnesty International, the Aire Centre and the International Commission of Jurists. Available at http://www.coe.int/t/dghl/stanardsetting/hrpolicy/accession/Working_documents/NGO_submissions_EU_accession_5Nov2012.pdf.

4

Problems and Challenges of the EU's Accession to the ECHR: Empirical Findings with a View to the Future

STELIOS ANDREADAKIS*

I. INTRODUCTION

AFTER MORE THAN 30 years of discussions and almost three years of negotiations, the accession of the European Union (EU) to the European Convention on Human Rights (ECHR) is close to becoming a reality following the successful completion of the negotiations and the Draft Accession Agreement on 5 April 2014. The much anticipated Opinion[1] of the Court of Justice of the European Union (CJEU) on the compatibility of the Draft Agreement with the EU Treaties was delivered on 18 December 2014 and it held that the Draft Agreement on the Accession of the European Union to the ECHR is incompatible with EU law. This was without a doubt an unwelcome development but at the same time it can be a wake-up call for both the EU and the Council of Europe that the accession is a much more daunting task than initially anticipated and that a more meticulous approach is required for resolving all the problems and facing the challenges of the accession. This chapter will revisit the problems and the challenges of the accession process, in an attempt to evaluate the steps made so far and reflect on how the post-accession scene is shaped.

* Lecturer in Law, University of Leicester. The author would like to thank all participants in the empirical phase for their views, insights and contribution. Special thanks to D.ssa Sonia Morano-Foadi and Professor Lucy Vickers for their comments on early drafts of this chapter.

[1] Opinion 2/13 of the Court (Full Court) of 18 December 2014 on the Compatibility of the draft agreement on the Accession of the European Union to the European Convention for the Protection of Human Rights and Fundamental Freedoms with the EU and FEU Treaties, available at http://curia.europa.eu/juris/document/document.jsf?text=&docid=160882&pageIndex=0&doclang=EN&mode=lst&dir=&occ=first&part=1&cid=106309.

Much has already been written[2] on the topic and a rigorous debate is currently conducted among academics and policy-makers on the emerging system of fundamental rights protection, the obstacles to the creation of a pan-European approach to human rights and the political interplay among the EU institutions, the Council of Europe and particularly the CJEU and the European Court of Human Rights (ECtHR). Although the significance of the accession cannot be underestimated, it remains a challenging task, a *bewildering riddle*, requiring sensitive handling, diplomatic manoeuvring and compromises at different levels. Its overarching aim is to fill the legal lacuna in the EU accountability system, according to which the Union cannot be sued before the Strasbourg Court for actions performed either by its institutions or other agents. The gradual transfer of competences from the Member States to the Union removed a considerable part of EU law from the scrutiny of the ECHR, so the accession will strengthen the external scrutiny exercised by the Strasbourg Court. This control mechanism of monitoring compliance with the standards set by the ECHR for fundamental rights protection is added and complements the existing internal system based on the Charter of Fundamental Rights of the European Union and the general principles of law, thus improving the EU's legitimacy, credibility and accountability.

Considering that the Convention has been for years recognised as 'a source of inspiration'[3] having 'special significance'[4] for EU law, the accession is not likely to bring radical changes, but it is of paramount importance that the Union agreed to voluntarily subject itself to the same external scrutiny as its Member States. Even if the instances that the EU is condemned turn out to be very few, the fear of condemn or the 'fruitful anger'[5] caused by the ECtHR judgments will be more than enough motivation for the Union to maintain the required (minimum) standards of protection. In this way, the citizens are placed at the centre of attention,

[2] S Morano-Foadi and S Andreadakis, Report on the Protection of Fundamental Rights in Europe—A Reflection on the Relationship between the Court of Justice of the European Union and the European Court of Human Rights post Lisbon, July 2014, available at http://www.coe.int/en/web/dlapil/news-dlapil; C Eckes, 'Accession to the ECHR: Between Autonomy and Adaptation' (2013) 76 *MLR* 254; T Lock, 'Accession to the ECHR: Implications for Judicial Review in Strasbourg' (2010) 35 *EL Rev* 777; T Lock, 'Walking on a Tightrope: The Draft ECHR Accession Agreement and the Autonomy of the EU Legal Order' (2011) 48 *CML Rev* 1025; T Lock, 'End of an Epic? The Draft Agreement on the EU's Accession to the ECHR' (2012) 31 *Yearbook of European Law* 162; N O'Meara, 'A More Secure Europe of Rights? The European Court of Human Rights, the Court of Justice of the European Union and EU Accession to the ECHR' (2011) 12 *German Law Journal*. 1813; W Weiß, 'Human Rights in the EU: Rethinking the Role of the European Convention on Human Rights after Lisbon' (2011) 7 *European Constitutional Law Review* 64–95.

[3] See Case C-4/73 *J Nold, Kohlen- und Baustoffgroßhandlungv Commission of the* European *Communities* [1974] ECR 491, para 13 and Case C-36/75 *Rutili* v *Minister for the Interior* [1975] ECR 1219. Some even talked about de facto accession of the EU to the ECHR, see A Verstichel, 'European Union Accession to the European Convention on Human Rights' in P Lemmens and W Vandenhole, *Protocol No 14 and the Reform of the European Court of Human Rights*, (Antwerp, Intersentia, 2005) 125.

[4] Case C-112/00 *Eugen Schmidberger, Internationale Transporte und Planzügev Republik Österreich* [2003] ECR I-5659, para 71. See also JL Murray, 'The Influence of the European Convention on Fundamental Rights on Community Law' (2011) 33 *Fordham International Law Journal* 1388–1422.

[5] P Sloterdijk, 'Die Revolution der Gebenden Hand', *Frankfurter Allgemeine Zeitung*, 13 June 2009, 8.

as, following the ratification of the Lisbon Treaty and once the accession is finalised. There will be three legal instruments, the Charter, the ECHR and the general principles of EU law, specially designed to ensure adequate protection within the EU legal order. In this way, not only will the citizens effectively get the same protection against EU acts as against national measures, but there will also be justified optimism for the creation of the envisaged 'Europe of Rights'.[6]

However, despite the importance of the accession and the substantial benefits for the EU system, the natural and legal persons in Europe, the negotiations proved to be a rather onerous balancing exercise of national interests, political concerns and other legal (or less legal) considerations regarding the relationship between the EU, ECHR and national legal orders and the allocation of powers between the Luxembourg and Strasbourg Court.

This chapter will use empirical findings based on interviews undertaken in the course of a three-year research project[7] with the CJEU and ECtHR judges and the EU and Council of Europe's officials involved in the negotiations of the Accession Treaty, in an attempt to reflect on the views expressed on the issue of the EU accession and European integration through the establishment of a robust and coherent fundamental rights protection regime.

The chapter is divided into three (Sections II, III and IV). The first part will discuss the rationale behind the accession and the three basic pillars on which this process is based. Then, the discussion will turn to examine three key area of concern that have been in the agenda of both the negotiations and the academic debates, as they involve issues of critical importance for the success of the accession and its overall functionality. Finally, the chapter will look at the future of the process, the next (final) steps towards the establishment of the new Europe based on rights, not merely economic considerations.

II. THE EU'S ACCESSION TO THE ECHR: THE THREE PILLARS AND THE OVERARCHING RATIONALE

The Union's accession to the ECHR will complete the EU system of fundamental rights protection as 'accession is not only an option, it is the destination'.[8] All the essential procedural and substantive mechanisms will be created with a view to bridging the existing gap in human rights protection in Europe and to

[6] A Stone Sweet and H Keller, 'The Reception of the ECHR in National Legal Orders' in H Keller and A Stone Sweet (eds), *A Europe of Rights: The Impact of the ECHR on National Legal Systems* (Oxford, Oxford University Press, 2008) 25.

[7] The research draws on a project funded by the British Academy (Small Research Grants (SRG) 2011 Round) and the School of Social Sciences and Law of Oxford Brookes University (internal funding 2009–10).

[8] V Reding in 'Reforming the European Convention on Human Rights: Interlaken, Izmir, Brighton and Beyond' (Council of Europe, 2014) 24, available at www.coe.int/t/dghl/standardsetting/cddh/reformechr/Publications/Compilation%20ReformECHR2014_en.pdf.

facilitate the development of the new characteristics that the EU wishes to add in its structure.

While Article 6(2) Treaty on European Union (TEU) provides a straightforward mandate, the accession was treated from the very beginning as a major undertaking which would require overcoming significant obstacles and constant challenges. Therefore, a set of principles was developed, in order to operate as a roadmap throughout this long and difficult process. These principles focused on highlighting the key aims and objectives of this process, the intended outcomes and the basic parameters to be taken into account at all stages.[9] More specifically, the three basic pillars on which the accession will be based on are as follows:

(a) The EU will accede on an equal footing and will become the 48th Contracting Party to the ECHR. 'Equal footing' means that the Union will enjoy no privilege and will be afforded no preferential or deferential treatment compared to the other Parties. The principle of equal treatment will be applied in all aspects of Union's participation in the Council of Europe.
(b) The accession of the EU will not bring any radical change to the existing ECHR mechanism, in the sense that it should be left as intact as possible and the EU will be just one more Party. This pillar together with the first one is clearly aimed at maintaining the pre-accession status quo in both the EU and the Council of Europe. As it will discussed later in the chapter, any change or adaptation essential for the realisation of the accession will be made, but it will not result in substantial changes in the organisational structure and operation of the two organisations. Both of them are successful and their success is due to their unique characteristics and distinctive features, which should be preserved at all costs.
(c) The accession should not affect the competences of the Union or the powers of its institutions.[10] This pillar is focused not on the EU-Council of Europe relationship, but on the EU itself; no new powers should be created for the Union and no alteration should be made to the existing obligations of Member States under the ECHR. The accession is intended to allow the Union to be part of the Council of Europe and fit the ECHR in its legal order.

Along with these three basic pillars, there is also an overarching aim, which links them together and its fulfilment is dependent on the stability of these pillars. More specifically, accession should be finalised as soon as possible, as any delay or disagreement, especially as a result of political deliberations, will destabilise the foundations of the whole project. To achieve this aim, the negotiations are to be carried out with a view to clarify and regulate only the most essential elements of the agreement. All the technicalities, practical details and procedural matters, for instance, in relation to the EU Member States, will be dealt with through the

[9] Morano-Foadi and Andreadakis, Report on the Protection of Fundamental Rights in Europe (n 1) at 67.

[10] Art 2 of Protocol 8 to the Lisbon Treaty.

internal rules of procedure. In this way, the EU will ensure that the accession will be completed without any Treaty amendments required as well as without any undue delays and with minimal disruption for the EU Member States and the Council's Contracting Parties.

Provided that all the above-mentioned conditions are fulfilled, the vision of the accession will be realised for the advantage of citizens and the adequate protection of those suffering from violations of their rights. Then, we will be able to talk about productive negotiations, fruitful exchange of views and a successful accession overall. As one of the respondents of the project mentioned, 'the most notable effect is that fundamental rights will be given the appropriate slot in the architecture of the EU. Accession should be seen as the key for completing this new architecture and a sort of counterbalance for what can be described as repressive powers in the exercise of its [EU] competences'.[11]

III. EMPIRICAL FINDINGS: VOICES FROM LUXEMBOURG, STRASBOURG AND BRUSSELS

The empirical findings are based on data collected during a British Academy funded project[12] investigating the post-Lisbon era in the EU in the area of fundamental rights protection. The initial theoretical phase focused on the interaction between the CJEU and the ECtHR and analysed the lack of convergence between the two Courts' approaches, applying the doctrine of legal and constitutional pluralism. Then, the second overlapping phase was aimed at reflecting on the views expressed by the judges of the two highest Courts in Europe, key informants and policy-makers ahead of the accession regarding the relationship between the two Courts and the new architecture of the EU.

During the second phase of the project, three rounds of semi-structured interviews were conducted with the CJEU and ECtHR judges as well as the EU and Council of Europe's officials involved in the negotiation, drafting and signing of the Accession Treaty. More specifically, 19 Judges and Advocates General of the CJEU, 10 ECtHR's judges and four officials from the Commission, the Council, the Council of Europe and the European Parliament were interviewed, offering their invaluable insights in relation to the process of the accession, their personal evaluations on the new era of rights in the EU and its impact on the lives of the 'peoples of Europe'.[13]

[11] Interview C (EU Commission, Brussels, 1 August 2012).

[12] See above n 6. Some of the empirical findings are also reported in ch 7 in this volume written by Sonia Morano-Foadi, which focuses on the relationship between the two Courts in the area of migration law.

[13] Treaty on European Union and the Treaty on the Functioning of the European Union [2012] C-326/01, Preamble.

Different interview templates were used for each category of respondents, covering questions about the dialogue between the two Courts and their overall relationship before and after the accession, the judicial approach in relation to fundamental rights protection, the three layers of fundamental rights protection (the Charter, the ECHR and the general principles of EU law), the nature of the external scrutiny, the interpretative tools used by the judges and legal and procedural aspects of the negotiating process for the accession of the EU to the ECHR. Other research questions involved issues of authority, autonomy of the two regimes, the new architecture of the EU, the challenges for all parties involved and concerns about the effectiveness of the new fundamental rights regime.

The empirical phase was designed to test the theoretical construct elaborated in the first stage of the research and reflect on its findings. The results of the empirical research were extremely valuable and thought-provoking, considering the fact that some of the interviews took place at the early stages of the process or when the negotiations had stopped. All participating interviewees provided a comprehensive overview of the accession, highlighting problematic areas, analysing practical aspects and technical details that allowed a thorough analysis and reflection of all the key and underlying issues of the accession.

Building on the findings of the empirical phase, this section will revisit the key issues related to the accession from the perspective of the judges, policy-makers and key informants. In this way, the academic analysis offered will be complemented by the more practical and pragmatic angle of those involved in the accession. Thus, the analysis that follows is based on empirical evidence reflecting on the issues of prior involvement of the CJEU, the newly-developed co-respondent mechanism before the ECtHR and the controversial presumption of comparable protection.

Both the judiciary and the policy-makers were optimistic about the conclusion of the negotiations and the finalisation of the accession. It is beyond any doubt that the benefits outweigh the possible drawbacks. Everybody in Europe is 'well-aware of the benefits and the added value of the Accession in the strengthening of the ECHR system and on the basis of a very careful scrutiny there will be practical concordance between them'.[14]

In its Opinion 2/94, the CJEU talked about the 'constitutional significance' of the accession and highlighted that it would 'entail a substantial change in the present Community system in that it would entail the entry of the Community into a distinct international institutional system as well as integration of all the provisions of the Convention into the Community legal order'.[15] The day after the accession will find the EU not only subjected to the external scrutiny and control of the ECHR, but also the ECHR regime will be formally added in its legal order, creating an integrated and multi-layered system of protection. The road will be

[14] Interview C (EU Commission, Brussels, 1 August 2012).

[15] Opinion 2/94 Accession by the Community to the European Convention for the Protection of Human Rights and Fundamental Freedoms [1996] ECR I-1759, paras 34–35.

open for achieving '*coherence and legal certainty among the different sources of fundamental rights which coexist in Europe*'.[16] At the same time, EU citizens will be able to bring complaints against EU institutions directly to the Strasbourg Court, which means that they will have another avenue of protection available against violations of their rights, while the consistency between the Courts in Luxembourg and Strasbourg will pave the way for a coherent approach towards human rights protection across Europe.

Overall, the accession should be seen as an opportunity for the Union to show to the world that it has the potential to transform an economic community of states into a modern international organisation characterised by transparency, accountability and legitimacy and effective commitment to fundamental rights protection.

A. Challenges and Obstacles

Despite the optimism and the positive comments expressed about the accession, all interviewees unanimously agreed on the need to wait until all issues are resolved. This is because the lessons learnt from the Constitutional Treaty, and to a certain extent the Lisbon Treaty, serve as a reminder that no agreement requiring unanimity is finalised before all parties sign and ratify it. The negotiation process revealed numerous problems and concerns in relation to institutional, procedural and substantive aspects of the accession, which delayed, undermined and temporarily halted the negotiations. Considering the specific characteristics of the Union as a *sui generis* candidate Contracting Party, the features of the ECHR mechanism and the Council of Europe's structure, it is not surprising that such obstacles have arisen and that there are still concerns. The accession is indeed a major step and requires the attention and cooperation of all interested parties in order to ensure that the EU will successfully fit into the existing ECHR system.

(i) Relationship between the Two Courts

The accession and the resulting subjection of the EU and its institutions to the judicial review of the ECtHR are not accompanied by the recognition of the Strasbourg Court as a superior body. It is, rather, a recognition as a specialised Court exercising external control over the international law obligations of the Union resulting from the accession to the ECHR.[17] The preservation of the Union's autonomy and its

[16] Interview No IV (ECtHR, Strasbourg, 19 June 2012).

[17] European Convention, 'Final Report of Working Group II' CONV 354/02, WG II 16, 12; see also European Parliament, 'Resolution on the Institutional Aspects of Accession by the European Union to the European Convention for the Protection of Human Rights and Fundamental Freedoms' P7_TA-PROV (2010) 0184, para 1; see also Morano-Foadi and Andreadakis, Report on the Protection of Fundamental Rights in Europe (n 1) at 101.

specific characteristics are guaranteed, as pursuant to Article 6(2) TEU the Union's competences shall not be affected.[18] Therefore, the EU institutions will continue being primarily responsible for implementing and enforcing the Convention rights without any involvement of the ECtHR. The Court will be called upon only after the CJEU has already exercised its powers in relation to the uniform interpretation and application of EU law. In this way, the legal autonomy of the Union will remain intact and the external scrutiny of EU acts by the Court in Strasbourg will be vigorous and independent.

If we look beyond the issue of the autonomy of the EU, there is an 'exceptional judicial interface'[19] between the CJEU and the ECtHR deriving from the fact that the two Courts have differing human rights protection mechanisms, although they have comparable jurisdiction *ratione personae*.[20] As one of the judges interviewed affirmed, 'the Courts are already close together not only because they study each other's judgements and also because there is no rivalry. One is the Supreme Court of the Union and the other is a specialised Court on human rights representing a wider range of states, but without having to deal with institutional questions like Luxemburg and to answer questions from the national judges. The ECHR represents the minimum standards of protection, but the CJEU, although not bound by the jurisprudence of the Strasbourg Court, is keen to use it when necessary. In certain issues, the Strasbourg Court has a large number of case-law and more expertise'.[21]

For decades, the two Courts have been independent from each other, serving completely different purposes, but at the same time their shared interests and values allowed them to develop a special relationship, including formal and informal dialogue between them.[22]

In the post-accession era, the ECtHR will operate as the ultimate arbiter and guarantor of the compatibility of EU law with the Convention. In the event that the Union and its institutions fail to apply their obligations under the Convention or guarantee the rights enshrined by the ECHR, the Strasbourg Court will have the power to intervene. Although the Court itself has always recognised these cases as being exceptional,[23] much emphasis has been given during the negotiation process on how to keep this relationship as harmonious as possible and minimise the risk of conflicting case law and interpretations.

[18] See also Art 1 of Protocol 8 relating to Art 6(2) TEU on the accession of the EU to the ECHR.

[19] P Gragl, *The Accession of the European Union to the European Convention on Human Rights* (Oxford, Hart Publishing, 2013), 50.

[20] Y Shany, *The Competing Jurisdictions of International Courts and Tribunals* (Oxford, OUP, 2003), 68.

[21] Interview No 4 (CJEU, Luxembourg, 14 December 2010).

[22] Morano-Foadi and Andreadakis, Report on the Protection of Fundamental Rights in Europe (n 1) at 41ff.

[23] The Rt Hon Kenneth Clarke, QC MP in 'Reforming the European Convention on Human Rights: Interlaken, Izmir, Brighton and beyond' (Council of Europe, 2014) 73, available at www.coe.int/t/dghl/standardsetting/cddh/reformechr/Publications/Compilation%20ReformECHR2014_en.pdf.

Mutual respect, good will and the recognition of the need for cooperation has been the common denominator among judges and policy-makers. 'We have seen some discrepancies between the two Courts … but both Courts are very careful in looking at each other. I am not sure they are working towards coherence but they tolerate each other; they aim at avoiding conflicts and frictions'.[24] There were some judges, who were more optimistic than others, claiming that divergence 'should be always a possibility and hopefully never an actuality if we are doing our job correctly in both Courts'.[25] Other judges were more pragmatic in their assertions for the future relationship between the two Courts: 'I think convergence is quite likely to happen whether we consciously work towards this or not. We take into account their case law and they do the same with ours. There are two regional supreme courts dealing with these issues of fundamental rights and it would be surprising if they did not take some interest on each other's case law'.[26]

The readiness for a common and harmonious approach towards human rights in Europe is a positive starting point and the judicial dialogue[27] constitutes the right means to achieve and maintain a stable and healthy relationship between the highest judicial authorities in the European continent. This gains additional importance, as the instances of conflict are rare and marginal, but realistically, the possibility of divergence and conflicts between the two Courts will continue to exist. The President of the CJEU has argued that 'the lack of efficiency and coherence resulting from the parallel application of three systems of protection of fundamental rights will be decisively reduced by the accession of the EU to the ECHR',[28] but their different methods of interpretation in combination with the variety of sources of law with often overlapping fields of application will always create uncertainty. Therefore, the dialogue between the two Courts is a very powerful instrument for a convergent human rights system in Europe, as in this way clashes impacting on each Court's sphere of jurisdiction and expertise are avoided.[29]

The judges interviewed shared the view that the two Courts have been mutually recognising and giving consideration to each other's case law in response to a sense of moral responsibility in the name of coherence, legal certainly and respect for the highest interest of the individuals in Europe.[30] 'There is a dialogue […] I think the dialogue is very important as we have to understand each other's

[24] Interview No 14 (CJEU, Luxembourg, 15 December 2010).

[25] Interview No 9 (CJEU, Luxembourg, 15 December 2010) and Interview No 17 (CJEU, Luxembourg, 15 December 2010).

[26] Interview No 10 (CJEU, Luxembourg, 15 December 2010).

[27] This issue is further discussed in ch 7 in this volume.

[28] V Skouris, 'The EU System of Judicial Protection after the Treaty of Lisbon' (2011) 7 *Croatian Yearbook of European Law and Policy* 1–9, 8.

[29] Morano-Foadi and Andreadakis, Report on the Protection of Fundamental Rights in Europe (n 1), at 42.

[30] S Morano-Foadi, 'Fundamental Rights in Europe: "Constitutional" Dialogue between the Court of Justice of the EU and the European Court of Human Rights' (2013) 5 *Oñati Journal of Emergent Socio-legal Studies* 64–88, 81.

few points and the approaches … For example, one of the areas that this Court [CJEU] needs is consciousness of human rights dimension as the last thing we have ever wanted is a situation where we were going to have a condemnation from Strasbourg'.[31]

Three forms of dialogue between the two Courts have emerged: the informal, the institutionalised, and the judicial dialogue.[32]

The judicial dialogue involves each Court looking at the case law of the other, when dealing with points of law that were raised in previous cases, and it is used as a tool for achieving coherence within the European human rights legal system as a whole. The informal dialogue involves regular meetings in both Strasbourg and Luxembourg and resembles a common practice between the CJEU and the constitutional or supreme courts of the Member States. The majority of the judiciary recognised the benefits of this initiative, as it has facilitated the creation of a forum of discussion on 'issues of common interests'[33] and 'exchange of information about jurisprudence'.[34] Finally, the 'institutionalised'[35] dialogue will be initiated after the accession, as it involves the joint appearance of the EU and its Member State(s) as defendants before the Strasbourg Court when the co-respondent (or co-defendant) mechanism will be set in motion. This mechanism is designed to ensure that all the parties involved in a case are able to present their views, participating in full, not through third party intervention, and, if necessary, to be held responsible.

The dialogue should continue at all three levels after the completion of the accession, as it offers substantial benefits and allows the establishment of an appropriate level of cooperation between the two institutions, thus minimising the the risk of clashes. However, as stated by one of the CJEU judges, 'dialogue cannot solve all problems between the two Courts. Cooperation is better, but anything else will be complicated. For instance, it will take time and given the principle of exhaustion of national remedies, it will not be the best solution to go to Luxembourg and then to Strasbourg or vice versa. It will be burdensome and it will be a problem of resources'.[36]

Establishing a deep relationship of mutual respect and common understanding without any interference in each other's sphere can be extremely effective. 'The relationship will not be hierarchical, but based on the principle of cooperation. The Court recognises that the ECtHR will have the "last word" as a logical consequence of the Convention on Human Rights. The Strasbourg court can ultimately

[31] Interview No 9 (CJEU, Luxembourg, 15 December 2010).

[32] Morano-Foadi and Andreadakis, Report on the Protection of Fundamental Rights in Europe (n 1) at 42–45. See also ch 7 of this book for a more detailed discussion of the judicial dialogue.

[33] Interview No 3 (CJEU, Luxembourg, 15 December 2010), Interview IX (ECtHR, Strasbourg 20 June 2012) and Interview IV (ECtHR, Strasbourg, 19 June 2012).

[34] Interview No 4 (CJEU, Luxembourg, 14 December 2010).

[35] Interview No V (ECtHR, Strasbourg, 20 June 2012).

[36] Interview No 5 (CJEU, Luxembourg, 14 December 2010) and Interview No 7 (CJEU, Luxembourg, 14 December 2010).

impose interpretation of human rights standards. In this sense, we should recognise the superior position of the Court in this field, but it is not the same to say that the ECtHR is higher or more important'. The Strasbourg Court will have the last word and 'we reasonably expect that we will have somehow the opportunity to have the "first word" [on EU law]'.[37]

This has been the only requirement made by the CJEU and it brings us to the second aspect of the relationship between the two Courts: the 'first-last' word relationship and the prior involvement mechanism.

The CJEU will be given the privilege of having the 'first word' in a case regarding an alleged violation of the ECHR by an EU act, based on the rationale that 'the assessment of the ECtHR should be based on the assessment of the legal system which is at stake'.[38] As the Presidents of both Courts highlighted in their Joint Statement in 2011, this mechanism is based on the 'respect to the principle of subsidiarity' and most importantly ensures that an internal review takes place before the external review without the need to amend the ECHR.[39] The Strasbourg Court, before performing its delicate balancing exercise, considers it essential to take into account the arguments, the interpretations and in general the perspective of the legal system under challenge. In this way, the CJEU 'preserves its role as regulatory court of the EU, even in cases involving human rights issues, which have not been submitted to its attention'.[40]

The CJEU made it clear from the beginning that its prior involvement is a *condition sine qua non* for the accession to take place and to be successful and the need to have the 'first word' was consistently highlighted by the judges in Luxemburg.[41] Both Courts as well as the negotiators consider this mechanism as an acceptable solution, as the CJEU will remain the jewel of the judicial crown of the EU while the 'the last word belongs to the ECtHR, not as compromise but as a realistic outcome'.[42] The consensus was widespread among the judiciary about the efficacy of this mechanism, even though it effectively elevates the Luxembourg Court to a privileged position compared to the courts of last resort of the Member States.[43]

Nevertheless, concerns were expressed during the empirical phase of the project as to the extent that the ECtHR, in exercising the external scrutiny and adjudicating on the EU law's conformity with the Convention, would abstain from ending up interpreting EU law. 'We have to be the arbiter of Union law and they have

[37] Interview No 12 (CJEU, Luxembourg, 15 December 2010).

[38] Interview C (EU Commission, Brussels, 1 August 2012).

[39] Joint Communication from Presidents Costa and Skouris, 24 January 2011, available at curia.europa.eu/jcms/upload/docs/application/pdf/2011-02/cedh_cjue_english.pdf.

[40] Interview B (EU Council, Brussels, 21 June 2012).

[41] Interview No 3 (CJEU, Luxembourg, 13 December 2010).

[42] Interview No 6 (CJEU, Luxembourg, 14 December 2010).

[43] C Timmermans, 'Will the Accession of the EU to the European Convention on Human Rights Fundamentally Change the Relationship between the Luxemburg and the Strasbourg Courts?' (Centre for Judicial Cooperation, 2013), Distinguished Lecture 2014/01, 14, available at http://www.admus.eui.eu/bitstream/handle/1814/31932/LAW_CJC_DL_2014_01.pdf?sequence=2.

to be the arbiter of whether that conforms to the Convention … [this is] very important because there is always a danger that they would ended up interpreting our law rather than testing its conformity'.[44]

The response given by the judges in Strasbourg is that there is no need to talk about loss of the EU law's autonomy after the accession: 'Problems resulting from the loss of CJEU's position as equal brother could make this court feel a little bit uneasy. This court will have the "last word" and this is actually the problem. Of course, we can promise we will hardly use it, but if there is a proper collision, then the situation will be different than now'.[45] It was broadly recognised that the CJEU will remain the EU Supreme Court and that the ECtHR, conscious of its delicate and sensitive task, will predominantly avoid interfering with the CJEU's role as interpreter of EU law, being conscious of its task to address failures in human rights protection. 'Judges are responsible people and, for obvious reasons, they want to avoid conflicts or create chaos. Judicial appreciation is more appropriate in the area of human rights'.[46]

This is where the multi-level dialogue is of critical importance and it has to be reminded that the dialogue is two-way, which means that the Luxembourg Court will have at least the opportunity to influence the ECtHR's interpretation.

Interestingly, the CJEU would be placed in a position which was fairly similar to that in which national constitutional courts found themselves as a result of the role of the CJEU as the final arbiter of the EU legal system.[47] At the same time, the Luxembourg Court will be running the risk of experiencing a 'sandwich effect', as it would be doubly scrutinised, on the one hand, by the national constitutional courts on the basis of the *Solange* principle[48] and, on the other hand, by the ECtHR, in the context of the external judicial scrutiny of the EU in the area of human rights. As it becomes apparent, there is no point in developing rivalry or showing animosity, as having an antagonistic relationship would not benefit any of the two institutions.[49] As affirmed by the judges, '… [Strasbourg] will have the last word but just concerning the minimum standards, i.e. the Convention. This does not mean that there is a restriction to protect at a higher level. It is clear that protection is higher at Union level'.[50]

[44] Interview No 9 (CJEU, Luxembourg, 15 December 2010). See also Morano-Foadi and Andreadakis, Report on the Protection of Fundamental Rights in Europe (n 1) at 101.

[45] Interview I (ECtHR, Strasbourg, 18 June 2012).

[46] Interview No 6 (CJEU, Luxembourg, 14 December 2010).

[47] J Martín and P De Nanclares, 'The Accession of the European Union to the ECHR: More than Just a Legal Issue' (Madrid, Instituto de Derecho Europeo e Integración Regional, 2013), Working Papers on European Law and Regional Integration No 15, 16.

[48] According to the presumption of equivalent protection, a transfer of competences to another international or supranational organisation is not prohibited 'as long as' fundamental rights receive an equivalent protection within the legal order of this organisation. See N Colneric, 'Protection of Fundamental Rights through the Court of Justice of the European Communities' (2002), available at http://www.denning.law.ox.ac.uk/themes/iecl/pdfs/working2colneric.pdf.

[49] Interview No 4 (CJEU, Luxembourg, 14 December 2010).

[50] Interview No 1 (CJEU, Luxembourg, 13 December 2010).

Each of the two Courts has a different position in this complex legal construction and creating tensions undermines the credibility of the EU as an international human rights actor and the suitability of the Council of Europe as a guarantor of efficient human rights protector. Establishing a relationship of mutual respect is in the interest of both Courts and will significantly contribute to good administration of justice in Strasbourg.[51] Showing animosity or having an antagonistic relationship would not benefit any of the two,[52] and it is worth mentioning that so far both institutions have shown that they value each other's authority and they are willing to work closely as evidenced by the creation of the prior involvement mechanism.

Before moving forward, irrespective of the motivation and merits for the adoption of such a mechanism, it important to note that this mechanism is designed to operate more as a safety valve rather than as an integral part of the Courts' operation, as elaborated by one of the policy makers, 'I think this will be rarely used because when it comes to the question of compatibility of the EU law with the ECHR, it will be very few national courts that will not make reference, when asked in national proceedings. This is an exercise of great superficiality. When it will happen, I am sure it will help the dialogue between the two courts. To me it is clear that the CJEU will decide these rights in a way which ensures the proper co-ordination with Strasbourg'.[53]

Extending the discussion about the relationship between the two Courts and their post-accession dialogue, the next section will touch upon the co-respondent, or co-defendant, mechanism, which will allow the Union to participate in the proceedings before the Strasbourg Court and potentially be held responsible for a violation of the Convention.

(ii) The Co-respondent Mechanism

The co-respondent, or co-defendant, mechanism was developed for instances where an alleged violation of fundamental rights may not be attributed to a Member State's fault or misconception of its obligations. If said violation has its roots in a provision of EU law, this means that the Member State, even if convicted by the Strasbourg Court, will be unable to remedy the violation. Therefore, 'all the parties involved in a case are given the opportunity to present their views, and to be held fully responsible, relieving in a way the ECtHR from the task of having to determine which party is really responsible for an alleged violation'.[54] The participation in the proceedings does not amount to acceptance of responsibility and it is at the Court's discretion to decide on the allocation of responsibility. Respondents and co-respondents shall be jointly responsible for a violation,

[51] Interview C (EU Commission, Brussels, 1 August 2012).
[52] Interview No 4 (CJEU, Luxembourg, 14 December 2010).
[53] Interview C (EU Commission, Brussels, 1 August 2012).
[54] Interview A (Council of Europe, Strasbourg, 18 June 2012).

unless the Court, on the basis of the reasons given by the respondent and the co-respondent, and having sought the views of the applicant, concludes that only one of them is to be held responsible. More specifically, 'the EU will be held liable for any primary law provisions which contravene the ECHR, while the Member State(s) will remain responsible only for national measures, which are adopted in application of EU law and they infringe the ECHR'.[55]

This mechanism attracted criticism and concerns have been raised regarding its complexity and overall the necessity to introduce another new mechanism instead of relying on the third-party intervention mechanism already set out in Article 36 ECHR.[56] Its inclusion in the Accession Agreement was justified firstly, because it recognises the Union as an autonomous legal order, and secondly it respects the distinctiveness and the specificities of this legal order together with the exclusivity of the CJEU's jurisdiction. It was also seen as a means to prevent the ECtHR from interpreting the Treaties and deciding upon competences.[57]

Once it was clarified that 'the co-respondent mechanism is maybe a complication, but it is a complication on the EU side'[58] and that the participation of the Union would not adversely affect the position of the individual applicants, it was included in the Accession Agreement. In the interviews it was stressed that 'judges will focus on the quality of the arguments presented, not at the number of participants to the procedure, which make that argument'[59] and in general this mechanism was not seen as an additional burden for the individual applicant, who would be required to overcome not only the defence of the Member State(s), but also the obstacle of the EU. In one of the interviews, the argument that the co-respondent mechanism can potentially create imbalance of powers was rejected on the presumption that the individual applicant will not have to 'preventatively pose himself with the question of distribution of competences', but to the contrary it has 'not only the party which is allegedly responsible for the violation in question, but also another party, which may be potentially responsible'; in other words, 'a full range of actors is at his disposal' as potential violators rather than a full range of powerful actors coming against him in a court of law.[60]

Furthermore, one of the policy-makers gave an alternative interpretation to the introduction of this mechanism, arguing that it will significantly contribute towards stronger enforcement of the ECtHR decisions: 'without the co-respondent mechanism in a case against an EU Member State, if the Court finds that there is a violation, the Member State would be under obligation to abide by the judgment, but then, since the EU is not party to the proceedings, it would not be legally

[55] ibid.

[56] See especially, S Douglas-Scott, 'The European Union and Human Rights after the Treaty of Lisbon' (2011) 11 *Human Rights Law Review* 645–82.

[57] N-L Arold Lorenz, X Groussot and GT Petursson, *The European Human Rights Culture—A Paradox of Human Rights Protection in Europe?* (Leyden, Brill, 2013) 261.

[58] Interview B (EU Council, Brussels, 21 June 2012).

[59] Interview C (EU Commission, Brussels, 1 August 2012).

[60] Interview B (EU Council, Brussels, 21 June 2012).

bound by that judgment. In other words, the enforcement of the judgment would effectively depend on the good will of the Union and its Member States'.[61]

Finally, some of the interviewees, being more pragmatic in their assessment, mentioned that since 'the assumption is that all the States and the EU institutions will do their best to ensure that their acts are already fully compliant with the Convention … the ECtHR is the last resort'[62] and it was additionally argued that out of all the cases brought before the Strasbourg Court, only a really small number, such as *Matthews* and *Bosphorus*,[63] would potentially trigger the application of the co-respondent mechanism.

The case of *Bosphorus* will be discussed in the next section, as it involves a very important issue, which has not been adequately clarified either during the negotiations or in the Accession Agreement, and there have been no indications about whether it will be upheld or not after the accession.

(iii) The Bosphorus Ruling: To be or Not to be (Upheld)?

Having discussed the relationship between the two Courts in detail, exploring the concerns expressed and the solutions put forward by the Accession Agreement, the last issue to be examined is the future of the *Bosphorus* presumption and, more specifically, the position of the EU within the Council of Europe's system following the completion of the accession.

In *Bosphorus*, the Strasbourg Court clarified that it has the jurisdiction to review applications against national measures, which directly or indirectly implement or derive from EU law obligations. In other words, it confirmed that it has the power to indirectly review the compatibility of EU acts with the standards of the Convention. However, instead of doing so, it declared that the EU offers fundamental rights protection of equivalent standard to that of the ECHR, thus introducing the 'equivalent protection test'[64] or the so-called *Bosphorus* presumption. Such an equivalent protection would only be presumed in cases where the states had no discretion at all in implementing the act in question.[65] The Court also mentioned that the presumption can be rebutted if there is evidence that the protection afforded by the EU is 'manifestly deficient'.[66] If the protection of fundamental rights becomes manifestly deficient, then the ECtHR, as a 'constitutional instrument of European public order' in the field of human rights, proceeds with an examination of the case, which can ultimately lead to a finding of violation.[67] In *Michaud v France* the ECtHR clarified that 'the presumption of equivalent protection is intended to ensure that a State Party is not faced with a

[61] Interview C (EU Commission, Brussels, 1 August 2012).
[62] Interview A (Council of Europe, Strasbourg, 18 June 2012).
[63] *Bosphorus Hava Yollari Turizm VeTicaret Anonim Sirketiv Ireland* App no 45036/98 [2005] 42 EHRR 1; *Matthews v United Kingdom* App no 24833/94 [1999] BHRC 686.
[64] ibid, para 155.
[65] ibid, para 156.
[66] ibid.
[67] ibid.

dilemma when it is obliged to rely on the legal obligations incumbent on it as a result of its membership of an international organisation which is not party to the Convention and to which it has transferred part of its sovereignty, in order to justify its actions or omissions arising from such membership vis-à-vis the Convention'.[68]

The presumption does not mean that the Union is free to ignore the Convention and/or its commitment towards respect and protection of human rights. The Court did not declare that the Union enjoys total immunity.[69] The equivalent protection formula basically applies only when the protection given is comparable to the one afforded under the ECHR regime. In practical terms, *Bosphorus* protects the Union against constant scrutiny, because the level of protection afforded by the EU is presumed to be the same as the one provided by all the existing Contracting Parties of the Council of Europe. The underlying rationale was not to create a 'double standards' system during the negotiation process, but to suspend treating the EU in the same way as the other Parties until its formal adherence to the ECHR.

Although at first glance the 'equivalent protection' doctrine appears to offer the Union a substantial and unprecedented privilege, a closer look would reveal that in practice it does not make a huge difference due to the CJEU's commitment to fundamental rights protection, the multi-level dialogue between the two Courts and the central role of the Charter in the EU legal order. Until then, the review of the equivalence of protection will be conducted on a case-by-case basis and the presumption remains rebuttable, if the protection afforded is found to be below the required threshold.[70] As recently demonstrated in the case of *MSS*,[71] the ECtHR did not abstain from exercising close scrutiny, despite the equivalent protection presumption in relation to the protection of fundamental rights within the EU legal system.

The *Bosphorus* presumption was an extremely positive development for the relationship between the two Courts and the two regimes and it is true that it ensured that the negotiations were carried out in an atmosphere of good faith and mutual respect. It was clearly intended to give some breathing space and a degree of flexibility to the Union during the period that the negotiations for the accession were conducted. Now that we are a few steps before the completion of the accession, it is time to revisit the question of the future of the presumption and

[68] *Michaud v France* App no 12323/11 [2012] ECHR 445, para 111.

[69] See L Scheeck, 'The Relationship Between the European Courts and Integration through Human Rights' (2005) 65 *ZeitschriftfürausländischesöffentlichesRecht and Völkerrecht* 837, 862–63. See also S Morano-Foadi and S Andreadakis, 'The Convergence of the European Legal System in the Treatment of Third Country Nationals in Europe: The ECJ and the ECtHR Jurisprudence' (2011) 22 *The European Journal of International Law* 1071, 1074 and Case C-127/02 *CooperatieveProducentenorganisatie van de NederlandseKokkelvisserij UA v The Netherlands* [2004] ECR I-7405.

[70] Joint Concurring Opinion of Judges Rozakis, Tulkens, Traja, Botoucharova, Zagrebelsky and Garlicki, and Concurring Opinion of Judge Ress, in *Bosphorus* (n 62).

[71] *MSS v Belgium and Greece* App no 30696/09 [2011] 53 EHRR 2. For a detailed discussion of this case, see chs 7 and 8 in this volume.

the principle of equivalent protection. 'The only thing we know for sure is that something different will have to be found from the *Bosphorus* approach because, the *Bosphorus* approach is still on the "equivalent level of protection", and something different has to be found'.[72]

The vast majority of the interviewees agreed that the *Bosphorus* presumption is incompatible with the basic principles-pillars on which the construction of the accession has been based. 'Personally I would find it very difficult to follow *Bosphorus* after the accession; otherwise accession does not make sense. But of course the Court here will have to say soon, what will happen to *Bosphorus*'.[73] The EU cannot accede on an *equal footing*, whilst maintaining the presumption of equivalent protection. Any preferential or deferential treatment will be in direct contradiction with the notion of equality among Contracting Parties, as it will not be treated in the same manner as any other of the 47 Contracting Parties. As a consequence, the Union's reputation and credibility will be diminished and its much-advertised commitment to adequate protection of fundamental rights will suffer serious damages. It would not be an exaggeration to argue that there will be no added value for the Union and the whole project of the accession will lose its importance. Even one of the judges, who adopted a more modest approach, argued that 'the Court after accession will carefully examine every case. The application of the doctrine will not change. This is the essence of the accession. There will still be the presumption of compatibility of EU law with the ECHR, but this will be tested on a case by case basis. It is a rebuttable presumption, not written on stone'.[74] The judge subsequently added that in all likelihood the *Bosphorus* presumption will be revised at the first given opportunity.

Overall, the future of *Bosphorus* has not yet been determined and this creates additional concerns. It constitutes one of the focal points of the accession, as it is linked with the very core of this process and a hasty handling can have detrimental effect for both the EU and the Council of Europe. The negotiators intentionally left this issue open, recognising that it is the ECtHR's responsibility to decide the fate of the presumption that the Court itself developed. Even though the answer to this pressing question and the most appropriate solution is considered to be straightforward, as confirmed by the empirical phase of the project, it has to be reminded that the Strasbourg Court will perform another sensitive balancing exercise before adjudicating on how the *sui generis* nature of the EU as a Contracting Party fits with the principles of equivalent protection and equality, the autonomy of the EU and the need for legal certainty in the area of fundamental rights in Europe.

[72] Interview No V (ECtHR, Strasbourg, 20 June 2012).

[73] Interview No VI (ECtHR, Strasbourg, 20 June 2012).

[74] Interview No IV (ECtHR, Strasbourg, 19 June 2012). A similar argument is discussed by Timmermans, 'Will the Accession of the EU to the European Convention on Human Rights Fundamentally Change the Relationship between the Luxemburg and the Strasbourg Courts?' (n 42) 18–19.

IV. LOOKING AT THE FUTURE: THE POST-ACCESSION ERA AND THE 'EUROPE OF RIGHTS'

Looking at the future, the accession constitutes a major step for Europe both in the context of the EU as well as the Council of Europe.

The negotiations regarding the accession of the EU to the ECHR have been a long and strained process, bringing to the surface a number of technical difficulties, legal problems, political concerns and other obstacles. The strong will of the negotiators and the commitment to the mandate contained in Article 6(2) TEU gave the necessary push to overcome some of the obstacles and reach a conclusion. These hurdles were not of a sufficient scale to frustrate the overarching aim of the accession, but there are still concerns about the post-accession era and it remains to be seen what course of action will be taken following the shock from the negative Opinion of the CJEU.

The accession was a conscious decision, in the sense that it was not imposed on the Union. It came more as a natural outcome of the Union's evolution and the recognition of the 'prime importance afforded to fundamental rights and the ECHR'.[75] Even so, the Union was not under an obligation to accede to the Convention, as confirmed in the *Solange I* decision,[76] but could opt for a special catalogue or Bill of Rights.[77] The introduction of the Charter as a binding instrument did not undermine the prospect of accession, as the EU saw it as a unique opportunity to inaugurate a new era of integration based on rights.[78] Article 53 of the Charter clearly refers to the role of the Convention in the EU legal order as a minimum standard of fundamental rights protection, while Article 52 prevents any polarisation between the minimum and the maximum standards by requiring that the Charter rights should be given the same interpretation as the corresponding Convention rights.

These arrangements allowed for a smooth incorporation of the ECHR in the EU law system and aim at minimising the risk of frictions. As discussed earlier, the unique nature of the Union made the negotiation process long, arduous and unpredictable, as there were numerous thorny issues to be ironed out, disagreements, tensions and details to be clarified. While the Accession Agreement forms an excellent basis to work on, the internal rules of procedure will fill in the remaining gaps and shed light on any unresolved issue. These rules are of

[75] Joint Declaration of the European Parliament, Council and Commission on Fundamental Rights, 5 April 1977, [1977] OJ C103/1.

[76] *InternationaleHandelsgesellschaft von Einfuhr- und VorratsstellefürGetreide und Futtermittel*, decision of 29 May 1974, BVerfGE 37, 271, [1974] CMLR 540.

[77] See JP Jacque, 'The Accession of the European Union to the European Convention on Human Rights and Fundamental Freedoms' (2011) *CML Rev* 995–1023, 999. See also Accession of the Communities to the European Convention on Human Rights: Commission Memorandum, Bulletin of the European Communities, Supplement 2/79, COM (79) final, para 8.

[78] S Morano-Foadi and S Andreadakis, 'Reflections on the Architecture of the EU after the Treaty of Lisbon: The European Judicial Approach to Fundamental Rights' (2011) 17 *European Law Journal* 607–22, 610.

paramount importance for 'balancing the interests of all the different parties involved in the accession process as well as for ensuring the "people(s) of Europe" enjoy more complete recognition and protection of their human rights'.[79]

The relationship between the two Courts seems to be based on 'consensus amongst judges' rather than rivalry. The Council of Europe is keen to continue playing the role of the 'benchmark for human rights, the rule of law and democracy in Europe'[80] and accepts the challenge of having Strasbourg transformed into the European capital of fundamental rights protection'.[81] At the same time, it is also aware that the Strasbourg mechanism is a subsidiary mechanism that can serve as a safety net following the exhaustion of all effective domestic remedies as the ECtHR has no mandate to act as Europe's primary constitutional court.[82] Likewise, the CJEU is unwilling to have a formally subordinate position vis-à-vis the ECtHR and seems to favour a more informal and mutually respectful arrangement, a kind of 'common supranational diplomacy'.[83] Thus, the Union becomes subject to the external review of the ECHR regime, while maintaining the autonomy and primacy of the CJEU within the EU realm.

Both Courts showed that they are good team players, willing to make necessary compromises and respect each other's' individuality: 'Competing interests? There are no frictions but emotions'.[84] 'There is no reason to believe that the relationship is not going to be harmonious'.[85] 'The relationship between the two Courts can be one of cooperation'.[86] Clarifying and streamlining the relationship of the two Courts is a key element for the success of the accession process and the sustainability of the 'Europe of Rights' project and, its implications are far wider than simply balancing the interests of these two powerful and influential institutions.

Before concluding, it is worth referring to the CJEU Opinion and its effect on the process of accession, although it is still quite early for conclusive remarks. This development has inevitably brought disappointment on both sides, not only because of the significance of the accession as a joint venture of the EU and the CoE, but also because of the lengthy and burdensome negotiation process. However, it does not have to be the tombstone of the EU accession to the ECHR;

[79] Interview B (EU Council, Brussels, 21 June 2012).

[80] Committee on Legal Affairs and Human Rights, 'European Union and Council of Europe Human Rights Agendas: Synergies Not Duplication!', 2 October 2013, Council of Europe, Parliamentary Assembly, available at assembly.coe.int/ASP/Doc/XrefViewPDF.asp?FileID=20173&Language=EN.

[81] V Reding, speaking at the Interlaken Conference held on 18 and 19 February 2010, in *Proceedings High Level Conference on the Future of the European Court of Human Rights* (Council of Europe, 2010) 26.

[82] M Kuijer, 'The Accession of the European Union to the ECHR: A Gift for the ECHR's 60th Anniversary or an Unwelcome Intruder at the Party' (2011) 3 *Amsterdam Law Forum* 17–32, 26.

[83] See G de Búrca, 'The Road Not Taken: The EU as a Global Human Rights Actor' (2011) 105 *American Journal of International Law* 649–93, 652. See also G Harpaz, 'The European Court of Justice and its Relations with the European Court of Human Rights: The Quest for Enhanced Reliance, Coherence and Legitimacy' (2009) 46 *CML Rev* 105.

[84] Interview No 13 (CJEU, Luxembourg, 15 December 2010).

[85] Interview No IV, (ECtHR, Strasbourg, 19 June 2012).

[86] Interview No 12 (CJEU, Luxembourg, 15 December 2010).

it is definitely a setback, but, as the experience from the Constitutional Treaty has taught us, the Union has the power to bounce back quickly and overcome the obstacles. The process of European integration is a long one and the EU has repeatedly proved that it has the ability to make things happen. The Opinion presents 'a clear and present danger to human rights protection'[87] and therefore '[i]t is clear that the drafters of the DAA [Draft Accession Agreement] will have to return to the negotiating table'.[88] After all, the accession has not been removed by the EU agenda, as the EU is still required by Article 6(2) TEU to accede to the ECHR. Failure to do so will leave the Commission exposed to an infringement action.

V. CONCLUSION

The present chapter reflected on the process of accession, focusing on the relationship between the CJEU and the ECtHR through the examination of the prior involvement mechanism of the CJEU, the co-respondent mechanism and the future of the *Bosphorus* presumption. Empirical data gathered from interviews with judges, negotiators and key informants was used, not in order to simply justify the presented arguments, but mainly to offer the insights of those heavily involved in the process of accession and thus complement the academic debate with procedural and practical elements.

Thus, the accession will undoubtedly signal a new chapter in the protection of rights in the EU and a new dimension to the inter-institutional judicial relationships.[89] It is a unique arrangement in the history of international and human rights law and will serve as an invaluable experience for the future. The words of Thorbjørn Jagland, the Secretary General of the Council of Europe, best describe the significance of such an achievement illustrating that the conclusion of the negotiations constitutes a milestone for the future of fundamental rights in Europe. 'This is a decisive step, paving the way to EU accession to the European Convention of Human Rights. It will contribute to the creation of a single European legal space, putting in place the missing link in the European system of fundamental rights protection'.[90]

[87] S Peers, 'The CJEU and the EU's Accession to the ECHR: A Clear and Present Danger to Human Rights Protection', EU Law Analysis, 18 December 2014, available at http://eulawanalysis.blogspot.co.uk/2014/12/the-cjeu-and-eus-accession-to-echr.html

[88] T Lock, 'Oops! We did it again—the CJEU's Opinion on EU Accession to the ECHR', VerfBlog, 18 December 2014, available at http://www.verfassungsblog.de/en/oops-das-gutachten-des-eugh-zum-emrk-beitritt-der-eu/

[89] P Craig, 'EU Accession to the ECHR: Competence, Procedure and Substance' (2013) 36 *Fordham International Law Journal* 1114–50, 1150.

[90] Council of Europe, 'Milestone Reached in Negotiations on Accession of EU to the European Convention on Human Rights', available at hub.coe.int/en/web/coe-portal/press/newsroom?p_p_id=newsroom&_newsroom_articleId=1394983&_newsroom_groupId=10226&_newsroom_tabs=newsroom-topnews.

The end is not as near as initially anticipated, but whenever there are political considerations and conflicting interests, 'nothing is over, until it is over'! All the remaining stages require consensus and strong motivation from the side of the CJEU, the EU Member States and the Council of Europe's Parties. All parties involved are reminded of this by the Opinion. Now the EU is obliged to send a strong message about the future of the accession and the whole process of integration based on rights. The EU's accession will create a common human rights approach across Europe setting an example for national courts and providing them with valuable guidance on how to deal with fundamental rights protection. If the two highest European Courts can find a common formula of cooperation and establish multiple channels of communication, then the same can (and should) happen with national courts, to guarantee adequate protection of individuals and deeper integration in the European continent.

The price for integration, uniformity and solidarity is high and the EU should be prepared to pay for it in the form of adaptations and compromises. As Robert Schuman famously stated in 1950, 'Europe will not be made all at once, or according to a single plan. It will be built through concrete achievements which first create a de facto solidarity'.[91]

[91] The Schuman Declaration, 9 May 1950, available at http://www.europa.eu/about-eu/basic-information/symbols/europe-day/schuman-declaration/index_en.htm.

5

The EU Human Rights Regime Post Lisbon: Turning the CJEU into a Human Rights Court?

WOLFGANG WEIß*

I. INTRODUCTION: CONTINUITY AND CHANGE IN THE LISBON EU HUMAN RIGHTS REGIME

THE LISBON TREATY brought about significant changes to the EU human rights regime and increased the overall importance of human rights. Their acknowledgement in the Treaty on European Union (TEU) preamble and their reference in the EU's objective and value provisions (Articles 2 and 3 TEU) give witness to their strengthened significance. Their respect became one of the EU's founding values, their promotion an explicit aim of the EU also with regard to external relations (Article 3(5) TEU). Respect for human rights now is part of the area of freedom, security and justice (Article 67(1) Treaty on the Functioning of the European Union (TFEU)). The EU Fundamental Rights Charter (the Charter) as a legally binding human rights catalogue added a completely novel development to the pre-existing, previously mainly forensic human rights edifice of the EU. Hence, some observers conclude that the Lisbon Treaty marks a new era of integration based on human rights.[1] The augmented relevance of human rights in EU law is reflected in the decisions of the Court of Justice of the European Union (CJEU) because human rights claims have considerably increased since Lisbon, fostering 'fundamental rights' arguments' in litigation before the Court.[2] In response to these developments, the Court appears challenged to deliberate

* Professor of European and Public International Law, German University of Administrative Sciences Speyer; and Honorary Research Fellow, Oxford Brookes University. I owe thanks to Sonia Morano-Foadi and Lucy Vickers for insightful comments.

[1] S Morano-Foadi and S Andreadakis, 'Reflection on the Architecture of the EU after the Treaty of Lisbon: The European Judicial Approach to Fundamental Rights' (2011) 17 *European Law Journal* 595, 599.

[2] S Iglesias Sánchez, 'The Court and the Charter: The Impact of the Entry into Force of the Lisbon Treaty on the ECJ's Approach to Fundamental Rights' (2012) 49 *CML Rev* 1565, 1588, 1609; Morano-Foadi and Andreadakis, 'Reflection on the Architecture of the EU after the Treaty of Lisbon' (ibid) 599.

anew the role and standards of EU fundamental rights protection, beyond merely taking the Charter as the first and foremost point of departure in its reasoning.[3]

Nonetheless, the Lisbon Treaty adduced a strange dialectic change to the EU human rights regime oscillating between continuity and change. This is simultaneously expressed within Article 6 TEU as its first paragraph brings about the Charter's binding force, whereas its third paragraph expresses continuity as the fundamental rights guaranteed by the European Convention on Human Rights and Fundamental Freedoms (ECHR) and resulting from the national constitutional traditions continue to constitute EU general principles. Article 6(3) TEU confirms the continuing relevance of the pre-Lisbon EU human rights heritage as it almost verbatim repeats the former Article 6(2) TEU (Nice) and reflects the settled case law according to which fundamental rights form an integral part of the general principles of law.[4] A further novelty is the EU destination[5] to accede to the ECHR (Article 6(2) TEU). The simultaneity of continuity and change is also reflected in the Charter itself, as on the one hand, it was drafted to produce greater coherence in European human rights protection by merely codifying and making more visible the already existing rights (see fourth recital of its preamble) so that the Charter was not primarily intended to raise the level of EU human rights protection or to introduce novel rights; whereas on the other hand, the Charter also contains true innovations like the prohibition of reproductive cloning (Article 3(2)(d) Charter), or social rights in Title IV on Solidarity.[6]

Against this background, the present contribution analyses the CJEU's application of human rights after Lisbon with the aim of determining how the Court has solved the tension between continuity and change. Does the CJEU continue in old patterns, or does it take the changes as an occasion for a re-orientation of its role, moving in the direction of a human rights court? This analysis will not look at the application of specific human rights, but will explore the CJEU's interpretive and methodical approaches in applying human rights because alterations in this regard appear more decisive for answering the question of whether the Court has fundamentally changed its approach in response to the novel developments and to criticism of its pre-Lisbon human rights case law. As the chapter focuses on methodological issues, it will compare the CJEU's pre- and post-Lisbon case law with regard to the structure of its proportionality control, the standard of review and judicial interpretive traditions.

[3] For this shift in argumentation discernible in post-Lisbon judgments, see Iglesias Sánchez, 'The Court and the Charter' (n 2) 1580, 1582; Morano-Foadi and Andreadakis, 'Reflection on the Architecture of the EU after the Treaty of Lisbon' (n 1) 600f.

[4] See Case C-521/09 P-DEP *Elf Aquitaine v Commission*, not yet published, para 112; Case C-571/10 *Kamberaj* not yet published, para 61.

[5] See M Dougan, 'Treaty of Lisbon 2007: Winning Minds, not Hearts' (2008) 45 *CML Rev* 617, 671.

[6] Many rights in the Charter were drafted in accordance with ECHR provisions, J Dutheil de la Rochère, 'Challenges for the Protection of Fundamental Rights in the EU at the Time of the Entry into Force of the Lisbon Treaty' (2011) 33 *Fordham International Law Journal* 1776, 1778. The Charter's chapter on social rights borrowed widely from that of the Community Social Charter and secondary legislation.

II. CJEU HUMAN RIGHTS ADJUDICATION AND PROPORTIONALITY ASSESSMENT

The first criterion for assessing whether the CJEU adopts the role of a constitutional human rights court is its application of the proportionality control.

A. Proportionality Review and Human Rights Protection

Public power has to respect the requirements of proportionality when interfering with human rights. As interferences in human rights need to be justified by public interests, the legality of public interferences is pivotally determined by a proportionate balancing of conflicting rights and interests (see also Article 52(1) Charter). The principle of proportionality serves as the overarching analytical tool insofar.[7] Thus, the standards of proportionality determine the effective level of human rights protection. The higher the scrutiny a court applies to proportionality assessment when reviewing acts of public power against human rights, the more meaningful proportionality requirements become as effective restraints to public power. If the Lisbon Treaty is to strengthen the substance of human rights protection in the EU, it has to add force to the requirements of proportionality assessment also with regard to the assessment of EU legal acts by the CJEU in view of human rights. As Stone Sweet has shown, the European Court of Human Rights (ECtHR) effectively turned into a human rights court by virtue of its intensified proportionality control. This development under the ECHR confirms the positive relation between judicial proportionality control and strengthened human rights protection.

The ECtHR requires a substantive, rather sophisticated judicial proportionality review of domestic measures which must serve legitimate aims, choose suitable and least restrictive means and strike a fair balance between means, ends and affected rights.[8] A mere reasonableness test under domestic courts would intervene in legislative assessments only where a legal act is so 'unreasonable that no reasonable body could so decide'[9] has been assessed by the ECtHR as in breach of ECHR rights because such a test is highly deferential and makes it almost impossible to give effect to the rights of the ECHR. Such control standards do not effectively allow any consideration by courts of the question of whether the

[7] B Schlink, 'Proportionality (1)' in M Rosenfeld and A Sajo (eds), *The Oxford Handbook of Comparative Constitutional Law* (Oxford, Oxford University Press, 2012) 729; A Stone Sweet, 'The European Court of Justice' in P Craig and G de Búrca (eds), *The Evolution of EU Law* (Oxford, Oxford University Press, 2011), 152; A Stone Sweet and J Mathews, 'Proportionality Balancing and Global Constitutionalism' (2008) 47 *Columbia Journal of Transnational Law* 68, 140f; M Wimmer, 'The Dinghy's Rudder: General Principles of European Union Law through the Lens of Proportionality' (2014) 20 *European Public Law* 331, 337.

[8] For more details, see J Christoffersen, *Fair balance: Proportionality, Subsidiarity, and Primarity in the European Convention on Human Rights*, International Studies in Human Rights 99 (Leiden, Nijhoff, 2009) 69f.

[9] The so-called Wednesbury unreasonableness test, see P Birkinshaw, *European Public Law* (London, Butterworths, 2003) 332.

interference with the Convention's rights was proportionate.[10] Rather, courts are required to engage in substantive review of the merits under the proportionality test. This means that the proportionality review demanded by the ECHR becomes highly intrusive on domestic legislative results and processes which gives the ECHR a constitutional character.[11] This kind of substantive proportionality review significantly increases the authority of judges relative to that of governments or legislatures.[12] One might object that the ECtHR acknowledges a margin of appreciation of domestic bodies which tempers its standard of review. The use of this concept by the ECtHR, however, lacks consistency,[13] and its scope varies according to the nature of the aims pursued by the interfering measure and of the activities restricted.[14] A margin of appreciation almost vanishes in situations of sufficiently common European standards and widens if there is no uniform European conception.[15]

B. Proportionality Review by the CJEU

(i) Criticism of Partisan Balancing and Loose Standards

The proportionality review by the CJEU is subject to constant criticism. The CJEU has been criticised for granting too high a role to merely economic interests and economic efficiency[16] and for neglecting the significance of social policy choices as a limitation to the exercise of economic freedoms.[17] This criticism

[10] *Smith and Grady v The United Kingom* ECHR 1999-VI 71, para 137f; See also *Hirst v The United Kingdom (No 2)* ECHR 2005-IX 62, para 73f.

[11] H Keller and A Stone Sweet, 'Assessing the Impact of the ECHR on National Legal Systems' in H Keller and A Stone Sweet (eds), *A Europe of Rights* (Oxford, Oxford University Press 2008) 699; A Stone Sweet, 'On the Constitutionalisation of the Convention: The European Court of Human Rights as a Constitutional Court' (2009) *Faculty Scholarship Series*, Paper 71, 6, available at www.digitalcommons.law.yale.edu/fss_papers/71.

[12] Stone Sweet, 'On the Constitutionalisation of the Convention' (n 11) 6.

[13] See the critique by CL Rozakis, 'Through the Looking Glass: An "Insider's" View of the Margin of Appreciation' in P Titiun (ed), *La conscience des droits: Mélanges en l'honneur de Jean-Paul Costa* (Dalloz, 2011) 527.

[14] *Smith and Grady v The United Kingdom* (n 10), para 88. For more details, see I de la Rasilla del Moral, 'The Increasingly Marginal Appreciation of the Margin-of-Appreciation Doctrine' (2006) 7 *German Law Journal* 611, 615f.

[15] Stone Sweet and Mathews, 'Proportionality Balancing and Global Constitutionalism' (n 7) 151; *İA v Turkey* ECHR 2005-VIII 29, para 25.

[16] See S Weatherill, 'The Internal Market' in S Peers and A Ward (eds), *The European Union Charter of Fundamental Rights* (Oxford, Hart Publishing, 2004) 201; G Majone, *Europe as the Would-be World Power: The EU at Fifty* (Cambridge, Cambridge University Press 2009) 1.

[17] See R Burchill, 'Assessing the European Union's Position on Human Rights: Is It a Desirable One?' in J Wetzel (ed), *The EU as a 'Global Player' in Human Rights?* (New York, Routledge, 2011), 20f and the seminal debate between J Coppel and A O'Neil, 'The European Court of Justice: Taking Rights Seriously?' (1992) 29 *CML Rev* 669 and J Weiler and N Lockhart, '"Taking Rights Seriously" Seriously: The European Court of Justice and its Fundamental Rights Jurisprudence', Parts I&II' (1995) 32 *CML Rev* 579. This criticism does not exclude, however, that there are cases in which one will find convergence between the two European Courts in relation to the proportionality principle, as with regard to detention of illegal migrants, see S Morano-Foadi, 'Migration and Human Rights: The European Approach', ch 7 in this volume.

again became particularly prevalent after the *Viking*[18] and *Laval*[19] decisions of the CJEU.[20] The criticism of biased and partisan balancing has been raised in particular when comparing the review of EU legal acts by the CJEU with its review of national measures which were adopted as a limitation to the exercise of EU fundamental freedoms. The case law of the CJEU tends to apply different standards of review insofar as national measures are reviewed very intensely, whereas the review of EU measures appears to be generally quite scarce. This applies in particular to the standard of review of proportionality. As regards EU secondary law, the Court is perceived as accepting, in great deference to the EU legislature, a broad margin of discretion on the part of the EU institutions for assessing whether a given measure is suitable or necessary to reach a certain end, in particular in areas which require complex economic assessments. As the CJEU only reviews whether there was a manifest error on the part of the EU institution, it restrains its control standard to a mere tenability or rationality control granting a considerable margin of discretion to EU institutions.[21] The CJEU rarely tests the adequacy of the measure (proportionality *strictu sensu* is the third step of the proportionality review, which is not explicitly mentioned in Article 52(1) Charter), and sometimes not even the necessity.[22] As a consequence of the inadequate proportionality control, the level of *effective* protection of EU human rights against EU acts is quite low. In contrast, the CJEU appears much more rigorous with regard to Member States' measures impeding the exercise of EU fundamental freedoms, in particular when reviewing their proportionality.[23] Proportionality review is rather strict[24] so that the Court is perceived to apply in its proportionality review of domestic measures a strong bias in favour of promoting European integration[25] and of preferring EU fundamental freedoms over EU fundamental rights.

[18] Case C-438/05 *International Transport Workers' Federation and Finnish Seamen's Union v Viking Line ABP and OÜ Viking Line Eesti* [2007] ECR I-10779.

[19] Case C-341/05 *Laval un Partneri Ltd v Svenska Byggnadsarbetareförbundet* [2007] ECR I-11767.

[20] See, eg, C Barnard, *The Substantive Law of the EU: The Four Freedoms*, 3rd edn (Oxford, Oxford University Press, 2010) 259; C Barnard, 'A Proportionate Response to Proportionality in the Field of Collective Action' (2012) 37 *EL Rev* 124; P Syrpis, 'The Treaty of Lisbon: Much Ado ... But About What?' (2008) 37 *Industry Law Journal* 228f.

[21] See also Birkinshaw, *European Public Law* (n 9) 145.

[22] See C Calliess, 'The Charter of Fundamental Rights of the European Union' in D Ehlers (ed), *European Fundamental Rights and Freedoms* (Berlin, de Gruyter Recht, 2007) 519; F Jacobs, 'Recent Developments in the Principle of Proportionality' in E Ellis (ed), *The Principle of Proportionality in the Laws of Europe* (Oxford, Hart Publishing, 1999) 3f; Barnard, 'A Proportionate Response to Proportionality' (n 20) 126 observes that only occasionally the CJEU reviews the third step of proportionality control, ie strict proportionality, if 'one of the parties raises the issue'; see also P Craig, *EU Administrative Law*, 2nd edn (Oxford, Oxford University Press, 2012) 602.

[23] See Jacobs, 'Recent Developments in the Principle of Proportionality' (n 22) 21; Weatherill, 'The internal market' (n 16) 195. For the difference in standard of review, see also Craig and de Búrca, *The Evolution of EU Law* (n 7) 532; R Streinz, *Europarecht* (Heidelberg, Müller, 2012), para 760; Coppel and O'Neil, 'The European Court of Justice' (n 17) 683–85.

[24] See also Birkinshaw, *European Public Law* (n 9) 145; T von Danwitz, 'Thoughts on Proportionality and Coherence in the Jurisprudence of the Court of Justice' in P Cardonnel and A Rosas and N Wahl (eds), *Constitutionalising the EU Judicial System* (Oxford, Hart Publishing, 2012), 378 stresses that the Member States are not awarded with a prerogative in assessing necessity, in contrast to what is conceded to the EU.

[25] T Tridimas, *The General Principles of EU Law* (Oxford, Oxford University Press, 2006) 193.

One might doubt whether such criticism does justice to more recent CJEU decisions which illustrate an equal ranking of human rights and treaty freedoms as the Court balanced, in a non-partisan way, treaty freedoms against fundamental rights invoked as lawful limitations to their exercise[26] and where it adopted quite a deferential approach to domestic measures for the sake of protecting national constitutional peculiarities.[27] Advocate General (AG) Trstenjak confirmed that in case of conflict between fundamental rights and treaty freedoms, the proportionality test has to ensure that neither of the colliding rights are interfered with in a disproportionate way. A fair balance between both has to be sought as fundamental right and freedoms are of equal rank.[28] She had to admit, however, that the approach adopted in the *Viking* and *Laval* cases is in need of further qualification.[29]

Despite such positive signs of striving for a fair balance between fundamental rights and treaty freedoms in some pre-Lisbon cases, one has to keep in mind that the overall CJEU case law still is far from being clear insofar.[30] Furthermore, a mere proclamation of equal rank of fundamental rights and treaty freedoms and of the need for respecting proportionality in balancing the two does not pronounce on the actual standard of review applied in the proportionality control and the extent of deference to deliberations of the national or EU legislature in justifying interference with fundamental rights or freedoms. Finally, with regard to the standard of review concerning EU acts, the CJEU sticks to its traditional approach that the EU measures' legality is affected only if the measure is manifestly inappropriate.[31]

(ii) Intensified Proportionality Review Post Lisbon?

Also after Lisbon, the CJEU, when reviewing the proportionality of EU acts in many cases first of all restates the traditional judicial approach of underscoring the leeway of the EU legislature and of confining itself to a review of whether

[26] See Case C-112/00 *Schmidberger v Republik Österreich* [2003] ECR I-5659; Case C-36/02 *Omega v Bonn* [2004] ECR I-9609; S Weatherill, 'From Economic Rights to Fundamental Rights' in S de Vries, U Bernitz and S Weatherill (eds), *The Protection of Fundamental Rights in the EU After Lisbon* (Oxford, Hart Publishing, 2013) 26 notices the reference of the *Schmidberger* ruling by the CJEU in the context of appraising the lawfulness of EU acts in Case-C-402/05 P and C-415/05 P *Kadi and Al Barakaat International Foundation v Council and Commission* [2008] ECR I-6351.

[27] For more details insofar, see S de Vries, 'The Protection of Fundamental Rights within Europe's Internal Market after Lisbon—An Endeavour for More Harmony' in de Vries et al, *The Protection of Fundamental Rights in the EU After Lisbon* (n 26) 63f, 82, 90.

[28] See Case C-271/08 *Commission v Germany* [2010] ECR I-7096, Opinion of AG Trstenjak, para 188.

[29] ibid, para 193.

[30] See de Vries, 'The Protection of Fundamental Rights within Europe's Internal Market after Lisbon' (n 27) 93.

[31] See also T Harbo, 'The Function of the Proportionality Principle in EU law' (2010) 16 *European Law Journal* 180. Craig, *EU Administrative Law* (n 22) 600f shows that this test no longer is applied in its very cursory initial version.

that measure was not manifestly inappropriate to reach the aim.[32] Nevertheless, there are some post-Lisbon decisions which give indications for a prudent re-orientation towards much more intense proportionality assessments and increased standards of review as the CJEU held that:

> [E]ven though [the legislature] has a broad discretion, the Community legislature must base its choice on objective criteria. Furthermore, in assessing the burdens associated with various possible measures, it must examine whether objectives pursued by the measure chosen are such as to justify even substantial negative economic consequences for certain operators.[33]

This is in line with the recent deepening of judicial control of Commission decisions in competition law. The CJEU explicitly confessed the need for an in-depth review of law and facts, irrespective of the Commission's margin of discretion.[34]

A rather explicit example of an intensified proportionality review of EU legislative acts is the *Schecke and Eifert* judgement about the protection of personal data in which the CJEU ruled that the EU legislator did not properly balance the public interest in transparency against the rights of natural persons under Article 7 and 8 of the Charter to respect for their private lives and their personal data.[35] Here, the CJEU stated that there was a lack of due balancing between the conflicting interests. It required an adequate consideration of the importance of the individual right at stake. The assessment of necessity of a measure demands reconciliation of the objective pursued by the legislature (here, transparency of public spending) with the fundamental rights of the individuals affected.[36] This test, even though classified by the CJEU under the criterion of necessity, actually reflects the third

[32] See Case C-343/09 *Afton Chemical Ltd v Secretary of State for Transport* [2010] ECR I-7027, para 46; Case C-58/08 *Vodafone and Others* [2010] ECR I-4999, para 52: 'With regard to judicial review … the Community legislature must be allowed a broad discretion in areas in which its action involves political, economic and social choices and … complex assessments and evaluations. *Thus … its legality can be affected only if the measure is manifestly inappropriate*' (emphasis added); Case C-221/09 *AJD Tuna* [2011] ECR I-1655, para 81; Case C-15/10 *Etimine* [2011] ECR I-6681, para 124; Case C-59/11 *Association Kokopelli*, not yet published, para 39, 59f; Case T-526/10, *Inuit Tapiriit Kanatami and Others v Commission*, not yet published, para 88.

[33] Case C-58/08 *Vodafone and Others* (n 32), para 53; the CJEU then (paras 54–71) reviews the proportionality assessments by the Commission and the Council when adopting the contested regulation, with regard to the legitimacy of the purpose, the appropriateness of the measure for the purpose pursued (para 60), its necessity (para 61ff) and its proportionality *stricto sensu* (para 69).

[34] Case C-386/10 P *Chalkor v Commission* [2011] ECR I-13085, para 62; Case C-389/10 P *KME Germany and Others v Commission* [2011] ECR I-13125, para 129; Case C-272/09 P *KME Germany and Others v Commission* [2011] ECR I-12789, para 102. The European Free Trade Association (EFTA) Court, ruling on Art 6 ECHR, expanded these statements of the CJEU by stating that 'the Court must be able to quash in all respects, on questions of fact and of law, the challenged decision': Case E-15/10 *Posten Norge AS v EFTA Surveillance Authority*, judgment of 18 April 2012, [2012] EFTA Ct Rep 246, para 98ff. See also J Temple Lang, 'Judicial Review of Competition Decisions under the European Convention on Human Rights and the Importance of the EFTA Court: The Norway Post Judgment' (2012) 37 *EL Rev* 464, 467f.

[35] Joined Cases C-92/09 and C-93/09 *Volker and Markus Schecke and Eifert* [2010] ECR I-11063, para 72f, 86.

[36] ibid, para 76.

step of proportionality review, ie the proportionality *strictu sensu*. The contention of the EU legislature that the objective of transparency could not be achieved by measures which interfere less with these rights,[37] was not accepted by the CJEU. It held that even though taxpayers in a democratic society had a right to be kept informed of the use of public funds, the legislator still had to:

> ascertain whether the publication … of data by name … did not go beyond what was necessary for achieving the legitimate aims pursued.… As far as natural persons … are concerned, … it does not appear that Council and the Commission sought to strike such a balance between the [EU]'s interest … and the fundamental rights.[38]

Thus, the CJEU did not accept the contention that the measure was necessary. Instead, it required a more elaborate analysis of the measure's balance with affected rights. The CJEU did not confine its legal assessment to an appraisal of whether the measure was manifestly inappropriate. Nor, however, did the Court second-guess the proportionality deliberations made by the EU legislature in order to develop, out of its own competence, a more proportionate solution to the conflict between privacy and transparency. The Court did in fact, by and large, only state that the deliberations of the EU legislature were insufficient, in particular since they lacked a consideration of other, less offensive methods.[39] The proportionality review by the CJEU in this case is said to be supportive of a 'more procedural approach' to the proportionality principle[40] instead of a review of the substance of proportionality, reflecting a newer trend discernible in the Court's proportionality control: the Court sometimes stipulates procedural requirements in the context of its proportionality control.[41] In the *Schecke* case the Court could indeed confine itself to rather formal, procedural stipulations as to how an adequate proportionality assessment by the EU legislature has to be performed; it required the consideration of alternatives. This approach avoids deep interference with the task of the legislature and does not prevent the Court, in other cases, engaging in a more substantive proportionality review, as it clearly showed its intention to apply stronger scrutiny insofar. Thus, the rather procedural stance in this case was rather particular and must neither be generalised nor misinterpreted as an implicit rejection of the need for substantive assessment of proportionality.[42] Judge Thomas von Danwitz pleads, as a consequence of the formulation in

[37] ibid, para 78.
[38] ibid, para 79f.
[39] ibid, para 81; see also C Barnard, 'The Protection of Fundamental Social Rights in Europe after Lisbon: A Question of Conflicts of Interests' in de Vries et al, *The Protection of Fundamental Rights in the EU After Lisbon* (n 26) 57.
[40] Barnard, 'A Proportionate Response to Proportionality in the Field of Collective Action' (n 20) 131.
[41] See S Prechal, 'Free Movement and Procedural Requirements: Proportionality Reconsidered' (2008) 35 *Legal Issues of Economic Integration* 203f; de Vries, 'The Protection of Fundamental Rights within Europe's Internal Market after Lisbon' (n 27) 68, 82; Wimmer, 'The Dinghy's Rudder' (n 7) 351f.
[42] von Danwitz, 'Thoughts on Proportionality and Coherence' (n 24) 374.

Article 52(1) of the Charter for a stricter, but also flexible and rights-specific proportionality review which still could allow for national margins of appreciation.[43]

Interestingly, the *Schecke* case dealt with an interference with Articles 7 and 8 of the Charter which correspond to Article 8 ECHR, and the CJEU explicitly referred to Article 52(3) of the Charter so that the meaning and scope of these rights had to be the same as in the ECHR.[44] Consequently, the CJEU referred several times to the jurisprudence of the ECtHR, both with regard to the scope of the protection of the fundamental right and its limitations,[45] and with regard also to the proportionality requirement.[46] Hence, one can infer that the stricter review of proportionality and the lack of reference to a leeway enjoyed by the EU legislature were also caused by the application of the review standards adopted by the ECtHR under the ECHR. In conformity with this, the CJEU in its most recent judgment on the validity of the Data Retention Directive 2006/24[47] held that with regard to proportionality review:

> where interferences with fundamental rights are at issue, the extent of the EU legislature's discretion may prove to be limited, depending on a number of factors, including, in particular, the area concerned, the nature of the right at issue guaranteed by the Charter, the nature and seriousness of the interference and the object pursued by the interference,[48]

referring again to a Strasbourg decision.[49] Due to the:

> important role played by the protection of personal data in the light of the fundamental right to respect for private life and the extent and seriousness of the interference with that right caused by Directive 2006/24, the EU legislature's discretion is reduced, with the result that review of that discretion should be strict ... the right to respect for private life ... requires ... in any event, that derogations and limitations in relation to the protection of personal data must apply only in so far as is strictly necessary ... Consequently, the EU legislation in question must lay down clear and precise rules governing the scope and application of the measure in question and imposing minimum safeguards so that the

[43] T von Danwitz, '§ 6 Gerichtlicher Schutz der Grundrechte' in C Grabenwarter (ed), *Europäischer Grundrechtsschutz*, (Baden-Baden, Nomos, 2014) paras 66–68. Accordingly, where von Danwitz functions as rapporteur, one can find a very diligent proportionality analysis, see, Case C-283/11 *Sky Österreich*, not yet published and Joined Cases C-293/12 and C-594/12 *Digital Rights Ireland and Seitlinger ua*, not yet published, which will be examined below.

[44] Joined Cases C-92/09 and C-93/09 *Volker and Markus Schecke and Eifert* (n 35), para 51.

[45] ibid, para 52; another example: Case C-279/09 *DEB* [2010] ECR I-13849, paras 35–53.

[46] Joined Cases C-92/09 and C-93/09 *Volker and Markus Schecke and Eifert* (n 35), para 72. Here the CJEU refers to *Gillow v The United Kingdom* (1986) Series A no 124-C, para 55, which defines the notion of necessary to mean 'proportionate to the legitimate aim pursued' which requires a weighing and balancing of the conflicting interests.

[47] Directive on the retention of data generated or processed in connection with the provision of publicly available electronic communications services or of public communications networks and amending Directive 2002/58/EC [2006] OJ L105/54.

[48] Joined Cases C-293/12 and C-594/12 *Digital Rights Ireland and Seitlinger ua*, not yet published, para 47. This is a rather verbatim reproduction of the rapporteur's (T von Danwitz) early reflections about the consequences flowing from the formulations used in Art 52(1) of the Charter for the CJEU's proportionality review, see T von Danwitz, 'Comment on Article 52' in PJ Tettinger and K Stern (eds), *Kölner Gemeinschaftskommentar zur Europäischen Grundrechte-Charta* (München, Beck, 2006) para 42.

[49] *S and Marper v The United Kingdom* [2008] ECHR 101, para 102, regarding Art 8 of the ECHR.

persons whose data have been retained have sufficient guarantees to effectively protect their personal data.[50]

The CJEU finally held that due to the general absence of limits for data retention and the lack of any objective criterion by which to determine the limits of the access of the competent national authorities to the data and their subsequent use, the wide-ranging and serious interference with the right to protection of personal data goes beyond what is strictly necessary.

The *Association Kokopelli* judgement of July 2012, however, exemplifies the contradictory simultaneity of old and new approaches also in post-Lisbon decisions. The CJEU had to rule on the legality of EU regulations establishing the common catalogue of plant varieties which excluded from the internal market certain vegetable seeds not listed there. The reason for their exclusion was the aim of increased productivity of agricultural production and of optimum utilisation of production factors. In assessing the proportionality of the EU acts, the Court, on the one hand, several times referred to the traditional standard of 'not manifestly inappropriate'[51] and only reviewed the tenability of the EU legislature's deliberations.[52] On the other hand, however, the Court took particular care to review the proportionality of the measure in view of severe negative economic consequences for Kokopelli whose old plant seeds no longer remained marketable so that it complained about a disproportionate interference with the right to pursue its economic activity (Article 16 of the Charter which the CJEU did not cite). These concerns had led AG Kokott to conclude that the measure was manifestly disproportionate as the EU legislature in her opinion failed to take account of these considerable negative effects.[53] The Court, however, was finally content to state that the measures did not appear, in view also of the economic interests of Kokopelli, to be 'manifestly disproportionate'.[54]

It is deplorable that the CJEU did not continue its intensified approach from *Schecke and Eifert* but returned to its rather superficial pre-Lisbon pattern of proportionality control of EU acts. Due to the explicit mention of Article 52(3) of the Charter and the Strasbourg standards of proportionality review in *Schecke*, one might speculate that the loose approach later adopted in *Kokopelli* was motivated by the fact that the CJEU might not be willing to apply higher scrutiny outside the scope of Article 52(3). If that was true, it would mean that the Court operates double standards of proportionality review, depending on whether EU fundamental rights are at stake which have a twin in the ECHR (as in *Schecke* or *Digital Rights Ireland*), or not (as in *Kokopelli*: the ECHR does not explicitly guarantee a right to conduct a business). Different standards in proportionality review of

[50] Joined Cases C-293/12 and C-594/12 *Digital Rights Ireland and Seitlinger ua*, not yet published, paras 48, 52, 54, again referring to Strasbourg case law.

[51] See Case C-59/11 *Association Kokopelli*, not yet published, paras 39, 60, 68.

[52] ibid, paras 59, 67.

[53] Case C-59/11 *Association Kokopelli*, not yet published, Opinion of AG Kokott, paras 87, 89f.

[54] Case C-59/11 *Association Kokopelli*, not yet published, para 68.

interferences with the same Charter rights, however, are not legitimate; there is no recognisable justification. In another recent judgment on Articles 7 and 8 of the Charter, ie on the same individual rights as affected in *Schecke and Eifert*, the CJEU neither alluded to any leeway on the part of the EU legislator, but confined its proportionality control to reviewing the suitability and necessity of the EU measure.[55] In another recent judgement on the freedom to conduct a business (Article 16 of the Charter, as in *Kokopelli*), in contrast, the CJEU employed a fully fledged, very elaborate proportionality review, as the proportionality principle was said to require that:

> [M]easures adopted by European Union institutions do not exceed the limits of what is appropriate and necessary in order to attain the objectives legitimately pursued by the legislation in question; when there is a choice between several appropriate measures recourse must be had to the least onerous, and the disadvantages caused must not be disproportionate to the aims pursued,[56]

which includes an analysis of proportionality *strictu sensu*, and as the Court did not mention the traditional reservation that the legality of a measure can be affected only if the measure is manifestly inappropriate. When comparing the contested EU provision to a less restrictive alternative, the CJEU took note of the lower effectiveness of the alternative.[57] Furthermore, the CJEU carefully considered whether an appropriate balance between the diverse interests was struck by the EU legislature.[58]

The overall strengthened significance of EU human rights post Lisbon requires a consistent reorientation of the CJEU in its proportionality review which is predictable in its application and standard of review and which must not depend on the personality of the judge rapporteur. Only then is proportionality review transformed into a tool of protecting individual human rights against EU public power as well. A mere tenability control no longer is acceptable as it does not allow for reviewing the conformity of EU acts with EU human rights, as the experience of the ECtHR illustrates.

III. CJEU HUMAN RIGHTS ADJUDICATION AND JUDICIAL INTERPRETIVE TRADITIONS

The alteration of judicial interpretive traditions regarding the CJEU's application of EU human rights would be a further indication of its reorientation. There are two traditions in particular which have a bearing on the effective implementation of EU human rights innovations. One of these traditions is the rather flexible handling of decisions of the Strasbourg human rights court by the CJEU

55 Case C-291/12 *Schwarz*, not yet published, para 40f.
56 Case C-283/11 *Sky Österreich*, not yet published, para 50.
57 ibid, paras 55–57.
58 ibid, paras 58–66.

(Section A below). The other one is the traditional interpretive way in the determination of EU general principles on fundamental rights (Section B below).

A. Conformity with the ECHR versus Established CJEU Case Law

One of the core aims of the Charter is consistency in the level of protection of human rights in Europe. The ECHR works as a minimum standard (Article 52(3) Charter). This provision even incorporates Convention standards into EU law insofar as Charter rights correspond to Convention rights. Accordingly, the CJEU confirms that as a consequence of Article 52(3) of the Charter, a Charter provision corresponding to a Convention right 'must therefore be given the same meaning and the same scope as [the corresponding ECHR provision], as interpreted by the case law of the European Court of Human Rights'.[59] As a consequence, the CJEU should not only consider ECtHR decisions on relevant issues and avoid contradictions to relevant interpretive statements of previous ECtHR decisions on like human rights issues, but should implement relevant ECtHR case law in order to attain the uniform protection of human rights sought. The CJEU, in some of its post-Lisbon decisions, however, does not appear to show this degree of preparedness to observe the Strasbourg case law. Hence, this mirrors the very eclectic traditional pre-Lisbon way the CJEU evinced with regard to Strasbourg decisions: even though the CJEU increasingly aligned its fundamental rights jurisprudence towards the ECHR, the Court did not want to be legally obliged to follow ECtHR case law in every respect as Strasbourg decisions merely had to be considered instead of being followed.[60] Such rather loose reception of Strasbourg decisions can still be found after Lisbon. This stance may also stand behind the recent Opinion 2/13 on the Accession to the ECHR where the court states that the rights of the Charter 'must … be interpreted and applied within the EU in accordance with the constitutional framework' (which, in the Court's view, comprises of 'significant distinctive features' like the autonomy of the EU legal order, its primacy over the laws of the Member States and the existence of a 'judicial system intended to ensure consistency and uniformity in the interpretation of EU law') where the Court, however, fails to note Article 52(3) and the thus constitutionally scheduled coherence with the ECHR (Opinion 2/13, nyr, paras 157–77). Even worse, there are decisions where the CJEU appears completely unaware of the new, post-Lisbon human rights regime as its decision was completely confined to determining a general EU principle on human rights.

The *Akzo Nobel* judgement[61] about the personal scope of the legal professional privilege is a remarkable example in this regard. Here, the CJEU did not mention

[59] Case C-400/10 PPU *MCB* [2010] ECR I-8965, para 53; see also Case C-279/09 *DEB* (n 45), para 35.

[60] See W Weiß, 'Human Rights in the EU: Rethinking the Role of the ECHR after Lisbon' (2011) 7 *European Constitutional Law Review* 64, 77–80.

[61] *Akzo Nobel Chemicals and Akcros Chemicals v Commission* [2010] ECR I-8309.

any relevant Charter provision, neither any relevant ECtHR case law, nor Article 52(3) of the Charter. This is astonishing given that the contested issue is also subject to ECtHR case law. The confidentiality of the communication between client and counsel is respected under Article 6(3) ECHR and under Article 8 ECHR.[62] As Articles 47 and 48 of the Charter recognise the right to a fair trial and the rights of defence, and hence correspond to Article 6 ECHR, the ECHR standards are highly relevant for their interpretation. The CJEU, however did not consider them in its decision, but applied the traditional legal comparative methodology of searching for a general principle of EU law. The CJEU recalled the general EU principle on legal professional privilege as developed in its landmark *AM & S* decision[63] and examined whether new developments in the Member States required an extension of the confidentiality of the client's communication with their lawyers also with regard to in-house lawyers, as contended by the parties.[64] The CJEU did not modify the general principle stated in *AM & S*. It did so by still confirming a lack of uniform tendency, or at least clear majority, in the Member States so that there was no need to recognise a new standard of the legal professional privilege.[65] Hence, the Court considered that the legal situation in the EU Member States has not evolved since *AM & S* to an extent which would justify a change in the case law.[66] The CJEU, however, failed to take note of the changes of the EU human rights regime since Lisbon.

The interpretive methodology applied by AG Kokott in her opinion was quite similar. Even though AG Kokott initially referred to the relevant Charter rights and the ECHR standards (including ECtHR case law),[67] she first focused on the question as to whether there was a clear trend in the Member States to also protect communication with in-house lawyers,[68] and only later dealt with the ECHR standards and Article 52(3) of the Charter stressing that relevant ECtHR decisions 'point to an understanding of the independence of lawyers which is not dissimilar to that on which the [CJEU] based its judgment in *AM & S*'.[69] The understanding of the ECtHR case law since *AM & S*, however, is subject to fierce controversy.[70] Even though the Strasbourg Court has not directly pronounced on a privilege for

[62] *Campbell* v *The United Kingdom* (1992) Series A no 233; *Niemietz v Germany* (1992) Series A no 251-B; *Foxley v The United Kingdom* App no 33274/96 (ECtHR, 20 June 2000); *Smirnov v Russia* App no 71362/01 (ECtHR, 7 June 2007) and *André and Other v France* App no 18603/03 (ECtHR, 24 July 2008), para 41. For its implication on Art 6(3) ECHR, see *S v Switzerland* (1992) Series A no 220-A, para 48. For more details, see E Gippini-Fournier, 'Legal Professional Privilege in Competition Proceedings' in B Hawk (ed), *International Antitrust Law and Policy: Fordham Corporate Law 2005* (New York, Juris Publishing, 2005) 613f.

[63] Case C-155/79 *AM & S v Commission* [1982] ECR I-1575.

[64] Case C-550/07 P *Akzo Nobel Chemicals and Akcros Chemicals v Commission* (n 61), para 65.

[65] ibid, para 71f.

[66] ibid, para 76.

[67] See Case C-550/07 P *Akzo Nobel Chemicals and Akcros Chemicals v Commission* (n 61), Opinion of AG Kokott, para 47f.

[68] ibid, para 100f.

[69] ibid, para 141f.

[70] See W Weiß, 'EU Competition Policy as an International Human Rights Issue' in J Wetzel (ed), *The EU as a 'Global Player' in Human Rights?* (New York, Routledge, 2011) 177 with further references.

in-house lawyers as well, the understanding of the ECtHR case law on legal privilege pertains to a more generous approach of the ECHR with regard to in-house lawyers.[71] Hence, the increased relevance of human rights in the EU post Lisbon should have prompted the CJEU to explicitly and carefully deal with pertinent Strasbourg decisions.

Another example where the CJEU neither considered the ECHR nor relevant case law is its *Samba Diouf* decision which dealt with the issue whether effective judicial protection in asylum procedures requires also that preparatory procedural decisions (ie the decision to deal with the asylum application under an accelerated procedure) are subject to judicial control separately and independently from the final decision. The CJEU noted that the right to effective judicial protection was now given expression in Article 47 of the Charter.[72] No mention was made of Article 6 and the relevant ECHR standards. Instead the CJEU only referred to its previous case law when answering the questions about the extent of the right to effective judicial protection referred to by the national court.

A most recent example is the CJEU *Fransson* decision. Here, the CJEU opined that the *ne bis in idem* principle of Article 50 of the Charter does not exclude the successive imposition of administrative and criminal penalties for the same act as long as the former is not criminal in nature. Only if the former is 'criminal in nature for the purposes of Article 50 Charter and has become final', does Article 50 then preclude criminal proceedings in respect of the same acts.[73] Again, the Court did not deal with ECHR standards and referred to its previous case law although AG Cruz Villalón in his opinion opined that:

> [T]he evolution of the [ECtHR] case-law shows that … Article 4 of Protocol No 7 to the ECHR precludes measures for the imposition of both administrative and criminal penalties in respect of the same acts … The current state of the case-law … is evidence of the existence of a conclusive statement of the law from Strasbourg.[74]

Despite such conclusive Strasbourg statements, the AG finally proposed to answer the questions referred to the Court in a different way not in line with Strasbourg. He stated that the *ne bis in idem* principle of Article 50 Charter 'does not preclude a Member State from imposing successively, for the same acts of non-compliance … a tax penalty and a criminal penalty in so far as the first penalty is not criminal in nature'.[75] The CJEU almost verbatim followed his proposal. The reason why the AG had not fully implemented Strasbourg case law was a peculiar methodical approach in interpreting the Charter: in the AG's view, Article 50 of the Charter calls for an interpretation partly independent from Strasbourg standards 'which

[71] See A Andreangeli, *EC Competition Enforcement and Human Rights* (Cheltenham, Edward Elgar Publishing, 2008) 120.

[72] Case C-69/10 *Samba Diouf* [2011] ECR I-7151, para 49. This case also raises issues with regard to the degree of scrutiny, see S Morano-Foadi, 'Migration and Human Rights: The European Approach', ch 7 in this volume.

[73] Case C-617/10 *Åkerberg Fransson*, not yet published, paras 34, 37.

[74] Case C-617/10 *Åkerberg Fransson*, not yet published, Opinion of AG Cruz Villalón, para 79.

[75] ibid, para 117(1).

is based exclusively on the wording and scope of Article 50 Charter'.[76] The reason he gave was the existence of national reservations of the Member States regarding Article 4 of Protocol No 7, which effected that the ECHR right was not fully incorporated into national law. Hence, the AG opined that in such circumstances 'the obligation of Article 52(3) Charter to place the level of protection provided for in the Charter on an equal footing to that provided for in the ECHR is not as effective'.[77] This statement does not consider the Explanations to Article 50 of the Charter given by the Presidium which explicitly state that the principle of *ne bis in idem* within a Member State has the same meaning and scope as Article 4 of Protocol 7.

The attitude shown by the CJEU has given rise to the suspicion by some observers that the impact of Article 52(3) of the Charter on the CJEU's methodological approach and the Court's willingness to adopt ECHR standards depend (inter alia) on the existence of already well established CJEU case law.[78] Where its own established case law exists, the CJEU allegedly does not consider ECHR standards to any noticeable extent. If this is the case, the attempt to attain conformity with ECHR standards reflected in the Charter and in particular in its Article 52(3) would fail exactly in cases where pre-existing case law might be in conflict with the ECHR.

However, with regard to *Samba Diouf*, there might be a different explanation for the resistance of the CJEU to address the relevance of ECHR standards to the issues present before the Court. As Article 6 ECHR is not applicable to fair trial issues in the expulsion of asylum seekers during their asylum procedures,[79] there might not have been matching ECtHR case law. But even if this was the case, the CJEU should have explicitly dealt with this, in the face of the demands of Article 52(3) of the Charter, and not completely renounced any mention of the ECHR.

B. Interpretation of the Charter and Traditional Interpretive Methods: Human Rights Ensured 'Within the Framework of EU Structure and Objectives'

Another judicial development causing concerns about the efficiency of EU human rights protection post Lisbon is related to the traditional interpretive approaches regarding general principles on EU human rights. The question is whether these approaches set down by the CJEU still prevail and impact upon the judicial interpretation and application of Charter rights. According to the CJEU, the protection of fundamental rights as general principles of EU law, 'whilst inspired by the constitutional traditions common to the Member States, must be ensured within

[76] ibid, para 87.
[77] ibid, para 85.
[78] Iglesias Sánchez, 'The Court and the Charter' (n 2) 1604.
[79] *Maaouia v France* ECHR 2000-X, paras 37–38.

the framework of the structure and objectives of the Community'.[80] This means that even though constitutional traditions and the common European heritage inspired the determination of EU fundamental rights, the CJEU employed a rather autonomous, 'creative and eclectic' methodology:[81] even if there was a human rights consensus shared by the national constitutional traditions of all Member States, this would not necessarily mean that the CJEU would transfer the content of such human rights to the EU level. As a consequence, the Court only applied human rights to the EU if and insofar as they conform to the structure and objectives of the EU.

In the same way, the CJEU felt free to adopt fundamental rights which were suitable for the EU's structure and objectives even though such rights had been recognised only by a minority of Member States. This autonomous approach reflects an appraisal of the EU as a self-standing polity and the search for a fundamental rights protection suitable to its essence as is confirmed by the duct of Opinion 2/13 where the Court again referred to the need for interpreting the Charter rights 'within the framework of the structure and objectives of the EU' (para 170).[82]

The question under the Charter now is whether such interpretive methodology and autonomy still persists as an instrument to safeguard the autonomy of EU law, leading to the EU human rights system and the Charter to become more and more self-referential, resulting in marginalisation of other international instruments like the Convention.[83] A hint in that direction might be Article 52(4) of the Charter according to which Charter rights which recognise fundamental rights as they result from common constitutional traditions of the EU Member States shall be interpreted in harmony with those traditions. This rule could be assessed as giving a comparable leeway to the CJEU in the interpretation of Charter rights. Such understanding, however, meets with severe objections.

Firstly, such understanding contradicts the idea of a codification. Whereas the CJEU could, in past times where there was no human rights catalogue in the EU, tailor the rights according to the needs, the structure and objectives of the EU in its determination of EU human rights, the raison d'etre of a codification demands a different methodical approach. For, the existence of a specific right enshrined in the codification of a human rights charter is not subject to any doubt at all, so that there is neither need nor room for genuinely defining this very right in the Court's case law. In addition, the wording itself of this specific right as formulated

[80] Case C-11/70 *Internationale Handelsgesellschaft mbH v Einfuhr- and Vorratsstelle für Getreide and Futtermittel* [1970] ECR-1125, para 4.

[81] Tridimas, *The General Principles of EU Law* (n 25) 6, 23; similarly Andreangeli, *EC Competition Enforcement and Human Rights* (n 71) 10; W Weiß, *Verteidigungsrechte im EG-Kartellverfahren*, Ius criminale 3 (Köln, Heymanns, 1996) 31–61; Case C-411/05 *Palacios de la Villa* [2007] ECR I-8535, Opinion of AG Mazák, para 87f; a telling example is Case C-144/04, *Mangold* [2005] ECR I-9981, para 74f.

[82] See insofar J Weiler, 'Fundamental Rights and Fundamental Boundaries' in J Weiler (ed) *The Constitution of Europe* (Cambridge, Cambridge University Press, 1999) 107–19.

[83] Burchill, 'Assessing the European Union's Position on Human Rights' (n 17) 24.

in the Charter forms the point of departure of its interpretation. Constitutional traditions may only inform the interpretation of the formulations in the Charter. Hence, the scope of the traditional methodological leeway must be confined to the interpretation of a Charter right. But even so, the question remains whether the CJEU still should enjoy the power to use the structure and objectives of the EU as one of the circumstances to be considered when interpreting a Charter provision as it did in Opinion 2/13. It is in line with recognised international rules (Articles 31–33 Vienna Convention on the Law of Treaties) to consider the object and purpose of EU provisions when interpreting EU rules like those on EU human rights in the Charter, but this can be done only within an interpretation of the formulations used in the wording of the Charter rights. Furthermore, interpreting a provision in light of the EU's object and purpose relates to the aims and objectives of the EU as a whole, which comprises the recognition of human rights, and is different to interpreting Charter provisions within the objects and purposes of specific EU policies. Besides, the rationale of the reservation as to structure and objectives of the EU does not fit to an original EU human rights codification. The autonomy of the method of the CJEU originally served to fend off expectations that national human rights should be applied to the EU's legal order. The reservation accordingly safeguarded the EU legal order's autonomy which is not threatened by an EU human rights catalogue.

Secondly, a reservation regarding the 'structure and objectives of the EU' in the interpretation of the Charter collides with Article 52(3) of the Charter because it prescribes conformity of interpretation and standard of protection between the Charter and corresponding ECHR rights. The ECHR as a minimum standard requires an EU level of protection not below the Convention. Consequently, the CJEU does not enjoy leeway to adopt an interpretation of Charter rights which stays behind ECHR standards. A reservation as to the appropriateness of a certain ECHR standard (with regard, for example, to the scope, the ambit, or the limitations of a right) to the structure and objectives of the EU is not provided for in the Charter.

Thirdly, the rationale of the codification idea rejects a persisting reservation as to the structure and objectives of the EU in the interpretation of the Charter. Codifications summarise and describe the current state of play, and form the point of departure for future developments and further progression. Consequently, the Charter text has to impact on the further development of the EU fundamental rights regime, including the future identification of general principles of EU law. Article 52(3) of the Charter is an expression of the flexibility and openness of the EU human rights law with regard to more extensive protection. Using the general principles and the traditional methodology applied in their determination in order to somehow petrify the Charter rights to the existing structures and objectives of EU policies would undermine the idea of codification and the harmonising purpose of the Charter. Hence, the Charter and the ECHR should have an impact on the future identification and interpretation of general principles of EU law, and general principles may not be used to lower their standards.

Despite these objections against transferring old reservations in the determination and application of EU general principles to the interpretation of Charter rights, some interpretive deliberations presented before the CJEU exactly transferred these traditional methodical approaches to the interpretation of Charter rights. Such may dilute the EU standards of fundamental rights protection.

In the already mentioned *Samba Diouf* case, AG Cruz Villalón stated that:

> [T]he right to effective judicial protection … has, though being recognised as part of EU law by virtue of Article 47 [Charter], acquired a separate identity and substance under that article which are not the mere sum of the provisions of Articles 6 and 13 of the ECHR. In other words, once it is recognised and guaranteed by the EU, that fundamental right goes on to acquire a content of its own, the definition of which is certainly shaped by the international instruments on which that right is based, including, first and foremost, the ECHR, but also by the constitutional traditions from which the right in question stems and, together with them, the conceptual universe within which the defining principles of a State governed by the rule of law operate.[84]

In his view, a Charter right's content has to be defined by referring to the ECHR, but 'once defined, its scope must be that described by the Charter',[85] although Article 52(3) of the Charter commands that the meaning and scope of a Charter right corresponds to the ECHR.

AG Bot in his opinion in the recent *Melloni* case stated that '[a]lthough it is true that the interpretation of the rights protected by the Charter must tend towards a high level of protection … it is nevertheless important to state that this *must be a level of protection which accords with EU law...*'[86] Here, he refers to a 'principle that has long guided the interpretation of fundamental rights within the Union, namely that the protection of fundamental rights … must be ensured within the framework of the structure and objectives of the Union'.[87] Hence, one has to take 'into account the requirements linked to the action of the Union and the specific nature of EU law', when determining the level of EU human rights protection.[88] As a consequence of his interpretive approach, since one of the EU objectives was the creation of an area of freedom, security and justice (see also the Charter preamble) the EU legislature set the level of fundamental rights protection so as not to compromise the effectiveness of the European Arrest Warrant.[89] In other words, the EU legislature determines the level of protection. Hence, the approach proposed by AG Bot means that the Court should not control whether the level of protection set by the EU legislature in the Framework Decision on the European Arrest Warrant is in conformity with the Charter and its right to a fair trial, but whether a domestic measure is in conformity with the level of protection set by the EU. As Article 3 of this Framework Decision provides, the Decision shall not

[84] Case C-69/10 *Samba Diouf*, not yet published, Opinion of AG Cruz Villalón, para 39.
[85] ibid, para 42.
[86] Case C-399/11 *Melloni*, not yet published, Opinion of AG Bot, para 106 (emphasis added).
[87] ibid, para 107, citing *Internationale Handelsgesellschaft* (n 79), para 4.
[88] ibid, para 108. See again also CJEU, Opinion 2/13, paras 170–72.
[89] ibid, para 119.

have the effect of modifying the obligation to respect fundamental rights. Here the reservation as to the appropriateness of human rights to the structure and objectives of the EU is used by AG Bot as a justification for attributing to the EU legislature in the realm of the area of freedom, security and justice a leeway to set the level of protection for the relevant fundamental rights which ensures the effectiveness of the cross-border execution of arrest warrants. This means that EU human rights are not a yardstick for EU legislature, but the level of protection of EU human rights is actually defined by the legislature with a view to the *effet utile* of an EU policy. Pointedly, EU regulations and directives have not to be in conformity with EU fundamental rights, but EU fundamental rights have to be interpreted so as to conform to EU secondary law. EU secondary law heavily impacts on the determination of the exigencies of the EU human rights regime, in contrast to the idea of human rights as constitutional rights.

Both opinions of the AGs reflect an autonomous approach in the interpretation of EU human rights which is not so much concerned with exigencies of the ECHR but much more with structural and institutional conditions of EU law and requirements of EU policies. Even though the CJEU's judgements did not explicitly take up these interpretive approaches presented by the AGs in their opinions, the Court in the *Melloni* judgement, by and large, confined its assessment of Article 4a of the Framework Decision's conformity with the right to a fair trial and the rights of defence (Articles 47 and 48(2) of the Charter) to a reflection of the aim and content of the Framework Decision.[90]

Besides, there are other cases in which the CJEU provides institutional restrictions to the application of Convention standards which amount to a reservation as to adapting EU human rights to the framework of the EU's structure and objectives. In the *NS* decision regarding the transfer of asylum seekers to Greece, the Court required 'systemic flaws' and 'systemic deficiencies' in the asylum procedure and reception conditions for asylum applicants in order to make a transfer incompatible with the prohibition against inhuman and degrading treatment in Article 4 of the Charter.[91] The Court stressed that not just any infringement of a fundamental right by the Member State responsible for reception of asylum applicants in the Common European Asylum system would affect the obligation of the other Member States to comply with the allocation of competences for asylum procedures and accordingly to send the asylum seekers back to the Member State where they first entered the EU. The rationale for such restrained effect of the protection of human rights in any individual case was the 'raison d'être of the European Union and the creation of an area of freedom, security and justice and, in particular, the Common European Asylum System'.[92] Hence,

[90] Case C-399/11 *Melloni*, not yet published, paras 50–52.

[91] Joined Cases C-411/10 and C-493/10 *NS and Others* [2011] ECR I-13905, paras 86, 89.

[92] ibid, para 82f. For further detail on the Common European Asylum System, see S Velluti, 'Who has the Right to have Rights? The Judgments of the CJEU and the ECtHR as Building Blocks for a European "ius commune" in Asylum Law', ch 8 in this volume.

for institutional reasons (the structure and certain objectives of the EU and its policy of establishing an area of freedom, security and justice), the value of individual human rights guarantees is diluted. In the perspective of the individual human being, the effectiveness of EU human rights protection against inhuman treatment depends on the circumstance whether the human rights violation also affects other individuals. In the name of the area of freedom, security and justice, a foreseeable single human rights violation does not meet the threshold erected by the Court against transfer to the offending Member State. This represents rather a cynical approach.

IV. CONCLUSION

The Lisbon Treaty augmented the importance of human rights in the EU legal order, but the new post-Lisbon human rights regime oscillates between tradition and change. Hence, the CJEU has the choice of either continuing with traditional ways of human rights adjudication or of making active use of Lisbon's innovations to redraft its position with regard to the application of human rights. The intensified importance of EU human rights after Lisbon justifies the expectation of a paradigm shift in the way the Court conceives EU human rights. In particular, EU human rights have to be taken seriously as effective restraints also for the exercise of EU public powers which require the Court to grant less deference to the EU legislator and to employ a higher standard of review, in particular with regard to proportionality assessments. A necessary re-conception of its role as a human rights court would redeem the Court from its obsession with the useful effect of EU policies which so easily come into conflict with respect for individual rights, all the more since the Court also has to consider the *effet utile* of EU human rights. The Charter, together with the clear foundation of the European integration process in the respect for human rights and rule of law as well as its commitment to the EU citizens,[93] stipulates changes in legal argumentation and reasoning, fostering constitutional human rights discourses in the Court.[94] The CJEU is required to function as a human rights court. If it does not do so by virtue of the changes brought by Lisbon, it will be forced to do so after the EU's accession to the ECHR. At least then, the pressure exerted by the ECtHR's control over the fundamental rights implementation by the CJEU will inevitably require the CJEU to intrude more deeply into EU legislative results and processes.[95]

[93] See second recital of Charter preamble according to which the EU 'places the individual at the heart of its activities'; see also Art 2 TEU on the values.

[94] Iglesias Sánchez (n 3) 1578f.

[95] Stone Sweet (n 7) 153.

The above analysis of post-Lisbon judgments of the CJEU shows that the CJEU has tentatively started reviewing EU acts much more robustly than before. The CJEU appears to have taken the first steps on the path to becoming a human rights court. The Court, at the same time, still might be tempted, based on the autonomy of EU law and the continuity side of the EU post-Lisbon human rights regime, to continue traditional interpretive approaches, which counter effective human rights protection with structural characteristics of the EU in order to limit the enjoyment of EU human rights. This attitude appears also to stand behind the Court's Opinion 2/13 on the accession to the ECHR (para 157ff). Besides, the Court should take all care to avoid the impression of a lax reception of the level of protection established by the Strasbourg Court.

Part II

6

European Judicial Dialogue and the Protection of Fundamental Rights in the New Digital Environment: An Attempt at Emancipation and Reconciliation

The Case of Freedom of Speech

ORESTE POLLICINO

I. MORE THAN AN INTRODUCTION: A METHODOLOGICAL DECLARATION OF INTENT

THE AIM OF the chapter is to answer the following questions. First, how is it possible to reconcile academic studies on Internet law with the broader debate on the multilevel protection of fundamental rights in Europe and the judicial interaction between autonomous yet interconnected legal orders, placing special emphasis on horizontal judicial conversation between the Luxembourg and Strasbourg Courts? Second, why is such an attempt expected to be valuable in attaining a better understanding of the process of European integration, with particular regard to scholarship focusing on European judicial dialogue?

The main assumption underlying the chapter is that the time seems to be ripe for an attempt to bridge the gap between the approach of Internet lawyers and that of constitutional and European studies scholars to judicial dialogue within a multilevel legal scenario. More precisely, it is clear from ongoing scholarly debate and in particular from the relevant case law of the European courts that the protection of fundamental rights on the Internet and the judicial enforcement of those rights goes far beyond what are considered to be the natural scope of Internet law, touching on crucial issues at the heart of EU law, human rights law and European constitutional law.

In light of these assumptions, the main purpose of the chapter is to emancipate the debate on legislation and case law relating to the Internet from the dominant position occupied by technicians, technocrats, IT experts and intellectual property lawyers. Such emancipation aims to instil a European and constitutional dimension into the topic under investigation and to reconcile the analysis of the relationship between new technologies and fundamental rights with the theoretical debate on the process of European integration, paying particular attention to the European judicial dialogue.

In order to answer the questions posed by this chapter, this chapter will explore these issues from the perspective of interaction between interconnected legal systems in the form of judicial dialogue.[1]

In order to justify the choice of the perspective of judicial dialogue as the most appropriate methodology for illustrating the dimension of Internet law rooted in fundamental rights, it is important to bring out the self-standing relevance of the two sides of the 'coin' (here the coin is the combined approach mentioned above of Internet law and studies on judicial dialogue). More precisely, it is necessary to elaborate further in this methodological introduction, on the one hand, why a judicial dialogue based approach would provide added and innovative value for Internet law studies (the first side of the coin). Secondly, it is also necessary to consider whether a consideration of European judicial interaction through the substantive parameter of Internet law (and the protection of fundamental rights within the digital environment) would be an advantage for research into judicial dialogue (the second side of the coin).

With regard to the first side of the coin, it should be clarified that the involvement of national and European courts in judicial dialogue is very rarely a spontaneous action and more often a reaction to a collision (or risk of a collision) between European legal systems as regards the identification of the most suitable level of effective protection for the fundamental rights at stake.

Nowadays more than ever it is the courts which, within their respective legal orders, occupy a privileged position that enables them to identify the risk of potential collisions that may encroach upon the effective protection of fundamental rights between interconnected legal systems. This consequently enables them to forge closer ties between different yet interacting systems. In fact, in times of judicial globalisation, the crucial position of the courts (and of judicial dialogue) is amplified yet further with regard to the protection of fundamental rights in the digital age. This is due to two peculiarities of the Internet.

The first peculiarity is substantive in nature and concerns the awareness that legal reforms tend to lag behind technological advances. The burden of making up for this necessary legislative inertia falls heavily on the shoulders of the courts. However, from our perspective, the novelty of the factual and legal context created by the Internet is even more interesting. Indeed, this is the main reason, along with the inertia of the legislature on national and supranational levels, why the courts increasingly seek assistance and inspiration (and ultimately dialogue) in

[1] This methodology has been developed in previous works: O Pollicino and G Martinico, *The Interaction between Europe's Legal Systems: Judicial Dialogue and the Creation of Supranational Laws* (Cheltenham, Edward Elgar Publishing, 2012) 350.

relation to the protection of fundamental rights on the Internet with courts of different yet interconnected legal orders even more than they do in the analogical world.

The second reason underlying the choice to focus on interaction between the courts is procedural in nature and is related to the jurisdictional issues brought about by the rise of the web. As will be noted in the first part of the chapter, these have had crucial implications for the protection of fundamental rights and led to a further amplification of the 'judicial dimension' in the field.

Against this background, it should be added that the Internet law has been the object of very specific technical studies, especially by US scholars who have long questioned first whether the web can be subject to legal regulation, and second, which entity has the power to impose such regulation.

The problem is that, particularly in Europe, this debate has been almost monopolised by Internet and IT lawyers who have explored the field from a very specific perspective, focusing mainly on the relationship between law and technology. In other words, the peculiarities of the topic have made it very fascinating for a specialist group of Internet lawyers, but much less attractive for scholars interested in the multilevel protection of fundamental rights from a European constitutional perspective. This is a natural consequence of the fact that the Internet represents an innovation, first and foremost from a technical point of view.

As regards the other side of the coin, there is at least one good reason why looking at European judicial interaction through the substantial parameter of Internet law (and protection of fundamental rights in the digital environment) it is considered to be an advantage for the research area related to judicial dialogue.

It is true that, especially in recent decades, relationships between courts have become one of the areas on which many scholars have focused their studies, particularly in the field of constitutional and European law. This approach has resulted in a variety of debates concerning the relationships that have developed between, in particular, the European courts (Court of Justice of European Union (CJEU) and the European Court of Human Rights (ECtHR)) and the national courts.

However, attention has mainly been paid to the reasons, effects and mode of operation of such interaction, whilst only a few cases have considered its substantive content. Court rulings have mainly been considered not because of the added value brought in terms of enhanced protection for certain rights, but primarily due to their importance in the relationships with other courts and, more generally, from the perspective of judicial interaction between interconnected legal orders.

The choice to focus on a substantive issue, such as the protection of freedom of speech on the Internet will hopefully help to instil scholarship on judicial dialogue with some concreteness, substance and unequivocal direction. The lack of these, along with the often overly vague and general theorisation of its specific features, has been identified—not wrongly—as the Achilles' heel of the studies on judicial dialogue.

As far as the structure of this chapter is concerned, the first part will emphasise how the provision of the First Amendment (freedom of speech) has been interpreted in the US legal experience, in both the analogue and digital realms.[2] The core part of the chapter will question how, in comparison also to the US experience, changes in technology affect the judicial protection of free speech afforded by the two European courts.

The closing section will provide brief remarks on the chapter's conclusion in the light of the more theoretical remarks on the relationship between the Internet and physical borders.

Although it may be objected that the study should nevertheless be limited to the European context, as it is mainly focused on the notion of European judicial dialogue, there at least two reasons why a comparative approach extending beyond Europe is advisable.

First of all, the rise of the Internet has, as mentioned above, established a link between these different views, in the sense that it is nowadays easier to cross national borders. It is thus crucial to consider the various potential conceptions of freedom of expression on the Internet. The conception enshrined in the First Amendment of the US Constitution represents a crucial parameter for comparison. In this regard, the relevant judicial case law of the US Supreme Court (which was the court to deal with the relationship between the protection of rights and the digital revolution) provides an unavoidable source of inspiration for the European courts.

The second reason why a comparative perspective should be adopted is that the advent of the Internet has exacerbated and over-amplified certain problems relating to jurisdiction that have been familiar to scholars studying freedom of speech also in the past, albeit to a lesser extent.

An example of how the European and US legal regimes interact in the context of the Internet can be seen in *Yahoo! v Licra*. Here, two French anti-racist organisations applied to the Court of Paris, which issued an order requiring Yahoo! to take down a website advertising the sale of Nazi memorabilia, which was hosted by its platform in France, where the Criminal Code prohibited the marketing of such products. The French court ruled in favour of the petitioners since the offending material was accessed (amongst other locations) in France and, accordingly, the harm was felt there.[3] Yahoo! subsequently sought a declaratory judgment from the Northern District of California[4] ruling that the French court lacked jurisdiction. Yahoo!'s argument was that the court order violated the First Amendment and was hence enforceable.

The US court found that the order issued by the French court breached the First Amendment of the US Constitution. However, the Ninth Circuit of Appeals[5]

[2] See for a recent more detailed analysis on this point, O Pollicino and M Bassini, 'Freedom of Expression and Defamation in Internet' in A Savjn and J Trzaskowski (eds), *Research Handbook on EU Internet Law* (Cheltenham, Edward Elgar Publishing, 2014) 508.

[3] *UEJF et LICRA v Yahoo! Inc and Yahoo! France*, Tribunal de Grande Instance de Paris, 22 May 2000.

[4] *Yahoo! Inc v La Ligue Contre le Racisme et L'Antisemitisme*, 169 F Supp 2d 1182 (ND Cal 2001).

[5] 433 F.3d 1199, *Yahoo! Inc, a Delaware Corp v La Ligue Contre Le Racisme et L'antisemitisme, a French Association; L'union Des Etudiants Juifs De France, a French Association* (9th Cir, 2006).

reversed the decision, finding that France had been within its rights as a sovereign nation to enact hate speech laws against the distribution of Nazi propaganda. Accordingly, the petitioners had been within their rights to bring a suit in France against Yahoo! due to the violation of French hate speech law.

The case revealed a crucial aspect, which is all too often overlooked within scholarly debate on the constitutional implications of Internet law. The procedural issue on the enforcement of jurisdiction conceals the substantive and value-based issue related to a potential clash between competing constitutional visions. More specifically, the above case involved a potential collision between, on the one hand, the 'holy' nature of freedom of expression protected in the First Amendment of the US Constitution and, on the other hand, the much more limited nature of the same freedom as embedded in the French Constitution and, more generally, in European constitutionalism.

II. FREEDOM OF SPEECH IN THE US AND ITS PROTECTION OFFLINE AND ONLINE: A CRITICAL ANALYSIS

The First Amendment of the US Constitution provides very extensive protection for freedom of speech:

> Congress shall make no law respecting an establishment of religion, or prohibiting the free exercise thereof; or abridging the freedom of speech, or of the press; or the right of the people peaceably to assemble, and to petition the Government for a redress of grievances.

This provision prohibits Congress from adopting any law which may amount to a restriction of freedom of speech. The Supreme Court has clarified that the ban also extends to the federal states and, therefore to their respective governments.

It is worth noting that there is no mention in the text of the First Amendment of any possible limitations based on the need to protect other fundamental rights that may have to be weighed against freedom of expression. The First Amendment seems to protect free speech as an absolute that cannot tolerate any restrictions or interference.[6]

A picture describing the US judicial approach to free speech can be obtained by applying these principles to some specific areas of law such as defamation, hate speech and sexually explicit speech.[7] Only once these principles have been

[6] The reasons why such extensive protection was granted to free speech in 1791 relate, at first glance, to the historical background of the settlement of the US. The Bill of Rights was adopted because some of the states had refused to sign the US Constitution without appropriate guarantees of civil liberties. The First Amendment, in particular, was supposed to meet the anti-Federalist states' expectation of their freedom to express (primarily political) opinions. At the time, the right in question was meant to be a freedom from any undue interference from public bodies in the enjoyment of free speech. It was thus a rule intended to produce 'vertical effects'.

[7] See in this respect M Ronsenfeld and A Sajo, 'Spreading Liberal Constitutionalism: An Inquiry into the Fate of Free Speech in New Democracies' in S Choudhry (ed), *The Migration of Constitutional Ideas* (Cambridge, Cambridge University Press, 2006) 146.

observed 'in action' it will be possible to understand how usage of the Internet has affected traditional categories and legal doctrine.

As far as defamation law is concerned, the decision taken in *New York Times v Sullivan*[8] ranks among the leading cases in this area. The case concerned the question as to whether the use of false or defamatory statements by the press against public figures was protected by freedom of expression. The Supreme Court pointed out that the statements made with actual malice or reckless disregard fell beyond of protection of freedom of speech (or more precisely, of the freedom of the press) and may therefore trigger liability for the author of such statements. Otherwise, where these criteria are not met, no limit can be imposed on public debate. This standard is based on the assumption that no advancement in public opinion can be achieved through the dissemination of false statements.

The judgment rendered in *Calder v Jones*[9] also has to be mentioned. In this case, the US Supreme Court applied the 'minimum contact' test[10] in finding that the Californian court (where the plaintiff resided) could hear a defamation complaint against a national magazine edited in Florida. The court of the state where the plaintiff resided was found to have personal jurisdiction over the defendants, who had 'certain minimum contacts' with the forum state.

The minimum contact test has played a significant role also in Internet cases, where jurisdictional problems have proved to be crucial.

The area of law that more than any other brings to light the broad scope of protection afforded to freedom of expression by the US courts is hate speech.[11] It would be impossible to refer here to the entire case law developed in relation to this issue. However, the common denominator of three leading cases concerning racial and religious hatred[12] is that only those expressions that are likely to result in an incitement to violence fall beyond the constitutional protection granted under the First Amendment. The adoption of this standard has led US courts to tolerate conduct that—as will be explored below—would in all likelihood be prohibited under the equivalent European provisions. In doing so, the Supreme Court has fixed a very high threshold for punishing hate speech: an incitement to hatred does not suffice, and only an incitement to violence justifies any restriction of freedom of expression.

The approach of US courts is consistent with the purpose of granting extensive protection to freedom of speech also in relation to sexually explicit and violent content. In *Miller v California*,[13] the Supreme Court established a three-prong test

[8] 376 US 254 (1964).

[9] 465 US 783 (1984).

[10] The 'minimum contact' doctrine was developed by the Supreme Court for the first time in *International Shoe Co v Washington*, 326 US 310. The purpose of this US doctrine is to determine the conditions under which a state court will not have personal jurisdiction over a defendant established in another state.

[11] For a more detailed analysis of hate speech and its relationship with freedom of expression, see the chapter by A Gillespie, 'Hate and Harm: The Law on Hate Speech' in Trzaskowski and Savin (eds), *Research Handbook on EU Internet Law* (Cheltenham, Edward Elgar Publishing, 2014).

[12] See *Brandeburg v Ohio*, 343 US 250 (1969); *RAV v City of St Paul*, 505 US 377 (1992); and *Virginia v Black*, 538 US 343 (2003).

[13] 413 US 15 (1973). See also *Roth v United States*, 354 US 476 (1957); *Ginsberg v New York*, 390 US 629 (1968).

for establishing whether content is to be defined as obscene: a work goes beyond the scope of protection of free speech and can therefore be regulated where that work, taken as a whole, appeals to the prurient interest in sex; portrays, in a patently offensive way, sexual conduct specifically defined by the applicable state law; and, taken as a whole, does not have serious literary, artistic, political, or scientific value. However, another landmark decision, *New York v Ferber*, excluded child pornography from free speech protection.[14]

A recent judgment concerned a California statute that had made it a criminal offence to sell to anyone under the age of 18 video games portraying the killing, maiming, dismembering or sexually assault of an image of a human being. The Supreme Court in *Brown v EMA*[15] struck down the law, finding that video games qualify for First Amendment protection in the same way as films, music and the other forms of literary or artistic expression. In this decision, the Supreme Court focused on one crucial aspect: the degree of protection for freedom of speech does not vary depending upon the medium, and legislation cannot create categories of unprotected speech, even for the purpose of child protection.

This brief exploration of the landmark categories related to the protection of freedom of speech as laid down in the case law of the US Supreme Court will enable the impact of the Internet on the level of protection for the fundamental right at stake to be considered. This will be done first with reference to the US, where the Internet first took root, and secondly from the European perspective—in order to study the implications raised by the new technologies, including matters of jurisdiction.

In order to answer the question as to whether the advent of the Internet has further extended the scope of freedom of expression in the US legal system as protected in the 'world of atoms', it is necessary to examine several cases.

The most important decision of the US Supreme Court, which is nowadays regarded as a landmark ruling for Internet freedom of expression, is *Reno v ACLU*.[16] The Supreme Court struck down as unconstitutional the provisions of the Communication Decency Act 1996 (CDA 1996), which outlawed the online distribution of obscene or indecent materials to any person under 18. In the Supreme Court's view, the CDA 1996 imposed excessively vague restrictions and lacked the precision required in order to limit free speech only to the extent necessary to protect children, in particular by failing to define 'indecent' and 'patently offensive' content properly.

It is worth noting that the decision expressly considered the difference between the nature of the Internet and that of other media such as radio and television:

> [R]adio and television, unlike the Internet, have, "as a matter of history [...] received the most limited First Amendment protection, [...] in large part because warnings could not adequately protect the listener from unexpected program content. [...] [On the Internet],

[14] 458 US 747 (1982).
[15] *Brown v Entertainment Merchants Association and Others*, 564 US 1 (2011).
[16] 521 US 844 (1997).

> the risk of encountering indecent material by accident is remote because a series of affirmative steps is required to access specific material.[17]

Similar nuances characterised another attempt by the US Government to regulate the protection of children online. After the US Supreme Court had struck down the most relevant part of the Communication Decency Act, the Child Online Protection Act (COPA), which pursued analogous purposes, came into force in 1998. This act was also reviewed by the Supreme Court, which held that it breached the First Amendment. Specifically, the COPA referred to 'material harmful to minors' as any material which was obscene or which, based on community standards, an average person would consider to appeal to the prurient interest. According to the Supreme Court,[18] this definition also failed to meet the standards required to circumscribe free speech limitations.

Another decision regarding the protection of freedom of speech on the Internet was taken in *Ashcroft v Free Speech Coalition.*[19] The case, which concerned the Child Pornography Prevention Act 1996 (CPPA 1996), was the last of the attempts to protect children from dissemination of explicit content, held that the restrictions on freedom of expression introduced by this Act were disproportionate and overbroad. Most notably, the decision focused on the provisions that prohibited the dissemination of images that appeared to represent children engaged in sexual activity as well as any form of speech conveying the impression that the images reproduced children involved in sexual conduct.

Free-speech activists complained that this legislation resulted in chilling effects. The Supreme Court held that Congress does of course have the power to enact legislation with the aim of preventing child pornography and the circulation of obscene content. However, since the provisions laid down by the CPPA 1996 went beyond this limit on admissibility, the restriction on freedom of speech was excessive and breached the First Amendment.

All of the above suggests that the advent of the Internet has not weakened the protection afforded to freedom of expression in the US courts, despite the possible threats to other interests caused by its use. On the contrary, it seems that the effectiveness of freedom of speech has been enhanced, in particular through a very strict scrutiny of the conditions that may constitute legal grounds for a restriction of this fundamental right.

Within the non-digital environment the courts had previously been suspicious of any potential restriction of free speech, whilst admitting that, subject to certain conditions, other interests could prevail. However, after the advent of the Internet another path seems to have been followed. As the three decisions on the publication of obscene content online demonstrate, even where there is another primary constitutional interest such as child protection, limitations of freedom of speech must be strictly proportionate with the aim pursued. In fact, the Supreme

[17] ibid, 868.

[18] *Ashcroft v American Civil Liberties Union*, 535 US 564 (2002).

[19] 535 US 234 (2002).

Court did not at any time rule that the protection of children from the dissemination of obscene content was not a protected legal interest; it simply required that restrictions based on this interest must not excessively undermine freedom of expression.

In conclusion, the picture portrayed of the US scenario establishes that the advent of the Internet has resulted in a further enhancement of the already huge protection enjoyed by freedom of speech in the non-digital environment. Thus, the First Amendment has not only retained but even increased its value within the new digital context. As the following sections will attempt to demonstrate, the opposite conclusions appear to apply in Europe.

III. FREEDOM OF SPEECH IN THE WORLDS OF 'ATOMS': THE EUROPEAN PERSPECTIVE

As the previous section has established, the First Amendment to the US Constitution speaks about freedom of expression in very absolute terms.[20] US court decisions have, in turn, confirmed this fairly broad protection, even where other fundamental rights are at stake. This has led authors like Ronsenfeld and Sajo, when referring to Bollinger,[21] to present free speech as 'the paramount right within the American constellation of constitutional rights'.[22]

Against this backdrop, the scenario is completely different in the European context. There are at least two reasons why this is so. The first concerns the degree of protection. The scope of constitutional protection for freedom of expression is more limited in Europe, where there is no provision carving out a sphere of protection as broad as that provided by the First Amendment. Better put, European constitutionalism pursues a more balanced approach to the arguments in favour of freedom of expression and those in favour of its competing rights.

The second reason why the European scenario is so different is due to the absence of a unique constitutional framework. While in the US the First Amendment is the sole sacred reference, the European model cannot be explained or understood without accounting for the combination between the EU, the European Convention on Human Rights (ECHR) and the decisions of the respective courts.

The European approach to freedom of expression, the exercise of which must be balanced with the protection of other fundamental rights, is clearly apparent from the relevant parameters which the Courts (both the CJEU and the ECtHR) have been called upon to enforce.

[20] For a more in-depth comparative study, see F Schaurer, 'Freedom of Expression Adjudication in Europe and America: A Case Study in Comparative Constitutional Architecture' in G Nolte (ed), *European and US Constitutionalism* (Cambridge, Cambridge University Press, 2005) 49–69.

[21] L Bollinger, *The Tolerant Society: Freedom of Speech and Extremist Speech in America* (Oxford, Oxford University Press, 1988) 7.

[22] Ronsefeld and Sajo, *Spreading Liberal Constitutionalism* (n 7) 152.

In particular, since the EU, at least at the outset, was intended as an economic community only, the constitutional background was provided by the system of the ECHR and the ECtHR. It is only in more recent times that the EU has acquired a new supranational dimension as a community that is no longer economic only, even though the road to constitutionalisation is still long.

Before the Treaty of Lisbon, there was no express acknowledgment of freedom of speech as a fundamental right. It was through the incorporation of the Charter of Fundamental Rights of the EU (the Charter) into treaty law that freedom of expression (under Article 11), amongst others, came to be regarded as a fundamental right of the EU.

Article 10 ECHR and Article 11 of the Charter are therefore the relevant parameters underlying protection for freedom of expression in Europe.

The courts of respectively the EU and ECHR systems have interpreted these parameters and handed down judgments that have clarified the scope of the protection afforded to free speech in Europe. Essentially, the task of the ECtHR has been primarily to scrutinise the relevant legislation of the states parties that is alleged to breach Article 10 of the Convention.

It is worth mentioning a very leading case in the ECtHR case law regarding freedom of expression: in *Handyside*[23] the Court rejected a complaint by an editor who had been convicted for publishing a school textbook with sexually explicit content. The Court found that the restrictions imposed on freedom of expression, including the seizure of the available copies of the book, met the criteria set forth under Article 10(2) of the Convention. However, it is important to note the Court's remarks obiter dictum in stressing that:

> Freedom of expression constitutes one of the essential foundations of such a society, one of the basic conditions for its progress and for the development of every man. Subject to paragraph 2 of Article 10 (art. 10-2), it is applicable not only to 'information' or 'ideas' that are favourably received or regarded as inoffensive or as a matter of indifference, but also to those that offend, shock or disturb the State or any sector of the population. Such are the demands of that pluralism, tolerance and broadmindedness without which there is no 'democratic society'.

We now turn to the CJEU.

As was noted at the start of this section, it has only been with the incorporation of the Charter into treaty law that freedom of expression and other fundamental rights have been given constitutional standing in the system of EU law. This fact reflects the approach of the CJEU, which has long been lacking a legal basis upon which to enforce the right to freedom of speech. In fact, the scope of the Luxembourg Court's scrutiny, conducted especially in response to preliminary proceedings, was generally limited to acts adopted in areas under EU competence in the economic sphere (including, amongst others, the E-Commerce Directive).

However in some cases the CJEU has, albeit indirectly, acknowledged freedom of expression as a fundamental right. For instance, this happened in the

[23] *Handyside v the United Kingdom* App no 5493/72 (ECtHR, 7 December 1976).

Schmidberger case.[24] The Court was asked to determine whether the domestic legislation at issue was compatible with the free movement of goods to the extent it permitted the temporary closure of a motorway for a demonstration intended to draw the public's attention to environmental issues. The judgment expressly referred to Article 10 of the Convention:

> [U]nlike other fundamental rights enshrined in that Convention, such as the right to life or the prohibition of torture and inhuman or degrading treatment or punishment, which admit of no restriction, neither the freedom of expression nor the freedom of assembly guaranteed by the ECHR appears to be absolute but must be viewed in relation to its social purpose. Consequently, the exercise of those rights may be restricted, provided that the restrictions in fact correspond to objectives of general interest and do not, taking account of the aim of the restrictions, constitute disproportionate and unacceptable interference, impairing the very substance of the rights guaranteed.[25]

However, taking into account the circumstances of the case, the Court said that various interests had to be weighed up and noted that an outright ban on the demonstration would have constituted 'unacceptable interference with the fundamental rights of the demonstrators to gather and express peacefully their opinion in public'.[26]

It is now time to see how European courts have enforced these general principles while handling cases emerged after the coming of the new technological scenario.

IV. THE IMPACT OF THE INTERNET ON THE PROTECTION OF FREE SPEECH IN EUROPE

A. The European Convention on Human Rights

In the light of the approach developed by the European courts in the 'world of atoms', it is now possible to analyse how the advent of the Internet has affected judicial protection of freedom of speech, and whether the new technological scenario has resulted in more or less protection for free speech. It was noted in the previous section that US courts have maintained a very broad level of protection, even though freedom of communication is now more likely to enter into conflict with other rights or interests. We shall now consider the impact which the Internet has had on the other side of the Ocean.

While the EU has enacted various legislative instruments concerning the use of the Internet in relation to the movement of goods and services, including the E-Commerce Directive and the Audiovisual Media Services Directive, and has recently incorporated freedom of expression into its very constitutional fabric in

[24] Case C-112/00 *Eugen Schmidberger, Internationale Transporte und Planzüge v Republik Österreich* [2003] ECR I-5659.

[25] Case C-112/00 *Schmidberger* (ibid) 80.

[26] Case C-112/00 *Schmidberger* (ibid) 89.

Article 11 of the Charter, the relevant parameter for the Strasbourg Court has thus far been provided by Article 10 of the Convention.

At the outset, it must be noted that the Strasbourg Court's flexible approach to possible limitations on freedom of expression is not of course anything new. The cases handled by the ECtHR prior to the development of new technologies, as said above, prove that Strasbourg's judges were already well inclined to enforce Article 10(2) of the Convention. However, if we analyse the most recent decisions taken by the Court, it appears that, contrary to the trend in the US Supreme Court, the advent of the Internet has further extended the ability to limit freedom of expression, provided that the conditions set forth under Article 10(2) have been complied with by the national legislation.

The assumption that freedom of speech works as a watchdog for democracy appears to have been revisited or at least relativised, as the ECtHR seems to be focusing more on cases in which the Internet is likely to pose new risks to the protection of fundamental rights, in which the restrictions were then found to be justified, than to those in which the Internet appeared as a new opportunity for the exercise of rights, in which free speech was thus to be upheld.

Even though the Court repeatedly held that the safe harbour entrusted to Article 10(2) must be construed strictly, the advent of the Internet has resulted in greater consideration being paid to restrictions on free speech. Specifically, according to the ECtHR, the specific medium of the Internet amplified threats to fundamental rights compared to the past. This point emerged, for the first time, in *Editorial Board of PravoyeDelo and Shtekel v Ukraine*,[27] concerning the particular segment of freedom of expression corresponding to freedom of press:

> The risk of harm posed by content and communications on the Internet to the exercise and enjoyment of human rights and freedoms, particularly the right to respect for private life, is certainly higher than that posed by the press. Therefore, the policies governing reproduction of material from the printed media and the Internet may differ. The latter undeniably have to be adjusted according to technology's specific features in order to secure the protection and promotion of the rights and freedoms concerned.

The assumption behind the Court's reasoning is that the Internet is likely to raise new problems for the protection of fundamental rights and that the measures applied to traditional media will not work effectively in the new digital environment. This means that a new balance must be struck between freedom of expression and other human rights. In a nutshell, since the Internet is raising unprecedented legal issues, restrictions on freedom of expression should be more broadly accepted.

This remark could per se be enough to describe how different the approach of the ECtHR is from that of the US Supreme Court, which expressed the completely opposite view in *Reno v ACLU*:[28]

> The record demonstrates that the growth of the Internet has been and continues to be phenomenal. As a matter of constitutional tradition, in the absence of evidence to the

[27] App no 33014/05 (ECtHR, 5 May 2011).
[28] 521 US 844, 885.

> contrary, we presume that governmental regulation of the content of speech is more likely to interfere with the free exchange of ideas than to encourage it. The interest in encouraging freedom of expression in a democratic society outweighs any theoretical but unproven benefit of censorship.

Also in *KU v Finland*,[29] the Court stressed the non-absolute nature of the protection of certain fundamental rights on the Internet. The case concerned the dissemination of personal data relating to a child by an anonymous individual who had posted an online advertisement in which he claimed to be looking for a sexual relationship. When the applicant filed a complaint with the local court, there were no legal grounds under domestic law to force an Internet service provider (ISP) to disclose personal data in cases involving criminal conduct such as that at issue. In addition, the domestic legislation failed to strike a balance between the right to data protection and other interests. Although the complaint was not based on Article 10, the ECtHR made significant remarks concerning the exercise of free speech on the Internet:

> Although freedom of expression and confidentiality of communications are primary considerations and users of telecommunications and Internet services must have a guarantee that their own privacy and freedom of expression will be respected, such guarantee cannot be absolute and must yield on occasion to other legitimate imperatives, such as the prevention of disorder or crime or the protection of the rights and freedoms of others [...] [I]t is nonetheless the task of the legislator to provide the framework for reconciling the various claims which compete for protection in this context.

It is only when the limitations imposed on freedom of expression are excessive compared to the aim pursued that the Court has adopted a stricter approach. It did so for instance in *Ahmet Yildirim v Turkey*,[30] where the Court concluded that Turkey had violated Article 10 of the Convention by imposing a disproportionate restriction on Internet access. In criminal proceedings against the owner of a website on which expressions insulting Ataturk's memory had been posted, an administrative authority had ordered that all Google sites be blocked in order to prevent access to the site in question, without ascertaining whether a less far-reaching measure could have been taken. The applicant, who owned a website where his academic works were published and which was affected by the blocking order, alleged a violation of his right to freedom of expression. The Court noted that the blocking of a website is one of the legitimate restrictions that contracting states may adopt in accordance with Article 10(2) of the Convention, but only upon the condition that such a restriction meets the requirement referenced in that provisions. In that case, there was neither a strict legal framework defining the scope of the ban or any provision for judicial review.

[29] App no 2872/02 (ECtHR, 2 December 2008).
[30] App no 3111/10 (ECtHR, 18 December 2012).

The approach of the ECtHR has proved to be very cautious. On the one hand, it has concluded that Article 10 will be violated if the restrictions on freedom of expression do not comply with the conditions set forth under Article 10(2). On the other hand, however, the Court has conceded that free speech is not an absolute, and does not enjoy greater protection compared to other fundamental rights: in fact, given the risks brought by the Internet, it is more likely that freedom of expression may be limited than in the non-digital context.

The same thinking lay behind the decision in the *Pirate Bay*[31] case, in which the ECtHR by contrast rejected an individual application based on Article 10. The applicants were the owners of a famous online platform where users were provided with links enabling the illegal downloading of copyrighted materials through peer-to-peer systems. They had been convicted under the Swedish law outlawing copyright infringements, but complained that their right to freedom of expression had been violated. The Court ruled the complaint inadmissible, as the restriction imposed on free speech complied with the conditions set forth under Article 10(2) and, in particular, was proportional to the legitimate aim pursued.[32]

Accordingly, the view taken by the Court of Strasbourg is that the advent of new technologies, and of the Internet in particular, has not generally expanded the scope of freedom of expression. On the contrary, it has created more opportunities for this right to conflict with other interests protected under constitutions.

This assertion can be confirmed, first if we consider how the ECtHR reacted to the use of the Internet with respect to the freedom of press, which is regarded as an essential pillar of freedom of speech and democracy. In the *Stoll* case,[33] the Court's reasoning was based on the assumption that new technologies have made the duties of journalists more demanding:

> [T]he safeguard afforded by Article 10 to journalists in relation to reporting on issues of general interest is subject to the proviso that they are acting in good faith and on an accurate factual basis and provide 'reliable and precise' information in accordance with the ethics of journalism [...] These considerations play a particularly important role nowadays, given the influence wielded by the media in contemporary society: not only do they inform, they can also suggest by the way in which they present the information how it is to be assessed. In a world in which the individual is confronted with vast quantities of information circulated via traditional and electronic media and involving an ever-growing number of players, monitoring compliance with journalistic ethics takes on added importance.[34]

Furthermore, these observations are confirmed even if it is assumed that similar conduct also occurred in the non-digital realm. Recalling the case of *Yildirim v Turkey*, such a broad limitation of freedom of expression as that adopted by the

[31] *Fredrik Neij and Peter SundeKolmisoppi (The Pirate Bay) v Sweden* App no 40397/12 (ECtHR, 19 February 2013).

[32] See also *Ashby Donald and Others v France* App no 36769/08 (ECtHR, 10 January 2013).

[33] *Stoll v Switzerland* App no 69698/01 (ECtHR, 10 December 2007).

[34] *Stoll v Switzerland* (ibid) pp 103–04.

Turkish authorities would not presumably have been necessary. If one single publication is found to be defamatory and there are legal grounds to prevent its circulation, the measures which must be adopted by the relevant authorities in the non-digital world must only relate to that publication, and not others. In other words, there will be no reason to block additional online content, which is equivalent to offline seizure, instead of blocking only the content regarded as an unlawful exercise of freedom of expression.

Naturally, the issue of proportionality (which is the key factor here) is related to the nature of the technology. Moreover, it is one of the leading factors, which means that it is critical for the protection of freedom of expression on the Internet.

The application of the proportionality principle was also crucial in the recent case of *Delfi v Estonia*,[35] in which the ECtHR was asked to consider whether the fining of an Internet news portal for defamatory comments posted by users, which the website failed to remove promptly, amounted to a restriction of freedom of expression. The Strasbourg Court found that Article 10 of the Convention does not afford protection to freedom of expression in absolute terms. Rather, Article 10 allows contracting states to interfere with the exercise of this right, provided that the said restrictions meet the conditions under paragraph 2, ie that they are prescribed by law, have a legitimate aim and are necessary in a democratic society. It is important to highlight that, whilst the Court held that the legislation at stake imposed a significant restriction, it nevertheless found that it did not violate Article 10. Since, in the Court's view, the protection of individual reputations ranks among the objectives that may justify a limitation on freedom of expression, it held that there had been no infringement of Article 10 because the interference was proportionate.

One final point needs to be stressed in conclusion. The relative (rather than absolute) consideration paid to the fundamental rights enshrined in the ECHR was not conjured up by the ECtHR, spurred on by the impact of new technologies. It has been the task of the ECtHR to balance fundamental rights since the outset. However, the new environment in which fundamental rights can be exercised has led the Court to stress more frequently its relative status, and also to justify restrictions that it would most likely not have tolerated in the 'world of atoms'.

B. The Court of Justice of the European Union

How would the CJEU have ruled in the *Delfi* case? This question is crucial in introducing the EU scenario against the background which, as we have seen, characterises the ECHR legal context.

As noted in the previous section, the case involved a claim by the owner of an Internet news portal, which had been sentenced in relation to defamatory

[35] App no 64569/09 (ECtHR, 10 October 2013). It should be pointed out that the Chamber's decision in *Delfi* was appealed to the Grand Chamber, whose decision is expected before the end of 2014.

statements posted by users as comments to an article. The ECtHR held that there had been no violation of Article 10. From a perspective other than scrutiny based on Article 10, the CJEU would have taken into account the E-Commerce Directive (Directive 2000/31/EC) when assessing whether Estonian legislation was compatible with the obligations imposed on and the liability exemptions accorded to ISPs. Moreover, it would now in all likelihood also consider Article 11 of the Nice Charter.

This brief comparison provides an opportunity for stressing the differences between the ECHR and EU systems, as well as the tasks of the respective courts.

The Strasbourg Court handles complaints based, inter alia, on Article 10, with which the relevant provisions of national constitutions on freedom of expression should comply. Thus, the ECtHR acts as a pan European constitutional court of fundamental rights. However, the parameter to be enforced was established in 1950, when the Convention came into force. This means that, when tackling cases involving new technologies, the Court has been required to conduct its review on the basis of a very long-standing parameter, which was designed to apply to a very different world. At the same time however, Article 10 (as well as the other provisions of the Convention) does lend itself to very flexible interpretation.

It is no accident that the legislation which the CJEU must enforce, including in particular the E-Commerce Directive, appears in some senses to be more obsolete than Article 10. In fact, the CJEU normally issues its decisions within proceedings relating to preliminary references. Since it is for courts of Member States to make a reference for preliminary ruling, the Court must remain within the limits of the question proposed and cannot conduct a broader scrutiny.

That said, the parameters on which the CJEU issues preliminary rulings are less flexible than Article 10 of the ECHR. Nonetheless, they are more specific. As regards protection of free speech, as noted above, with the exception of a few provisions contained in the Audiovisual Media Services Directive, there is no *hard law* at the EU level. Rather, it is noted that the E-Commerce Directive regulates the responsibility of ISPs, and is the sole legal framework that deals specifically with the Internet. Yet, as noted above, it is difficult to enforce these provisions since they have proved, albeit quite recently, to be obsolete compared to Article 10 of the Convention. The problem concerns in particular the liability exemptions set forth under the E-Commerce Directive, which were adopted in relation to technology that was very different from today. The rise of for instance user-generated content platforms or peer-to-peer systems has brought up unprecedented issues, which the E-Commerce Directive does not seem to be able to resolve satisfactorily.[36]

To return to our question, at the time of the *Delfi* case, it would most likely have been resolved on the basis of the liability exemptions. Rather than examining whether convicting the news portal for offensive comments violated freedom

[36] See, in this respect, Joint Cases C-236/08, C-237/08 and C-238/08 *Google France SARL and Google Inc v Louis Vuitton Malletier SA, Google France SARL v Viaticum SA and Luteciel SARL, and Google France SARL v Centre national de recherche en relations humaines (CNRRH) SARL and Others* [2010] ECR I-02417. See also Case C-324/09 *L'Oréal SA and Others v eBay International AG and Others* [2011] ECR I-06011.

of expression, the CJEU would have focused, it may be supposed, on the absence of any control by the website's owner over the (unlawful) activity of users. In all likelihood, no consideration would have been paid to freedom of speech, since the Court's task is not to ascertain whether a violation has occurred, but rather whether the provider can be held responsible for the conduct of users who have posted defamatory comments.

This does not however mean that freedom of expression has not been considered in certain judgments of the CJEU. Even without a specific policy laying down substantive regulations, we can in fact assess how freedom of expression has been weighed against other fundamental rights in certain recent decisions involving the Internet. First, the case law of the Luxembourg Court shows that freedom of expression has been considered in judgments concerning copyright protection. This is also a result of the incorporation of the Charter into EU treaty law, which expressly protects intellectual property as fundamental right under Article 17(2). The fact that intellectual property ranks among the rights protected under the Charter means that copyright is a competing interest with freedom of expression and is thus likely to be weighed against it.

This factor has an important consequence: whereas in the past freedom of expression, as an individual fundamental right, by no means competed with copyright, the latter having been regarded as a property right and subsequently as an economic interest, the scenario is completely different now. With the advent of the Internet, this factor has escalated the conflict between copyright protection and freedom of expression. Thus, both the CJEU and the ECtHR have been faced with an increase in cases where these rights are in conflict.[37]

Two almost identical cases (*Scarlet v Sabam* and *Sabam v Netlog*,[38] or the *Sabam saga*) addressed the issue as to whether the courts were entitled, as a matter of EU law, to subject ISPs to an obligation to adopt a filtering system aimed at detecting potential copyright infringements on the assumption that the heavy use of an Internet connection was indicative of the illegal downloading of content.[39]

Both cases questioned whether such injunctions were compatible with the relevant EU law, and specifically with users' right to the protection of their personal data; ISPs' freedom to carry out economic activity and, finally users' freedom of expression (as the filtering may not distinguish between illegal and legal content).

Surprisingly, the CJEU only considered the freedom of speech on a residual basis, having first examined the question with reference to the other two aspects. The CJEU found that the requirement to adopt a filtering system such as that at issue in this case was not proportionate with the objective of copyright protection. This is because it resulted in a restriction, first, of the ISP's right to engage in economic activity, which is protected under Article 16 of the Charter. Secondly,

[37] *Ashby Donald and Others v France* (n 32).

[38] Case C-70/10 *Scarlet Extended SA v SABAM* [2011] ECR I-11959 and Case C-360/10 *SABAM v Netlog NV*, 16 February 2012.

[39] For a commentary, see S Kulk and F Borgesius, 'Filtering for Copyright Enforcement in Europe after the SABAM Cases' (2012) 11 *European Intellectual Property Review*.

the Court held that the system also violated Articles 8 and 11 of the Charter, which refer, respectively, to right to personal data and freedom of expression. Copyright is of course protected as a fundamental right under the Charter. However, it is significant that the compatibility of measures aimed at copyright protection has only been reviewed at a secondary stage after individual rights.

These decisions seem to downgrade the role of freedom of expression, which is considered as a fundamental right alongside others, especially entrepreneurial freedom. The fact that no particular prominence has been given to this right can perhaps be related to the emancipation of the EU from a predominantly economic dimension, which has still not been fully completed.

The analysis of the CJEU case law concerning online copyright enforcement has revealed the emerging judicial tendency, in Luxembourg, to downgrade the role of freedom of expression within a digital context compared to the prominence afforded to that freedom in the analogue context.

Similar conclusions can be reached in relation to the very recent and already renowned judgment of the CJEU on the protection of the so-called 'right to be forgotten' on the Internet,[40] in which the Court took the emergence of a digital right to privacy very seriously. Maybe, one could object, too seriously, especially if this judgment is read in conjunction with the no less famous[41] ruling which struck down the Data Retention Directive a few weeks earlier[42] on the grounds that it breached, inter alia, Articles 7 and 8 of the Charter. Such a radical privacy-based approach that risks the protection of the rights that may conflict with the new digital right to privacy may not be taken seriously, and secondly, the implications of such a (radical) choice for the web. With regard to this first point, it must not be forgotten that excessive protection for the right to be forgotten risks removing the necessary protection afforded to the right of expression, and, and particularly to the right of each Internet user to be properly and fully informed. The CJEU does provide a few guidelines in its reasoning on how the balance may be struck between these conflicting rights.

Moreover, the Court does make several references to Articles 7 and 8 of the Charter and to the relevant provisions of the Directive. Nevertheless, in contrast with the much more balanced approach of the Advocate General,[43] Article 11 of the Charter, which protects freedom of expression, was not expressly mentioned

[40] Case C-131/12 *Google Spain SL, Google Inc v Agencia Espanñola de Proteccioón de Datos, Mario Costeja Gonzaález*, 13 May 2014, Opinion of AG Niilo Jääskinen, 25 June 2013.

[41] Joined Cases C-293/12 and C-594/12 *Digital Rights Ireland and Seitlinger and Others*, 8 April 2014.

[42] Directive 2006/24/EC of the European Parliament and of the Council of 15 March 2006 on the retention of data generated or processed in connection with the provision of publicly available electronic communications services or of public communications networks and amending Directive 2002/58/EC, in [2006] OJ L105/54.

[43] Case C-131/12 (n 40), Opinion of AG Niilo Jääskinen, 25 June 2013, It is worth mentioning at least one passage of the opinion in which the AG clearly considered, in contrast with the approach of the CJEU the need to balance the enforcement of the right to privacy in Internet use with the need to assure the protection of freedom of expression online. Specifically, as regards to the possible implementation of a notice and take-down procedure based upon individual complaints, Mr Jääskinen clearly noted that the imposition of such a system for the removal of the indexed content would undermine the freedom of expression of the owners of the websites, as it would amount to a private form of censorship.

in the judgment at any point. This does not seem to be a coincidence, but rather a confirmation of the asymmetrical balancing described above.

Secondly, with regard to the implications of the judgment more broadly on the 'web status quo', the chilling effect of the decision on the business model and practical functioning of search engines should not be underestimated. If search engines want to avoid being overwhelmed by take-down requests, the only alternative is to decide, *ex ante*, only to publish news that could never be related to users' private lives. Thus, a tangible risk of self-censorship is immediately apparent. If however search engines decide to wait for take-down requests to be submitted, it will be for the search engines themselves to strike the delicate balance between the individual right of being forgotten and the right of all the other users to be informed regarding facts or opinions of public interest. This is precisely the balancing test that is carried out by the courts, or, in the worst case scenario, by the national data protection authorities. However, surely it is too dangerous to delegate this highly delicate task to private (non-impartial) actors?

V. CONCLUSIONS

This chapter has assessed how the exponential growth of new technologies and the use of the Internet in particular have affected, through the privileged methodological perspective of judicial interaction between interconnected legal systems, the classical (offline) standards of protection for the fundamental right to freedom of expression. Regardless of whether an expansive or narrow constitutional scrutiny is adopted, it goes without saying that the Internet has led to the emergence of new opportunities and has thus extended both the quality and quantity of speech that can be enjoyed by individuals. On the other hand, however, a broader exercise of this freedom is likely to increase conflicts with other interests, which likewise enjoy the same status of fundamental rights. Opportunities and risks must therefore to be weighed up against each other, as the analysis of case law has shown.

More precisely, the most important relevant decisions of the US and European courts have been compared in order to investigate whether or not the traditional approach to freedom of speech pursued in the world of atoms has changed and, more succinctly, whether the margin of constitutional protection has expanded or shrunk.

In this respect, a necessary starting point has been a consideration of how the US and Europe approach freedom of speech in a very different light. Taking account of the advent of the Internet, the distance becomes even more significant. The most important decisions of the US Supreme Court adopted in relation to the Internet confirm that freedom of speech still enjoys broad protection. Better—an even wider margin of protection than that one (already 'huge') enjoyed by the First Amendment in the world of atoms.

In Europe, the use of the Internet seems able to mark a turning point in the courts' approach to freedom of expression. Both the ECtHR and the CJEU have in fact handed down a number of rulings in which it is assumed that new technology brings with it more risks than opportunities in terms of the exercise of freedom of expression. The same outcome, then, is reached through different judicial paths by the two European courts.

On the one hand, we have seen that the ECtHR has left room for restrictions that fulfil the requirements of Article 10(2) of the Convention less narrowly than under the Court's classical analogue approach to freedom of expression. The recent *Delfi* case proves that limitations on freedom of expression are not subject to any preclusion where they amount to a proportional manner of pursuing legitimate aims. The Strasbourg Court's position is thus a long way from the US Supreme Court's strict scrutiny for the First Amendment.

On the other hand, the CJEU has been called upon to balance fundamental rights such as freedom of expression, data protection, entrepreneurial freedom and copyright, even in the light of the Charter that now forms part of EU treaty law. And yet the Court appears to pay even more attention to economic rights or those compatible with the original conformation of the EU. However, the very recent acceleration of the CJEU in the radical enforcement of the digital right to be forgotten, with its inevitable implication of the downgrading of the competing right to access information, seems to lead to the same conclusion: freedom of expression does not have the same value as the Luxembourg Court would have reasonably afforded in the 'worlds of atoms'. Nor does such value seem likely to change in view of the forthcoming accession of the EU to the ECHR: there is a common restrictive approach in the EU and ECHR legal systems towards freedom of expression in the digital age, despite the different paths taken by the respective courts.

Thus, the age of the Internet, which was initially regarded as a new frontier for the exercise of fundamental rights and of freedom of expression, has not led, within the European context, to the 'promised land' that might have been expected.

If it is observed that the US view is so different and if the borderless nature of the Internet is considered, it can be understood why a single theory of freedom of speech on the Internet is still a distant prospect. Accordingly, as long as so different views co-exist, any EU regulation of content will be very hard to achieve and, most of all, to enforce. In addition, jurisdictional problems also need to be considered. The difference between the constitutional visions of free speech in Europe and the US is a tough, and perhaps insuperable, obstacle in this respect.

This is a difference that is surely based, as the case law analysis has attempted to demonstrate, on the fact that European courts seem to be much more worried than their US counterpart that the excessive protection of freedom of expression on the Internet may result in an irreversible diminution of the countervailing rights at stake, namely privacy, child protection, reputation and copyright. However, at least one other reason justifies a different approach. This reason is related to the importance of physical borders and domestic control in the Internet age. While the US Supreme Court appears not to be overly concerned about the fact that, by definition, the trans-national nature of the Internet can have a substantial effect on the efficiency and even feasibility of domestic regulations striking a national balance between contrasting fundamental rights, the same concern emerges even more clearly in the relevant case law of the European courts.

More precisely, one of the (not yet explicitly expressed) arguments behind the attitude of the ECtHR to downgrading the level of protection for freedom of expression on the Internet seems to be an acknowledgment that, contrary to the position for traditional media, the contracting states lack the power to strike a proper national balance for the new digital media between protection of freedom of expression and the individual rights (privacy, reputation) or collective rights (national security, public order) that contrast with it. Consequently, given the necessary absence of a balancing test on national level, it falls to the Strasbourg Court to strike that balance at supranational level.[44]

The same concern regarding a lack of territorial control and a need for a European vision of Internet law emerges in a very similar way in the case law of the CJEU, albeit expressed in different judicial terms. Again, notwithstanding the different judicial model (and the different nature of the relevant legal parameters to be enforced, as well), it is unlikely that the CJEU and the ECtHR would deliver contradictory judgments.

Until recently, the main concern of the Luxembourg Court was that the relevant European legislation should have applied to all Internet operators whose activity has effects in the EU territory, irrespective of where the ISP server is located. This approach is quite reasonable, because it would otherwise be sufficient for a web operator to establish its premises outside the EU in order to avoid the application of European law to its activities (which is more restrictive in its protection of fundamental rights).

However, in its decision on the Data Retention Directive, the Luxembourg Court added a new, very crucial, stone to the building of a European Internet fortress. More precisely the CJEU clarified that the Directive should been deemed to be invalid also because it '(…) does not require the data in question to be retained within the European Union, with the result that it cannot be held that the control, explicitly required by Article 8(3) of the Charter, by an independent authority of compliance with the requirements of protection and security (…)'.[45]

The step forward compared to the previous position of the Luxembourg Court is quite evident. The discussion concerns the opportunity, from a legal point of view, over whether there should be a European Internet law regulating online activities with an impact on European territory, in addition to the need, from a physical point of view, for all the personal data related to individual residents in Europe to be retained within the EU. This will then be a physical territorial constraint which is added to the legal constraint regarding the application of

[44] The said 'substitution' clearly led to the emergence of the crucial issue, which cannot be addressed in this chapter, on the legitimacy of the ECtHR to perform this role.
[45] Joined Cases C-293/12 and C-594/12 *Digital Rights Ireland and Seitlinger* (n 41) 68.

European law. It will represent a further reinforcement of the European Internet fortress, which risks becoming invincible internally, yet lacking any external drawbridge, in order to guarantee the effectiveness, within a global scenario, of the ambitious aims of affording the highest possible protection to the human rights at stake.

Focusing on the relevant case law of the European courts does actually prove to be an effective tool to measure the reach of the European integration in the context of fundamental rights, with specific regard to their protection in the digital age. The analysis carried out with specific regard to the judicial protection of freedom of expression when the 'playing field' moves from the world of atoms to the world of bits has in fact revealed that judicial dialogue constitutes one of the keys, and likely the most valuable, to interpret and, especially, contextualise the case law of the European courts.

Yet, apart from the announced accession of the EU to the ECHR, it has been first of all a task of the European courts to put these spheres in connection and to lead such connection to such a degree so as to qualify it as an authentic judicial interaction.

7

Migration and Human Rights: The European Approach

SONIA MORANO-FOADI

I. INTRODUCTION

THE CURRENT CHAPTER, which draws on research undertaken by the author,[1] explores the interplay between fundamental rights and migration laws and policies at the EU and Council of Europe's (CoE) levels. It contributes to a broader discussion about the place of human rights in Europe after the entry into force of the Treaty of Lisbon,[2] aiming at an understanding of the relationship between control of migration and respect of fundamental values. Combining empirical findings and case law on migration and human rights, this chapter reflects on the extent to which the European Court of Human Rights (ECtHR) and the Court of Justice of the EU (CJEU), in addressing issues of migration when a human rights element is under scrutiny, take a coherent approach.

The debate underpinning the nexus between human rights and immigration law, concerns, above all, the scope of the European Convention of Human Rights (ECHR) and EU laws at the national level. There is a human right of every person, citizen or foreigner, to leave a country, which can be found in the Universal Declaration of Human Rights, International Covenant on Civil and Political

[1] The research draws on two projects, one funded by the British Academy (Small Research Grants (SRG) 2011 Round) and Oxford Brookes University internal funding and the other funded by the European Science Foundation (EW09-259). Some of the empirical findings are also reported in ch 4 of this volume written by Stelios Andreadakis. In fact, sometimes the same quotes are used but they are looking at different issues. In ch 4, empirical evidence is directed to illustrate implications in relation to the EU's accession to the ECHR, and the present chapter is an example of how the relationship between the two Courts plays out on migration law.

[2] The Treaty of Lisbon, which came into force on December 2009, has strengthened the protection of human rights, conferring binding effect to the Charter of Fundamental Rights and Freedoms and providing the legal basis for the EU's accession to the ECHR. Within this new architecture, the minimum standard of protection is guaranteed by the Convention and a more extensive safeguard is guaranteed by the Charter. Thus, in the application of EU law, Member States are committed to uphold respect for human rights through the binding effect of the Charter.

Rights, International Convention on the Elimination of All forms of Racial Discrimination and Article 2 of Protocol 4 to the ECHR.[3] However, non-EU citizens' rights to enter and reside in a Member State are not as such guaranteed by the Convention, international or EU law, although immigration control has to be exercised in Europe consistently with the Convention's obligations and the EU Charter of Fundamental Rights (the Charter). For example, concerns might occur in relation to returning a person to any country where there is a real risk that he or she would be subjected to torture, inhuman or degrading treatment or punishment (Article 3 ECHR or Article 19 Charter) or when there is a risk of extrajudicial killing and following the entry into force of Protocol 13, where there is a risk of death penalty (Article 2 ECHR or Article 2 Charter). In addition, expulsion or deportation of a person from a state where members of his/her family reside might raise an issue relating to the protection of his/her family life[4] (Article 8 ECHR or Article 7 Charter).

The European approach to these areas of law in the continent is largely influenced by decisions taken by the ECtHR and the CJEU as respectively interpreters of the Convention and the EU Charter, treaties and secondary legislation. Yet, the institutional overlap between the EU and the CoE in the field of fundamental rights raises concerns about the relationship between the two European legal systems, the traditional autonomy and integrity of nation states and the role of the judiciary as inspired by European human rights law.[5] Understanding whether the two European Courts speak the same 'language' is crucial to the development of human rights and represents the key for social cohesion and integration in Europe. Lack of coherence and legal certainty would weaken the European human rights protection in favour of the loosest approach taken by one of the two Courts.[6]

In the following pages this chapter engages with current debates on migration and human rights, focusing on the tensions emerging in their interactions. The interplay between migration on the one hand, and human rights on the other, deserves consideration and raises a number of issues. Thus, the chapter reflects on the various layers of 'citizenship' accorded to non-EU nationals legally residing within the EU borders. Then, inspired by empirical research, it explores and critiques the dual protection of human rights in Europe through an assessment of the approaches adopted by the two European Courts to non-EU citizens. Four

[3] Commissioner for Human Rights, 'The Right to Leave a Country', Issue Paper (Strasbourg, CoE, 2013) 63.

[4] See the case *Abdulaziz, Cabales and Balkandali v UK* (1985) 7 EHRR 471.

[5] S Morano-Foadi and S Andreadakis, Report on the Protection of Fundamental Rights in Europe—A Reflection on the Relationship between the Court of Justice of the European Union and the European Court of Human Rights post Lisbon, July 2014, available at http://www.coe.int/en/web/dlapil/news-dlapil.

[6] For a detailed analysis of the potential effect of the CJEU aligning to the ECtHR approach in the area of religious expressions in the public sphere, see MLP Loenen and L Vickers 'More is Less? Multiple Protection of Human Rights in Europe and the Risks of Erosion of Human Rights Standards', ch 9 in this volume.

strands of decisions involving the two Courts that have coherently addressed some migration and human rights related issues at European level are analysed.

The chapter concludes highlighting tensions and synergies that emerge from the CJEU-ECtHR symbiosis and evoking a coherent European human rights system.

II. HUMAN RIGHTS AND MIGRATION IN EUROPE

There are conceptual differences between the EU and the CoE in dealing with migration.

The EU's approach proposes a framework based on citizenship entitlements, with various layers of protection and classification placing EU nationals at the top of the hierarchy and the CoE suggests a legal regime based on rights for all individuals regardless of their nationality.

Two elements need to be considered in relation to the EU. The *first* is the complex framework of the EU regional entity, historically, created as an economic agreement between Member States and slowly expanding its own competences to encompass more subject areas as a consequence of the 'spill over' effects of economic issues. Following this, the introduction of Union citizenship as a concept was mainly related to free movement of workers and thus based on an exclusive idea, linked to the internal market's project. Consequently, people were considered (and to a certain extent still are) as factors of production and non-EU citizens were not covered by this area of law, unless part of an EU citizen's family.[7] The *second* relates to the competences' expansion over the years. This expansion first followed the entry into force of the Treaty of Amsterdam through the creation of the area of freedom, security and justice. Further expansion then followed with the binding effect of the Charter and the introduction of the legal basis for the EU's accession to the ECHR.

A stratification of rights and entitlements based on different migrants' statuses is still a dominant aspect of the EU legislative framework. Under the legal basis provided by Article 79 Treaty on the Functioning of the European Union (TFEU), a number of legal measures were introduced mainly to regulate the 'conditions of residence' of third-country nationals (TCNs) within the territory of the EU,[8] but the

[7] S Morano-Foadi, 'Un-nesting the "Matrioska" Doll: Problems and Paradoxes at the Intersection Between Citizenship, Migration and Human Rights' (2014) 27 *Revista de Derecho de la Unión Europea* 301–20.

[8] The main pieces of secondary legislation in force in this field are: Council Directive 2003/109 on the status of third-country nationals who are long-term residents [2004] OJ L16/44; Council Directive 2003/86 on the right to family reunification [2003] OJ L251/12 (known as the Long-Term Residence Directive); Council Directive 2003/9 laying down minimum standards for the reception of asylum seekers [2003] OJ L31/18; Council Directive 2004/83 on minimum standards for the qualification and status of third country nationals or stateless persons as refugees or as persons who otherwise need international protection and the content of the protection granted [2004] OJ L304/12 (known as the Qualification Directive); Directive 2011/95/EU of the European Parliament and of the Council on standards for the qualification of third-country nationals or stateless persons as beneficiaries of

volume of legal migration still remains a Member State's prerogative. Thus, Article 79(4) TFEU allows the EU to provide incentives and actions in support of Member States for the integration of non-EU nationals legally residing within the EU.

A constituent part of the EU's objective of progressively establishing an area of freedom, security and justice open to those who, forced by circumstances, legitimately seek protection in the Union, is the creation of a common policy on asylum, ex Article 78(a) and (b) TFEU.[9] This policy must be in accordance with the Geneva Convention of 28 July 1951 and the Protocol of 31 January 1967 relating to the status of refugees, and other relevant treaties.

However, despite the creation of such an EU area and with the exception of long-term resident TCNs who enjoy equal treatment with EU nationals[10] and TCNs requiring international protection, Union citizens still have privileged treatment on entering, residing and moving within the EU compared to legally residing TCNs.[11]

The post-Lisbon era is characterised by two important developments aiming at strengthening the human rights protection in Europe: the Charter's upgrade to primary law and the introduction of the legal basis for the EU's accession to the Convention.[12] The Charter has indeed improved coherence and visibility of rights[13] within the Union. It was introduced to protect all

international protection, for a uniform status for refugees or for persons eligible for subsidiary protection, and for the content of the protection granted [2011] OJ L337/9 (known as the Recast Qualification Directive); Council Directive 2005/71/EC on a specific procedure for admitting third-country national for the purposes of scientific research [2005] OJ L289/15; Council Directive 2009/50/EC on the conditions of entry and residence of third country nationals for the purposes of highly qualified employment, [2009] OJ L155/17; Directive 2011/98/EU of the European Parliament and of the Council on a single application procedure for a single permit for third-country nationals to reside and work in the territory of a Member State and on a common set of rights for third-country workers legally residing in a Member State [2011] OJ L343/1.

[9] The main EU measures in the field of refugees law are: Convention Determining the State Responsible for Examining Applications for Asylum lodged in one of the Member States of the European Communities (Dublin Convention) [1997] OJ C254/1; Council Regulation (EC) No 343/2003 of 18 February 2003 establishing the criteria and mechanisms for determining the Member State responsible for examining an asylum application lodged in one of the Member States by a third-country national [2003] OJ L50/1 (known as the Dublin II Regulation); Regulation (EU) No 604/2013 of the European Parliament and of the Council of 26 June 2013 establishing the criteria and mechanisms for determining the Member State responsible for examining an application for international protection lodged in one of the Member States by a third-country national or a stateless person [2013] OJ L180/31 (recast, known as the Dublin III Regulation).

[10] Council Directive 2003/109 (n 8).

[11] S Morano-Foadi and M Malena, 'Integration Policy at European Union Level' in S Morano-Foadi and M Malena (eds), *Integration for Third-Country Nationals In The European Union The Equality Challenge* (Cheltenham, Edward Elgar, 2012).

[12] S Morano-Foadi, 'Fundamental Rights in Europe: "Constitutional" Dialogue between the Court of Justice of the EU and the European Court of Human Rights' (2013) 5 *Oñati Journal of Emergent Socio-legal Studies* 64–88.

[13] European Commission, 'Strategy for the Effective Implementation of the Charter of Fundamental Rights by the European Union, 19 October 2010, available at http://ec.europa.eu/justice/news/intro/doc/com_2010_573_en.pdf, at 3 (accessed 13 April 2011); D Chalmers, G Davies and G Monti, *European Union Law*, 2nd edn (Cambridge, Cambridge University Press, 2010) 237; A Torres Pérez, *Conflicts of Rights in the European Union: A Theory of Supranational Adjudication* (Oxford, Oxford University Press, 2009) 10.

individuals and not to reaffirm distinctions with the effect of marginalising non-EU citizens.[14]

This can be contrasted with the approach of the CoE, which proposes an inclusive model of rights within the continent, suggesting a holistic regime based on 'individual rights' and not on 'citizenship entitlements'. It regards human rights as universal, indivisible and interdependent, protecting rights of minority groups, old and young people, women and children, migrants to name just a few.

The two European regimes of the CoE and the EU have generally co-existed in harmony in some areas[15] with no major conflicts as the two Courts have generated a strong relationship of cooperation. However, the 'citizenship' approach adopted within the EU legal system, when not properly addressed, has differentiated individuals and it is likely to create further problems in future cases. It should not be ignored that the CJEU has set different objectives from the ECtHR. Luxembourg speaks the language of freedoms and it is committed to offering a teleological interpretation of the treaties and facilitating the functioning of the internal market. It is devoted to ensuring that EU citizens enjoy all the rights and freedoms provided and protected by the European legal order.[16]

By contrast, the ECtHR is a specialised Court, focusing on human rights and the ECHR. Therefore, differences in the approach, the interpretative methods, the justification of judgments, as well as the analysis of provisions and legal terms are likely to appear.

However, minimising differences between nationals and non-nationals, thus overcoming inequality of treatment to strengthen protection, is possible. Against the theoretical backdrop of an 'exclusive' concept of EU citizenship, there is a more extensive and progressive protection of rights afforded by the CJEU when interpreting specific EU migration law measures, such as, for example, the Qualification Directive[17] and indeed the Charter, as compared to the Convention, even though complete equality between the EU and non-EU citizens is still so

[14] S McInerney, 'The Charter of Fundamental Rights of the European Union and the Case of Race Discrimination' (2002) 27 *EL Rev* 484.

[15] For example, the right to protection for property, the right to freedom of expression, the right to respect for private and family life, the right to a fair trial. See N Krisch, 'The Open Architecture of European Human Rights Law' (2008) 71 *MLR* 183; L Scheeck, 'The Relationship Between the European Courts and Integration through Human Rights' (2005) 65 *Zeitschrift für ausländisches öffentliches Recht and Völkerrecht* 837; J Callewaert, 'The European Convention on Human Rights and European Union Law: A Long Way to Harmony' (2009) 6 *European Human Rights Law Review* 782.

[16] S Morano-Foadi and S Andreadakis, 'The Convergence of the European Legal System in the Treatment of Third Country Nationals in Europe: The ECJ and the ECtHR Jurisprudence' (2011) 22 The *European Journal of International Law* 1071.

[17] Council Directive 2004/83/EC of 29 April 2004 on minimum standards for the qualification and status of third country nationals or stateless persons as refugees or as persons who otherwise need international protection and the content of the protection granted [2004] OJ L304/12. This Directive has been replaced by the Recast Directive 2011/95/EU of the European Parliament and of the Council of 13 December 2011 on standards for the qualification of third-country nationals or stateless persons as beneficiaries of international protection, for a uniform status for refugees or for persons eligible for subsidiary protection, and for the content of the protection granted [2011] OJ L337/26. However, Directive 2011/95 does not apply to the UK, Ireland and Denmark.

far to be achieved. This would potentially ensure a more extensive protection in Europe, as the ECtHR has considered the Convention to be a 'living document' and the Court has been extending its interpretation over the years and will continue to do so in the future. Within this framework, it is thus of high relevance the application of the law and the implementation at national level of a coherent European framework. It is extremely important that the two European Courts, the interpreters of the Convention and the EU Charter, convey the same message on European human rights protection.

Despite emerging common approaches between the two Courts, a full harmonisation of the human rights standards in the field of migration is yet to be achieved. However, recently, in the area of TCNs' migration the two Courts have started to respond to points of law raised by one another, when necessary, to increase human rights protection of migrants. This has now occurred in several instances and constitutes an element of synergy between the Courts.

The research presented in this chapter covers the interplay between the CJEU and ECtHR in the fundamental rights sphere through the means of empirical investigations.[18] Three rounds of interviews have been undertaken. The first round was held with 19 judges and Advocates General of the CJEU; the second with 10 ECtHR's judges; and the third round of interviews was conducted with the Commission, the Council and the CoE's officials engaged in the drafting of the Accession Treaty to the ECHR. Key respondents from the European Parliament have also been involved in the research.

The following pages reflect on the Courts' attempts to align to each other's case law at the interplay between human rights and migration.

III. JUDICIAL VIEWS ON HUMAN RIGHTS AND MIGRATION

The first relevant reflection emerging from the empirical work conducted with the judiciary at European level is the importance of co-operation between the two European Courts to ensure a high standard of human rights protection around the continent. This is seen as a necessity rather than an aspiration, as legal certainty is paramount. The national judiciary should be inspired by the rule of law in Europe. This is crucial, as most of the issues related to migration have a human rights dimension.

Neither of the two European Courts is an asylum and immigration tribunal, but each of them has been dealing with immigration cases. The ECtHR in fact has been labelled as 'a refugee court'.[19] Its first judgment on asylum and immigration

[18] For detailed commentary on EU's accession to the ECHR, see S Andreadakis, 'Problems and Challenges of the EU's Accession to the ECHR: Empirical Findings with a View to the Future', ch 4 in this volume.

[19] M Bossuyt, 'The Court of Strasbourg Acting as an Asylum Court' (2012) 8 *European Constitutional Law Review* 219.

was taken in 1991; since then the number of cases on the subject has increased following its decision in the *Mamatkulov and Askarov v Turkey* judgment.[20]

Most of the cases deal with indirect violations of Article 3 of the Convention, usually when a refugee or an asylum seeker would be expelled or extradited to a country where he or she would be exposed to treatment that is contrary to that Article. There are also cases dealing with deportation of foreign criminals and their Article 8 rights. It has been argued that such a Court, being a human rights court, leans more towards the protection of the individual rather than the underlying interest of the state.[21] However, often this Court is cautious and applies the margin of appreciation in immigration cases, particularly when there is a wide discretion.[22]

By contrast, the CJEU has not been acting either as a human rights court or as an asylum and immigration tribunal.[23] Yet, after the entry into force of the Treaty of Lisbon important changes to the architecture of Europe have made the Court deal with preliminary ruling procedures in the field of immigration. Many issues of interpretation in relation to the implementation of pieces of secondary legislation, such as, for example, Regulation 343/2003[24] (also known as Dublin II Regulation) or Directive 2004/83[25] (also known as the Qualification Directive) have been brought to the attention of the CJEU. In particular, questions were raised by the national judges as to the meaning of specific provisions aimed at ensuring an effective intra-Union system dealing with asylum seekers' applications (Dublin II Regulation) or establishing common rules for determining who qualifies as a refugee or as a person eligible for subsidiary protection (Qualification Directive).

Moreover, although the directives/regulations constitute the *lex specialis* in the field of immigration, the Charter constitutes the *lex generalis*, and its binding effect has invested this institution with more responsibility in relation to human

[20] App nos 46827/99 and 46951/99 (ECtHR, 4 February 2005).

[21] N Blake and R Husain, *Immigration Asylum and Human Rights* Blackstone's Human Rights (Oxford, Oxford University Press, 2003) 80–83; N Blake and L Fransman (eds), *Immigration, Nationality and Asylum under the Human Rights Act 1998* (London, Butterworths, 1999) 11–20.

[22] A Farahat, 'The Exclusiveness of Inclusion: On the Boundaries of Human Rights in Protecting Transnational and Second Generation Migrants' (2009) 11 *European Journal of Migration and Law* 253; D Stevens, 'Asylum-Seeking Families in Current Legal Discourse: A UK perspective' (2010) 32 *Journal of Social Welfare and Family Law* 5.

[23] W Weiss, 'Human Rights in the EU: Rethinking the Role of the European Convention on Human Rights after Lisbon' (2011) 7 *European Constitutional Law Review* 64–95. For an interesting analysis on this point, see also W Weiss, 'The EU Human Rights Regime Post Lisbon: Turning the CJEU into a Human Rights Court?', ch 5 in this volume.

[24] At n 9 above. A new Regulation, the Dublin Regulation Recast, coined 'Dublin III' has also been introduced. On a more detailed discussion on the Dublin II and II Regulations, see S Velluti, 'Who Has the Right to Have Rights? The Judgments of the CJEU and ECtHR as Building Blocks for a European "ius commune" in Asylum Law', ch 8 in this volume.

[25] Directive 2004/83 and Directive 2011/95 (n 8).

rights.[26] In fact, issues have been raised in relation to the scope of the right to asylum as protected by Article 18 of the Charter and the meaning of Article 4 of the Charter on the prohibition of torture and inhuman or degrading treatment or punishment.[27]

Despite the Courts' approach, the interpretative methods, the justification of judgments in the migration field at the intersection with human rights seem to differ; elements of convergence between the two Courts are evident. This is confirmed by the following quotes taken from the interviews with the judges and also jurisprudence of the two Courts, which is addressed in the next section.

The judges interviewed were aware of the complexity of their work in relation to migration and human rights, when the protection based on the set of norms under scrutiny, would not treat individuals equally.[28]

Judges were inclined to expand interpretation to strengthen protection of rights, as suggested in the following quote:

> As far as asylum seekers are concerned, great if the EU gives more protection. We say that migrants should have rights protected under the minimum standard. What we say, when migrants are staying in one of the countries which is a Member State of EU and is also a Party to the Convention, they have some rights which go further if the Member State is also an EU country. But for me it is the same when the EU gives more protection like when any other CoE Member State does at the national level.[29]

Some of the CJEU's judges affirmed that indeed reinforcing the protection of human rights in Europe after the Lisbon Treaty was possible due to competence expansion:

> … the changes connected to the strengthening of the powers of the CJ in the area of freedom, security and justice … which contains measures taken to protect the external borders of the EU, asylum, immigration […] Prior to Lisbon the judicial control of acts in this area was in many ways limited. As a result of the Lisbon Treaty many of the limitations to the powers of the CJ have been deleted.[30]

Express mention was accorded by the CJEU judges to the Charter, as a Bill of rights:

> […] first of all, the Charter is binding and more cases on fundamental rights issues [have reached this Court] because some areas [such as] immigration, civil and criminal procedure are sensitive to human rights.[31]

[26] S Morano-Foadi and S Andreadakis, 'Reflections on the Architecture of the EU after the Treaty of Lisbon: The European Judicial Approach to Fundamental Rights' in Special Issue edited by S Morano-Foadi and F Duina, entitled 'The Institutionalisation of Regional Trade Agreements Worldwide: New Dynamics and Future Perspectives' (2011) 17 *European Law Journal* 595–610. See also Loenen and Vickers, 'More is Less?' (n 6).

[27] For further discussion on this point, see Velluti, ch 8 in this volume.

[28] Interview III (ECtHR, Strasbourg, 19 June 2012).

[29] Interview V (ECtHR, Strasbourg, 20 June 2012).

[30] Interview 14 (CJEU, Luxembourg, 15 December 2010).

[31] Interview 1 (CJEU, Luxembourg, 13 December 2010).

> The biggest [change] is that we refer to the Charter more freely. Now there is the Charter, then the ECHR and then the general principles of EU law, whereas before the Court was hesitant to use the Charter as it had no legal standing.[32]

> There are several cases … even now before the Court, dealing either with citizens of the Union or TCNs, especially those coming from countries having a special agreement with EU such as Turkey. I think there is a great difference between the two rights in competition. Even if the Court decides that the TCNs are in a situation different than the EU citizens, the Court must ask itself if the particular case is in compliance with the Charter, because the Charter applies to everybody, and the Charter is the same as the ECHR (Arts 31 ff Charter). The Court at the moment is shifting the scope of the interpretation and application to the Charter.[33]

The CJEU judges have also stressed that more national judges address questions having some human rights implication:

> The subject has [….] changed. [National judges raise not] only questions of internal market, but […] also questions on rights of third country nationals, criminal law, internet and consumer law … as a result of the change in the focus and the body of EU legislation.[34]

The relationship between the two Courts has not over the years been antagonistic. The two Courts have acted more as allies than as enemies, working 'in parallel' and within their respective legal systems. The general impression emerging from the interviews with the judges is the presence of ongoing dialogue between the Courts in an attempt to achieve coherent protection of human rights in Europe. This is reflected in the following quotes from some Strasbourg judges:

> I would like to see this relationship not as a Kelsenian relationship, but rather a dialogue between specialised Courts, the CJEU is specialised in the EU law, the ECtHR specialised in HR and the national courts specialised in national constitutional law, but sometimes it is difficult to draw the lines.[35]

> … extreme care is taken not to disappoint each other … not to interfere with each other's business. When, it comes to HR protection under Convention, the last word is with this Court and Luxembourg has always agreed on that by not giving an interpretation to the Convention which goes in another direction than the interpretation by our Court. However, what is possible is that the Luxemburg Court applies and interprets directly the Charter which gives more protection than minimum rights of Convention. So in this respect they can now take the lead in interpreting the provisions of the Charter that go further than the Convention.[36]

[32] Interview 6 (CJEU, Luxembourg, 14 December 2010).
[33] Interview 11 (CJEU, Luxembourg, 15 December 2010).
[34] Interview 4 (CJEU, Luxembourg, 14 December 2010).
[35] Interview VI (ECtHR, Strasbourg, 20 June 2012).
[36] Interview V (ECtHR, Strasbourg, 20 June 2012).

However on the question whether the CJEU is now speaking the 'language' of rights, the Luxembourg judges were divided, as these quotes demonstrate:

> It never was and it has not suddenly become a HR Court. It is a Court with a mandate to observe the law in all matters that it deals with, including fundamental rights.[37]

> The question, whether the Court will speak more the language of rights rather than the language of the common market, is a horrible cliché to be honest. This Court has been speaking about rights since the beginning, since Van Gend en Loos. These rights might be economically driven if you look at the area of social law, if you look at the free movement of persons these are 'very' human rights.[38]

> There has been no significant change in the Court's operation. It is still responsible for the uniform application and interpretation of EU law as well as for the control of the powers of the EU institutions in carrying out their tasks. Human rights' ideals were always a source of inspiration.[39]

> The Court will remain the Court of the internal market [...] it will remain the General Court of the EU [...] it is not going to be a fundamental rights' Court. That is Strasbourg's mandate. The context is changing we have so many things to do, we are not dealing any longer with the sole common market because we have now the area of freedom, security and justice but I think we will remain a general court as a subject matter. It would be a terrible disaster if we translate all cases we get here in terms of fundamental rights. It would be a nonsense.[40]

The perception of the judges about the Courts having a different role and yet aiming at achieving a coherent human rights approach in Europe is clearly expressed in the following quotes:

> I think it is quite likely to happen whether we consciously work towards this or not. We take into account their case law and they do the same with ours. There are two regional supreme courts dealing with these issues of fundamental rights and it would be surprising if we did not take some interest on each other's case law.[41]

> Yes, until now our Court has referred to the jurisprudence of the ECtHR, by applying the general principles which formed after the Convention; the question in relation to the future—there might be some difficulties, which should be solved by the Accession Treaty.[42]

> We have seen some discrepancies between the two Courts for example in relation to the access to privacy such as *Hoeck* case … but both Courts are very careful in looking

[37] Interview 10 (CJEU, Luxembourg, 15 December 2010).
[38] Interview 14 (CJEU, Luxembourg, 15 December 2010).
[39] Interview 10 (CJEU, Luxembourg, 15 December 2010).
[40] Interview 14 (CJEU, Luxembourg, 15 December 2010).
[41] Interview 10 (CJEU, Luxembourg, 15 December 2010). This quote has also been used by Andreadakis, ch 4 in this volume, to illustrate mutual respect and cooperation between the judges.
[42] Interview 16 (CJEU, Luxembourg, 16 December 2010).

> at each other. I am not sure they are working towards coherence but they tolerate each other. They aim at avoiding conflicts and frictions. There are informal meetings where we discuss problems of fundamental rights if there is a need for research, the research department can do that, can find cases.[43]

In light of these findings, thought goes to the extent to which harmony could be fully realised. Legal scholars have often contemplated the answer to this question;[44] the simplest answer was for the EU to accede formally to the ECHR, which has, of course, been made possible by the Treaty of Lisbon.[45] And whilst this is indeed true, the answer also lies with the EU and the CoE and their respective Courts whom must learn how to interact completely, not just co-exist.

IV. THE 'HUMAN RIGHTS MEETING POINT' IN MIGRATION LAW CASES

Each of the two Courts has already responded to points of law raised by the other Court, when necessary, to increase human rights protection. This has occurred in several instances and constitutes an essential tool for the Courts. The dialogue between these two Courts is a very powerful instrument for the convergence argument.[46] Three levels of dialogue between the two Courts have been developed. These are the 'informal' dialogue, consisting of regular meetings between the two Courts; the 'institutionalised' dialogue, to be enacted if and when the EU's accession to the ECHR will occur and ensuring that the EU and its Member States may appear jointly as defendants before the Strasbourg; and the 'judicial' dialogue, based on the scrutiny by each of the two European Courts of the case law of the other, when dealing with points of law that were raised in previous case law by any of the two fora.[47]

It is submitted that the last form of dialogue is an excellent tool, bringing coherence within the European human rights legal system as a whole.

[43] Interview 14 (CJEU, Luxembourg, 15 December 2010). This quote has also been used by Andreadakis, ch 4 in this volume.

[44] See D Spielmann, 'Human Rights Case Law in the Strasbourg and Luxembourg Courts: Conflicts, Inconsistencies, and Complementariness' in P Alston, M Bustelo and L Heenan (eds), *The EU and Human Rights* (Oxford, Oxford University Press, 1999) ch 23 at 777.

[45] The Accession Treaty has been considered by the CJEU as incompatible with EU law. See Opinion 2/13 of the Court (Full Court) of 18 December 2014 pursuant to Article 218(11) TFEU on the compatibility of the draft agreement with the EU and FEU Treaties, available at http://curia.europa.eu/juris/liste.jsf?num=C-2/13. For a commentary on the accession, see K Raba, 'Closing the Gaps in the Protection of Fundamental Rights in Europe: Accession of the EU to the ECHR', ch 2 in this volume.

[46] Interview VI (ECtHR, Strasbourg, 20 June 2012).

[47] S Morano-Foadi, 'Fundamental Rights in Europe: "Constitutional" Dialogue Between the Court of Justice of the EU and the European Court of Human Rights' (2013) 5 *Oñati Journal of Emergent Socio-legal Studies* 64–88, available at http://www.sortuz.org/content/pdfs2013/4%20Morano%20-%20human%20rights.pdf. For a detailed analysis of the institutionalised dialogue, see Andreadakis, ch 4 in this volume.

When talking about the 'judicial dialogue', one of the ECtHR judges interviewed in the project affirmed:

> [W]e are looking at our respective case law […] The example I gave is of a real dialogue, because we responded to what the CJEU said in *Elgafaji* and in *Sufiand Elmi* we increased the protection thanks to this judicial dialogue.[48]

Four strands of cases are now the object of the following analysis as an example of convergence between the two European Courts' approaches in the field of migration, when a human rights element is considered.

A. Article 15 Qualification Directive and Article 3 ECHR

The CJEU has provided interpretation of some provisions contained in the Qualification Directive. The main scope of this legal measure is to ensure that all Member States apply common criteria for the identification of persons genuinely in need of international protection, and, on the other hand, to ensure that a minimum level of benefits is available for these persons in all Member States. In order to qualify for subsidiary protection,[49] a TCN or a stateless person does not need to be a refugee but needs to prove that substantial grounds have been shown for believing that the person concerned, if returned to his or her country of origin, or in the case of a stateless person, to his or her country of former habitual residence, would face a 'real risk' of suffering 'serious harm'. Article 15 of the Qualification Directive defines the meaning of 'serious harm'.[50] Then, to qualify for subsidiary protection, the individual concerned should not benefit of the protection of the country of origin or habitual residence.[51]

[48] Interview VIII (ECtHR, Strasbourg, 20 June 2012).

[49] See European Migration and Network (EMN) Glossary & Thesaurus for a definition of subsidiary protection which is available at http://ec.europa.eu/dgs/home-affairs/what-we-do/networks/european_migration_network/glossary/index_a_en.htm.

[50] The text of Art 15 of the Qualification Directive states: 'Serious harm consists of: (a) death penalty or execution; or (b) torture or inhuman or degrading treatment or punishment of an applicant in the country of origin; or (c) serious and individual threat to a civilian's life or person by reason of indiscriminate violence in situations of international or internal armed conflict'.

[51] The text of Art 17 of the Qualification Directive states: '1. A third country national or a stateless person is excluded from being eligible for subsidiary protection where there are serious reasons for considering that: (a) he or she has committed a crime against peace, a war crime, or a crime against humanity, as defined in the international instruments drawn up to make provision in respect of such crimes; (b) he or she has committed a serious crime; (c) he or she has been guilty of acts contrary to the purposes and principles of the United Nations as set out in the Preamble and Articles 1 and 2 of the Charter of the United Nations; (d) he or she constitutes a danger to the community or to the security of the Member State in which he or she is present. 2. Paragraph 1 applies to persons who instigate or otherwise participate in the commission of the crimes or acts mentioned therein. 3. Member States may exclude a third country national or a stateless person from being eligible for subsidiary protection, if he or she prior to his or her admission to the Member State has committed one or more crimes, outside the scope of paragraph 1, which would be punishable by imprisonment, had they been committed in the Member State concerned, and if he or she left his or her country of origin solely in order to avoid sanctions resulting from these crimes'.

The CJEU, in the *Elgafaji* decision,[52] has provided an 'interpretative guidance' on the requirement of the existence of a 'serious and individual threat' (Article 15(c) Qualification Directive), in light of the fact that 'the relevant provisions were found to be compatible with the ECHR'.[53]

The applicants, Mr and Mrs Elgafaji required temporary residence permits in the Netherlands. In support of their application and based on their personal circumstances, they argued that, were exposed to a real threat to their life, if expelled to Iraq, their country of origin. On refusal of temporary residence permits by the Minister, they brought actions before the court (Rechtbank te's-Gravenhage), which were successful. An appeal was seized by the Minister, who held that there were difficulties in interpreting the relevant provisions of Directive 2004/83/EC. The appeal judge raised preliminary questions to the CJEU addressing the issue of whether the existence of a 'serious and individual threat' to the life or the person of the applicant for subsidiary protection,[54] is subject to the condition that the applicant adduce evidence that he is specifically targeted by reason of factors particular to his circumstances; and, if not, to indicate the criterion on the basis of which the existence of such a threat can be considered to be established.

The CJEU claimed that Article 15(c) of the Qualification Directive has its own field of application and held that protection under that Article goes beyond that of Article 3 of the Convention, which is covered by Article 15(b).[55] It held that, in line with Article 15(c) of the Directive, the concept of 'individual threat' is interpreted quite broadly, as it is not linked to the condition that 'the applicant adduces evidence that he is specifically targeted by reason of factors particular to his personal circumstances'.[56] Substantial grounds to the 'individual threat' are shown in situations where a civilian who is returned to the relevant country would face a 'real risk' of being subjected to the threat of serious harm solely for his presence in the country or region at stake.[57] However, to demonstrate such a risk the applicant would not be required to adduce 'evidence' of him being specifically targeted by reason of factors particular to his personal circumstances.[58]

The CJEU specified that such a situation would be 'exceptional' and as such occurring in the context of high level of indiscriminate violence on civilians in the territory where armed conflicts are in place. Thus, the 'more the applicant is able to show that he is specifically affected by reason of factors particular to his

[52] Case C-465/07 *Meki Elgafaji and Noor Elgafaji v Staatssecretaris van Justitie* [2009] ECR I-00921.

[53] ibid, para 44. The CJEU in an obiter dictum held that the interpretation given in *Elgafaji* of the relevant provisions of Directive 2004/83 was fully compatible/compliant with the ECHR, including the case law of the ECtHR relating to Art 3 of the ECHR. See in the same sense, F Ippolito, 'The Contribution of the European Courts to the Common European Asylum System and its Ongoing Recast Process' (2013) 20 *Maastricht Journal* 2; P Tiedemann, 'Subsidiary Protection and the Function of Article 15(c) of the Qualification Directive' (2012) 31 *Refugee Survey Quarterly* 138.

[54] See n 49 for a definition of subsidiary protection.

[55] See n 50 for the text of Art 15 of the Qualification Directive.

[56] Case C-465/07 *Elgafaji* (n 52), para 30.

[57] ibid, para 34

[58] ibid, para 35.

personal circumstances, the lower the level of indiscriminate violence required for him to be eligible for subsidiary protection'.[59]

In *NA v the United Kingdom*,[60] the ECtHR expressly considered the earlier decision in *Vilvarajah v the United Kingdom*[61] and stated that Article 3 ECHR should not be interpreted so as to require an applicant to prove the existence of special distinguishing features if he could otherwise show that his country of destination's general situation of violence was of a sufficient level of intensity to create a 'real' risk that any removal to that country would violate Article 3 ECHR. Such an approach was adopted by the Court in extreme cases of general violence, ie in the presence of a real risk to be exposed to ill-treatment simply by virtue of generalised violence in the return country.

The interesting dynamic that makes this case particularly relevant to the discussion on the 'judicial' dialogue between the two Courts, is that although the scope of Article 15(c) of the Qualification Directive is apparently broader than Article 3 ECHR, the ECtHR had a similar interpretation in *NA v the UK* and has explicitly referred to the interpretation given by the CJEU in *Elgafaji* and *Sufi and Elmi v the United Kingdom.*

In the case of *Sufi and Elmi v the United Kingdom*,[62] the Strasbourg Court had to examine whether the deportation of the applicants to Somalia would expose them to a 'real' risk of being subject to treatment contrary to Article 3 ECHR on account of the general situation of violence.

It followed the interpretation given by the CJEU stating that comparable protection was offered and thus widening its interpretation of Article 3. It stated:

> However, based on the CJEU's interpretation in *Elgafaji*, the Court is not persuaded that Article 3 of the Convention, as interpreted in *NA*, does not offer comparable protection to that afforded under the Directive. In particular, it notes that the threshold set by both provisions may, in exceptional circumstances, be attained in consequence of a situation of general violence of such intensity that any person being returned to the region in question would be at risk simply on account of their presence there.[63]

Although, the *Elgafaji* case is an example of convergence between the case law of the ECtHR and the CJEU in relation to general violence and between the Qualification Directive and Article 3 ECHR, scholars argue that the CJEU did not comprehensively answer the preliminary question on the 'criteria' for determining subsidiary protection under Article 15(c) of the Directive.[64]

[59] ibid, para 39.

[60] App no 25904/07 (ECtHR, 17 July 2008), para 115.

[61] Series A no 215 (ECtHR, 30 October 1991).

[62] App nos 8319/07 and 11449/07 (ECtHR, 28 June 2011) at 7.

[63] ibid, para 226.

[64] B Zalar, 'Comments on the Court of Justice of the EU's Developing Case Law on Asylum' (2013) 25 *International Journal of Refugee Law* 377, 378.

In fact, four years later, in the *Diakite* case the question on the criteria for assessment was raised and the CJEU:

> [A]cknowledged that an internal armed conflict exists, for the purposes of applying that provision [Article 15(c)], if a State's armed forces confront one or more armed groups or if two or more armed groups confront each other … It is not necessary for that conflict to be categorised as 'armed conflict not of an international character' under international humanitarian law; nor is it necessary to carry out, in addition to an appraisal of the level of violence present in the territory concerned, a separate assessment of the intensity of the armed confrontations, the level of organisation of the armed forces involved or the duration of the conflict.[65]

Thus, in the *Diakite* case, in an attempt to assist the national judges in making migration decisions, the CJEU has elaborated clear interpreting guidelines on when subsidiary protection should be given.

B. EU Dublin II Regulation and Article 3 ECHR

In examining the compliance of an asylum application with Article 3 ECHR, the Grand Chamber of the ECtHR in *MSS v Belgium and Greece*,[66] reflected on the implementation of the EU Dublin II Regulation.[67] The aim of this measure is to lay down criteria and mechanisms for determining the Member State responsible for examining an application for asylum lodged in one of the Member States by a TCN.

MSS, an Afghan national who, in 2008, left Kabul and entered the EU via Greece, then moved to Belgium and applied for asylum. In applying the Dublin II Regulation, the Belgium Government sent the applicant straight back to Greece. The applicant argued that in returning him to Greece, Belgium had violated Article 3 (on prohibition of torture and of inhuman or degrading treatment), Article 2 (on the right to life), and Article 13 (on the right to an effective remedy) of the Convention. The ECtHR found that Greece had violated the Convention by maintaining detention and living conditions that offend a person's dignity. Then, the Court noted that the processing of asylum applications was inadequate and found that Belgium had violated the Convention, causing the applicant to endure inhumane detention and living conditions in Greece. The ECtHR also decided that the applicant lacked, in Belgium, an adequate right to an effective remedy in order to protect his rights—this was due to the lack of examination that was made of his asylum application.

[65] Case C-285/12 *Diakité v Commissaire général aux réfugiés et aux apatrides*, Judgment of the Court (Fourth Chamber) of 30 January 2014, not yet reported.

[66] App no 30696/09 (ECtHR, 21 January 2011).

[67] The Dublin II Regulation, issued in 2003 by the EU, includes the principle that an asylum-seeker's application can be examined in only one Member State of the EU. When it becomes clear that the applicant has entered the EU via another Member State or has already applied for asylum in another state, the applicant is returned to that state and the process is handled by that state's authorities.

This is how one of the judges interviewed has commented on this case:

> One recent example of migration was [the] *M.S.S.* case on [the] Dublin Regulation. There the Court delivered a very significant judgement finding that if the expulsion investigation and decision making is not proper in the receiving country (the first state) the state cannot rely on [the] Dublin Regulation. The message was clear and strong.[68]

The joined cases *NS* and *ME*[69] represent the CJEU's reply to the *MSS* case and were decided on 21 December 2011.[70] The CJEU was asked to rule on 'Dublin transfers' from the UK and Ireland to Greece. Although it found the Dublin II system compatible with international human rights law, the Court asserted that if a *de facto* overload of a Member State's asylum system was to mean that rights protected under the EU Charter would be adversely affected, then the other Member State should be obliged not to deport asylum seekers to that state in order to apply the Dublin II Regulation in accordance with EU primary law.[71] The aim of Dublin II was to expedite the examination of asylum seekers' applications in the interest of both the asylum applicant and the respective Member States, and prevent a situation wherein multiple Member States process applications by the same applicant.

Some commentators[72] argue that the CJEU concluded that not every infringement of a fundamental right by the Member State will affect obligations to comply with the Dublin II Regulation,[73] but only systemic flaws in the asylum procedure and reception conditions, resulting in inhuman or degrading treatment within the meaning of Article 4 of the Charter, would be incompatible with that provision.[74] It was questioned whether the interpretation given by the CJEU in this case was comparable to the ECtHR's standard of protection in line with the *Bosphorus* case, which clearly states that 'domestic judicial procedure [should] respect and protect individuals against any infringement of absolute human rights no matter whether systemic flaws are involved or not'.[75]

[68] Interview VII (ECtHR, Strasbourg, 20 June 2012).

[69] Joined Cases C-411/10 *NS v Secretary of State for the Home Department* and C-493/10 *ME and Others v Refugee Applications Commissioner, Minister for Justice, Equality and Law Reform* (ECtHR, 21 December 2012).

[70] J Laffranque, 'Who Has the Last Word on the Protection of Human Rights in Europe?' (2012) XIX *Juridica International* 117–34, 119.

[71] Joined Cases *NS* and *ME* (n 69) paras 114, 122, 131 and 135–36.

[72] Zalar, 'Comments on the Court of Justice of the EU's Developing Case Law on Asylum' (n 64) at 381.

[73] Joined Cases *NS* and *ME* (n 69), para 82.

[74] ibid, para 86.

[75] App No 45036/98, *Bosphorus Hava Yollari Turizm Ve Ticaret Anonim Sirketi v Ireland* [2005] 42 EHRR 1; Zalar, 'Comments on the Court of Justice of the EU's Developing Case Law on Asylum' (n 64) at 381.

The question has been solved by the CJEU in the *CIMADE* case,[76] which clearly states that asylum seekers may not be deprived, even for a temporary period of time, of the protection of the minimum standards concerning respect and protection of human dignity.[77] It is clear that even within the EU there could be protection flaws, as affirmed by a Strasbourg judge:

> ... we cannot create any double standards. ... in the *M.S.S v. Belgium and Greece* case of the ECtHR; and then reported in [the] *NS* case before the CJEU it was decided that there should be mutual trust and recognition, but at the same time there is a need of a compliance check, it cannot take it for granted even in EU countries.[78]

In fact, at national level, a very recent UK Supreme Court judgement, *R v Secretary of State for the Home Department,*[79] concluded that the Court of Appeal was wrong in considering that only a 'systemic breach' by the receiving country of its human rights obligations would justify not returning an asylum seeker to that EU country. The Supreme Court suggested that it is 'forbidden' to send an asylum seeker to a country where there is a *risk* that he could be subjected to inhuman or degrading treatment. It is not necessary to demonstrate a 'systematic breach in the facilities system' for the violation of Article 3 ECHR. The UK authorities should consider possible violations, case by case.[80] This Court affirmed that, the CJEU's judgment in *NS* had to be read according to the context in which it was given. While it did refer to a 'systemic breach', such a breach was well established on the facts of the case. The CJEU's focus was, therefore, not on the sort of breach that had to be established, but rather on EU Member States' awareness of such a breach.[81] There was no warrant for concluding that CJEU's judgment was that there had to be a systemic breach; it only meant that a systemic breach would be enough. The CJEU was not calling into question the well-established test applied in human rights law, which is that the removal of a person from a Member State of the CoE to another country is forbidden, if it is shown that there is a 'real risk' that the person transferred will suffer treatment contrary to Article 3 of the ECHR.[82]

[76] Case C-179/11 *Cimade and Groupe d'information et de soutien des immigrés (GISTI) v Ministre de l'Intérieur, de l'Outre-mer, des Collectivités territoriales et de l'Immigration*, Judgment of 27 September 2012, not yet reported.

[77] ibid, para 56.

[78] Interview VI (ECtHR, Strasbourg, 20 June 2012).

[79] *R (on the application of EM (Eritrea) v Secretary of State for the Home Department* [2014] UKSC 12.

[80] See http://supremecourt.uk/decided-cases/docs/UKSC_2012_0272_PressSummary.pdf and see also http://www.bbc.co.uk/news/uk-26267245.

[81] However, Member States may not transfer an asylum seeker to a 'responsible Member State' if they know that in the said state an asylum seeker could face a real risk of being subjected to inhuman or degrading treatment within the meaning of Art 4 of the Charter. The CJEU found that the Member States have at their disposal sufficient instruments to allow them to assess compliance with fundamental rights and, thereby, should be aware of the real dangers to which an asylum seeker would be subjected in the event that he or she is sent to the country in question. Additionally, the CJEU found that the matter belongs to the domain of EU rights application, that Member States must apply the Charter's principles, and that the application of the Charter in the UK is not questioned (Protocol (No 30) on the application of the Charter to Poland and to the UK ([2010] OJ C83/313).

[82] *R (on the application of EM (Eritrea)* (n 79) at [56]–[58].

C. EU Returns Directive and Article 5 ECHR

Another example of convergence of approach between the two Courts is offered by the *El Dridi* case,[83] on deprivation of personal liberty.[84] The Prefect of Turin issued a deportation decree against Mr El Dridi, a TCN who had entered Italy irregularly. Consequently, the head of police of Udine issued an order requiring his removal. As revealed by investigations carried out, Mr El Dridi did not comply with the removal order and consequently was sentenced to one year's imprisonment by the District Court of Trento, under a provision of an Italian Legislative Decree.[85] He appealed against this decision and the Appeal Court of Trento decided to stay proceedings and refer the question of whether a criminal penalty imposed on the appellant for non-compliance with stages of administrative procedures concerning the return to his country of origin, was contrary to EU law—in particular to the principle of sincere cooperation and the objectives of the Returns Directive.[86] Moreover, the CJEU had to ascertain whether the penalty was proportionate, appropriate and reasonable.

In this judgment, to interpret the Returns Directive, the CJEU applied both the ECtHR case law and CoE's guidelines,[87] as referred to in recital 3 of its preamble. The CJEU referred to the *Saadi v the United Kingdom* case,[88] on the principle of proportionality,[89] according to which:

> [D]etention of a person against whom a deportation or extradition procedure is under way should not continue for an unreasonable length of time, that is, its length should not exceed that required for the purpose pursued.[90]

Then, it reported the guideline affirming that:

> [A]ny detention pending removal is to be for as short a period as possible.

[83] Case C-61/11 PPU *Hassen El Dridi* (alias Karim Soufi), 28 April 2011.

[84] Zalar, 'Comments on the Court of Justice of the EU's Developing Case Law on Asylum' (n 64) at 379.

[85] No 286/1998 of 25 July 1998 consolidating the provisions regulating immigration and the rules relating to the status of foreign national (Ordinary Supplement to GURI No 191 of 18 August 1998), as amended by Law No 94 of 15 July 2009 on public security (Ordinary Supplement to GURI No 170 of 24 July 2009) ('Legislative Decree No 286/1998').

[86] Directive 2008/115/EC of the European Parliament and of the Council of 16 December 2008 on common standards and procedures in Member States for returning illegally staying third-country nationals [2008] OJ L348/98. The objective of this Directive as stated in recital 20 of its preamble: 'to establish common rules concerning return, removal, use of coercive measures, detention and entry bans, cannot be sufficiently achieved by the Member States and can therefore, by reason of its scale and effects, be better achieved at Community [now Union] level, the Community [now Union] may adopt measures, in accordance with the principle of subsidiarity as set out in Article 5 of the Treaty. In accordance with the principle of proportionality, as set out in that Article, this Directive does not go beyond what is necessary to achieve that objective'.

[87] Committee of Ministers of the CoE, 'Twenty Guidelines on Forced Return' adopted on 4 May 2005.

[88] (2008) 47 EHRR, paras 72 and 74.

[89] Case C-61/11 PPU *Hassen El Dridi* (n 83), para 43.

[90] ibid, para 43.

Moreover, the Court suggested that under the Returns Directive[91] and its case law, proportionality means that the measure of detention must pass the 'necessity test' with due regard to the means used and objectives pursued.[92]

This seems to suggest that 'protection under the EU law is higher than under Article 5 of the Convention',[93] and thus in line with the Charter.[94]

D. Qualification Directive, Procedure Directive and Article 13 ECHR: Revocation of the Refugees' Status

In dealing with applicants' revocation of refugee status by Germany for Iraq's changing conditions in August 2006,[95] the CJEU in the *Abdulla* case[96] was called upon to interpret Article 11(1)(e) of the Qualification Directive.[97] It stated that the national court should evaluate the extent of the risk of persecution.

The assessment should be carried out:

> [W]ith vigilance and care, since what are at issue are issues relating to the integrity of the person and to individual liberties, issues which relate to the fundamental values of the Union.[98]

However, the CJEU did not introduce an examination test with concrete criteria and standards, but rather offered a very loose guideline, ie assessment of the risk must in all cases be carried out with 'vigilance and care'.[99]

By contrast, in terms of risk examination, when the *Abdulla* case was pending before the CJEU, the ECtHR had already developed concrete standards offered to the national authority. This includes the need to apply an independent and rigorous scrutiny for any claim, for example, where there exist substantial grounds for fearing a real risk of being treated in a manner contrary to Article 3 ECHR (or

[91] Directive 2008/115 (n 86).

[92] Case C-61/11 PPU *Hassen El Dridi* (n 83), para 57, and Art 15 of the Returns Directive.

[93] Zalar, 'Comments on the Court of Justice of the EU's Developing Case Law on Asylum' (n 64) at 379.

[94] See Art 52(3) of the Charter.

[95] For an understanding of the changes in Iraq, see the Report to Congress, 'Measuring Stability and Security in Iraq', November 2006, in accordance with the Department of Defense Appropriations Act 2007 (Section 9010, Public Law 109-289). As stated at p 1 of the Report: 'The period covered in this report (August 12, 2006 to November 10, 2006) saw incremental progress in the Government of Iraq's willingness and ability to take over responsibility, to build institutions, and to deliver essential services'. Available at http://www.defense.gov/pubs/pdfs/9010quarterly-report-20061216.pdf.

[96] Joint cases C-175/08 (*Aydin Salahadin Abdulla*), C-176/08 (*Kamil Hasan*), C-178/08 *(Ahmed Adem, Hamrin Mosa Rashi)* and C-179/08 *(Dler Jamal) v Bundesrepublik Deutschland* [2010] ECR I-01493; see para 36 for reference to the changing conditions as mentioned by the appeals court.

[97] Directive 2004/83 (n 8).

[98] Joint cases C-175/08 (n 96) at para 90.

[99] ibid.

Article 2) in the event of an applicant's expulsion.[100] It also refers to providing an 'effective remedy before a national authority' under ex Article 13 ECHR.[101]

However, in the later *Diouf* judgment,[102] the CJEU introduced more rigorous standards in dealing with the interpretation of Article 39 Procedures Directive.[103] Mr Samba Diouf, a Mauritanian national was rejected, under an accelerated procedure, an application for refugee status. Reflecting on the objective of the Procedures Directive, which is to establish a common system of safeguards to ensure that the Geneva Convention and the fundamental rights are observed, the Court stressed that EU law regulates only minimum standards—leaving procedural autonomy and a margin of assessment in the implementation of the Procedures Directive at the national level.[104]

Thus, it stated that:

> [T]he organisation of the processing of applications for asylum is … left to the **discretion of Member States**, which may, in accordance with their national needs, prioritise or accelerate the processing of any application, taking into account the standards provided for by the directive … to an **adequate and complete examination.**[105]

It then stressed that:

> [T]he right to an effective remedy is a fundamental principle of EU law. In order for that right to be exercised effectively, the **national court** must be able to **review the merits of the reasons** which led the competent administrative authority to hold the application for international protection to be unfounded or made in bad faith, there being no irrebuttable presumption as to the legality of those reasons.[106]

The Court continued that:

> It is also within the framework of that remedy that the national court hearing the case must establish whether **the decision to examine** an application for asylum under an accelerated procedure **was taken in compliance with the procedures** and basic guarantees laid down in Chapter II of Directive 2005/85, as provided for in Article 23(4) of the directive.[107]

[100] Zalar, 'Comments on the Court of Justice of the EU's Developing Case Law on Asylum' (n 64) at 379. See also case law, at 381.

[101] See the following cases: *Gebremedhin v France* App no 25389/05 (ECtHR, 26 April 2007) (suspensive effect of domestic remedy for asylum claims in transit zone); *Hirsi Jamaa and Others v Italy* [GC] App no 27765/09 (ECtHR, 23 February 2012), paras 197–207 (absence of suspensive effect of domestic remedies against military personnel operating a 'push back at sea'); *Abdolkhani and Karimnia v Turkey* App no 30471/08 (ECtHR, 22 September 2009) (right to an effective remedy: domestic remedy needs to deal with the substance of the claim), *IM v France* App no 9152/09 (ECtHR, 2 February 2012), paras 136-1 (procedural safeguards for accelerated asylum procedures); *CG and Others v Bulgaria* App no 1365/07 (ECtHR, 24 April 2008) (lack of procedural safeguards in deportation proceedings).

[102] Case C-69/10 *Brahim Samba Diouf v Ministre du Travail, de l'Emploi et de l'Immigration* [2011] ECR I-07151.

[103] Council Directive 2005/85/EC of 1 December 2005 on minimum standards on procedures in member states for granting and withdrawing refugee status [2005] OJ L326/13.

[104] Case C-69/10 *Brahim Samba Diouf* (n 102), para 29. For a commentary on this case and its application, see Weiss Op cit. footnote no (n 23).

[105] ibid, para 30. See also para 44 referring to the AG Opinion points 53 and 54.

[106] ibid, para 61.

[107] ibid.

Although in the later cases of *Y and Z*[108] the CJEU returned to the loose guideline on 'vigilance and care',[109] it can be concluded that the standards and rules on the rigorous examination test and effective legal remedy under both Courts' case law are of a comparable standard.[110]

V. CONCLUDING REMARKS

Although human rights protection is intended to shape (even more than before) the migration dimension at European and national levels, liberal states strongly control unwanted migration by imposing restrictive laws and policies often limiting individual rights.

Thus, any incongruent and incoherent message coming from the European judiciary could potentially have a strong impact on the national legal system. This is why there is a need to have a solid 'dialogue' between the two European Courts, which represents a very powerful instrument for convergence in Europe.

This chapter has shown how this 'dialogue' works in the specific field of migration and human rights and has reported the views of the judiciary on the 'convergence' element and on the actual development at the intersection between these two areas of law.

As there are two different European systems to abide with, the minimum standard to be achieved in Europe is the protection guaranteed by the Convention, and EU law will enhance it. Thus, when necessary, the Convention being a 'living document' will be interpreted in accordance with EU law raising the human rights benchmark and strengthening their protection in Europe. This was also confirmed by the judges interviewed in the project, as the following quote shows:

> The ECHR can be seen as a part of general principles of the EU law, as a source of interpretation, as an international treaty as a minimum standard. There is, then, the question of case developing under the Charter and in how much of its case law the EU Courts will refer to the ECHR, not only when they say that the Charter is not applicable in the area of Member States, but also as a minimum standard for this relationship.[111]

[108] Joined Cases C-71/11 and C-99/11 *Bundesrepublik Deutschland v Y and Z*, 5 September 2012, para 48.

[109] See n 105.

[110] *Bosphorus Airways v Ireland* (n 75). In Joined Cases C-411/10 *NS* and *ME* (n 69), the CJEU implicitly reaffirms the Opinion of AG Trstenjak that the minimum content of the right to an effective remedy includes the requirements of effectiveness. According to that principle the realisation of the rights conferred by EU law 'may not be rendered practically impossible or excessively difficult' (Joined Cases C-411/10 *NS* and *ME* (n 69), Opinion of AG Trstenjak, paras 160–61). However, according to the Opinion of AG Villalón in Case C-69/10 *Brahim Samba Diouf* (n 102), 'the recourse to the courts should be effective, both in the sense that it must be legally capable of securing reparation, where appropriate, for the loss complained of, and in the sense that it must be a practical remedy, that is to say, that its pursuit must not be subject to conditions that make it impossible or extremely difficult to exercise' (Case C-69/10 *Brahim Samba Diouf* (n 102), Opinion of AG Cruz Villalón, para 43).

[111] Interview VI (ECtHR, Strasbourg, 20 June 2012).

However, questions still remain open. First, it still remains to be seen how this broader interpretation of the Convention, in line with EU law, will play out in countries that are not part of the EU. The extent to which an extensive interpretation of Convention rights, such as, for example, in the case of equivalent protection given by Article 11(c) of the Qualification Directive and Article 3 ECHR, can be applied to countries which are not part of the EU and how, in such an instance, the margin of appreciation would work. Second, interviewees were puzzled by questions in relation to the margin of appreciation and its application to the EU as a whole, following its accession to the Convention if and when it occurs.

A clear message coming from the project is that judges tend to prefer a case-by-case approach as they are trained to decide cases, as the following quote clearly demonstrates:

> Judges have very specific personalities ... they are trained to decide cases ... I think it is good exchanging ideas, but not necessarily in a very formalistic way.[112]

Thus, it seems clear that not many judges, at the time of the interviews, had clearly thought about the new architecture after accession. Most of them were not concerned with the possibility of reaching conflicting decisions, echoing the Convention as a source offering a minimum standard of protection.

Moreover, it remains necessary to examine more closely the impact that the 'dialogue' of the two Courts has on national and European policies. It is likely that national judges will share the author's argument that a coherent approach is necessary to guarantee some consistency in the protection of human rights in Europe and that the European judiciary would be a source of inspiration for the national one. It is still questionable whether to achieve social cohesion and equality in Europe the conceptual difference between EU citizens and legally residing TCNs will be overcome through legislative measures.

What has become crystal clear is that a great deal hinges on the 'dialogue' between the two Courts being consistent, as a CJEU judge noted upon interview:

> ... it is extremely important to find a mechanism of co-operation between the Courts, which can resolve the open conflicts between the two jurisprudences. If not, it might be quite dangerous for the coherence of the EU legal system.[113]

But as things move forward, how is harmonisation to be realised, if not guaranteed? It is possible to make two final remarks in relation to this. First, and the simplest answer, is for the EU to accede formally to the ECHR; this has, of course, been made possible by the Treaty of Lisbon but unfortunately the Accession Treaty in its current form has been declared by the CJEU as incompatible with EU law. Second, is the answer that also lies with the EU and the CoE whom, in an attempt to strengthen human rights protection within Europe, must learn how to interact

[112] Interview II (ECtHR, Strasbourg, 19 June 2012).
[113] Interview 17 (CJEU, Luxembourg, 16 December 2010).

completely, not just co-exist. This means that the two entities should inaugurate a new era where the citizenship's philosophy would reverse the relationship between the refugee (TCN) and the national, proposing an 'inclusive' rather than 'exclusive' caveat for combating social exclusion and achieving integration.[114] Thus, the human rights dimension cannot be ignored and should be the *trait d'union* between the two regimes in Europe in any migration law case.

[114] Case C-34/0 *Ruiz Zambrano v Office national de l'emploi (ONEm)* [2011] ECR I-1177, Opinion of AG Sharpston.

8

Who has the Right to have Rights?

The Judgments of the CJEU and the ECtHR as Building Blocks for a European 'ius commune' in Asylum Law

SAMANTHA VELLUTI

I. INTRODUCTION

IN *THE ORIGINS of Totalitarianism*[1] Arendt provides an influential examination of the plight of stateless people, invoking the 'right to have rights' as the one fundamental human right. Her central argument is that 'statelessness' corresponds not only to a situation of 'rightlessness' but also to a life devoid of public appearance and legal personhood making it impossible for those excluded from politics to claim the right to have rights, namely a status of *homo sacer*.[2] In the European Union (EU), the increased number of migrants, displaced people and asylum seekers have refocused public discourse on the Arendtian question of 'who has the right to have rights'. In particular, to what extent do asylum seekers effectively have standing to evoke the set of rights provided under the European Convention on Human Rights (ECHR) and the EU Charter of Fundamental Rights (EUCFR)?

This chapter draws on Rancière's[3] critique of Arendt's vision of human rights according to which the subject of human rights emerges through a process of political action and speech in order to verify the existence of and exercise those rights 'that are inscribed within the self-understanding of the political community'.[4] More specifically, for Rancière it is precisely through this process that

[1] H Arendt, *The Origins of Totalitarianism* (Cleveland, World Pub Co, 1958).

[2] In Latin 'the sacred man' or 'the accursed man' under ancient Roman law referred to a person who was banned from society and deprived of all rights and all functions in civil religion. For a study of *homo sacer* in contemporary times, see G Agamben, *Homo Sacer: Sovereign Power and Bare Life* (Turin, Einaudi, 1995).

[3] J Rancière, 'Who is the Subject of the Rights of Man?' (2004) 103 *South Atlantic Quarterly* 297–310.

[4] A Schaap, 'Enacting the Right to Have Rights: Jacques Rancière's Critique of Hannah Arendt' (2011) 10 *European Journal of Political Theory* 22, 34.

political subjects demonstrate the reality of both their 'equality' as humans within the order of nature and their 'inequality' within the social order. On this account, asylum seekers can demonstrate, on the one hand, that they do not enjoy the rights that they are supposed to have according to various international human rights treaties: by making public their political exclusion asylum seekers draw attention to their plight and the ways in which they are denied the same universal human rights from which states claim to derive their legitimacy. On the other hand, by raising awareness of their situation they act as political subjects and demonstrate, therefore, that they have legal entitlements despite the fact that they cannot enjoy them. In so doing, they demonstrate their 'equality' as humans despite being excluded from politics and thus being deprived of legal personhood.

Against this background, the question addressed by this chapter is the extent to which the EU context provides the required process of political and legal[5] action to effectively enable asylum seekers to demonstrate the reality of both their 'equality' as humans within the order of nature and their 'inequality' within the social order. In particular, the chapter is set to examine the way the European Courts are attempting to reduce the present gap between the protection of fundamental rights and legal remedies, in relation to the possibility of individuals and courts to rebut the 'presumption' of mutual trust between Member States in the context of the Common European Asylum System (CEAS). Recent judgments on asylum seem to suggest that—despite different jurisdictions, differing methodologies in interpretation and degree in decisional autonomy and, not least, a different relationship with national courts—both the Court of Justice of the EU (CJEU) and the European Court of Human Rights (ECtHR) are equally concerned with ensuring better protection of asylum seekers' fundamental rights as an attempt to tackle the legislative deadlock in the EU.[6]

The focus of analysis is the Dublin system, which is one of the most important components of CEAS and where mutual trust has been given a key role in the way that individual asylum applications within the EU are allocated to and decided by Member States. As the chapter will go on to show, CEAS is under construction and there are still significant differences between national authorities' practices. Hence, in a juridical landscape where the approximation of national laws is still far from being achieved, the application of mutual trust—which presupposes that all Member States are 'safe countries'—threatens and in many instances reduces the effective protection of asylum seekers' fundamental rights. Arguably, mutual trust has become one of the fallacies of the Dublin system. Unsurprisingly, in a

[5] Author's addition.

[6] On the relationship between the two European Courts and their role in relation to the protection of fundamental rights, see S Morano-Foadi, 'Migration, Integration and Equality: The European Approach', ch 7 in this volume; for detailed commentary on the relationship between the European Courts also in light of EU accession to the ECHR, see S Morano-Foadi and S Andreadakis, Report on the Protection of Fundamental Rights in Europe—A Reflection on the Relationship between the Court of Justice of the European Union and the European Court of Human Rights post Lisbon, July 2014, available at http://www.coe.int/en/web/dlapil/news-dlapil.

series of landmark rulings both European Courts made clear that 'non-rebuttable trust' is not allowed when this jeopardises the protection of an asylum seeker's fundamental rights.

The chapter proceeds as follows: the first section examines the Dublin Regulation including its recast and the application of the principle of mutual trust; the second section provides a comparative analysis of key cases of the ECtHR and the CJEU considering also their intrinsic differences; the final section explores the relationship between the two European Courts and reflects on whether the body of asylum rulings of both courts is paving the way towards a 'ius commune' in asylum law.

II. THE DUBLIN REGULATION AND MUTUAL TRUST

A. The Dublin II Regulation

The Dublin system is a key component of CEAS and was designed to prevent two undesirable phenomena namely that of 'refugees in orbit', ie refugees circulating between Member States or within one Member State neither being allowed to stay within its territory, nor being able to leave it, and 'asylum shopping', ie protection-seekers lodging applications in several Member States or choosing the one having the most lenient policy or practice in this respect. Hence, the main objective of the Dublin system was to ensure an effective process of examining asylum applications in the EU and, more generally, reduce asylum seekers' incentive to move and encourage them to remain in the first Member State in which they could seek protection.

The Dublin II Regulation,[7] replacing the Dublin Convention,[8] has been widely criticised for failing to adequately protect asylum seekers' fundamental rights.[9] The responsibility determination rules under the Dublin II Regulation linked responsibility for asylum applications to border management by compelling the return of individuals to third countries for the sole reason of having transited through those countries. In so doing, they have ended up overburdening less well-equipped asylum systems as well as creating pressure for irregular or illegal migration within the EU. In particular, the Dublin II Regulation provided that after

[7] Council Regulation (EC) No 343/2003 of 18 February 2003 establishing the criteria and mechanisms for determining the Member State responsible for examining an asylum application lodged in one of the Member States by a third-country national (Dublin II Regulation) [2003] OJ L50/1.

[8] Convention Determining the State Responsible for Examining Applications for Asylum lodged in one of the Member States of the European Communities (Dublin Convention), 15 June 1990, [1997] OJ C254/1.

[9] F Maiani and V Vevstad, 'Chapter 1: Distribution of Applicants for International Protection and Protected Persons' in European Parliament, Directorate-General for Internal Policies, Policy Department C, Citizens' Rights and Constitutional Affairs, 'Setting up a Common European Asylum System. Report on the Application of Existing Instruments and Proposals for the New System', PE 425.622, Brussels 2010.

the consideration of any family links or whether a prior visa or residence permit exists, if it could be established that an asylum seeker had irregularly entered the border of a Member State by land, sea, or air having come from a third country, the Member State thus entered would be responsible for examining the request for asylum.[10]

One of the main shortcomings of the Dublin system is that it is based on the idea that asylum seekers can rely on equal access to protection and justice in each Member State.[11] In this context, the principle of mutual trust remains a fundamental foundational principle underlying the operation of the Dublin system and a key building block of CEAS. In its most basic meaning, this principle implies that Member States establish mutual confidence in relation to the quality and lawfulness of each other's laws.[12] According to Battjes, in the Dublin system mutual trust is based on 'the assumption that each Member State will treat asylum-seekers and examine their claims in accordance with the relevant rules of national, European and International Law'.[13] It finds its legal expression in the so-called 'presumption of equivalent protection' or more generally a 'presumption of safety' among those Member States, which joined the Dublin system.[14]

Under the Dublin rules, responsibility entails the obligation to take charge of (or to take back) the (failed) asylum seeker who turns up in a non-responsible state and to examine the claim for asylum. Mutual trust also concerns the examination of the request for asylum by the other Member State, ie the procedure for sorting out whether or not the third-country national (TCN) fulfils the requirements for international protection[15] and it extends to the treatment of the asylum seeker during this examination.[16] The justification for mutual trust is enshrined

[10] Art 10(1) of the Dublin II Regulation, now Art 13(1) Dublin III Regulation.

[11] For a detailed examination of the Dublin II Regulation's compliance with international refugee law, see UN High Commissioner for Refugees (UNHCR), The Dublin II Regulation: a UNHCR Discussion Paper, Geneva, UNHCR, April 2006, available at http://www.unhcr.org/refworld/docid/4445fe344.html; UNHCR, 'Comments on the European Commission's Proposal for a recast of the Regulation of the European Parliament and of the Council establishing the criteria and mechanisms for determining the Member State responsible for examining an application for international protection lodged in one of the Member States by a third country national or a stateless person (Dublin II) (Com(2008) 820, 3 December 2008) and the European Commission's Proposal for a recast of the Regulation of the European Parliament and of the Council concerning the establishment of 'Eurodac' for a comparison of fingerprints for the effective application of [the Dublin II Regulation] (COM(2008) 825, 3 December 2008)', 1–2 March 2009, available at http://www.unhcr.org/cgi-bin/texis/vtx/search?page search&query=COM%/ 2 82 0 0 8% 29+825%2C+3+December+2008&x=0&y=0.

[12] E Brouwer, 'Mutual Trust and the Dublin Regulation: Protection of Fundamental Rights in the EU and the Burden of Proof' (2013) 9 *Utrecht Law Review* 135, 138.

[13] H Battjes, 'Mutual Trust in Asylum Matters: The Dublin System' in Meijers Committee, (Standing Committee of Experts on International Immigration, Refugee and Criminal Law), *The Principle of Mutual Trust in European Asylum, Migration and Criminal Law* (Utrecht, FORUM, Institute for Multicultural Affairs, December 2011) 8–18, 9.

[14] F Maiani and C Hruschka, 'Le partage des responsabilités dans l'espace Dublin, entre confiance mutuelle—et sécurité des demandeurs d'asile' (2011) 2 *Revue suisse pour la pratique et le droit d'asile* (ASYL) 12, 12.

[15] Battjes, 'Mutual Trust in Asylum Matters' (n 13) 9–10.

[16] ibid, 10.

in the Preamble to the Dublin Regulation where it is stated inter alia that 'Member States, all respecting the principle of *non-refoulement*, are considered as safe countries for third-country nationals'.[17] The mechanism of mutual recognition as applied in the field of asylum implies a practice of non-interference with decisions already made on applications for asylum within the EU.[18] This can be seen also in the context of the Asylum Procedures Directive where Member States may declare an application for international protection inadmissible if a decision on the same application has already been made in another Member State.[19]

An exception to mutual trust is represented by the so-called 'discretionary clauses'[20] according to which Member States may freely decide to examine an application, although they are not legally bound to do so. Moreover, as examined further below, both European Courts have made it clear that Member States will have to put it aside when this is necessary to guarantee non-*refoulement*. Nevertheless, mutual trust—and, in particular, mutual recognition of decisions—is a means to ensure the preservation of states' exercise of sovereign powers. In addition, within CEAS there are significant differences between Member States as to the level and standard of protection. Consequently, great disparities and inequality affecting asylum seekers as well as certain Member States persist.[21]

The Dublin system has failed to produce the effects of mutual recognition that it was hoped for. In particular, the application of the Dublin system has led to an unequal distribution of displaced persons across Europe and to an increased number of asylum seekers being returned to Member States on the borders of the enlarged Union, which have been unable to deal with flows of asylum seekers,[22] as well as a resort to onward and illegal transit.[23] Under the Dublin system, entry controls have been linked to the allocation of responsibility creating unequal burdens depending on a country's geographical position.[24] This is contrary to the principle of solidarity and fair sharing of responsibility as per Article 80 Treaty on the Functioning of the European Union (TFEU). In addition, this has led some Member States such as Greece to adopt restrictive asylum measures thus denying

[17] Recital 3 of the Dublin III Regulation.

[18] I Staffans, 'Convergence and Mutual Recognition in European Asylum Law' in J Klabbers and M Sellers (eds), *The Internationalisation of Law and Legal Education* (Heidelberg, Springer, 2008) 149, 161.

[19] Art 33(2)(a) and (d) of the Asylum Procedures Directive (Directive 2013/32/EU of the European Parliament and of the Council [2013] OJ L180/60).

[20] Arts 3(2) (the 'sovereignty clause') and 15 (the 'humanitarian clause') Dublin II Regulation (now Art 17 Dublin III Regulation).

[21] U Brandl, 'Distribution of Asylum-Seekers in Europe? Dublin II Regulation Determining the Responsibility for Examining an Asylum Application' in C Dias Urbano de Souza and P De Bruycker (eds), *The Emergence of a European Asylum Policy* (Brussels, Bruylant, 2003) 33–69.

[22] M Symes, 'Challenging "Dublin" Removals—Human Rights and European Law Arguments' (2010) 24 *Journal of Immigration Asylum and Nationality Law* 29, 36.

[23] S Kneebone, C McDowell and G Morrell, 'A Mediterranean Solution? Chances of Success' (2006) 18 *International Journal of Refugee Law* 492, 506.

[24] S Da Lomba, *The Right to Seek Refugee Status in the European Union* (Antwerpen, Intersentia, 2004), 137; see also European Parliament, Report on the Evaluation of the Dublin system, Committee on Civil Liberties, Justice and Home Affairs 2 July 2008, A6-0287/2008, 12.

access to a fair and effective asylum procedure.[25] The Dublin II Regulation also incentivised countries to use detention as a means to securing transfers. Moreover, there are major differences between Member States as to the level of reception conditions.[26]

Overall, the operation of the Dublin II Regulation has been inefficient, expensive and time-consuming in spite of efficiency being one of its main objectives[27] and it has failed to achieve its goal of reducing the number of multiple applications.[28] In particular, the findings of the European Council on Refugees and Exiles (ECRE) show that the implementation of the Dublin Regulation has added a lengthy and cumbersome procedure to the beginning of the asylum process.[29] This lengthy process unnecessarily prolongs the state of uncertainty in which asylum seekers find themselves as well as delaying refugees' integration in the host country.[30]

B. The Dublin Regulation Recast

One of the most visible changes introduced by the Dublin Regulation Recast,[31] coined 'Dublin III' is that, in line with the objectives of CEAS, it places greater emphasis on the humanitarian dimension of the Dublin system. The amendments expand the definition of 'family members' as the definition no longer encompasses only family links that already existed in the country of origin.[32] Family unification is also included in the hierarchy of responsibility criteria. Specifically, Member States are required to reunite unaccompanied minors or dependant relatives with other relatives present in Member States.[33] Moreover, the Regulation introduces general safeguards for children and specifies that the best interests of the child are a primary consideration in the transfer of an individual.[34]

[25] PN Papadimitriou and IF Papageorgiou, 'The New "Dubliners": Implementation of European Council Regulation 343/2003 (Dublin-II) by the Greek Authorities' (2005) 18 *Journal of Refugee Studies* 299; see also UNHCR, 'The Return to Greece of Asylum-Seekers with "Interrupted" Claims' (Geneva, UNHCR, July 2007), available at http://www.unhcr.org/refworld/pdfid/46b889b32.pdf.

[26] Amnesty International, 'The Dublin II Trap', March 2010, available at http://www.amnesty.org/en/library/info/EUR25/001/2010/en, 35–41.

[27] ECRE, 'Sharing Responsibility for Refugee Protection in Europe: Dublin Reconsidered', 15 March 2008, available at http://www.ecre.org/component/content/article/57-policy-papers/1 34-sharing-responsibility-for-refugee-protection-in-europe-dublin-reconsidered.html, at 10.

[28] ibid, at 11.

[29] ibid.

[30] ibid, at 26.

[31] Regulation (EU) No 604/2013 of the European Parliament and of the Council of 26 June 2013 establishing the criteria and mechanisms for determining the Member State responsible for examining an application for international protection lodged in one of the Member States by a third-country national or a stateless person (recast) [2013] OJ L180/31.

[32] Recitals 17 and 18, Arts 4(1)(c), 7(3), 9, 31(2)(b) and 34(2)(a) Dublin III Regulation.

[33] Arts 6(4) and 8 Dublin III Regulation.

[34] Recitals 13 where there is explicit reference to the 1989 UN Convention on the Rights of the Child, 16 and 24, Art 6 Dublin III Regulation; see also Case C-648/11 *MA, BT, DA v Secretary of State for the Home Department*, Judgment of 6 June 2013 (nyr).

However, it still fails to sufficiently address the underlying weaknesses of the Dublin system.[35] As mentioned earlier, the main limitations of the Dublin Regulation are associated with the way it has been conceptualised: mainly as an administrative tool for establishing Member States' responsibility for examining asylum claims rather than as a burden-sharing instrument for protecting refugees in the EU and again Dublin III reproduces this intrinsic logic. This problem combined with the (untouched) responsibility determination rules for examining an asylum application may hinder the completion of CEAS, which is based on solidarity and integration. The maintenance of the same responsibility determination rules in the Dublin III Regulation and the lack of harmonisation in relation to protection standards—as the European Parliament has observed—may mean that 'the Dublin system [even in its revised form][36] will continue to be unfair both to asylum-seekers and to certain Member States'.[37] In terms of ensuring access to a substantive and fair asylum procedure, this state of affairs is of great concern especially when considering that the processing of applications may take several months leaving asylum seekers waiting in uncertainty for a rather long period of time. An important change, which constitutes a significant improvement in comparison with its predecessor is amended Article 3(2) subparagraph 2 containing the so-called 'sovereignty clause'. The latter has been amended so as to explicitly envisage the possibility of a transfer being stopped to the Member State primarily designated as responsible where there are substantial grounds for believing that there are systemic flaws in the asylum procedure and in the reception conditions for applicants in that Member State, resulting in a risk of inhuman or degrading treatment within the meaning of Article 4 EUCFR. The revised Regulation, therefore, seems to acknowledge the unequal standards of national asylum systems and the obligation to prevent systematic flaws in the asylum procedure, combined with the explicit reference to the EUCFR, could force Member States to make more use of this clause in the future.[38]

Moving to the key changes introduced by the Dublin III Regulation, one of the most significant amendments is the extension of the scope of the Regulation to applicants for all forms of international protection.[39] Moreover, the Regulation also applies to transit zones.[40] With regard to the guarantee of legal safeguards for persons falling within the scope of the Dublin system, there is reference

[35] ECRE, 'Comments on the European Council on Refugees and Exiles on the European Commission Proposal to Recast the Dublin Regulation' (Brussels, ECRE, April 2009), available at http://www.ecre.org/files/ECRE_Response_to_Recast_Dublin_Regulation_2009.pdf.

[36] Author's addition.

[37] European Parliament, Evaluation of the Dublin system (Own Initiative Report), INI(2008) 2262, 2 July 2008, para 2.

[38] The revised provision in Art 3(2) subpara 2 illustrates the influence that both European Courts have exerted on the EU legislature (see cases *MSS* for the ECtHR and *NS* and *ME* for the CJEU, examined further below in Section III).

[39] Arts 1 and 2(b) and (c) Dublin III Regulation.

[40] Art 3(1) Dublin III Regulation.

throughout the Recast Regulation to the right to an effective remedy[41] and in this context to free legal assistance and representation. According to Article 27 Dublin III Regulation applicants have the right to judicial review of a transfer decision. In particular, the new provisions included in paragraphs 3 and 4 have added some clarity in relation to the right of appeal or review of a transfer decision, particularly in relation to the issue of whether lodging an appeal has an automatic suspensive effect, which was the subject of much discussion under the Regulation.[42] Paragraphs 3 and 4 provide for national law concerning appeals or reviews to envisage one of the following four scenarios, namely: the right for the applicant to remain in the Member State concerned pending the outcome of the decision; automatic suspension of the transfer for a certain reasonable period of time and when such suspension lapses a judicial decision is to follow on whether to grant suspensive effect to an appeal or review; a request within a reasonable period of time to a court or tribunal to suspend the implementation of the transfer decision pending the outcome of his/her appeal or review; and that the competent authorities may decide, acting *ex officio*, to suspend the implementation of the transfer decision pending the outcome of the appeal or review. While Article 27 of the Dublin III Regulation represents a positive step forward from the perspective of the applicant's right to an effective remedy it still leaves Member States with considerable discretion. As a consequence, the procedural guarantees for asylum seekers against decisions of the Member States remain rather weak in practice. Differences between Member States have not been removed and the main objective of having a harmonised Dublin system remains far from being achieved.

As to the suspension of transfers, the Commission's Recast proposal contained a procedure which would have allowed the Commission—on its own initiative or on the initiative of another Member State—to suspend Dublin transfers to a Member State when 'circumstances prevailing in the Member State concerned may lead to a level of protection for applicants for international protection which is not in conformity with Community legislation, in particular with the Reception Conditions Directive[43] and the Asylum Procedures Directive'.[44] According to the proposal, the Commission would have based a decision to suspend transfers on 'an examination of all the relevant circumstances prevailing in the Member State', state the reasons for the decision, and specify among other things 'any particular conditions attached to such suspension'. The proposed Article 31 stated that the Commission would have to determine whether the grounds for the suspension persisted after a six-month period.[45] The Commission proposal on the

[41] Recital 19 (where there is also reference to Art 47 EUCFR), Arts 18(2) and 27 Dublin III Regulation.

[42] Case C-19/08 *Migrationsverket v Edgar Petrosian and Others* [2009] ECR I-495, where the CJEU was asked by the referring court to clarify the meaning of Art 20(1)(d) and (2) of the Dublin II Regulation.

[43] Directive 2013/33/EU of the European Parliament and of the Council of 26 June 2013 [2013] OJ L180/96.

[44] Art 31(2)–(3) of the Recast Proposal (COM (2008) 820, 3 December 2008).

[45] Art 31(8) of the Recast Proposal.

above 'suspension mechanism', as amended by the European Parliament,[46] was met with opposition from the Council.[47] A so-called 'early warning system' has replaced the Commission's proposed suspension mechanism, which envisages an important role for the European Asylum Support Office (EASO) and it enables the Commission to make recommendations to a Member State with problems in its asylum system, inviting it to draw up a 'preventive action plan'.[48] Overall, the said 'early warning mechanism' is a more nuanced measure than the one proposed by the Commission, which does not provide for any specific time frame and is open to flexibility and discretion. Moreover, the involvement of so many EU institutions and the different stages envisaged also make it a rather hefty and lengthy process. Hence, once again not only the fundamental rights of a protection seeker are in jeopardy but the objective of securing efficiency is also seriously undermined. The Dublin III Regulation also introduces some safeguards against the arbitrary or excessive use of detention in the context of the transfer procedure to the responsible Member State[49] as asylum seekers are frequently detained in the context of these procedures. However, Member States still retain quite a lot of discretion as to how to interpret and apply the new rules. Hence, despite these changes the risk of arbitrary detention remains.

The foregoing seems to suggest that the Dublin III Regulation embraces a more human rights-based approach compared with its predecessor. However, the security paradigm underlying the overall Dublin system remains strong and the changes introduced fail to guarantee sufficient safeguards against non-*refoulement*. As Costello observes 'CEAS enshrines more mutual recognition of negative than positive decisions. The recognition of an asylum-seeker as a refugee in one Member State does not create EU obligations for the others. [...] Member States use mutual recognition as a selective tool, to limit responsibility, rather than to share it'.[50] In particular, the criteria for determining the Member State responsible for examining asylum applications rather than expressing the principle of solidarity as per Article 80 TFEU have in fact resulted in 'burden shifting' from the northern to the southern or eastern Member States located at the borders of the Union's territory. As the 2014 events in the southern Italian island of Lampedusa

[46] European Parliament, Position adopted at first reading on 7 May 2009 with a view to the adoption of Regulation (EC) No ... /2009 of the European Parliament and of the Council establishing the criteria and mechanisms for determining the Member State responsible for examining an application for international protection lodged in one of the Member States by a third-country national or a stateless person (recast) [2010] OJ C/212, E/371.

[47] Council of Ministers, Discussion Paper No 15561/10, 29 October 2010.

[48] Council of the European Union, Position of the Council at first reading with a view to the adoption of a Regulation of the European Parliament and of the Council establishing the criteria and mechanisms for determining the Member State responsible for examining an application for international protection lodged in one of the Member States by a third-country national or a stateless person (recast), Brussels 31 May 2013, Doc No 15605/2/12 REV 2, Art 33; see also Council of Ministers, Discussion Paper No 16782/11, 14 November 2011.

[49] Recital 20 and Art 28 Dublin III Regulation.

[50] C Costello, 'Courting Access to Asylum in Europe: Recent Supranational Jurisprudence Explored' (2012) 12 *Human Rights Law Review* 287, 335.

illustrate,[51] this is less of a legal issue than a political one with a financial dimension. CEAS is 'burdened by these issues, particularly those with a financial dimension, creating illusions regarding solidarity and burden sharing ideals'.[52]

III. THE ROLE OF THE EUROPEAN COURTS IN ENSURING ADEQUATE STANDARDS OF ASYLUM SEEKERS' HUMAN RIGHTS PROTECTION

A. The ECtHR, the Presumption of Equivalent Protection and EU Asylum Law

In cases concerning Contracting States' responsibility whilst implementing EU law the Strasbourg Court has developed the notion of presumption of 'equivalent protection', namely that under EU law fundamental rights are protected in a way, which could be considered 'equivalent' to that provided for by the Convention.[53] This concept was fully developed in the well-known case of *Bosphorus*[54] where the concept of 'equivalency' (of protection under EU law) was associated with that of 'comparable' (rather than identical level) of protection of human rights. Linked to the latter, it also went on to develop the other equally important notion of 'presumption of conventionality', namely, once it is demonstrated that an equivalent protection is provided within an international organisation, the presumption will be that a country has not departed from the requirements of the ECHR when it does no more than implement legal obligations flowing from its membership of the organisation.

As to EU asylum law, the Strasbourg Court has been called to decide on a number of cases concerning the Dublin system. In the case of *TI v the United Kingdom*,[55] concerning a Dublin transfer of a Sri Lankan asylum seeker by the UK to Germany, the ECtHR held that the transferring state could also be accountable vis-à-vis the protection of *non-refoulement* despite the notion of 'safe country' under the Dublin mechanism. This was the first decision where the Court referred to 'indirect' *refoulement* and it held that the fact that Germany was a party to the ECHR did not absolve the UK from the responsibility to ensure that by transferring the asylum seeker to Germany he would not be exposed to the risk of *refoulement*. The judgment, therefore, made clear that mutual trust based on the Dublin system cannot be absolute and that states are not only responsible for protecting asylum seekers against 'direct' *refoulement* but also against 'indirect' *refoulement*.

[51] G Orsini et al, 'Lampedusa: A Cruel and Corrupt System', *Discover Society*, 6 May 2014, available at http://www.discoversociety.org/2014/05/06/lampedusa-a-cruel-and-corrupt-system/.

[52] J Lenart, '"Fortress Europe": Compliance of the Dublin II Regulation with the European Convention for the Protection of Human Rights and Fundamental Freedoms' (2012) 28 *Merkourios Utrecht Journal of International and European Law* 4, 7.

[53] Eg *M & Co v Federal Republic of Germany* App no 13258/87 (ECtHR, 9 February 1990).

[54] *Bosphorus v Ireland* App no 45036/98 (ECtHR, 30 June 2005), at paras 155–57.

[55] App no 43844/98, ECHR 2000-III (ECtHR, 7 March 2000).

That said, the ECtHR found that there was no evidence to suggest that Germany would breach Article 3 ECHR and, specifically, that it would fail to protect the applicant from removal to Sri Lanka. Moreover, the ECtHR did not clarify when, exactly, mutual trust must be considered to be 'rebutted'. It held that German law provided sufficient safeguards for the applicant to prevent his expulsion to Sri Lanka in breach of Article 3 ECHR.

In *KRS*,[56] concerning an Iranian asylum seeker's application against expulsion by the UK to Greece under the Dublin Regulation, the Strasburg Court reiterated its earlier position with regard to a country's responsibility under Article 3 ECHR, when transferring an asylum seeker to another country. The Court reached the same conclusion as in *TI* and found no violation of Article 3 ECHR because of the lack of sufficient evidence suggesting that the asylum seeker, in being transferred, would face the risk of being exposed to ill-treatment. The ECtHR held that the EU asylum system protects fundamental rights, as regards both the substantive guarantees offered and the mechanisms controlling their observance.

However, this presumption was considered rebutted for the first time in the landmark *MSS* ruling concerning an Afghan asylum seeker who was returned by Belgium to Greece under the Dublin II Regulation.[57] The Strasbourg Court held that there should be a proper ad hoc assessment every time there is a serious doubt for the sending state that the Asylum Procedures and Reception Directives are not being implemented effectively in the destination state to the extent that there are 'major structural deficiencies' in the asylum procedure and reception conditions for asylum applicants, which result in inhuman or degrading treatment.[58] The Strasbourg Court gave considerable weight to a series of reports published since 2006 by the Council of Europe, the EU, the UN High Commissioner for Refugees (UNHCR) and non-governmental organisations (NGOs).[59] Moreover, the ECtHR not long before the delivery of its judgment in *MSS*, had found degrading detention conditions in three cases against Greece.[60]

The presumption upon which CEAS was based was no longer considered per se a sufficient basis for intra-EU transfers of asylum seekers and the ECtHR held that the practical implementation of protection standards by the Member State concerned must be considered. The protection of human rights in the EU—and

[56] *KRS v the United Kingdom* App no 32733/08 (ECtHR, 2 December 2008).

[57] *MSS v Belgium and Greece* App no 30696/09 (ECtHR, 21 January 2011). Space precludes an exhaustive review of this landmark ruling; for case comment and critical analysis, see G Clayton, 'Asylum-Seekers in Europe: *MSS v Belgium and Greece*' (2011) 11 *Human Rights Law Review* 758; Maiani and Hruschka, 'Le partage des responsabilités dans l'espace Dublin' (n 14); P Mallia, 'Case of *MSS v. Belgium and Greece*: A Catalyst in the Re-thinking of the Dublin II Regulation' (2011) 30 *Refugee Survey Quarterly* 107; V Moreno-Lax, 'Dismantling the Dublin System: *MSS v Belgium and Greece*' (2012) 14 *European Journal of Migration and Law* 1.

[58] *MSS* (ibid), at para 300.

[59] *MSS* (ibid), para 160.

[60] *SD v Greece* App no 53541/07 (ECtHR, 11 June 2009); *Tabesh v Greece* App no 8256/07 (ECtHR, 26 November 2009); *AA v Greece* App no 12186/08 (ECtHR, 22 July 2010).

chiefly the protection against indirect *refoulement*[61]—was ensured by the Court on the basis of a derogation clause as per Article 3(2) of the Dublin II Regulation.[62] Hence, it may be argued that following *MSS* the clause has been re-conceptualised from being a mere residual guarantee of Member States' sovereignty to a necessary guarantee for ensuring compliance with EU and international human rights law.[63]

In addition, the Strasbourg Court stressed the need for a 'comprehensive reconsideration of the existing European legal regime' and how such a needed on-going reform process of CEAS' instruments was aimed in particular, 'at substantially strengthening the protection of the fundamental rights of asylum-seekers implementing a temporary suspension of transfers under the Dublin Regulation to avoid asylum-seekers being sent back to Member States unable to offer them a sufficient level of protection of their fundamental rights'.[64] Significantly, EU asylum standards set out in the Asylum Procedures and Reception Directives have been used by the ECtHR in order to identify the lack of adequate protection *beyond* the traditional Conventional rights and, specifically, to extend the notion of inhuman and degrading treatment to 'living conditions' of asylum seekers, such as destitution and poverty,[65] the 'particularly serious' deprivation of material reception conditions (including accommodation, food and clothing, in kind or in the form of monetary allowances) sufficient to protect the asylum seekers. In *MSS*, failure by Greece to comply with the Reception Directive influenced the Court's reasoning and it was used as an aggravating factor.[66]

Hence, with *MSS* the ECtHR has made it clear that the rebuttal of the presumption of equivalence is necessary whenever it ensures the effective protection of asylum seekers' fundamental rights.

B. The CJEU and Asylum

The Luxembourg Court from being a court predominantly preoccupied with matters concerning the EU internal market and, more generally, the European integration process, has progressively and increasingly been considering cases of a more fundamental rights nature. In so doing it has attributed 'special significance'

[61] The *non-refoulement* obligation under Art 3 ECHR includes also 'indirect' *refoulement* which entails return to a country from where there is a risk of onward return to ill-treatment, see *TI v the United Kingdom* (n 55) 15; see also *Salah Sheekh v The Netherlands* App no 1948/04 (ECtHR, 11 January 2007), para 141; in *KRS v the United Kingdom* (n 56) 16; and in *Abdolkhani and Karimnia v Turkey* App no 30471/08 (ECtHR, 22 September 2009), at paras 88–89.

[62] Now Art 17(1) of the Dublin III Regulation.

[63] This is an observation made by Ippolito in F Ippolito and S Velluti, 'The Relationship Between the European Court of Justice and the European Court of Human Rights: The Case of Asylum' in K Dzehtsiarou, T Konstadinides, T Lock and N O'Meara (eds), *Human Rights Law in Europe: The Influence, Overlaps and Contradictions of the EU and ECHR* (London, Routledge, 2014) 156, 177.

[64] *MSS* (n 57) para 350.

[65] See ibid, para 250; see also *Budina v Russia* App no 45603/05 (ECtHR, 18 June 2009).

[66] G Clayton, 'Asylum-Seekers in Europe: *MSS v Belgium and Greece*' (2011) 11 *Human Rights Law Review* 758, 768.

to the ECHR in the EU legal order relying on Convention rights as setting minimum standards for developing EU fundamental rights.[67] With the legally binding status acquired by the EUCFR and EU accession to the ECHR on the agenda, following the entry into force of the Treaty of Lisbon (TL), the approach of the CJEU towards the European Convention and the ECtHR's jurisprudence is gradually changing.[68] To a certain extent, as explained further below, the CJEU clearly intends to interpret EU asylum legislation in a manner, which is consistent with the ECtHR asylum jurisprudence. On the other hand, the Luxembourg Court is also concerned with preserving the autonomy of its own jurisdiction and, more broadly, the EU legal order. The EUCFR is thus becoming a vehicle for expanding the scope of protection of 'EU' fundamental rights and the CJEU will not refrain itself from adopting a more 'progressive' approach in interpreting relevant provisions to ensure this end.

The *NS* and *ME* cases constitute the CJEU's 'response' to the *MSS* ruling. They concerned Afghan, Iranian and Algerian asylum seekers who challenged their return from the UK and Ireland to Greece under the Dublin Regulation.[69] The judgments make it clear that a Member State may potentially infringe Article 4 EUCFR if it transfers an asylum seeker to another Member State in certain circumstances. The decision is also important in clarifying the applicability of the EUCFR to the UK and Poland according to Protocol 30. In particular, it was held that Article 1(1) of Protocol 30 merely 'explains' Article 51 EUCFR and is not a provision, which amounts to an opt-out. However, as noted by Mellon neither the Grand Chamber nor the Advocate General considered in much detail the more contentious issue of the applicability of Title IV (on 'Solidarity') concerning social and economic rights, where Article 1(2) of Protocol 30 is likely to have more effect.[70]

[67] For further discussion, see S Morano-Foadi, 'Reflections on the Architecture of the EU after the Treaty of Lisbon: the European Judicial Approach to Fundamental Rights' in Special Issue edited by S Morano Foadi and Francesco Duina, 'The Institutionalisation of Regional Trade Agreements Worldwide: New Dynamics and Future Perspectives' (2011) 17 *European Law Journal* 595; see also W Weiß, 'The EU Human Rights Regime Post Lisbon: Turning the CJEU into a Human Rights Court?', ch 5 in this volume.

[68] Weiß argues that the TL challenges the substance and methodology of human rights protection in the EU, W Weiß, 'Human Rights in the EU: Rethinking the Role of the European Convention on Human Rights after Lisbon' (2011) 7 *European Constitutional Law Review* 64. However, the ruling of the CJEU regarding the EU's accession to the ECHR seems to alter and hinder this process; see Opinion 2/13 of the Court (Full Court), 18 December 2014, Opinion pursuant to Article 218(11) TFEU—Draft international agreement—Accession of the European Union to the European Convention for the Protection of Human Rights and Fundamental Freedoms—Compatibility of the draft agreement with the EU and FEU Treaties, not yet published, available at http://curia.europa.eu/juris/document/document.jsf?text=&docid=160882&pageIndex=0&doclang=en&mode=lst&dir=&occ=first&part=1&cid=40247.

[69] Joined Cases C-411/10 and C-493/10 *NS v Secretary of State for the Home Department* and *ME and Others v Refugee Applications Commissioner and Minister for Justice, Equality and Law Reform* (nyr); for case comment and critical analysis, see J Buckley, 'Case Comment on *NS v Secretary of State for the Home Department* (C-411/10)' (2012) 2 *European Human Rights Law Review* 205; C Costello, 'Dublin-case NS/ME: Finally, an End to Blind Trust Across the EU?' (2012) 2 *Asiel and Migrantenrecht* 83; G Mellon, 'The Charter of Fundamental Rights and the Dublin Convention: An Analysis of *N.S. v Secretary of State for the Home Department* (C-411/10)' (2012) 18 *European Public Law* 655.

[70] Mellon, 'The Charter of Fundamental Rights and the Dublin Convention' (ibid), at 661.

The Opinion of Advocate General Trstenjak examines to some extent the relationship between mutual trust and fundamental rights under the Dublin system.[71] In particular, the Advocate General took the view that if there is a serious risk that the fundamental rights under the EUCFR of the asylum seeker to be transferred may be breached in the Member State having primary responsibility, the other Member States may not transfer an asylum seeker to that Member State. Rather, the other Member States are, in principle, obliged to exercise the right to assume responsibility under Article 3(2) of the Dublin Regulation and must themselves examine the asylum application.

The Opinion was instead silent in relation to the question of whether the protection afforded by the rights set out in Articles 1, 18 and 47 EUCFR was wider than that afforded by Article 3 ECHR. The Advocate General merely referred to Article 52(3) EUCFR and stated that the protection guaranteed by the Charter in the areas in which its provisions overlap with those of the ECHR must be no less than the protection granted by the ECHR[72] and that 'particular significance and high importance' had to be attached to the ECtHR case law in connection with the interpretation of the relevant provisions of the EUCFR by the CJEU.[73] This silence can be explained by the fact that the question had lost salience since the *MSS* ruling where it was held that transfers to Greece were in breach of Article 3 ECHR.[74]

Similarly, the Court did not enter into the merit of whether the right to asylum under Article 18 EUCFR overlaps with Articles 1 (right to dignity) and 47 (right to an effective remedy and fair trial), as well as Articles 4 (prohibition of torture and inhuman or degrading treatment or punishment) and 19(2) (protection in the event of removal, expulsion or extradition). In addition, the CJEU also stated that the judgments of the ECtHR 'essentially always constitute case-specific judicial decisions and not rules of the ECHR themselves, and it would therefore be wrong to regard the case-law of the European Court of Human Rights as a source of interpretation with full validity in connection with the application of the Charter'.[75] The CJEU also remained silent on the scope of the right to asylum in Article 18 EUCFR.[76] Instead, it merely upheld the need to exercise the sovereignty

[71] Joined Cases C-411/10 and C-493/10 *NS* and *ME* (n 69), Opinion of AG Trstenjak, 22 September 2011.

[72] ibid, para 148.

[73] ibid, para 146.

[74] Costello, 'Courting Access to Asylum in Europe' (n 50), at 327.

[75] Joined Cases C-411/10 and C-493/10 *NS* and *ME* (n 69), Opinion of AG Trstenjak, at para 146.

[76] On the content of the right to asylum in Art 18 EUCFR and the right to an effective remedy in Art 47EUCFR, see UNHCR, UNHCR Oral Submissions in Joined Cases of NS (C-411/10) and ME and Others (C-493/10) Hearing of the Court of Justice of the EU Luxembourg, 28 June 2011 available at http://www.refworld.org/pdfid/4e1b10bc2.pdf. The Court did not use either the indicators for the determination of the breach's seriousness developed by the UNHCR in its oral submission or the points on the impact of the breach on the individual. The Court has been asked to clarify the content of the right to asylum in Art 18 EUCFR and whether it amounts to a free-standing right in other cases but has so far left the question unanswered, see Case C-245/11 *K v Bundesasylamt*, Judgment of the Court (Grand Chamber) of 6 November 2012 (nyr); Case C-528/11 *Zuheyr Frayeh Halaf v Darzhavna agentsia za bezhantsite pri Ministerskia savet*, Judgment of 30 May 2013 (nyr).

clause and, in particular, it held the responsibility of the sending state under Article 3(2) Dublin Regulation for the asylum seeker's application when there are 'systemic deficiencies in the asylum procedure and reception conditions for asylum applicants' resulting in inhuman or degrading treatment, within the meaning of Article 4 EUCFR.[77] On the contrary, 'serious' risks of infringements of individual provisions of CEAS Directives in the Member State primarily responsible are not sufficient to create an obligation on the part of the transferring state to assume responsibility for the asylum examination, provided these infringements do not also violate the Charter rights of the asylum seeker to be transferred.[78] The extent to which breaches of other EU fundamental rights should prevent transfer remains to be seen. In contrast to the Opinion of the Advocate General, the CJEU decided to focus on Article 4 EUCFR probably in consideration of the fact that, given the inclusion therein of important fundamental social rights, including other breaches could have opened the floor to different non-*refoulement* claims.[79] The Court clarified that the EU asylum system cannot operate on the basis of a 'conclusive presumption' that all EU Member States 'observe the fundamental rights of the European Union'.[80] Moreover, the CJEU referred to 'the extent of the infringement of fundamental rights described in *MSS*[81] and, in particular, the absence of any guarantee that the asylum application would be seriously examined by the Greek authorities and the exposure of the applicant to conditions of detention and living conditions that amounted to degrading treatment',[82] to determine that the existence of 'systemic deficiencies' in the asylum procedure and reception conditions for asylum applicants resulting in inhuman or degrading treatment form a basis for rebuttal of the presumption of equivalent protection.

However, in defining the burden of proof test to rebut the presumption of safety according to which a Member State 'cannot be unaware' of such systemic deficiencies, it did not refer to the part of the *MSS* judgment where the ECtHR, in consideration of the inherent vulnerability of asylum seekers as a group, developed the concept of a 'shared burden of proof'.[83] Similarly, it did not refer to *MSS* when it argued that a country may gather information from the reports of international organisations, the UNHCR[84] as well the European Commission,

[77] Joined Cases C-411/10 and C-493/10 *NS* and *ME* (n 69) at paras 84, 86, 94 and 106.

[78] This mirror's the Opinion of the AG (at para 127).

[79] On this point, see Costello, 'Courting Access to Asylum in Europe' (n 50) at 332.

[80] Joined Cases C-411/10 and C-493/10 *NS* and *ME* (n 69) at para 105.

[81] *MSS* (n 57).

[82] Joined Cases C-411/10 and C-493/10 *NS* and *ME* (n 69) at paras 86 and 94.

[83] See *MSS* (n 57) at paras 352 and 359. This was in line with the position of the UN Committee against Torture (UNCAT), see *Agiza v Sweden* (2005, at para 13.7); *AS v Sweden* (2000, at para 8.6) and with the view of the UN Sub-Commission for the Promotion of Human Rights, namely that once a *general* risk situation is established, there is a 'presumption' that the person would face a real risk, see UN Sub-Commission on the Promotion and Protection of Human Rights (2005), Resolution 2005/12 on Transfer of Persons, 10 August 2005, para 4.

[84] In *MSS* (n 57) the Grand Chamber of the ECtHR attached 'critical importance' to UNHCR's views, see *MSS* at para 349.

which were the same as mentioned by the ECtHR.[85] Likewise, in relation to the standard of proof the CJEU relied on its own autonomous interpretation of 'serious risk' and did not refer to the concept of 'substantial grounds for a real risk' developed by the ECtHR.[86] According to the Meijers Committee, in relation to assessing whether the national authorities of the sending state 'knew or ought to have known' about the risk of ill-treatment in the country of destination, Member States should be obliged to report on the length of the procedure, the detention conditions and reception capacity in relation to the inflow of asylum seekers to EASO and the Commission statistical data (the Asylum Management Reporting System), on a quarterly basis.[87] What transpires from the foregoing analysis of *NS* and *ME* is that both the CJEU and the Advocate General are emphasising the importance of the EUCFR's provisions and the autonomy of the EU legal order whilst at the same time being mindfully respectful of the ECHR and the case law of the ECtHR.

In *Puid*,[88] concerning an Iranian national who applied for asylum in Germany, the key question was whether an asylum seeker could be said to have a personal enforceable right against a Member State deriving from Article 3(2) of the Dublin Regulation. In particular, the question posed by the national referring court was whether a duty of the Member States to exercise the sovereignty clause under Article 3(2) Dublin Regulation can also be inferred from reasons not directly associated with the asylum seeker himself or other particularities of an individual case, but which result from a legal or administrative situation in the Member State assuming responsibility that pose a threat to the fundamental rights of asylum seekers under the EUCFR. As already seen above, in *MSS* the ECtHR, in assessing the risk of ill-treatment in the Member State responsible according to the criteria set out in the Dublin Regulation, took into consideration the general country's situation in order to establish the risk of ill-treatment, rather than the individual circumstances of the asylum seeker.

However, the CJEU took a different approach. While the Court reiterated its finding in *NS*—according to which Member States may not transfer an asylum seeker to a Member State which the criteria set out in the Regulation indicate is

[85] In *MSS* (n 57), the ECtHR mentioned the European Commission's infringement procedures against Greece, in 2006 and 2008, regarding the country's failure to apply the Reception Conditions Directive and to comply with its obligations under the Dublin Regulation by not adopting the laws, regulations and administrative measures necessary to ensure the examination of applications by asylum seekers transferred back to Greece under the terms of the Regulation.

[86] This concept was first developed by the ECtHR outside EU asylum cases (*Soering v the United Kingdom*, App no 14038/88 (ECtHR, 7 July 1989)) and has subsequently been applied to Dublin returns (*TI v the United Kingdom* (n 55), *KRS v the United Kingdom* (n 56) and *MSS* (n 57)).

[87] Mejiers Committee, Letter to the European Parliament (LIBE Committee): The recast of the Dublin Regulation (2008/0243 COD) and the proposal for a process for early warning, preparedness and management of asylum crisis, available at http://www.statewatch.org/news/2012/mar/meijers-cttee-letter-EP-dublin.pdf.

[88] Case C-4/11 *Federal Republic of Germany v Kaveh Puid*, Judgment of the Court (Grand Chamber) of 14 November 2013 (nyr).

responsible, where they cannot be unaware that systemic deficiencies in the asylum procedure and in the reception conditions for asylum seekers in that Member State provide substantial grounds for believing that the asylum seeker would face a real risk of being subjected to inhuman or degrading treatment within the meaning of Article 4 EUCFR—in a somewhat cautious manner it refused to acknowledge that an asylum seeker could have a personal enforceable right against a Member State deriving from Article 3(2) of the Dublin Regulation.[89] In particular, the CJEU held that although the Member State, which is determining the Member State responsible has the right referred to in Article 3(2) of the Dublin II Regulation (commonly referred to as the sovereignty clause) to itself examine the application, the Member State is not required to do so.

The decision of the Court more or less follows the Opinion of Advocate General Jääskinen[90] who seems to be concerned with the effects that the *NS* and *ME* 'exception' could have on the principle of mutual trust. In his own words: 'the Court has aimed at establishing a high barrier against the setting aside of the principle of mutual trust underlying Regulation No. 343/2003. This means that *the principle of mutual trust may not be placed under question through systematic examination*, in each procedure entailing an application for asylum'.[91] What transpires from this case is that non-*refoulement* is clearly of great concern to both the Court and the Advocate General. At the same time, the circumstances such as the one in the present case are considered as 'exceptional situations' whereas great importance is given to the need to preserve the principle of mutual trust in the Dublin system.[92] In addition, in both the judgment of the Court and the Opinion of the Advocate General there is no reference to the ECHR or the ECtHR's case law but only to EU legal instruments, which seems to confirm a preference for an autonomous interpretative approach.

NS has nonetheless been a very influential judgment and the Dublin III Regulation explicitly provides for the possibility to suspend transfers to Member States with 'systemic flaws' in their asylum procedures and reception conditions therefore foreseeing the possibility for the determining Member State to become the responsible Member State for a person's asylum application.[93]

[89] Case C-4/11 *Federal Republic of Germany v Kaveh Puid* (ibid), paras 25–35.
[90] Case C-4/11 *Federal Republic of Germany v Kaveh Puid* (ibid), Opinion of AG Jääskinen.
[91] ibid, para 62 (emphasis added).
[92] A similar approach as in *Puid* was taken in Case C-394/12 *Shamso Abdullahi v Bundesasylamt*, Judgment of the Court (Grand Chamber) of 10 December 2013 (nyr).
[93] Art 3(2) subpara 2 Dublin III Regulation.

IV. CONCLUDING REMARKS: THE EUROPEAN COURTS AND ASYLUM SEEKERS' HUMAN RIGHTS

As examined elsewhere,[94] despite some significant changes, we are still far from the 1999 Tampere goals of having a common asylum procedure and a uniform status for those who are granted asylum valid throughout the Union. However, the EUCFR, particularly since it became legally binding,[95] has had and is having a significant impact on the development of CEAS. In particular, the CJEU's judicial activism combined with the equally important 'monitoring' function of the ECtHR is filling in the *lacunae* of EU asylum legislation, which in spite of the recast process remain. With regard to asylum seekers' human rights the role of both European Courts, therefore, remains key to ensuring their effective protection.

What seems 'to emerge is a shared view and understanding that human rights should be better protected through the development of a "European" *ius commune* and that a certain optimization of "judicial cooperation" may contribute to this aim'.[96] Arguably, more than 'a parallel interpretation' of the EUCFR and the ECHR has started taking place: a 'kind of bilateral interplay between the EU and Convention law, thereby producing a twofold process of "conventionalization" of Union law and "unionization" of Convention law, though with different timings and intensities'.[97]

At the same time, the prominence of the EUCFR has led to a decrease in importance of references made to the ECHR and the ECtHR case law and to an increased significance of the CJEU's interpretative autonomy and distinctiveness of the EU legal order. Moreover, both the CJEU and the Advocate General seem reluctant to give the right to asylum enshrined in Article 18 EUCFR the meaning of an enforceable subjective right as evidenced by their refusal to enable an asylum seeker to use the 'sovereignty clause' of the Dublin Regulation as a means to impose a duty on a transferring Member State not to return him/her to another EU country if the former 'cannot be unaware' of existing systemic deficiencies in the asylum procedure and in the reception conditions for asylum seekers in that other Member State which provide substantial grounds for believing that the asylum seeker would face a real risk of being subjected to inhuman or degrading treatment within the meaning of Article 4 EUCFR. In other words, the 'sovereignty clause' remains a kind of regulatory mechanism solely to be applied to relationships between Member States.

[94] S Velluti, *Reforming the Common European Asylum System—Legislative Developments and Judicial Activism of the European Courts* (Heidelberg, Springer, 2013).

[95] Art 6(1) Treaty on European Union (TEU).

[96] Ippolito and Velluti, 'The Relationship between the European Court of Justice and the European Court of Human Rights' (n 63).

[97] J Callewaert, '"Unionisation" and "Conventionalisation" of fundamental rights in Europe' in J Wouters, A Nollkaemper and E De Wet (eds), *The Europeanisation of Public International Law: the Status of Public International Law in the EU and its Member States* (The Hague, TMC Asser Press, 2008) 109, 114.

More generally, the application of mutual trust within the Dublin system is problematic. While this principle should be in the interest of the individual and specifically, to protect asylum seekers' basic rights and thus prohibit *refoulement*, its application in practice has not achieved its purported goals. A higher level of harmonisation is necessary for the effective implementation of mutual trust 'or, where such a harmonized approach cannot be attained, a lower threshold for the applicant with regard to the burden of proof [that he or she will be treated in violation of Article 3 ECHR or Article 4 EUCFR if transferred][98] is necessary'.[99] However, as the chapter has shown, CEAS is still under construction and significant differences between Member States' asylum laws remain. Recent judgments of both European Courts have made it clear that when it is necessary to fully protect asylum seekers' fundamental rights and, specifically, when there is a real risk of *refoulement*, mutual trust must be rebutted. While this is to be welcomed as a positive development, there needs to be further clarification from the European Courts about the nature of the duties of the transferring state, including the national courts, in assessing the situation and risks for the individual in the other Member State and further procedural guarantees safeguarding asylum seekers against a Dublin transfer have to be developed.[100]

The legal implications of EU accession to the ECHR,[101] such as the ECtHR's increased scrutiny of EU law and an alignment of CJEU judgments with ECtHR case law, will undoubtedly contribute to strengthening a Rancièrean process of political and legal action for asylum seekers, which will nonetheless be hampered by an underlying security paradigm and by its contextualisation within the particularistic framework of the territorial state. However, the ruling of the CJEU regarding the EU's accession to the ECHR makes it difficult for the EU to proceed with accession and should the EU do so on the terms of the CJEU accession would diminish rather than strengthen the protection of human rights within the EU legal order; see Opinion 2/13 (n 68).

[98] Author's addition.

[99] Brouwer, 'Mutual Trust and the Dublin Regulation' (n 12) 138.

[100] ibid, 145–46. In this context, the revised Commission's Implementing Regulation of the Dublin rules does little to assist national authorities, including national courts; Commission Implementing Regulation (EU) No 118/2014 of 30 January 2014 amending Regulation (EC) No 1560/2003 laying down detailed rules for the application of Council Regulation (EC) No 343/2003 establishing the criteria and mechanisms for determining the Member State responsible for examining an asylum application lodged in one of the member States by a third country national [2014] OJ L39/1.

[101] For detailed analysis, see Morano-Foadi and Andreakis, Report on the Protection of Fundamental Rights in Europe (n 6) at 64–93; P Gragl, *The Accession of the European Union to the European Convention of Human Rights* (Oxford, Hart Publishing, 2013).

9

More is Less? Multiple Protection of Human Rights in Europe and the Risks of Erosion of Human Rights Standards

TITIA LOENEN AND LUCY VICKERS

I. INTRODUCTION

HUMAN RIGHTS ARE generally well protected in Europe. Since World War II human rights protection mechanisms have been set up and improved over time, both nationally and at the European level. In the latter context the European Convention of Human Rights (ECHR) has played the most prominent role, but more recently the European Union (EU) has become an ever more important player in the field. This is borne out by the place accorded to human rights in the Lisbon Treaty, in accordance with which the Charter of Fundamental Rights (the Charter) became a binding piece of primary EU law,[1] and the EU may accede to the Convention, a process discussed elsewhere in this volume.

The increased human rights scope of EU law and concomitant competence of the Court of Justice of the European Union (CJEU) aims to bring more protection for EU citizens. Although the enlarged opportunities to invoke human rights would suggest that this aim will be fulfilled, this chapter argues that this may not, in the event, be the case. This is because of the risk of adverse effects from the fusing of European competencies, in particular the risk of a lowering of substantive human rights protection notwithstanding increased procedural possibilities to make human rights claims.

The reason for doubt about the effects of the additional connections between the two legal systems stems from the impression that the pluralism in national human rights standards seems to be putting increasing pressure on the European Court of Human Rights (ECtHR) to abstain from real scrutiny in politically sensitive cases. The ECtHR's use of the margin of appreciation doctrine regarding the regulation of religious expressions in the public sphere, such as regulation of the wearing of a headscarf, face veil and other religiously inspired dress, is a case in point.

[1] Art 6(1) Treaty on European Union (TEU).

In these cases the Court has granted the states concerned a wide margin of appreciation, which gives them a broad competence to limit the human rights at issue. Whilst this may be understandable in any particular case, nonetheless a wide margin accorded to one state can have important spill over effects to other states, as other states feel able to limit human rights in the area at hand, even if they did not do so before.

The expectation of this chapter is that the CJEU, though working in a different context from the ECtHR, will follow the latter Court in leaving states a wide discretionary competence in sensitive areas. It is argued that the result may be potential lowering of substantive human rights standards, and that this may be encouraged by the authority accorded to the ECHR in the Treaty of Lisbon.

This chapter will try to substantiate the above expectations by looking in more detail into the case of the public official who invokes human rights to back her claim to be allowed to wear a headscarf or other religious symbol at work for religious reasons.[2] This is a highly controversial and sensitive matter and in human rights terms it is met with widely divergent approaches as between European countries. On the one hand, in France no public servant is allowed to wear any visible signs of adherence to a religion as this is regarded to be incompatible with the principle of *laïcité*, a rather strict notion of state neutrality.[3] This policy is even applied to publicly-employed cleaning personnel, even though it is difficult to see them as representing the state. On the other hand, in the United Kingdom even judges, if anything the ultimate representatives of state power, are allowed to wear a turban in court.[4] In the Netherlands the picture is mixed. Most public servants are allowed to express their religion in dress or other attire, yet specific categories of public officials, such as judges or police officers, are not allowed to do so. The regulation of this matter falls under the scope of application of both EU law and the ECHR and thus provides an excellent opportunity for a comparison.

In the next section, the main characteristics of the current EU competence in human rights matters and the relationship with the ECHR are sketched. The chapter then presents a short overview of the main case law of the ECtHR on headscarf issues and identifies the wide margin of appreciation accorded to the national authorities to regulate such matters (Section III). This is followed by an exploration of how the headscarf issue could be addressed under EU law (Section IV). The section concludes that the way in which any legal review of a ban on headscarves and other religious symbols for public servants will take place under EU law will be very similar to the test to be applied under the ECHR. The actual outcome of the review by the CJEU regarding the legitimacy of such

[2] Referred to as 'the headscarf issue' in what follows.

[3] For an overview of the approaches to this matter in France, England and the Netherlands, see H van Ooijen, *Religious Symbols in Public Functions: Unveiling State Neutrality. A Comparative Analysis of Dutch, English and French Justifications for Limiting the Freedom of Public Officials to Display Religious Symbols* (Antwerpen, Intersentia, 2012).

[4] Reportedly Rabinder Singh was the first judge to sit at the High Court wearing a turban. See http://www.guardian.co.uk/uk/2003/mar/24/race.world (last accessed 21 April 2013).

a ban, however, may well depend on the question of how much discretion it will leave to the Member States. Section V addresses the arguments for and against a deferential approach. It concludes with the concern that if the CJEU follows the deferential line of the human rights court, human rights protection will not be enhanced by having an additional supervising mechanism of the EU, but instead that protection may in some ways be reduced.

II. EU COMPETENCE REGARDING HUMAN RIGHTS

It is well known that the EU project started with an economic focus, but this has gradually been broadened significantly to include social issues. More recently human rights have taken on greater importance, as clearly reflected in the Treaty of Lisbon. First, several provisions in the Treaty on European Union (TEU), as amended by the Lisbon Treaty, give human rights a prominent position. First and foremost Article 6 gives the Charter the status of binding, primary law[5] and provides the legal basis for the future accession of the EU to the ECHR.[6] In addition, the rights, freedoms and principles included in the ECHR and in the constitutional traditions common to the Member States are to be regarded as general principles of EU law.[7] Though the precise relationship between the ECHR and the Charter may be complex, as the two human rights documents differ in many respects, the Charter gives a prominent position to the ECHR and the interpretation given to it by the ECtHR by providing that the meaning and scope of Charter rights that correspond with rights protected in the ECHR 'shall be the same' as the latter.[8]

[5] Article 6(1): 'The Union recognizes the rights, freedoms and principles set out in the Charter of Fundamental Rights of the European Union of 7 December 2000, as adapted at Strasbourg, on 12 December 2007, which shall have the same legal value as the Treaties. The provisions of the Charter shall not extend in any way the competences of the Union as defined in the Treaties. The rights, freedoms and principles in the Charter shall be interpreted in accordance with the general provisions in Title VII of the Charter governing its interpretation and application and with due regard to the explanations referred to in the Charter, that set out the sources of those provisions'.

[6] Article 6(2): 'The Union shall accede to the European Convention for the Protection of Human Rights and Fundamental Freedoms. Such accession shall not affect the Union's competences as defined in the Treaties'. After almost three years of negotiations between the 47 Member States of the Council of Europe and the European Commission, a draft agreement was reached in April 2013. See http://www.coe.int/t/dghl/standardsetting/hrpolicy/accession/Meeting_reports/47_1%282013%29008_final_report_EN.pdf. The European Court of Justice gave its opinion on 18 December 2014. The whole procedure is now on hold.

[7] Article 6(3): 'Fundamental rights, as guaranteed by the European Convention for the Protection of Human Rights and Fundamental Freedoms and as they result from the constitutional traditions common to the Member States, shall constitute general principles of the Union's law'.

[8] Article 52(4): 'In so far as this Charter contains rights which correspond to rights guaranteed by the Convention for the Protection of Human Rights and Fundamental Freedoms, the meaning and scope of those rights shall be the same as those laid down by the said Convention. This provision shall not prevent Union law providing more extensive protection'.

So the case law of the ECtHR has an important role to play in the interpretation of the Charter. This certainly holds true for the subject of this chapter, which has already been addressed in a series of cases.

EU competence in human rights issues can be seen beyond the Charter too. For example, the Framework Directive 2000/78 on equality and non-discrimination will involve the ECtHR in determining matters that relate to religious rights, albeit in the context of religious equality; and the EU's competence on sex discrimination is also a human rights matter. The position of the ECHR provided for in the Lisbon Treaty suggests that the equality directives[9] be interpreted to comply with the human rights norms of the ECHR. Any future accession of the EU to the ECHR will give a strengthened significance to the EU's human rights competence.[10] In the context of the headscarf issue discussed below, cases which come to the CJEU for determination will come under the equality directives which prohibit discrimination on grounds of religion and belief and/or gender and race or ethnic origin. In determining whether there has been discrimination, the CJEU will need to consider the jurisprudence of the ECHR, discussed below.[11]

III. THE HEADSCARF JURISPRUDENCE OF THE ECHR

The ECtHR has heard a number of cases concerning headscarves, which will not be dealt with in detail here.[12] Instead, only the main cases will be considered, as they suffice to demonstrate that the ECtHR has accorded the national authorities a very wide margin of appreciation to regulate such matters.

The first case of specific relevance to public officials was the case of *Dahlab*,[13] a Swiss public primary school teacher. The case was decided in 2001. The Swiss

[9] Directive 2006/54/EC of the European Parliament and of the Council of 5 July 2006 on the implementation of the principle of equal opportunities and equal treatment of men and women in matters of employment and occupation (recast) [2006] OJ L204/23; Council Directive 2000/43/EC of 29 June 2000 on the implementation of equal treatment irrespective of race or ethnic origin in employment and regarding access to and supply of goods and services (Race Directive) [2000] OJ L180/22; Council Directive 2000/78/EC of 27 November 2000 establishing a general framework for equal treatment in employment and occupation (Framework Directive) [2000] OJ L303/16.

[10] See W Weiß, 'The EU Human Rights Regime Post Lisbon: Turning the CJEU into a Human Rights Court?', ch 5 in this volume and S Morano-Foadi and S Andreadakis, Report on the Protection of Fundamental Rights in Europe—A Reflection on the Relationship between the Court of Justice of the European Union and the European Court of Human Rights Post Lisbon, July 2014, available at http://www.coe.int/en/web/dlapil/news-dlapil.

[11] See E Howard, 'Protecting Freedom to Manifest One's Religion or Belief: Strasbourg or Luxembourg?' (2014) 32 *Netherlands Quarterly of Human Rights* 159–82 for a comparison between the position of the two Courts on the headscarf issue.

[12] For details, see: D McGoldrick, *Human Rights and Religion—The Islamic Headscarf Debate in Europe* (Oxford, Hart Publishing, 2006); S Haverkort-Speekenbrink, *European Non-Discrimination Law. A Comparison of EU Law and the ECHR in the Field of Non-Discrimination and Freedom of Religion in Public Employment with an Emphasis on the Islamic Headscarf Issue* (Antwerpen, Intersentia, 2012); and E Howard, *Law and the Wearing of Religious Symbols: European Bans on the Wearing of Religious Symbols in Education* (London, Routledge, 2012).

[13] *Dahlab v Switzerland* App no 42393/98 (ECtHR, 15 February 2001) (decision on admissibility).

authorities had invoked the necessity of protecting the neutrality of public education to dismiss her because she refused to put away her headscarf in class. The Court held that the dismissal did not infringe the ECHR. The complaint was considered 'manifestly ill founded' and thus inadmissible.

In 2005 the Grand Chamber judgment in the case of *Sahin v Turkey*[14] clearly set the standard to be applied in this type of case. The case concerned a university student who objected to the dress regulations of a Turkish state university that prohibited religious attire being worn in the university. Turkey's main arguments for the ban focused on the protection of state neutrality as enshrined in its Constitution and the importance of this principle for guaranteeing peaceful relations among (different strands of) religions. Turkey also emphasised its commitment to the principle of sex or gender equality. In its view, religious prescripts to wear a headscarf are not compatible with the latter. The ECtHR upheld the ban as compatible with the rights enshrined in the ECHR. In its decision the Court kept its distance and emphasised that 'where questions concerning the relationship between State and religions are concerned, on which opinion in a democratic society may reasonably differ widely, the role of the national decision making body must be given special importance'.[15] As a consequence, it left a wide margin of appreciation to the Turkish government to decide whether it is indeed 'necessary' in the Turkish context to prohibit the wearing of religious symbols in teaching institutions. The Court accepted the arguments put forward by the Turkish government, especially those which referred to the specific Turkish history regarding *laïcité* and the strong political significance that wearing a headscarf had taken on in Turkey with the growing influence of extremist political movements in that country.

The dissenting opinion by Judge Tulkens illustrates the far reaching nature of the margin of appreciation left in this case to the national authorities.[16] According to Tulkens, the Court accepted the Turkish arguments at face value and did not assess even marginally whether they did indeed hold water in the Turkish context. According to her '(…) European supervision seems quite simply to be absent from the Judgment'.[17] In her view, if the Court had been less deferential it would have concluded that both Sahin's right to freedom of religion and her right to education were infringed by the Turkish state.

The consequences of the Court's approach for other bans on religious symbols in other countries became apparent in a series of French cases concerning the

[14] *Leila Sahin v Turkey* App no 44774/98 (ECtHR, 10 November 2005).

[15] ibid, s 109.

[16] This also seems to have been the main critique of comments in legal journals. See, eg, K Altiparmak and O Karahanogullari, 'After *Sahin*: The Debate on Headscarves is Not Over', case note European Court of Human Rights [2006] 2 *European Constitutional Law Review* 268–92; T Lewis, 'What Not to Wear: Religious Rights, the European Court, and the Margin of Appreciation' [2007] 56 *International and Comparative Law Quarterly* 395–414; N Gibson, 'An Unwelcome Trend: Religious Dress and Human Rights Following Leyla Sahin vs. Turkey' (2007) 25 *Netherlands Quarterly of Human Rights* 599–640.

[17] Dissenting opinion section 3.

law of 2004 banning all ostentatious religious symbols from the public school classroom to uphold the principle of *laïcité*. The law drew worldwide attention.[18] This time several complaints were brought to the ECtHR by both Muslim girls and Sikh boys. Again stressing the margin of appreciation to be left to the national authorities in this context, the Court declared all complaints 'manifestly ill founded' and thus inadmissible.[19]

Though the *Sahin* judgment and the French complaints did not concern a public official who wishes to wear a headscarf or other religious symbol at work, it seems only logical to allow states similar leeway in the latter type of case as the argument of protecting state neutrality will even be stronger regarding persons who are actually in the service of the state. Thus it would seem that a wide margin of appreciation would protect the French policy of precluding any public servant from wearing religious symbols at work.[20]

This conclusion seems to be corroborated by subsequent case law. In the judgment of the Court in the case of *Lautsi v Italy* a wide margin of appreciation was affirmed once more as the standard of review for the regulation of religious symbols in the public sphere.[21] The case concerned a complaint of a non-religious pupil and its parent against the Italian practice of hanging crucifixes in public school classrooms. The Grand Chamber of the Court overruled a unanimous judgment by a chamber of the Court that this constituted a violation of the ECHR. Again, the Grand Chamber gave pride of place to a very wide margin of appreciation for the states and held that Italy was allowed to continue its practice. Similarly, in *Eweida and Others v the United Kingdom* the Chamber of the Court hearing the case reiterated its deferential line.[22] In fact, four different complaints were addressed in this single judgment. The first complaint concerned a staff member of British Airways, Ms Eweida, who was not allowed to wear a visible cross to express her Christian faith, whereas Sikh men were not barred from wearing a turban nor Muslim women from donning a headscarf. The wearing of a Christian cross was also at issue in the second complaint. This time Ms Chaplin, a nurse working in a state hospital, was not allowed to have a necklace with a cross dangling from her V-necked uniform for hygiene and safety reasons. The other two cases concerned a quite different matter. Ms Ladele, who was a registrar of births, deaths and marriages, complained because the local authorities were not

[18] Law 2004-228 of March 15, 2004, concerning, as an application of the principle of the separation of church and state, the wearing of symbols or garb which show religious affiliation in public primary and secondary schools.

[19] The cases were all decided on the same day (ECtHR, 30 June 2009); on Muslim women's complaints: *Aktas v France* App no 43563/08; *Bayrak v France* App no 14308/08; *Gamaleddyn v France* App no 18527/08; *Ghazal v France* App no 29134/08; on complaints by Sikh pupils: *Javir Singh v France* App no 25463/08; *Ranjit Singh v France* App no 27561/08.

[20] For an overview of the divergent practices and debates on the acceptability of public school teachers, police officers and judges with headscarves or other religious attire in the UK, France and the Netherlands, see van Ooijen, *Religious Symbols in Public Functions* (n 3).

[21] App no 30814/06 (ECtHR, 18 March 2011).

[22] App nos 48420/10; 59842/10; 51671/10; 36516/10 (ECtHR, 15 January 2013).

willing to accommodate her wish to abstain from registering same sex couples for a civil partnership for religious reasons. The last complainant, Mr McFarlane, was also a Christian objecting to homosexual activity. His employer, a private organisation providing sex therapy and relationship counselling, did not accept his unwillingness to work with same sex couples.

In its assessment, the Court again emphasised that the domestic authorities enjoy a wide margin of appreciation in dealing with the matters at hand. The Court held that the refusal to accommodate the religion based wishes of the employees was not incompatible with the ECHR, except in the case of Eweida. In this case the Court rejected the national court's appraisal. The latter should have prioritised Eweida's wish to wear a visible cross as an expression of her religion over the interest of British Airways to project a certain corporate image. This conclusion was influenced by the fact that the company did not object to the wearing of headscarves and turbans for religious reasons and in the meantime in fact had already altered its uniform code to allow for the visible wearing of crosses and other religiously inspired jewellery. This showed that the employer's interest in its corporate image was very weak.[23]

The final case to consider is *SAS v France*[24] which involved a ban on the more contentious religious dress of the full face veil, known in France as the burqa-ban. In 2010 following the national debate on headscarves, legislation was introduced in France and Belgium to ban altogether the niqab or face veil in public spaces. This was significantly more far reaching than the headscarf bans considered above as it imposed a criminal sanction on the manifestation of religion, and was to be enforced not just in the more limited context of work or school, but much more generally, as the ban applied to concealing the face in public. The ban would mean that Muslim women who veil would be unable to go out to the shops, to take children to school or to the park or to the doctors. In its judgment in the case, the Court noted that there was almost total consensus in Europe not to ban the veil in all public spaces, that a ban was inconsistent with international human right norms and European values, that it was not necessary to uphold human dignity nor gender equality, and that such a generalised ban on the veil in public would need careful justification. However, it then concluded that the aim of 'living together', could justify the ban as long as it was proportionate. Despite such strong reasons to the contrary, the Court then concluded that the wide margin of appreciation meant that the ban was proportionate. Yet again, the ECtHR relied on a very wide margin of appreciation in upholding the compatibility of the ban with human rights norms.

As these cases show, then, the approach of the ECHR to religious issues such as the veil and headscarf is to leave a very broad discretion to national authorities to determine levels of protection. To an extent, this reflects the lack of consensus

[23] ibid, para 94.
[24] App no 43835/11 (ECtHR, 1 July 2014).

across Europe about how religion should be treated.[25] Although there was not really a lack of consensus in the case of the ban on face coverings, with only two states imposing a total ban, the Court noted that the issue is subject to extensive debate in many more states. This lack of consensus is then matched with a corresponding desire to allow states flexibility in their interpretation of the Convention. Whilst the granting of discretion may be an understandable reaction to the lack of consensus in Europe on the issue of religious dress, this flexible approach does nonetheless mean that the ECtHR is weak in terms of setting robust standards of protection, and the margin of appreciation can be criticised on this basis. Indeed, the decision in *SAS v France* provides perhaps the greatest support yet for Judge Tulken's proposition in her dissent in *Sahin* that reliance on a wide margin of appreciation can mean an absence of genuine European supervision.[26]

IV. THE HEADSCARF ISSUE UNDER EU LAW

The case of the pupils who are not allowed to wear religious symbols in public education does not seem to fall under the scope of application of EU law so far, as they do not relate to employment. However, the case of public officials being denied this possibility clearly does, as the EU directives on equal treatment and non-discrimination in employment also cover public employment. As the Member States are responsible for the implementation of these directives, the Charter is also applicable on the basis of Article 51(1).[27] Nevertheless, given the *lex specialis* character of the directives in relation to the Charter, the directives provide the main set of fundamental rights norms applicable to the case of headscarves in the workplace, and so they will be the focus of what follows.[28]

The applicability of the EU equality directives to the headscarf issue is no simple story, due to the intersectional character of the headscarf controversy. The position of the women who want to wear a headscarf for religious reasons and are affected by a ban on religious symbols in public employment may involve their identity and rights as religious persons, as females and as members of non-western minority groups.[29]

[25] C Evans, *Freedom of Religion under the ECHR* (Oxford, Oxford University Press, 2001) 143–44.

[26] See H Yourow, *The Margin of Appreciation Doctrine in the Dynamics of European Human Rights Jurisprudence* (Leiden, Martinus Nijhoff Publishers, 1996) and T O'Donnell, 'The Margin of Appreciation Doctrine: Standard in the Jurisprudence of the European Court of Human Rights' (1982) 4 *Human Rights Quarterly* 474; T Jones, 'The Devaluation of Human Rights Under the European Convention' (1995) *Public Law* 430. See also PW Edge, 'The European Court of Human Rights and Religious Rights' (1998) 47 *ICLQ* 680–87.

[27] Article 51(1): The provisions of this Charter are addressed to the institutions and bodies of the Union with due regard to the principle of subsidiarity and to the Member States only when they are implementing Union law'.

[28] See S Morano-Foadi, ch 7 in this volume for an analysis in relation to migration.

[29] See on this intersection, L Roseberry, 'Religion, Ethnicity and Gender in the Danish Headscarf Debate' in D Schiek and V Chege (eds), *European Union Non-Discrimination Law. Comparative Perspectives on Multidimensional Equality Law* (London, Routledge/Cavendish, 2009) 327–51.

In fact, three EU directives dealing with equality in employment could be applicable, depending on the framing of the issue in terms of either potential religious discrimination, sex discrimination or discrimination on grounds of race or ethnic origin.[30]

The most obvious basis for a claim by a public official who is denied the possibility of wearing any religious symbols at work would be the Directive 2000/78 that covers equal treatment in employment irrespective of religion, sexual orientation, disability and age.[31] This directive does not prohibit all distinctions on grounds of religion *tout court*, but allows for the possibility of justifying both direct and indirect discrimination on grounds of religion. Where indirect discrimination is concerned all of the EU equality directives provide for the possibility of putting forward an 'objective justification',[32] and the same applies in the case of religious discrimination. As far as direct discrimination is concerned, however, the directive covering religious discrimination contains in Article 2(5) another general justification clause that is absent in the other directives:

> This Directive shall be without prejudice to measures laid down by national law which, in a democratic society, are necessary for public security, for the maintenance of public order and the prevention of criminal offences, for the protection of health and for the protection of the rights and freedoms of others.

The close similarity between this provision and the limitation clause in Articles 8–11 ECHR is obvious.[33]

If a claim by a public servant who is not allowed to wear a headscarf at work were to be advanced under the directive covering religious discrimination, the compatibility of such a policy would be assessed either under Article 2(5) (if the policy targets religious expressions as such) or under the 'objective justification' clause (if the policy constitutes potential indirect discrimination). Notwithstanding the differences between the two types of review, both tests are very similar in their focus on the assessment of the legitimacy of the goals put forward and of the proportionality of the means employed to achieve those goals.[34]

In addition to the directive covering religious discrimination, the directives on discrimination concerning sex and race/ethnic origin could be relevant.[35] Leaving

[30] For an exploration of these issues, see MLP Loenen, 'Framing Headscarves and other Multicultural Issues as Religious, Cultural, Racial or Gendered: The Role of Human Rights Law' (2012) 30 *Netherlands Quarterly of Human Rights* 472–88.

[31] See n 9 above.

[32] For an extensive overview of the directives and the case law of the CJEU, see E Ellis and P Watson, *EU Anti-Discrimination Law*, 2nd edn (Oxford, Oxford University Press, 2012).

[33] For instance, Art 9(2) reads: 'Freedom to manifest one's religion or beliefs shall be subject only to such limitations as are prescribed by law and are necessary in a democratic society in the interests of public safety, for the protection of public order, health or morals, or for the protection of the rights and freedoms of others'.

[34] For a detailed comparison between justification or exception clauses in European equal treatment and non-discrimination law, see S Haverkort-Speekenbrink, *European Non-Discrimination Law. A Comparison of EU Law and the ECHR in the Field of Non-Discrimination and Freedom of Religion in Public Employment with an emphasis on the Islamic Headscarf Issue* (Antwerpen, Intersentia, 2012).

[35] See n 9 above.

aside the rather unlikely construction of a ban on public officials wearing religious symbols such as headscarves as constituting *direct* discrimination on grounds of race/ethnic origin or sex,[36] an argument could be made that in particular cases such bans could perhaps amount to *indirect* discrimination on those grounds. This would be possible if the ban at stake in fact has a disparate impact on women (in quite a few countries, a ban on religious symbols would mainly affect Muslim women, not Muslim men) or if it has a disparate impact on non-western minority groups (in most countries it seems the persons affected would be members of immigrant groups of non-western origin). If disparate impact can be established, the test under EU law would then revolve around an assessment of the presence of an objective justification for the ban. Generally speaking, the CJEU requires a rather strict scrutiny where indirect discrimination on grounds of sex or race/ethnic origin is concerned.[37] In the context of these other equality grounds for any potentially indirect discrimination to be justified there must be a legitimate aim for any restriction, and the means chosen for achieving that aim must correspond to a real need, must be appropriate with a view to achieving the objective in question and must be necessary to that end.[38] Matters such as customer preference or corporate image, for example, would not be adequate to justify any indirect discrimination.

An important question is whether application of the provisions of any of the above EU directives on the headscarf issue would necessarily result in a different outcome, compared with application of the ECHR. If so, this could be problematic. It is difficult to imagine the CJEU interpreting EU law to provide less protection than the ECHR, given the wide margin of appreciation the human rights court leaves to the states. Yet, if the CJEU provides more protection to public officials than the ECtHR, which is no doubt allowed as the ECHR only provides minimum standards, this may also create difficulties.

The first issue here is to consider what 'more protection' might mean: more protection for whom? More freedom to wear the headscarf may be understood to be more protection for religious freedom; but equally, it is arguable that greater religious freedom for these women comes at the price of the protection of others' interests, and proponents of headscarf bans often invoke the protection of the rights of others to limit the right to manifest one's religion.[39] The rights of others can include a right to a religiously neutral public space, or rights of women to be

[36] Direct discrimination could arguably be established if a specific ethnic group or a specific sex would be the ban's only victim or in fact would be intentionally targeted. Direct discrimination on grounds of race/ethnicity and sex is prohibited except for very limited situations that are not applicable in the headscarf case. For an overview, see Ellis and Watson, *EU Anti-Discrimination Law* (n 32).

[37] For sex discrimination the area of social policy has been a major exception. For a detailed overview of the complexities, see C Tobler, *Indirect Discrimination. A Case Study into the Legal Development of the Concept of Indirect Discrimination under EU Law* (Antwerpen, Intersentia, 2005).

[38] Case C-170/84 *Bilka-Kaufhaus vWeber von Hartz* [1986] ECR 1607-1631.

[39] The protection of the rights of others figured also prominently in the French debate on the law banning ostentatious religious symbols in public education, see the report of the Stasi-Commission, which advised the French Government on the ban: Commission de réflexion sur l'application du principe de laïcité dans la République, Rapport au président de la République, 11 December 2003, at http://www.ladocumentationfrancaise.fr/rapports-publics/034000725/index.shtml (last accessed 21 April 2013).

free from pressure to wear the headscarf, both interests that have been identified in the ECHR case law as requiring protection.[40]

In addition, the pejorative nature of discrimination arguably poses a problem if different standards of protection are allowed under the ECHR and EU law. If the CJEU gives public officials more protection for religious freedom by deciding, for instance, that the French practice of not allowing any public servant to wear a headscarf constitutes unjustified indirect discrimination on grounds of either religion, sex or race/ethnic origin, it would seem rather strange for the ECtHR to accept it under the ECHR.

A detailed study of the similarities and differences to be expected between the CJEU and the ECtHR in this type of case shows that application of the EU equality directives could, but surely need not, lead to different outcomes.[41] As pointed out above, the 'objective justification test' of the CJEU under the directives and the 'necessary in a democratic society' test of the ECtHR under Article 9 ECHR have a very comparable structure. Both require an assessment of the legitimacy of the goals pursued and the proportionality of the means employed to achieve those goals. In addition, both tests turn out to be flexible instruments in the hands of the courts that apply them.[42] In those circumstances an important question will be how much discretion the CJEU will leave to the Member States in this area. For example, it is arguable that the French ban on headscarves for all public servants would not survive a strict scrutiny on gender discrimination grounds on the basis that it is overbroad by including any publicly employed person whatever his or her specific function. A less discriminatory version of the rule can be easily imagined, and is indeed widely practiced elsewhere in Europe.[43]

Formally, of course, in a preliminary procedure the Court will leave it up to the national courts to apply the criteria it has formulated, but in practice the Court can formulate its criteria in such a way that it can leave them either much or hardly any leeway.[44] The section below considers first whether the EU can introduce discretion into its reasoning, and second whether such an approach would be desirable.

[40] Eg *Leyla Sahin v Turkey* (n 14).

[41] See Haverkort-Speekenbrink, *European Non-Discrimination Law* (n 12) ch 9: a comparison of non-discrimination law (EU) and the rights to freedom of religion (ECHR), at 271–87. The general limitation clause in the Art 52(1) of the Charter of Fundamental Rights is also very similar to the ECHR: 'Any limitation on the exercise of the rights and freedoms recognised by this Charter must be provided for by law and respect the essence of those rights and freedoms. Subject to the principle of proportionality, limitations may be made only if they are necessary and genuinely meet objectives of general interest recognised by the Union or the need to protect the rights and freedoms of others'.

[42] See especially ch 11 in Haverkort-Speekenbrink, *European Non-Discrimination Law* (n 12).

[43] See van Ooijen, *Religious Symbols in Public Functions* (n 3), and D McGoldrick, *Human Rights and Religion—The Islamic Headscarf Debate in Europe* (Oxford, Hart Publishing, 2006).

[44] '[I]t is well established that the Court often gives the national courts such specific "guidance" regarding how to apply EC law, that it appears to perform that task of application of the law for itself': Tobler, *Indirect discrimination* (n 37) 243.

V. A DEFERENTIAL APPROACH BY THE CJEU?

The preliminary question here is whether the CJEU is legally obliged to follow the deferential line of the ECtHR. It would seem not. By leaving the national authorities a wide margin of appreciation the ECtHR has allowed states to ban headscarves, but nothing in the Court's judgments and decisions suggests that they are required to do so. So both prohibiting and allowing headscarves and other religious symbols in the public service seems compatible with the jurisprudence of the ECHR. This leaves the CJEU free to follow its own line in the context of its EU competence from the point of view of complying with the ECHR.

A second question is whether the CJEU is able to follow the ECHR lead of leaving matters of detail to be decided by national authorities, or whether it is required to set the same standard, whatever that may be, for all Member States. Here the answer is less clear. In the case of the interpretation of EU equality law, the CJEU has been fairly strict in setting standards for all Member States. For example, there has never been any suggestion that the standard of review set for indirect sex discrimination in *Bilka*[45] might not apply to all Member States. However, in the context of balancing economic rights against fundamental freedoms, a 'margin of discretion' has been allowed in the interpreation of EU laws where they intersect with fundamental rights. This can be seen in *Schmidberger v Austria*,[46] and confirmed in the *Omega* case[47] where the CJEU accepted that EU law must be interpreted in the light of fundamental human rights principles. It accepted that there is a margin of discretion in reaching a fair balance between competing economic and social interests, and that it is not necessary that states all agree on a shared conception of how to protect the interests in question. These cases from beyond the equality sphere show that as long as the standard of protection provided does not fall below a minimum standard, there is room for different standards of protection for fundamental rights to be accepted as legitimate within the EU Member States to reflect different national contexts and traditions.

It seems then from both the point of view of compliance with the ECHR and general principles of EU law, that it is open to the CJEU to take a deferential approach to national practice when faced with the headscarf issue if it so chooses. This brings us to the question of whether deference is desirable on the part of the Court.

A. Reasons to Support a Deferential Approach

The simplest reason for the CJEU to take a deferential approach similar to that of the ECtHR, even if it is not strictly required to, is to avoid any disparities between

[45] Case C-170/84 *Bilka-Kaufhaus v Weber von Hartz* (n 38).

[46] Case C-112/00 *Schmidberger Internationale Transporte Planzüge v Republik Österreich* [2003] ECR I-5659.

[47] Case C-36/02 *Omega v Oberburgermeisterin der Bundesstadt Bonn* [2004] ECR I-9609.

the two Courts in terms of their protection of fundamental rights, which could arise from a different approach. But more substantive reasons can also be found. First, is the need to the respect of national identity as guaranteed in Article 4(2) TEU. The first sentence of this provision reads as follows:

> The Union shall respect the equality of Member States before the Treaties as well as their national identities, inherent in their fundamental structures, political and constitutional, inclusive of regional and local self-government.

The relationship between state and religion and the regulation of religious manifestations is closely intertwined with a country's history and culture and as such is often enshrined in its constitutional norms and values. In this way they can be considered to belong to national identity. This explains why emotions may run high on the headscarf issue, as was the case in reaction to the *Sahin* and *Lautsi* judgments. A parallel with the emotions around moral issues such as the approach to same sex marriage could be drawn. In the latter case the CJEU has been careful to respect the divergent national practices and feelings.[48]

A further argument for a deferential approach by the CJEU derives from the perspective of a proper division of power between democratically elected legislative bodies and the judiciary. Courts, and especially international courts, should be careful to stay away from politically sensitive issues. In the present case, a less deferential approach may involve the CJEU in having to pronounce itself in detail on a large variety of highly sensitive rules and policies concerning the relationship between state and religion and religious manifestations. Indeed, concern for entering territory that is better seen as the preserve of democratic government explains in part the deferential reasoning of the ECtHR in the cases of *Sahin*, *Lautsi*, and *SAS v France*. The CJEU may consider it relevant that no 'common ground' exists in Europe regarding the regulation of religious manifestations in the public sphere.

Of course, establishing whether or not a common ground exists is not always straightforward. In *SAS v France*, the Court noted that only two out of the 47 Member States of the Council of Europe had criminalised the veil, demonstrating that France was very in much a minority position on the issue, and suggesting a good deal of common ground. However, the Court then concluded that there was a lack of consensus due to existence of public debate on the issue in a number of other states.[49]

Moreover, the choice of the comparators will also influence the outcome of the comparison. Thus in the case of *Sahin* the comparative research showed that forbidding university students to wear religious symbols at state universities was in fact very exceptional. Even in France the law banning ostentatious religious symbols in public education is limited to primary and secondary education and

[48] *Cf* M Bell, *Anti-Discrimination Law and the European Union* (Oxford, Oxford University Press, 2002) 120.

[49] *SAS v France* (n 24), para 156.

does not include the university level. This suggests that allowing the wearing of religious symbols by university students might be the 'common ground' in European countries. Nevertheless, by focusing on more overall policies regarding religious symbols in public education, including policies regarding teachers, the Court could conclude that no common ground existed.[50]

Nonetheless, although the detail may be contested, few would dispute that there is a huge variance in the approach to religious issues in the public sphere across Europe, a result of different political settlements being reached after centuries of war and bloodshed over issues of religion and its relationship with the state. In this context, an approach which is deferential to different states' practice is certainly understandable.

An additional element to add to these arguments relates to the authority and status of the CJEU in political terms. The EU currently faces a deficit in terms of its democratic legitimacy. Trust in the EU is at an all time low, and a significant proportion of European citizens have a negative image of the EU.[51] That the EU itself is under increasing attack is borne out by the threat of a British withdrawal.[52] Moreover, the current discussions on the ECtHR may provide a clear warning for any international court perceived to be overstepping its competence and encroaching on the sovereignty of the national state. Given this political context, it is not unreasonable to suppose that any European institution, including the CJEU is unlikely to wish to stir up further unpopularity by making decisions which will be viewed with hostility by some of the EU's major players. A critical approach to bans on headscarves and other religious symbols by the CJEU could stir up exactly this type of hostility. For example, it is unlikely that the Court will want to alienate France by making a negative judgment on its *laïcité* approach, *laïcité* being so much part and parcel of French identity. This may help account for the decision of the ECtHR in *SAS v France* which indeed made specific reference to its unwillingness to intervene on matters that had been subject to the democratic process.[53]

It is clear, then, that powerful arguments exist that would favour a deferential approach by the CJEU in cases involving religious matters. The arguments are both legal and political. They involve deference to the already established jurisprudence of Europe's primary human rights court, as well as a recognition that now may not be a good time politically to reopen debates on religion and the state which have a long and conflict-ridden history. However, before advocating this deferential

[50] See the remarks in this respect by F Tulkens in her dissenting opinion in *Sahin v Turkey* (n 14).

[51] 'Public Opinion in the European Union', Standard Eurobarometer 77 Spring 2012, European Commission.

[52] In his speech of 23 January 2013 on the future of the EU, Prime Minister David Cameron announced he will hold a referendum in 2017 on British membership of the EU. He said that to keep the British on board the EU will have to reform and Brussels will have to return part of its power to the national states. See http://www.guardian.co.uk/politics/2013/jan/23/david-cameron-eu-speech-referendum (last accessed 21 April 2013).

[53] See *SAS v France* (n 24), para 154.

approach, it is worth considering the case for the Court requiring more exacting scrutiny of the compatibility of a ban on headscarves or other religious symbols for public servants with the EU equality directives, and ultimately, the Charter.

B. Reasons for Not Following a Deferential Line

In the first place, EU law and the concomitant supervisory role of the CJEU serve a different purpose compared to the human rights court. The role of the human rights court is basically to assess the conformity of state action with the state's obligations flowing from the ECHR in individual cases. The ECHR has no overarching purpose in terms of European integration. The EU, in contrast, has a much more encompassing agenda and therefore requires a different role for its CJEU. The Court is the ultimate authority on the proper interpretation of EU law to ensure the uniformity and efficacy of EU law.[54] Efficacy and uniformity may be endangered by a wide margin of discretion for the Member States as it allows for or may even promote widely diverging outcomes of transposing EU law. The judgment in the case of *Melloni* shows that the CJEU is very well aware of this danger and is prepared to affirm its authority in this regard:[55] the CJEU did not allow discretion to a Member State to apply a higher human rights standard (provided for in its Constitution) than was provided for in the EU rules regarding the European Arrest Warrant, which were in themselves compatible with the Charter, as deviation would undermine the primacy, unity and effectiveness of this part of EU law. In the case of the equality directives and their application to the headscarf issue, the effective transposition of the EU equality directives is at risk if different states impose different standards of protection. A wide margin of appreciation may well turn out to mean that protection against discrimination will encompass entirely different things in different countries. Any sense of uniformity and efficacy in the implementation of EU law would be lost.

A second reason for suggesting that the CJEU may wish to take a more interventionist stand on the implementation of the equality directives as they apply to the headscarf issue is that such an approach may help achieve other aims of EU social policy. For example, the EU has developed a strong strand of social policy on promoting inclusion and integration of migrant groups across the EU,[56] many of

[54] See the *Simmenthal* case (Case 106/77 *Amministrazione delle Finanze dello Stato v Simmenthal* [1978] ECR 629).

[55] Case C-399/11 *Melloniv Ministerio Fiscal*, 26 February 2013.

[56] See S Morano-Foadi and M Malena, 'Integration Policy at European Union Level' in S Morano-Foadi and M Malena (eds) *Integration for Third-Country Nationals in the European Union: The Equality Challenge* (Cheltenham, Edward Elgar, 2012). See also Council document 14615/04, 19.11.2004, and Conclusions of the European Council, 25/26 March 2010, EUCO 7/10, CO EUR 4, CONCL 1. See also Communication from the Commission to the European Parliament, the Council, the European Economic and Social Committee and the Committee of the Regions, European Agenda for the Integration of Third-Country Nationals (Brussels, 20.7.2011, COM (2011) 455 Final), p 5.

whom are from religious minorities. The equality directives can clearly be understood to form part of this process, as the employment sphere is recognised as a key area for promoting integration. This is in part because it is a common meeting point for those from different communities within a state who might not otherwise interact much, but also because improved employment levels for migrant populations will directly improve their levels of integration in society. Low employment rates are particularly marked in the case of migrant women,[57] many of whom are from religious minorities, and so it would seem that removing barriers to the employment of migrant female workers would be a step towards fulfilling the EU social policy agenda regarding migration and integration. Allowing different states to provide different levels of access to employment for women from religious minorities could thus be viewed as detrimental to the achievement of the EU social policy on integration.

The free movement of workers could provide further reasons for refusing the Member States much leeway, and imposing strict scrutiny when it comes to the interpretation of the equality directives. Banning headscarves in public functions or more generally limiting religious manifestations may well affect this EU pillar of EU integration. For example, some Muslims or Sikhs may be inhibited from moving to countries where they are refused jobs in public employment or where their children are not allowed to express their religion in public education;[58] thus, a doctor or teacher in the UK who wishes to wear of headscarf or turban to work may not enjoy full freedom to move to work in the EU if they are unable to do so without removing the turban or headscarf. An acceptance of the development over time of different practices relating to religion and work in Europe, which would be the result of a deferential approach by the Court, may well have implications for the EU right to free movement of workers.[59]

Another area of EU social policy which may be undermined by a wide margin of discretion relates to the notion of European citizenship which the EU endeavours to develop. Religion belongs to the common values of the European heritage and to the core of personal identity. Protection of its expression would thus seem to be an important part of any notion of European citizenship.[60] In this respect, how to deal with religious and cultural pluralism is one of the major challenges

[57] See Communication from the Commission to the European Parliament, the Council, the European Economic and Social Committee and the Committee of the Regions, European Agenda for the Integration of Third-Country Nationals (Brussels, 20.7.2011, COM (2011) 455 Final), p 5.

[58] Such claims have already been made, albeit unsuccessfully so far: see *R (Baradaran) v Secretary of State for the Home Department* [2014] EWCA Civ 854 where the argument was made in an asylum case that removal of a Muslim child to France should not be allowed because of the headscarf ban in school. The claim was dismissed.

[59] This argument is countered by some with the reasoning that free movement also means that one has an exit option if one does not like the limitations in a specific country. See I Cameron, 'Competing Rights?' in S de Vries, U Bernitz and S Weatherill (eds), *The Protection of Fundamental Rights in the EU After Lisbon* (Oxford, Hart Publishing, 2012) 181–213.

[60] This ties in with S Morano-Foadi, 'EU Citizenship and Religious Liberty in an Enlarged Europe' (2010) 16 *European Law Journal* 417–38.

contemporary Europe faces. Leaving this matter largely to national regulation could be seen as an admission of weakness.

Last but not least, as far as indirect sex discrimination or race/ethnic discrimination may be involved, a deferential approach would not be in line with the case law so far. As mentioned above, the approach of the CJEU to gender equality is very strict: any requirement must have a legitimate aim, the means chosen for achieving that objective must correspond to a real need on the part of the undertaking, must be appropriate with a view to achieving the objective in question and must be necessary to that end.[61] It is difficult to imagine how such a strict approach would have developed if the CJEU had accepted in the context of gender that the practice of states may legitimately vary according to each state's history and political situation, given that historically most of Europe has had well established practices and traditions in which gender discrimination has flourished. If the CJEU decides to take a deferential approach to equality when religious issues are involved, then, it will effectively introduce a hierarchy as between equality rights.[62] It would also create particular problems in cases of intersectional discrimination, as the result would differ depending on whether the claim were framed as gender discrimination, where there would be strict scrutiny, or religious discrimination, where there would not.

In sum, a deferential approach to the varieties of states' practice by the CJEU would have the effect of undermining both human rights and equality conceptions within EU law. The changes introduced by the Treaty of Lisbon, under which the Charter became binding and the EU has acceded to the Convention, were designed to give human rights a much more prominent place in the EU. The explicit purpose of these changes was the strengthening of human rights protection and human rights scrutiny. This move to enhancing the human rights protection at EU level will be undermined if the CJEU takes an approach to implementation which is deferential to variation in national states' practice. In effect, then, a wide margin of discretion would seem to imply that what is given with one hand is taken away with the other.

VI. CONCLUSIONS

From the above analysis it would seem that although powerful arguments exist in favour of the CJEU taking a deferential approach to national practice in cases involving religious matters, equally powerful arguments exist for a stricter standard to be applied. The arguments in favour of deference are partly based on

[61] *Bilka-Kaufhaus v Weber von Hartz* (n 38).

[62] M Bell and L Waddington, 'Reflecting on Inequalities in European Equality Law' (2003) 28 *EL Rev* 349; M Bell and L Waddington, 'More Equal Than Others: Distinguishing European Equality Directives' (2001) 38 *CML Rev* 587; and D Schiek, 'A New Framework on Equal Treatment of Persons in EC Law?' (2002) 8 *European Law Journal* 290.

consistency between the two legal systems and partly political. The arguments against deference are based on the need to uphold strict scrutiny of measures which involve equality norms, in part because of the potential for equality law to help achieve EU social policy objectives of citizenship and integration, but perhaps most importantly because of the importance that the EU has rightly put on upholding high equality standards in the case of gender and more recently race.

Despite what can be seen as the strength of the case for strict scrutiny, it is likely that the CJEU will take a deferential approach in cases involving religious symbols such as the headscarf. This is because in the current political climate, with increasingly critical voices being raised against the dominant role of the EU institutions, the arguments for a deferential approach in politically sensitive matters such as those discussed in this chapter could very well take the upper hand, especially since the CJEU may feel backed by the authority of the ECtHR. Given the reasonably weak democratic legitimacy of the EU,[63] the Court is unlikely to relish threatening European cohesion by stirring up issues of state autonomy on religious matters. This is even more the case given that the context in which these rights arise is the workplace, in which all the rights are, in any event, contingent.[64] In this context, it is suggested that the Court is likely to leave these issues to the discretion of the Member States.

If this is a correct assessment, however, the dangers identified in the case against deference, above, remain. Moreover, there is an additional danger: human rights standards could not only fail to enjoy enhanced protection; the standards themselves could in fact be eroded in those states where the protection has so far been high. An illustration of how this might happen can be seen in the current discussions in the Netherlands on the accommodation of religious manifestations in the public sphere. Despite a traditionally tolerant approach to religion in the public sphere, the general mood seems to be changing into a much less tolerant and accommodating attitude towards religious manifestations and maybe even towards religion as such.[65] Where there is a strong lead from EU law in favour of protection of rights, domestic attitudes matter less, as the EU law will take precedence over national laws in any event. For example, protection for sexual orientation equality at EU level has led some countries within the EU to implement protection which might well not have been implemented if left to national discretion.[66] However, where the approach of the EU is more deferential to states'

[63] See R McCrea, *Religion and the Public Order of the European Union* (Oxford, Oxford University Press, 2011).

[64] The religious rights in issue are usually rights to manifest, rights which are not in themselves absolute and the work context also means that residual protection is provided by a right not to work.

[65] For an overview of developments in the Netherlands, see M van den Brink and MLP Loenen, 'The Netherlands: Neutral But Not Indifferent' in P Cumper and T Lewis (eds), *Religion, Rights and Secular Society: European Perspectives* (Cheltenham, Elgar Publishing, 2012) 17–37.

[66] For discussion of the role of political actors in the development of sexual orientation protection, see R Uitz, 'Lessons from Sexual Orientation Discrimination in Central Europe' (2012) 60 *American Journal of Comparative Law* 235. See also R Wintemute, ch 10 in this volume.

practice, proponents of further limitations on equality law will not be curbed by the need to comply with European standards.

In effect, then, where public debate moves to restrict human rights protection, human rights advocates have been able to invoke the Court's case law to resist such moves. The same can apply to moves to erode equality rights. However, if the EU law moves to a position equivalent to the ECtHR and accepts a wide margin of appreciation in the level of protection afforded to certain human rights, those supporting the protection of equality rights will no longer be able to put up the barrier of EU law to the erosion of rights. There is then a real danger that some majorities will not hesitate to use this flexibility and deference to limit the human rights of minority groups.

10

In Extending Human Rights, which European Court is Substantively 'Braver' and Procedurally 'Fitter'?

The Example of Sexual Orientation and Gender Identity Discrimination

ROBERT WINTEMUTE*

I. INTRODUCTION

IT IS INCREASINGLY common for cases raising the same issue of human rights (or fundamental rights) to be presented both to the European Court of Human Rights (ECtHR) and the Court of Justice of the European Union (CJEU). In deciding these cases, is one European Court substantively 'braver' in extending the protection of human rights law than the other? Is one European Court procedurally 'fitter' to handle novel cases? A complete answer to that question would require a comprehensive survey of all human rights issues that have been addressed by both Courts. But a contribution towards an answer can be provided by examining a single, relatively novel question of human rights law, ie, protection against discrimination based on sexual orientation or gender identity. In doing so, this chapter will compare the timing of extensions of protection by each Court (Section II), consider what factors might explain the relative substantive

* Professor of Human Rights Law, King's College London. This chapter is based on a presentation at the conference 'Fundamental Rights in Europe: A Matter for Two Courts' held at the School of Law, Oxford Brookes University, on 18 January 2013. It also draws on the author's participation in cases before the Court of Justice of the European Union and the European Court of Human Rights, as an adviser to the lawyer(s) for the applicant (*Lisa Grant*, *EB v France*, *Maruko*), as the lawyer for the applicant (*Fretté v France*), or as the lawyer for third-party interveners (*Fretté v France*, *Karner v Austria*, *EB v France*, *Schalk and Kopf v Austria*, *Gas and Dubois v France*, *X and Others v Austria*, *Vallianatos and Others v Greece*).

'bravery' or caution of each Court (Section III), and assess the procedural advantages of raising a novel question in one Court or the other (Section IV).[1]

II. IN THIS AREA, DOES THE CJEU WAIT FOR ECtHR CASE LAW THAT IT CAN FOLLOW?

Some cases of discrimination based on sexual orientation or gender identity, especially in the areas of criminal and family law, fall outside the scope of EU law, and can only go to the ECtHR. But other cases have the potential to be referred to the CJEU, or to be submitted to the ECtHR, either directly in the absence of a reference to the CJEU, or after a reference in which the CJEU has found no violation of EU human rights standards. When an issue falls within the jurisdiction of both European Courts, but reaches the CJEU before the ECtHR has had a chance to consider it, how confident is the CJEU in finding a violation of EU human rights standards (including the Charter of Fundamental Rights and the anti-discrimination provisions of the Treaty on the Functioning of the European Union (TFEU) and related Directives), without any guidance from the ECtHR? An examination of the CJEU's case law with regard to sexual orientation and gender identity discrimination suggests that, in these circumstances, the CJEU has generally waited for ECtHR case law that it could follow.

With regard to gender identity discrimination, the timing of litigation has resulted in ECtHR precedents that have provided a foundation for subsequent favourable CJEU judgments, and spared the CJEU from having to strike out on its own. The first successful case involving a transsexual person was *B v France*,[2] in which the ECtHR held that France's refusal to change the legal sex of a transsexual woman (from male to female) on her birth certificate, and other identity documents, violated Article 8 (respect for private life) of the European Convention on Human Rights (ECHR). *B* provided a foundation for *P v S and Cornwall County Council*,[3] in which the CJEU found that 'dismissal of a transsexual for a reason related to a gender reassignment' was (presumably direct) sex discrimination contrary to Directive 76/207/EEC. Although *P* concerned the potentially less controversial question of a transsexual person's right to remain in employment after gender reassignment, rather than the question of their legal sex after gender reassignment, it is unlikely that the CJEU would have 'stretched' Directive

[1] The terms 'braver' and 'fitter' in the title are used metaphorically, not to describe attributes of courts that can be measured objectively. In this chapter, 'braver' means 'willing to take difficult decisions in a sensitive area without receiving prior guidance from another court of equal stature'. 'Fitter' means 'rules of procedure that make it easy for individuals, and civil society organisations supporting them, to raise novel human rights claims'. On the 'bravery' of national human rights institutions, see Kirsten Roberts (forthcoming publications).

[2] App no 13343/87 (ECtHR, 25 March 1992). All judgments and admissibility decisions of the ECtHR are available at http://hudoc.echr.coe.int. All cited cases are judgments, unless otherwise indicated.

[3] Case C-13/94 [1996] ECR I-2143. All judgments of the CJEU are available at http://eur-lex.europa.eu/en/index.htm (simply search by document number, ie case number).

76/207/EEC to protect Ms P if the ECtHR had not already protected Ms B. Indeed, in his Opinion, Advocate General Tesauro asked the CJEU 'to make a "courageous" decision', having previously cited the precedent set by the ECtHR in *B*.[4]

Did *B* and *P* mean that a transsexual person had the right to marry a person of the sex opposite to their reassigned sex (rather than their birth sex), and to enjoy all the rights and benefits of married different-sex couples? In *KB v National Health Service Pensions Agency*,[5] a non-transsexual female employee (Ms KB) sought the same survivor's pension for her transsexual male partner (Mr R, whom she could not legally marry) as would be paid to her husband, if she had married a non-transsexual man. When *KB* reached the CJEU on 15 March 2001, the most recent answer from the ECtHR, with regard to Ms KB's right to marry Mr R, was a resounding 'No', by 18 votes to two in *Sheffield and Horsham v the United Kingdom*.[6] As for the CJEU's own case law, Ms KB and Mr R were legally a same-sex couple, of which one member was transsexual, putting the facts midway between *Lisa Grant v South–West Trains* (a case, to be discussed below, in which a same-sex couple sought equal employment benefits) and *P* (which involved treatment of a transsexual person as an individual, rather than as a member of a couple).

Fortunately for Ms KB, the ECtHR had decided to review its case law on the right of transsexual persons to a change of legal sex, and access to different-sex marriage, by scheduling a Grand Chamber hearing in *Christine Goodwin v the United Kingdom*[7] for 20 March 2002, just before the 23 April 2002 hearing in *KB* (two of Ms Goodwin's barristers also represented Ms KB at her hearing). The ECtHR's judgment of 11 July 2002 held that the UK's failure to permit Ms Goodwin to request legal recognition of her gender reassignment violated Article 8 (respect for private life), and that her exclusion from different-sex marriage violated Article 12. After a delay to determine that the England and Wales Court of Appeal (EWCA) wished to proceed with the *KB* reference,[8] despite *Christine Goodwin*, the Advocate General (on 10 June 2003) and the CJEU (on 7 January 2004) found in Ms KB's favour, both citing *Christine Goodwin*. The effect of the CJEU's judgment (based on the right to equal pay without sex discrimination, now found in Article 157 TFEU) was to grant Ms KB and Mr R a temporary exemption from the marriage requirement, until the UK amended its legislation to comply with *Christine Goodwin*, which would permit Ms KB and Mr R to marry.

Having been guided by the ECtHR twice, the CJEU had no trouble dealing with its third case of gender identity discrimination, *Richards v Secretary of State for Work and Pensions*,[9] which it received after deciding *KB*. If a transsexual employee has a right not to be dismissed (*P*), and the transsexual partner of an employee has a right to a survivor's pension from an occupational scheme (*KB*), it must

[4] Opinion of 14 December 1995, paras 12 and 24.
[5] Case C-117/01 [2004] ECR I-541.
[6] App nos 22885/93, 23390/94 (ECtHR, 30 July 1998).
[7] App no 28957/95 (ECtHR, 11 July 2002).
[8] *KB* (n 5), Opinion of AG Ruiz-Jarabo Colomer, paras 12–14.
[9] Case C-423/04 [2006] ECR I-3585.

follow that a transsexual individual has a right to equal treatment with regard to state pensions. Indeed, the CJEU concluded in *Richards* that Directive 79/7/EEC requires the payment of a state pension to a transsexual woman from the age of 60, the same age as for a non-transsexual woman, rather than 65, the age for a non-transsexual man at the time. The CJEU's reasoning was supported less than a month later, when the ECtHR decided *Linda Grant v the United Kingdom.*[10] *Linda Grant* was virtually identical to *Richards*, but had been dismissed by the EWCA in 2003, without a reference to the CJEU, because *KB* had not yet been decided. In *Linda Grant*, the ECtHR found the refusal to pay a state pension to the applicant, a transsexual woman, at the same age as a non-transsexual woman, violated Article 8, but only from 5 September 2002, the date that 'the Department for Work and Pensions refused to award the applicant a State pension in light of the judgment in *Christine Goodwin*'.[11] Thus, the CJEU and the ECtHR decided essentially the same issue of gender identity discrimination within less than a month of each other, and reached the same result, except that the CJEU allowed Ms Richards to claim for the period between her 60th birthday (28 February 2002) and the *Christine Goodwin* judgment (11 July 2002), as well as the period after the judgment.

With regard to sexual orientation discrimination, the historical pattern is different, because the CJEU twice had to decide cases regarding the treatment of cohabiting or registered same-sex couples, *before* the ECtHR had found a violation of the ECHR in such a case. The CJEU's *P* judgment in 1996 on transgender equality immediately inspired a reference in a lesbian, gay and bisexual equality case: *Lisa Grant v South-West Trains Ltd*,[12] which concerned an employer's refusal to pay the same rail travel benefits to the unmarried female partner of a female employee (Lisa Grant) as to the unmarried female partner of a male employee, whose partner would qualify as a 'common law opposite sex spouse' if they had been in a 'meaningful relationship' for two years.[13] At the time of the CJEU's judgment, the only guidance from the ECtHR was that blanket bans on all private, consensual, adult, same-sex sexual activity violated Article 8 ECHR.[14] The opinion of the European Commission of Human Rights (EComHR) that a higher, and therefore unequal, age of consent for same-sex sexual activity, compared with different-sex sexual activity, violated Article 14 combined with Article 8, had not yet been confirmed by the ECtHR, and in any case did not require equal treatment outside the criminal law.[15] On the contrary, in six cases in which same-sex couples had been denied the same immigration or housing rights as unmarried

[10] App no 32570/03 (ECtHR, 23 May 2006).

[11] ibid, see paras 12 and 43. The ECtHR did not cite *Richards*, of which it was not necessarily aware, having adopted its *Linda Grant* judgment on 4 May 2006, only seven days after *Richards* was published.

[12] Case C-249/96 [1998] ECR I-621.

[13] ibid, para 5.

[14] *Dudgeon v the United Kingdom* App no 7525/76 (ECtHR, 22 October 1981) (ban in Northern Ireland).

[15] *Sutherland v UK* App no 25186/94 (1 July 1997) (non-binding report of former EComHR).

different-sex couples, the EComHR had found no violation of the ECHR, especially because same-sex couples did not enjoy 'family life' under Article 8.[16] Thus, it should have come as no surprise that, despite a favourable Advocate General's Opinion,[17] the CJEU rejected Lisa Grant's arguments. The CJEU held that refusing employment-related benefits to an unmarried female-female couple did not constitute direct sex discrimination with regard to pay, contrary to Article 157 TFEU (formerly Article 119 EC Treaty), because an unmarried male-male couple would have been treated in the same way.[18] Citing the negative decisions of the EComHR, as well as the ECtHR's negative judgments (before *Christine Goodwin*) on the exclusion of transsexual persons from different-sex marriage, the CJEU concluded that, 'in the present state of [EU] law…, stable relationships between two persons of the same sex are not regarded as equivalent to marriages or stable relationships outside marriage between persons of opposite sex'.[19]

The CJEU's second case of less favourable treatment of a same-sex couple was *D and Sweden v Council*,[20] in which a Swedish official of the Council argued that he and his same-sex registered partner (under Swedish law) should receive the same household allowance as a married different-sex couple. Had there been any developments in ECtHR case law that might support Mr D's case? Since *Lisa Grant*, the ECtHR had found that the UK's ban on lesbian, gay and bisexual individuals serving in the armed forces violated Article 8 ECHR,[21] and that courts violate Article 14 combined with Article 8 ECHR if they treat sexual orientation as a negative factor in making decisions about the custody of the genetic children of gay fathers and lesbian mothers. But neither case concerned the rights of a same-sex couple, as opposed to a lesbian, gay or bisexual individual.[22] And, far from departing from the EComHR's case law, the ECtHR had confirmed it by declaring *Mata Estevez v Spain*[23] inadmissible, albeit in a case in which the applicant did not have a lawyer, and in which there were no third-party interventions arguing that the EComHR's case law should be overruled. Although the CJEU did not cite and was probably not aware of *Mata Estevez*, it had received no signals from

[16] See *X and Y v the United Kingdom* App no 9369/81 (3 May 1983); *S v the United Kingdom* App no 11716/85 (14 May 1986); *WJ and DP v the United Kingdom* App no 12513/86 (11 September 1986); *C and LM v the United Kingdom* App no 14753/89 (9 October 1989); *B v the United Kingdom* App no 16106/90 (10 February 1990); *Röösli v Germany* App no 28318/95 (15 May 1996).

[17] Opinion of AG Elmer of 30 September 1997, para 50 (he urged the CJEU to find 'discrimination on the basis of gender' contrary to Art 119 EC Treaty).

[18] *Lisa Grant* (n 12), para 27. The reasoning used by the CJEU is flawed, because it is based on a misleading comparison: R Wintemute, 'Recognising New Kinds of Direct Sex Discrimination: Transsexualism, Sexual Orientation and Dress Codes' (1997) 60 *MLR* 334; R Wintemute, 'Sex Discrimination in *MacDonald* and *Pearce*: Why the Law Lords Chose the Wrong Comparators' (2003) 14 *King's College Law Journal* 267.

[19] *Lisa Grant* (n 12), paras 33–35.

[20] Joined Cases C-122/99 P and C-125/99 P [2001] ECR I-4319.

[21] *Smith and Grady v the United Kingdom* Application nos 33985/96 and 33986/96 (ECtHR, 27 September 1999).

[22] *Mouta v Portugal* App no 33290/96 (ECtHR, 21 December 1999).

[23] App no 56501/00 (ECtHR, 10 May 2001).

the ECtHR that it should consider departing from its approach in *Lisa Grant*. Thus, the CJEU rejected all of the appellants' pleas in *D and Sweden*, especially 'infringement of the principle of equal treatment of officials irrespective of sexual orientation', because 'the situation of an official who has registered a partnership in Sweden cannot be held to be comparable, for the purposes of the Staff Regulations, to that of a married official'.[24]

The CJEU's third case of less favourable treatment of a same-sex couple was *Maruko*,[25] in which a German public sector occupational pension scheme paid survivors' pensions only to surviving different-sex spouses, and not to surviving same-sex registered partners (even though Germany's state pension scheme treated registered partners equally). Had there been any developments in ECtHR case law that might support Mr Maruko's case? Since *D and Sweden*, the ECtHR had extended protection for lesbian, gay and bisexual *individuals* against discrimination from access to military and other employment, and child custody decisions, to the age of consent to sexual activity,[26] and adoption of children by unmarried individuals.[27] But more importantly, on 11 September 2001, a few months after *D and Sweden*, the ECtHR departed from *Mata Estevez* by declaring *Karner v Austria*[28] admissible. In its *Karner* judgment of 24 July 2003, the ECtHR found discrimination against a same-sex couple for the first time: failure to extend to an unmarried same-sex partner the right of an unmarried different-sex partner to succeed to the tenancy of a house or flat violated Article 14 combined with Article 8. The ECtHR required 'particularly serious reasons' to justify a difference in treatment based on sexual orientation,[29] and applied its proportionality test strictly. It was not enough that Austria's rule was suitable (or appropriate) to achieve the 'weighty and legitimate' aim of 'protecting the family in the traditional sense': 'It must also be shown that it was necessary to exclude persons living in a homosexual relationship … in order to achieve that aim'.[30]

As for developments in EU law, the CJEU was clearly too cautious in its *Lisa Grant* and *D and Sweden* judgments, because in each case it took less than three years for the EU legislature to remedy the discrimination that had been challenged. After *Lisa Grant* (February 1998), the Council adopted Directive 2000/78 in November 2000, which prohibits direct discrimination based on sexual orientation in relation to 'pay', including free travel, survivor's pensions, and other employment benefits of financial value. It is almost certain that, today, applying

[24] *D and Sweden* (n 20), paras 47–52.

[25] Case C-267/06 [2008] ECR I-1757.

[26] *SL v Austria* App no 45330/99 (ECtHR, 9 January 2003) (higher age of consent for male-male sexual activity violated Art 14 combined with Art 8 ECHR, confirming the EComHR's opinion in *Sutherland*).

[27] *EB v France* App no 43546/02 (ECtHR, 22 January 2008) (rejection of openly lesbian woman's application for approval as a potential adoptive parent, because of her sexual orientation, violated Art 14 combined with Art 8 ECHR).

[28] App no 40016/98 (ECtHR, 24 July 2003).

[29] ibid, para 37.

[30] ibid, paras 40–43.

Karner, the CJEU would reach the opposite conclusion in a case with facts like *Lisa Grant*. Similarly, after *D and Sweden* (May 2001), the Staff Regulations were amended in March 2004 to provide that a 'non-marital partnership shall be treated as marriage provided that … the couple produces a legal document recognised as such by a Member State … acknowledging their status as non-marital partners … [and provided] that the couple has no access to legal marriage in a Member State'.[31]

At the hearing in 2007, Mr Maruko's lawyer cited *Karner* to the CJEU. Did it make a difference? In its judgment of 1 April 2008, the CJEU did not cite *Karner*, but clearly departed from (and effectively overruled) its judgments in *Lisa Grant* and *D and Sweden*, without referring to them, by finding discrimination against a same-sex couple for the first time. The CJEU was unwilling to accept the argument of Mr Maruko's lawyer that restricting an employment-related pension benefit to married different-sex spouses was indirect discrimination based on sexual orientation in all member states in which same-sex couples could not marry (in 2008, 24 out of 27, or all but the Netherlands, Belgium and Spain). This was probably because the ECtHR has yet to accept an indirect discrimination argument of this kind, involving a comparison between a married different-sex couple and a registered or cohabiting same-sex couple.[32] Instead, the CJEU accepted the narrower argument of the Commission and the Advocate General (because it would apply to fewer member states) that Directive 2000/78/EC only prohibits (as direct or indirect discrimination based on sexual orientation) differences in treatment between spouses and registered partners in member states that have voluntarily introduced registered partnership, and voluntarily treat it 'in the same way' as marriage, or give it 'substantially the same [effects]' as marriage.[33] The CJEU thus held that *if* a member state decides to pass a registered partnership law for same-sex couples (as Germany had done, but Italy, Poland and other member states had not done), *and if* the law 'places persons of the same sex in a situation comparable to that of spouses so far as concerns that survivor's benefit' (as Germany had done, but some member states with registered partnership laws might not have done), then the prohibition of direct discrimination based on sexual orientation with regard to pay, in Directive 2000/78/EC, requires that a same-sex registered partner receives the same survivor's pension as a married different-sex spouse.[34] Unlike the Advocate General, the CJEU characterised the

[31] Staff Regulations of officials of the European Communities, Article 1d(1) and Annex VII, Article 1(2)(c), as amended by Council Regulation 723/2004/EC of 22 March 2004 [2004] OJ L124/1.

[32] The ECtHR rejected such an argument in *Gas and Dubois v France* App no 25951/07 (ECtHR, 15 March 2012), paras 42, 67–68. A French court asked about indirect discrimination in Case C-267/12 *Frédéric Hay v Crédit agricole mutuel de Charente-Maritime et des Deux-Sèvres* [2013] ECR I-0000, in which a gay man entered a 'civil solidarity pact', but was denied the extra paid holidays and cash bonus granted to employees who enter a marriage (restricted to different-sex couples at the time).

[33] Opinion of AG Ruiz-Jarabo Colomer of 6 September 2007, paras 27, 111.

[34] *Maruko* (n 25), para 72. See G Toggenburg, '"LGBT" go Luxembourg: On the Stance of Lesbian Gay Bisexual and Transgender Rights before the European Court of Justice' (2008) 5 *European Law Reporter* 1–17.

discrimination as direct rather than indirect, because it was between couples in comparable legal situations (as in *Karner*) and implicitly because the difference in name (marriage versus registered partnership) was immaterial. In so doing, the CJEU avoided a voyage into the uncharted (by the ECtHR) territory of indirect discrimination based on sexual orientation.

Since *Maruko*, can we see the same pattern of the CJEU following the lead of the ECtHR? In *Schalk and Kopf v Austria*, the ECtHR ruled (by seven votes to zero) that the ECHR did not require Austria to allow same-sex couples to marry,[35] and (by four votes to three) that the ECHR did not require Austria to bring a registered partnership law for same-sex couples into force earlier than it had done (1 January 2010),[36] but (by seven votes to zero) that 'a cohabiting same-sex couple living in a stable de facto partnership, falls within the notion of "family life" [in Article 8 ECHR], just as the relationship of a different-sex couple in the same situation would'.[37] As will be noted below, the ECtHR's statement regarding 'family life' in *Schalk and Kopf* had no discernible effect on the terminology used by the CJEU in *Römer*,[38] its fourth case of less favourable treatment of a same-sex couple, in which it applied and clarified *Maruko*. The only factual difference in *Römer* was that the employee was still alive and was receiving a smaller monthly pension because he had a registered same-sex partner, rather than a married different-sex spouse. The CJEU explained that 'comparable' in *Maruko* did not mean an identical legal situation. Instead, it is enough if the 'relevant' legal rights and obligations of registered partners and spouses are the same, ie, if registered partners 'have [legal] duties towards each other, to support and care for one another and to contribute adequately to the common needs of the partnership by their work and from their property, as is the case between spouses'.[39] In its fifth case of less favourable treatment of a same-sex couple, *Frédéric Hay*,[40] the CJEU found that denying a same-sex couple an employment benefit linked to marriage was direct discrimination based on sexual orientation, as in *Maruko* and *Römer*, even though the *pacte civil de solidarité* was also open to different-sex couples, because marriage was not open to same-sex couples at the relevant time.

The ECtHR's most recent judgments on sexual orientation discrimination are *X and Others v Austria*[41] and *Vallianatos and Others v Greece*.[42] In *X and Others*, the Grand Chamber applied its *Karner* principle to second-parent adoption for

[35] App no 30141/04 (ECtHR, 24 June 2010), paras 61–63.

[36] ibid, paras 104–06 and the joint dissenting opinion. The ECtHR decided in *Vallianatos and Others v Greece* App nos 29381/09 and 32684/09 (ECtHR, 7 November 2013) that the Greek Parliament discriminated based on sexual orientation, violating Article 14 combined with Article 8, when it passed a (weak) registered partnership law for unmarried different-sex couples in 2008 (it is the only implemented alternative to marriage in Europe that excludes same-sex couples).

[37] ibid, para 94.

[38] Case C-147/08 [2011] ECR I-3591.

[39] ibid, paras 41–47.

[40] Above n 32.

[41] App no 19010/07 (ECtHR, 19 February 2013).

[42] ibid (n 36).

same-sex couples in countries that allow unmarried different-sex couples to propose such an adoption, and confirmed the statement of the Chamber in *Schalk and Kopf* that same-sex couples enjoy 'family life'.[43] In *Vallianatos*, the Grand Chamber applied its *Karner* principle to new couple registration systems created as an alternative to marriage, holding that they must be open both to unmarried different-sex couples and same-sex couples.

The CJEU's most recent judgments are its first not to involve the rights of a same-sex couple, but rather the easier questions of hypothetical lesbian, gay and bisexual individuals applying for employment, and lesbian, gay and bisexual asylum seekers. In *Asociaţia ACCEPT v Consiliul Naţional pentru Combaterea Discriminării*,[44] a shareholder of a football club told the mass media that:

> Not even if I had to close [FC Steaua] down would I accept a homosexual on the team … There's no room for gays in my family, and [FC Steaua] is my family. Rather than having a homosexual on the side it would be better to have a junior player. This isn't discrimination … I have the right to work with whoever I choose … Even if [player X's current club] gave him to me for free I wouldn't have him! … [I]f he's a homosexual I don't want to know about him.

The CJEU held that Directive 2000/78/EC does not require 'an identifiable complainant', that an employer 'cannot deny the existence of facts from which it may be inferred that it has a discriminatory recruitment policy merely by asserting that statements suggestive of the existence of a homophobic recruitment policy come from a person who … is not legally capable of binding it in recruitment matters', and that an employer is not required to prove hiring of lesbian, gay or bisexual employees in the past, but may instead rebut a presumption of discrimination simply by demonstrating the non-discriminatory factors on which their recruitment policy is based.[45] In *ACCEPT*, no particular guidance from the ECtHR was required, because the decision had a solid foundation in the text of Directive 2000/78/EC, which was adopted just over a year after the ECtHR's 1999 judgments on exclusion from military employment.[46]

In Joined Cases *X, Y and Z*[47] the CJEU did not wait for ECtHR case law, but could be said to have followed national case law. Despite the negative admissibility decision of the ECtHR in *F v the United Kingdom*,[48] which permitted a man claiming to be gay to be deported to Iran, the CJEU had no trouble concluding that, under Directive 2004/83/EC on minimum standards for qualification as a refugee 'the competent authorities cannot reasonably expect, in order to avoid the risk of persecution, the applicant for asylum to conceal his homosexuality in his country of origin or to exercise reserve in the expression of his sexual orientation'.

[43] *X and Others* (n 41), paras 95, 151.
[44] Case C-81/12 [2013] ECR I-0000.
[45] ibid, at paras 36, 49, 56.
[46] See, eg, *Smith and Grady v the United Kingdom* (n 21).
[47] Joined Cases C-199/12 to C-201/12 *X, Y and Z v Minister voor Immigratie en Asiel, intervening parties: United Nations High Commissioner for Refugees* [2013] ECR I-0000.
[48] App no 17341/03 (ECtHR, 22 June 2004).

This reasoning had been adopted by the UK Supreme Court in *HJ (Iran) and HT (Cameroon) v Secretary of State for the Home Department*,[49] and was supported by a third-party intervener in the Dutch courts, the United Nations High Commissioner for Refugees.

The ECtHR will have an unusual opportunity to catch up with the CJEU, when the Grand Chamber hears *M.E. v Sweden*.[50] The Chamber held, 'by six votes to one that the expulsion of the applicant to Libya would not give rise to a violation of Article 3 [ECHR]'. The majority considered it acceptable that the applicant, a man married to a man in Sweden, would have to return to Libya, wait at least four months for a family reunion visa, and 'be discreet about his private life during this time'. Judge Power-Forde wrote a strong dissent, which cited *X, Y and Z*:

> What counts, for the CJEU, is the fact of having to exercise greater restraint and reserve than would be required of a heterosexual … not the length of time for which the discriminatory restraint and reserve would have to be endured … Sexual orientation is fundamental to an individual's identity … and no one should be forced to renounce it—even for a while.

The following two tables summarise the chronology of the case law of the two European Courts:

A. Gender Identity Discrimination

Table 1

Year	European Court of Human Rights (ECtHR)	Court of Justice of the European Union (CJEU)
1992	*B v France* (25 March 1992) (violation of Art 8 ECHR: refusal to change legal sex of transsexual woman on birth certificate)	
1996		Case C-13/94 *P v S and Cornwall County Council* (30 April 1996) ('dismissal of a transsexual for a reason related to a gender reassignment' was sex discrimination contrary to the Equal Treatment Directive)

(Continued)

[49] [2010] UKSC 31. See also Joined Cases C-148/13, C-149/13 and C-150/13 *A, B and C*, 17 July 2014.

[50] *M.E. v Sweden*, Chamber judgment of 26 June 2014, paras 88–89; Grand Chamber hearing scheduled for 22 April 2015.

Table 1: (*Continued*)

Year	European Court of Human Rights (ECtHR)	Court of Justice of the European Union (CJEU)
2002	*Christine Goodwin v the United Kingdom* (11 July 2002) (violations of Arts 8 and 12 ECHR: refusal to change legal sex of transsexual woman on birth certificate and allow her to marry a non-transsexual man)	
2004		Case C-117/01 *KB v National Health Service Pensions Agency* (7 January 2004) (Art 157 TFEU requires survivor's pension for transsexual male partner of non-transsexual female employee, even though they could not yet marry)
2006	*Linda Grant v the United Kingdom* (23 May 2006) (violation of Art 8 ECHR: refusal to pay state pension to transsexual woman at age of 60)	Case C-423/04 *Richards v Secretary of State for Work and Pensions* (27 April 2006) (Directive 79/7 requires payment of state pension to transsexual woman at age of 60)

B. Sexual Orientation Discrimination

Table 2

Year	European Court of Human Rights (ECtHR)	Court of Justice of the European Union (CJEU)
1981	*Dudgeon v the United Kingdom* (22 October 1981) (violation of Art 8 ECHR: blanket ban on male-male sexual activity in Northern Ireland)	
1997	*Sutherland v the United Kingdom* (1 July 1997) (non-binding report of former EComHR; violation of Art 14 combined with Art 8 ECHR: higher age of consent to male-male sexual activity)	
1998		Case C-249/96 *Lisa Grant v South-West Trains* (17 February 1998) (employment benefit provided to employees' unmarried different-sex but not same-sex partners was not sex discrimination contrary to Art 157 TFEU)

(Continued)

Table 2: (*Continued*)

Year	European Court of Human Rights (ECtHR)	Court of Justice of the European Union (CJEU)
1999	*Smith and Grady v the United Kingdom* (27 September 1999) (violation of Art 8 ECHR: dismissal of lesbian, gay and bisexual members of armed forces) *Mouta v Portugal* (21 December 1999) (violation of Art 14 combined with Art 8 ECHR: custody of girl transferred from her gay father to her heterosexual mother; distinction based on sexual orientation'not acceptable under the Convention')	
2001		Joined Cases C-122/99 P and C-125/99 P *D and Sweden v Council* (31 May 2001) (EU law did not require that a household allowance for different-sex spouses be extended to same-sex registered partners)
2003	*SL v Austria* (9 January 2003) (violation of Art 14 combined with Art 8 ECHR: higher age of consent to male-male sexual activity; 'differences [in treatment] based on sexual orientation require particularly serious reasons by way of justification') *Karner v Austria* (24 July 2003) (violation of Art 14 combined with Art 8 ECHR: housing succession right for surviving unmarried different-sex but not same-sex partners)	
2008	*EB v France* (22 January 2008) (violation of Art 14 combined with Art 8 ECHR: lesbian woman ineligible to apply to adopt a child as an unmarried individual)	Case C-267/06 *Maruko* (1 April 2008) (*if* a member state decides to pass a registered partnership law for same-sex couples, *and if* the law 'places persons of the same sex in a situation comparable to that of spouses so far as concerns that survivor's benefit', then Directive 2000/78 requires that a registered partner receives the same survivor's pension as a spouse)

(Continued)

Table 2: (*Continued*)

Year	European Court of Human Rights (ECtHR)	Court of Justice of the European Union (CJEU)
2010	*Schalk and Kopf v Austria* (24 June 2010) (no violation of Art 12 or Art 14 combined with Art 8 ECHR: same-sex couples enjoy 'family life' and Art 12 is applicable but no right to marry yet for lack of European consensus; question of whether an alternative to marriage is required left open)	
2011		Case C-147/08 *Römer* (10 May 2011) (similar to *Maruko* with clarification regarding what makes situations comparable)
2012	*Gas and Dubois v* France (15 March 2012) (no violation of Art 14 combined with Art 8 ECHR: second-parent adoption restricted to married different-sex couples)	
2013	*X and Others v Austria* (19 February 2013) (violation of Art 14 combined with Art 8 ECHR: second-parent adoption open to unmarried different-sex but not same-sex couples) *Vallianatos and Others v Greece* (7 November 2013) (violation of Art 14 combined with Art 8 ECHR: alternative registration system for unmarried different-sex couples only)	Case C-81/12 *Asociaţia ACCEPT* (25 April 2013) (statements by person associated with football club that he would not have a gay player on his team could be 'facts from which it may be presumed that there has been … discrimination' under Directive 2000/78) Joined Cases C-199/12 to C-201/12 *X, Y and Z v Minister voor Immigratie en Asiel* (7 November 2013) (no need to conceal sexual orientation in country of origin to avoid persecution) Case C-267/12 *Frédéric Hay* (12 December 2013) (denial to same-sex couple of employment benefit linked to marriage was direct discrimination based on sexual orientation, as in *Maruko* and *Römer*, even though *pacte civil de solidarité* is also open to different-sex couples)

III. IN THIS AREA, IS THE ECtHR SUBSTANTIVELY 'BRAVER' THAN THE CJEU?

The preceding analysis of the European Courts' case law on sexual orientation and gender identity discrimination suggests that the CJEU has generally done nothing for lesbian, gay, bisexual or transgender (LGBT) individuals and same-sex couples, with regard to a particular issue, unless the ECtHR had already provided some protection. *P* (CJEU, 1996) was made possible by *B* (ECtHR, 1992), which was cited by the Advocate General in *P. KB* (CJEU, 2004) and *Richards* (CJEU, 2006) were made possible by *Christine Goodwin* (ECtHR, 2002). *Lisa Grant* (CJEU, 1998) and *D* (CJEU, 2001) failed because there was not yet any favourable case law from the ECtHR on couples that are factually and legally same-sex (ie, where neither partner has undergone gender reassignment). *Maruko* (CJEU, 2008) and *Römer* (CJEU, 2011) succeeded because of *Karner* (ECtHR, 2003). However, the CJEU used narrow reasoning based on direct discrimination, which limits the impact of *Maruko* and *Römer* to the minority of member states that have registered partnership laws for same-sex couples, but do not already provide equal treatment with regard to benefits for employees' same-sex partners. The CJEU's reasoning might change in the future, if the ECtHR finds a violation in a case of indirect discrimination based on sexual orientation. The exceptions to this pattern are *ACCEPT* (proving employment discrimination) and *X, Y and Z* (asylum), which did not concern same-sex couples, and where guidance was available either from the CJEU's prior decisions on racial or ethnic origin (*Firma Feryn*[51] in *ACCEPT*) or religion (*Y and Z*[52] in *X, Y and Z*), or from the UK Supreme Court (in *X, Y and Z*).

What factors explain the relative 'bravery' of the ECtHR, compared with the CJEU, when addressing the legally, politically and socially controversial issues raised by cases of sexual orientation and gender identity discrimination? One factor could be specialisation and its effect on 'judicial self-confidence'. The ECtHR is a full-time human rights court with primary responsibility for interpreting the ECHR. The CJEU is a part-time human rights court that seeks to apply the minimum standards of the ECHR but, just like a national court, is often cautious about anticipating improvements in the ECtHR's case law, or being 'more generous' than the ECtHR, ie setting a higher standard than the ECtHR for EU member states, with regard to a particular human rights issue.[53]

A second factor could be the limited jurisdiction of the CJEU, which protects the human rights of individuals against EU institutions, and against member

[51] Case C-54/07 *Centrum voor gelijkheid van kansen en voor racismebestrijding v Firma Feryn NV* [2008] ECR I-5187.

[52] In Joined Cases C-71/11 and C-99/11 *Bundesrepublik Deutschland v Y and Z*, 5 September 2012, paras 79–80, the CJEU ruled that Ahmadi Muslims are not obliged to abstain from certain religious practices to avoid persecution in Pakistan.

[53] Compare *R v Special Adjudicator, ex p Ullah* [2004] UKHL 26, para 20 (Lord Bingham), with *Re P* [2008] UKHL 38 and *EM (Lebanon)* [2008] UKHL 64.

states 'only when they are implementing Union law'.[54] The ECtHR does not have to ask itself whether a member state 'is implementing Council of Europe law'. Under Article 1 ECHR, all acts and omissions of all public authorities in the territory of each Council of Europe member state, and in other territories where they have effective control,[55] can be reviewed for compliance with the rights in the ECHR and its Protocols. It makes no difference whether the act or omission relates to criminal law, family law, immigration law, tax law or social security law. All legislation on all subjects, including the national constitution, is potentially subject to review.

Because the CJEU has a limited jurisdiction over acts and omissions of public authorities in EU member states, it must constantly ask itself whether a particular extension of a human right will trespass on member state competences. In the area of sexual orientation and gender identity discrimination, the particular concern is always whether an extension would trespass on member state competence over family law. The CJEU's hesitation is reflected not only in its waiting for guidance from the ECtHR, but also in the terminology used in its judgments. In *Karner*, the ECtHR referred to 'a couple of the same sex'.[56] In *Schalk and Kopf*, after finding that same-sex couples enjoy 'family life', the ECtHR observed that 'same-sex couples are just as capable as different-sex couples of entering into stable committed relationships. Consequently, they are in a relevantly similar situation to a different-sex couple as regards their need for legal recognition and protection of their relationship.'[57] Yet in *Maruko* and *Römer*, the CJEU insisted on referring to 'persons of the same sex' (or 'persons of the same gender') rather than 'couples of the same sex'.[58] The same was true in *Lisa Grant* and *D and Sweden*.[59] In *Hay* (2013), the CJEU finally referred to 'same-sex couples' and 'homosexual couples'.[60] And in *Römer* (2011) and *Hay* (2013), the CJEU did not cite the ECtHR's extension of 'family life' to same-sex couples in *Schalk and Kopf* (2010).

A good example of the limit on the CJEU's jurisdiction over sexual orientation and gender identity discrimination in family law was a statement by Advocate General Jääskinen in *Römer*:

> It is the Member States that must decide whether or not their national legal order allows any form of legal union available to homosexual couples, or whether or not the institution of marriage is only for couples of the opposite sex. In my view, a situation in which a Member State does not allow any form of legally recognised union available to persons of the same sex may be regarded as practising [indirect?] discrimination on the basis of sexual orientation, because it is possible to derive from the principle of equality, together with the duty to respect the human dignity of homosexuals, an obligation

[54] Charter of Fundamental Rights of the EU, Art 51(1).
[55] *Al-Skeini v the United Kingdom* App no 55721/07 (ECtHR, 7 July 2011), paras 130–42.
[56] *Karner* (n 28), para 42.
[57] *Schalk and Kopf* (n 35), paras 94, 99.
[58] *Maruko* (n 25), paras 67, 73; *Römer* (n 38), paras 44, 52.
[59] *Lisa Grant* (n 12), para 35; *D and Sweden* (n 20), para 48.
[60] *Hay* (n 32), paras 36, 43.

[a positive obligation?] to recognise their right to conduct a stable relationship within a legally recognised commitment. However, in my view, this issue, which concerns legislation on marital status, lies outside the sphere of activity of Union law.[61]

In *Schalk and Kopf*, three out of seven judges of the ECtHR, in dissent, would have imposed on member states 'an obligation to recognise [the] right [of same-sex couples] to conduct a stable relationship within a legally recognised commitment'. The four judges forming the majority found it unnecessary to rule on this question: 'Given that at present [from 1 January 2010] it is open to the applicants to enter into a registered partnership, the Court is not called upon to examine whether the lack of any means of legal recognition for same-sex couples [in Austria] would constitute a violation of Article 14 taken in conjunction with Article 8 if it still obtained today'. Unlike the CJEU, the ECtHR will have to examine this question in future cases from member states with no registered partnership law for same-sex couples (such as Italy), and will not be able to dismiss it as 'outside the sphere of activity of [Convention] law'.[62]

IV. IS THE ECtHR PROCEDURALLY 'FITTER' TO EXTEND HUMAN RIGHTS THAN THE CJEU?

For a court to extend the protection of human rights law, it must not only be willing to engage in 'brave' substantive reasoning, it must have procedures that make if 'fit' to handle the cases that might permit extension. Its procedures affect (i) the access of individual applicants to the court, (ii) the possibility of participation by third parties, including non-governmental organisations, (iii) the languages that may be used in written and oral pleadings, (iv) the form of its judgment, and (v) the length of time it takes to process a case. Taking into account these five factors, which of the ECtHR or the CJEU is procedurally 'fitter' to extend the protection of human rights law?

First, there can be no doubt that it is much easier for an individual to take a case to the ECtHR than to the CJEU. Although Protocol No 15 to the ECHR will tighten access to the ECtHR, especially by shortening the application deadline from six months to four months after the final decision at the national level,[63] it will remain the case that an individual who has exhausted domestic remedies (or has no effective domestic remedies) in their national courts, meets the deadline, and can 'claim[] to be the victim of a violation' of a Convention right causing them 'significant disadvantage', has a right to lodge an application with the ECtHR against a Council of Europe member state, under Article 34 ECHR. No such

[61] Opinion of AG Jääskinen of 15 July 2010, para 76.

[62] See the pending ECtHR cases of *Oliari v Italy* App no 18766/11 and *Orlandi v Italy* App no 26431/12, communicated in 2013.

[63] CETS No 213, opened for signature on 24 June 2013, http://conventions.coe.int.

general right of direct access exists for the CJEU and its General Court, because the strict standing requirements of Article 263(4) TFEU preclude most cases brought by individuals (especially regarding the interpretation of treaty articles and directives) from beginning in the General Court. Instead, most such cases must begin in a national court, and it is impossible to force a national court to make a reference to the CJEU, even when Article 267(3) TFEU applies.[64] While the ECHR permits individuals to join the (very long) queue for human rights justice at the ECtHR, EU law provides that no amount of pounding on the door, or going on hunger strike in front of the door, will get an individual's case into the CJEU, without 'a note' from their national court, no matter how novel or important the question of EU law they wish to present. If and when the EU accedes to the ECHR, the ECtHR will also be able to provide 'a note', ie, the ECtHR may decide to refer to the CJEU questions of EU law that a national court failed to refer.

Second, if an individual's case makes it to the CJEU, as the result of a reference, they are often on their own, apart from the lawyers they can afford to pay, or who are willing and able to handle the case for free, who in either case will not necessarily be experts on EU human rights law. If the individual must pay and cannot afford to send a lawyer to Luxembourg, in some cases they will not be represented at the hearing.[65] The fact that the individual is not well represented, or not represented at all, might be mitigated by the fact that the Commission supports their case, and will make arguments that might persuade the CJEU. But this is not always so. Sometimes, the Commission might oppose the individual,[66] or might support an intermediate position that it considers more likely to be accepted by EU member states.[67] Are non-governmental organisations (NGOs) with expertise on the particular human rights issue permitted to support the individual, and make his or her struggle against (in some cases) the Commission and multiple intervening governments less unequal, by applying to the CJEU for leave to intervene in the reference proceedings? The answer is no.[68] Third-party intervention is only possible with leave of a national court (often the one that made the reference), which assumes that a procedure for authorising interventions already exists at the national level.[69]

[64] Case C-224/01 *Köbler v Republik Österreich* [2003] ECR I-10239 provides a theoretical possibility of claiming damages in a national court for a failure to refer. See also *Dhahbi v Italy* App No 17120/09 (ECtHR, 8 April 2014), where a national court's refusal to consider a request for a reference violated Art 6 ECHR.

[65] See, eg, Case C-13/05 *Chacón Navas v Eurest Colectividades SA* [2006] ECR I-6467.

[66] See, eg, *P v S and Cornwall County Council* (n 3), para 14.

[67] See, eg, *Lisa Grant* (n 12), para 23.

[68] Applications by private parties to intervene may only be made in direct actions that start in the General Court: Statute of the Court of Justice, Art 40; Rules of Procedures of the Court of Justice, rr 129–131. See also O De Schutter, 'Le tiers à l'instance devant la Cour de justice de l'Union européenne' in H Ruiz Fabri and J-M Sorel (eds), *Le tiers à l'instance* (Paris, Pedone, 2005).

[69] See Carrera, De Somer and Petkova, 'The Court of Justice of the European Union as a Fundamental Rights Tribunal' pp 14–16, available at http://www.ceps.eu/book/court-justice-european union fundamental-rights-tribunal-challenges-effective-delivery-fundamen (29 August 2012).

This is true of the UK,[70] but not of all EU member states,[71] which detracts from the uniform enforcement of EU human rights law. The position in CJEU references contrasts sharply with that in applications to the ECtHR. Under Article 36(2) ECHR, 'the Court may, in the interest of the proper administration of justice, invite … any person concerned who is not the applicant to submit written comments or take part in hearings'.[72]

Third, an NGO granted leave to intervene in a case before the ECtHR may use the official languages of the ECtHR, English or French, in any written document or at a hearing. It is therefore possible for a lawyer from any country in Europe to work on a case against Azerbaijan, Hungary or Ukraine, without being able to read, write or speak Azeri, Hungarian or Ukrainian. Before the CJEU, despite its large staff of interpreters and translators, linguistic freedom is highly restricted. EU institutions and private parties must respect the language of the case, which is that of the national court that made the reference, unless special permission to use another language is requested and granted.[73] This means that, even if a European-level NGO were granted leave to intervene by the referring national court, they would be expected to submit their written observations in Estonian, Greek or Hungarian, if that were the language of the case. Only a member state is permitted to use another language, and then only its official language,[74] not another official EU language that it would prefer to use. For example, a lawyer representing the Estonian government might prefer to speak in English, French or German, so that more than one judge would be able to understand their arguments without the need for interpretation. At hearings, judges and Advocates General are free to use any official EU language.[75]

Fourth, the form of CJEU judgments resembles that of the French legal system (the most influential among the first six EU member states), which does not permit dissenting judgments. Although the appearance of unanimity is intended to enhance the authority of the judgment, it gives a false impression that there was an obviously correct answer, and often has the effect of diminishing the clarity of the reasoning, compared with a system in which the majority and minority judges are allowed to express their reasoning in their own way. Moreover, the rigidity of compulsory unanimity is not well suited to human rights law, which evolves over time, as the weight given to competing arguments shifts with changing legal, political and social conditions. Dissenting judgments can point out weaknesses in the majority's reasoning

[70] See, eg, Case C-192/99 *The Queen v Secretary of State for the Home Department (SSHD), ex p Manjit Kaur, intervener: Justice* [2001] ECR I-1237; Case C-411/10 *NS* [2011] ECR I-13905 (four intervening parties); Case C-529/11 *Alarape v SSHD, intervening party: AIRE Centre* [2013] ECR I-0000; *X, Y and Z* (n 47).

[71] See, eg, *Maruko* (n 25), in which there was no procedure permitting ILGA-Europe (the European Region of the International Lesbian, Gay, Bisexual, Trans and Intersex Association) to apply to the German court that referred the case for leave to intervene.

[72] See also Rules of Court, r 44(3).

[73] Rules of Procedure of the Court of Justice, Arts 37(3), 38(1).

[74] ibid, Art 38(4).

[75] ibid, Art 38(8).

(which might be addressed and removed in future cases), might eventually persuade the majority to adopt the dissenters' interpretation, or might come to be seen as ill-founded. Defeat after raising a novel human rights issue is much less devastating if a dissenting judgment offers a glimmer of hope to the individual and NGOs supporting them, because they can see that they persuaded one or more judges, and that they might persuade more in a future case. The monolithic, unanimous rejection of the discrimination arguments in *Lisa Grant* (1998) and *D and Sweden* (2001), followed by their monolithic, unanimous acceptance in 2008 in *Maruko* (without acknowledging or explaining the departure from the two prior judgments), contrasts sharply with *Sheffield and Horsham v the United Kingdom* (1998) (no violation of Article 12 ECHR by 18 votes to two) and *Christine Goodwin* (2002) (violation by 17 votes to zero), or *Fretté v France* (2002) (no violation of Article 14 combined with Article 8 by four votes to three) and *EB v France* (2008) (violation by 10 votes to seven). The hybrid form of a judgment of the ECtHR (a French-style, unsigned judgment of 'the Court' for the majority, with British-style, signed, concurring and dissenting opinions of individual judges), probably reflects the UK's participation in the ECHR from the outset. This hybrid form might also have been adopted by the CJEU, if the UK had not excluded itself from the EEC in 1957.

Fifth, the main procedural advantage of the CJEU's reference procedure is speed. A particularly quick example is *ACCEPT*, in which the CJEU received the request for a preliminary ruling from the Romanian court on 14 February 2012, and delivered its judgment around one year and two months later, on 25 April 2013. This process can be compared with *X and Others v Austria*, in which the application lodged with the ECtHR on 24 April 2007 led to a judgment nearly six years later, on 19 February 2013. However, it would seem that speed and direct access to a European Court are mutually exclusive. The price of the CJEU's speed is the absence of direct access for individuals, which reduces the CJEU's caseload. The price of the ECtHR's direct access is waiting in the queue (subject to its priority policy)[76] with up to 100,000 other applicants.

Having compared the ECtHR and the CJEU with respect to these five factors, it is clear that (apart from the question of speed, which comes at a high price), the ECtHR is much more 'applicant/NGO-friendly', and therefore procedurally much 'fitter' to extend the protection of human rights law. By having procedures for third-party interventions, it shows that it is able and willing to listen to representatives of civil society, who can offer a broader perspective on a human rights issue that might affect millions of other Europeans in the same position as the individual applicant. It facilitates their participation by permitting the use of two international languages, regardless of the language of the country against which the case was brought. And the form of its judgments makes transparent the debate amongst its judges about difficult human rights issues, allowing concurring and dissenting judges to point to possible future developments in its case law. The CJEU should consider: (a) introducing its own procedure for third-party

[76] Rules of Court, r 41.

interventions, at least in references raising questions of human or fundamental rights (including the right to be free from discrimination); (b) allowing any party to any case (including third-party interveners) to use any official EU language in written or oral observations; and (c) giving each judge the option of writing or joining a concurring or dissenting opinion in each case. This would create a more level playing field for individuals and NGOs, compared with EU institutions and member state governments, and would be entirely in keeping with the spirit of *van Gend en Loos*: 'The vigilance of individuals concerned to protect their rights [using 'direct effect' and Article 267 TFEU] amounts to an effective supervision in addition to the supervision entrusted by Articles [258 and 259 TFEU] to the diligence of the Commission and of the Member States'.[77]

The following table summarises the procedural differences between the two European Courts:

Table 3

European Court of Human Rights (ECtHR)	**Court of Justice of the European Union (CJEU)**
(1) Art 34 ECHR right of direct application after exhausting domestic remedies;	(1) impossible to force a national court to make an Art 267 TFEU reference;
(2) full-time human rights court with primary responsibility for interpreting the ECHR;	(2) part-time human rights court that seeks to apply minimum standards of the ECHR but is often cautious (see above); potential problem if ECtHR applies *Bosphorus v Ireland*[78] to novel question first considered by the CJEU without guidance from the ECtHR;
(3) third-party interventions permitted;	(3) third-party interventions possible in reference proceedings only if they exist at the national level and the national court grants leave to intervene;
(4) any party may use English or French in a written document or at a hearing;	(4) EU institutions and private parties must respect the language of the case; only governments may use another language (their own, not English, which some might prefer); at hearings, judges and Advocates General may use any official EU language;
(5) dissenting/concurring opinions permitted;	(5) all judgments unanimous;
(6) a judgment can take five years or more.	(6) quicker procedure but only because of point (1).

[77] Case 26-62 [1963] ECR 1 (English special edition).
[78] App no 45036/98 (ECtHR, 30 June 2005).

V. CONCLUSION

This chapter is not meant to show disrespect for the CJEU, which has produced many valuable and influential human rights judgments, especially in the area of sex discrimination law. However, its tendency to be substantively cautious, combined with the rigidity in its procedures that reduces its procedural 'fitness', makes it a risky choice of forum for a novel human rights issue. Choice is possible because, while most human rights issues can only go to the ECtHR, others fall within the scope of EU law and could go either to the CJEU, or to the ECtHR, or to both courts at the same time (see *Richards* and *Linda Grant* above). A national court is less likely to make a reference if the party that might benefit from it does not request it, which might sometimes make sense if the individual's prospects seem better in the 'braver', more experienced and more applicant/NGO-friendly ECtHR than in the more cautious and less applicant/NGO-friendly CJEU.

If a novel issue reaches the CJEU (because it made sense to request a reference, or the national court decided of its own motion to make one), the individual might lose because the CJEU can find no judgment of the ECtHR to support finding a violation of EU human rights law, even though such a judgment might have been delivered if the novel issue had been presented first to the ECtHR. If the individual loses in the CJEU, they might like a second chance, ie an 'appeal' to the European Court with greater expertise on human rights law. Fortunately, the ECtHR's judgment in *Bosphorus v Ireland* should not present an obstacle. *Bosphorus* deference to the CJEU, unless the CJEU's 'protection of Convention rights was manifestly deficient',[79] only applies if the CJEU has interpreted EU law as *requiring* a certain act, rather than merely *permitting* it, at the discretion of the public authority in question. The ECtHR stressed that 'a State would be fully responsible under the Convention for all acts falling outside its strict international legal obligations', and that there was no 'exercise of discretion by the Irish authorities' in *Bosphorus*.[80] A CJEU finding of 'no discrimination' would generally mean that the public authority in question 'may' discriminate, not that it 'must'. Whether or not *Bosphorus* deference will be maintained after the planned accession of the EU to the ECHR, under Protocol No 14 to the ECHR and Article 6(2) Treaty on European Union, it should not apply to a challenge to a discriminatory act that was merely permitted, but not required, by the CJEU's interpretation of EU law.

There are reasons why some human rights litigants might prefer the ECtHR to the CJEU. But this could change. If the CJEU takes seriously Article 52(3) of the Charter of Fundamental Rights (the ECHR's minimum standards 'shall not prevent Union law providing more extensive protection'), it could become substantively 'braver'. And if it adopts some of the reforms suggested above, it could become procedurally 'fitter'. Having direct or conditional access to two, equally attractive European Courts would benefit all potential human rights litigants in the EU.

[79] ibid, paras 156, 165, 166.
[80] ibid, paras 157 and 148.

11

Access to Justice in the Recent Grand Chamber Judgments of the European Court of Human Rights

DRAGOLJUB POPOVIĆ*

I. INTRODUCTION

ARTICLE 6 OF the European Convention on Human Rights provides for the right to a fair trial.[1] Its provisions supplement the fundamental guarantees existing in this respect at the level of Member States of the Council of Europe.[2] The Grand Chamber of the European Court of Human Rights has recently developed its case law on Article 6, while dealing with cases of different kinds. The cases were mostly about the requirements of Article 6, as well as its scope of application.

II. ARTICLE 6 OF THE CONVENTION: APPLICATION REQUIREMENTS

A. The Evolution

It has been remarked among academics that 'access to justice has come a long way towards its recognition as a true enforceable right under international law'.[3]

* Judge at the European Court of Human Rights.

[1] For purposes of brevity the Convention for the Protection of Human Rights and Fundamental Freedoms will hereinafter be referred to as 'the Convention' and the European Court of Human Rights as 'the Court'.

[2] A remark was made in scholarly works on the existence of a certain tension between the 'growing national guarantees' of the fair trial and the Convention requirements. *Cf* S Boyron and W Lacey, 'Procedural Fairness Generally' in M Tushnet, Th Fleiner and Ch Saunders, *Routledge Handbook of Constitutional Law* (London, Routledge, 2013) 272.

[3] F Francioni, 'The Right of Access to Justice under Customary International Law' in F Francioni (ed), *Access to Justice as a Human Right* (Oxford, Oxford University Press, 2007) 54; *cf* also D Shelton, *Remedies in International Human Rights Law* (Oxford, Oxford University Press, 2006) 8–9.

The Court, while applying the Convention has made an important contribution in following that path. Some of the most recent developments of the Court's case law provide evidence in this regard.

It should be noted at the outset that the right to a fair trial, as provided for by Article 6 of the Convention has a broader meaning than similar guaranties in the constitutions of the Member States of the Council of Europe. The beginning of its text reads as follows:

> In the determination of his civil rights and obligations or of any criminal charge against him, everyone is entitled to a fair and public hearing within a reasonable time by an independent and impartial tribunal established by law.

It has been observed that the wording of the provision mentioned was influenced by the Anglo-American legal tradition of procedural safeguards.[4] The requirements for the application of Article 6 have been subject to evolution in the Court's case law.

Respective legal developments find their origin in the case of *Ringeisen v Austria*.[5] The applicant was involved in trading real estate, selling land plots in Austria. To resolve certain disputes arising from his activity he had to seize administrative units in two instances, first the District Administration and the Regional Real Property Transactions Commission at a later stage.[6] The applicant had been speculating with land. He was purchasing plots of lands belonging to farmers with the idea to convert those into building sites. To achieve such a goal he had to obtain permission from the administrative authorities. He had first seized an administrative body at the district, and subsequently at the regional level. As he had been refused, he filed a constitutional complaint (*Verfassungsbeschwerde)*. The Constitutional Court had ruled for the applicant on procedural grounds and the administrative bodies had to reopen proceedings. However, the applicant lost in the new set of proceedings. He filed once again with the Constitutional Court, this time on substantial grounds, but lost his case.[7]

The question before the Court was whether the case concerned the determination of civil rights and obligations within the meaning of Article 6 of the Convention? The Court's ruling was that despite the fact that 'it was applying rules of administrative law the Regional Commission's decision was to be decisive in the relations in civil law'.[8] The Court's approach in *Ringeisen* was criticised among

[4] *Cf* C Grabenwarter, *Europäische Menschenrechtskonvention* (Munich, CH Beck, 2003), 326. For construing a procedural right of access to justice as a corollary of a State positive obligation under the Convention, *cf* D Xenos, *The Positive Obligations of the State under the European Convention of Human Rights* (London, Routledge, 2012) 175–76.

[5] App no 2614/65 (ECtHR, 16 July 1971). For bibliography on the case, see V Berger, *Jurisprudence de la Cour européenne des droits de l'homme* (Paris, Dalloz-Sirey, 2009) 331–32.

[6] ibid, paras 17–20.

[7] ibid, paras 19–21.

[8] ibid, para 94.

academics for having qualified as 'civil' the rights which were by and large subject to administrative regulation.[9]

The rule in *Ringeisen* determined the subject matter to which Article 6 was applicable; what remained was the scope of persons that were entitled to enjoy the protection of the provision. The meaning of the notion of 'civil rights and obligations' in respect of Article 6 embraced both aspects. Namely, it was not important only to find that a certain relation fell within the scope of civil rights and obligations, but also to determine who was entitled to protection of the respective provision.

As to the scope of persons who could enjoy the protection of Article 6 of the Convention, the case of *Pellegrin v France* was at the turning point of developments.[10] The facts of the case are as follows. The applicant, who was a management and accountancy consultant, was recruited by a French ministry in charge of co-operation and development to become a technical adviser of the governments of Equatorial Guinea and Gabon. He was subsequently examined by a doctor and declared permanently unfit to serve overseas.[11] As he had been recruited by the French government and was supposed to take part in a cooperation programme aimed at helping African countries, he was considered to be a civil servant, under French law.

The principal issue in *Pellegrin* was whether disputes relating to the recruitment, careers and termination of services of civil servants fell outside the scope of Article 6.1 of the Convention? The Court applied the so-called functional criterion, based on the nature of the employee's duties and responsibilities.[12]

The starting point in the Court's reasoning was that certain posts in the public sector involved 'responsibilities in the general interest or participation in the exercise of powers conferred by public law'. Persons holding posts of that kind were indeed in the position to 'wield a portion of the State's sovereign power', the fact which made it legitimate for the State to demand 'a special bond of trust and loyalty' from such civil servants.[13] Following this line of reasoning the Court formulated a general rule in *Pellegrin*. It excluded the disputes 'raised by public servants whose duties typify the specific activities of the public service in so far as the latter [was] acting as the depositary of public authority responsible for protecting the general interests of the State' from the scope of Article 6.1.[14] The Court nevertheless remarked that a restrictive interpretation of the exception to the safeguards afforded by Article 6.1 should apply.[15] The dissenting judges in *Pellegrin* were of

[9] *Cf* E Kastanas, *Unité et diversité: notions autonomes et marge d'appréciation des Etats dans la jurisprudence de la Cour européenne des droits de l'homme* (Brussels, Bruyant, 1996), 376. For the influence of this approach in English law, see: D Harris, M O'Boyle and Harris, O'Boyle and C Warbrick, *Law of the European Convention on Human Rights* (Oxford, Oxford University Press, 2009) 210–11.

[10] App no 28541/95 (ECtHR, 8 December 1999).

[11] ibid, paras 8–16.

[12] ibid, para 64.

[13] ibid, para 65.

[14] ibid, para 66.

[15] ibid, para 64.

opinion that the introduction of the functional criterion clearly led the Court in the opposite direction. In their view the 'guarantees set forth in Art. 6 should be broadly construed'.[16] The dissenters were also of opinion that the 'introduction of the criterion of participation in the exercise of powers conferred by public law [did] not avoid the risk of arbitrariness and [created] a new zone of uncertainty'.[17] The requirements of the application of Article 6 of the Convention thus remained disputed to some extent and called for further clarification.

B. Overruling Previous Stance

The Grand Chamber has recently taken a stand on the requirements for the application of Article 6 on two occasions. First it was in a judgment given in 2007, which overruled the Court's previous stance on the issue raised in *Pellegrin*. Subsequently the Court overruled another of its previous rulings in a judgment, rendered in 2009. The first was the judgment in *Vilho Eskelinen and Others v Finland*, the second the one in *Micallef v Malta*.[18]

The issue that had once been entrenched in *Pellegrin* reappeared and was revisited by the Court in *Eskelinen*. A group of Finish policemen had instituted proceedings at national level claiming wage supplements and bonuses for their salaries alleging they were entitled to remote-area allowances. They had been entitled to such allowances under a collective agreement regulating their service. The administrative bodies refused their claim. They filed with the administrative courts, but were unsuccessful before two instances.[19] Having lost the case at the national level they turned to Strasbourg, complaining under Article 6.1 of the Convention. The respondent government invoked the rule in *Pellegrin* claiming inapplicability of Article 6 to the case.

The applicants combated the government's stance, which was based on the rule in *Pellegrin* that excluded applicability of Article 6 to the case. Although they were policemen, they claimed 'that their service and their salaries were not related to the exercise of powers conferred by public law'.[20] The applicants' thesis was that the dispute exclusively concerned the salaries and that such a right was of a private law character. The amount of the salaries was indeed a matter of a contract between the employee and employer, also regulated by a respective collective agreement in terms of labour law.[21]

The respondent government contested the applicability of Article 6 of the Convention on the ground that the applicants' duties 'entailed direct participation

[16] ibid, para 1 (judges Tulkens, Fischbach, Casadevall and Thomassen dissenting).
[17] ibid, para 4.
[18] *Vilho Eskelinen and Others v Finland* App no 63235/00 (ECtHR, 19 April 2007); *Micallef v Malta* App no 17056/06 (ECtHR, 15 October 2009).
[19] *Vilho Eskelinen* (ibid), paras 10–21.
[20] ibid, para 32.
[21] ibid.

in the exercise of powers conferred by public law and duties designed to safeguard the general interests of the State'. In doing so the government referred to the rule in *Pellegrin*.[22] The government went further to invoke the case law developments following the rule and confirming its validity in the Court's jurisprudence.[23]

The Grand Chamber of the Court first stated that the applicants 'could claim to have a right on arguable ground' and then turned to the problem of the nature of the right.[24] Revisiting its previous case law the Court found the rule in *Pellegrin* to be 'categorical in its wording' as well as that it was intended to be subject to restrictive interpretation. Such interpretation was supposed 'to limit the cases in which public servants could be denied the practical and effective protection' of Article 6 of the Convention.[25]

The Grand Chamber of the Court highlighted the fact that 'the application of the functional criterion (stemming from *Pellegrin*, DP) may itself lead to anomalous results'. The Court therefore reversed its previous stance, stating that it was not apparent to what extent the 'inclusion in a particular sector of public service was sufficient to remove applicability of Art. 6'. It was also underlined that the applicants 'all had access to a court under national law'. These circumstances taken as a whole made the Grand Chamber conclude that Article 6 was applicable to the case.[26]

This method of reasoning provided grounds for the Court to introduce a new rule, which laid down two requirements for applicability of the Convention provision mentioned. The first was that the respondent State in its national law must have expressly excluded access to court for the post or category of staff in question. The second condition was that such exclusion had to be justified on objective grounds in the State's interest.[27]

The dissenting judges in this case expressed the opinion that abandoning a solid precedent without reference to new social developments would create legal uncertainty.[28] Some scholars are of the opinion that the new rule is not coherent with the Court's jurisprudence in general.[29] Others on the contrary, declare themselves favourable to the new rule, suggesting that the Court should go further and consider disputes concerning employment in public service subject to Article 6

[22] ibid, para 35.

[23] *Eodem loco*. The reference was made to the Court's decision in *Verešovà v Slovakia* App no 70497/01 (ECtHR, 1 February 2005) in which the Court declined applicability of Art 6 to the case of a lawyer serving in the police.

[24] *Vilho Eskelinen* (n 18), paras 40–50.

[25] ibid, paras 48–49. On following the *Pellegrin* rule before it was overruled, in cases against Turkey and France, *cf* J Casadevall, *El Convenio europeo de Derechos humanos, el Tribunal de Estrasburgo y su jurisprudència* (Valencia, Tirant lo Blanch, 2012) 268.

[26] *Vilho Eskelinen* (n 18), paras 51–52 and 63.

[27] ibid, para 66.

[28] Judges Costa, Wildhaber, Türmen, Borrego-Borrego and Jočiene, dissenting. On dissenters' arguments, *cf* D Popović, *The Emergence of the European Human Rights Law* (The Hague, Eleven International Publishing, 2011) 97–98.

[29] See F Sudre, *Droit européen et international des droits de l'homme* (Paris, Presses Universitaires de France, 2012) 393–94.

without exception.[30] It should be noted that the Court, by introducing the second of the requirements mentioned above stressed its own scrutiny over the fulfilment of the conditions of application of Article 6.

C. Injunction Proceedings

Another issue was at stake in *Micallef.* The case concerned relations between neighbours. Its background was somewhat trivial, for at the origin of the case there was a dispute related to an objection of a neighbour to the applicant's sister's habit of hanging out wet clothes to dry over the neighbour's yard. Such a habit allegedly interfered with the property rights of the yard's owner. An injunction to restrain hanging out clothes to dry over the neighbour's yard was issued by a domestic court. The applicant filed with the Court in Strasbourg as the heir of his sister.[31] The object of dispute before the Court was whether Article 6 of the Convention could apply to the injunction proceedings?

The Government of Malta invoked the rule in *Eskelinen* to claim inapplicability of Article 6 of the Convention in this case. The argument was that the applicability of Article 6 should be recognised by the Court only if the domestic system had accepted it formerly and in this regard the government submitted that the right 'to be heard in injunction proceedings was not established in Maltese law'.[32] The respondent government's main argument was that preliminary proceedings aimed at the granting of an interim measure, such as an injunction, were not 'normally considered to determine civil rights and obligations'. Therefore they 'do not normally fall within the protection of Art 6'.[33]

The Court's effort aimed to deal with the issue of applicability of the civil limb of Article 6 of the Convention in this case. The Court deliberated not only on general principles, but also on the classification of the proceedings, concerning the case, before raising the question whether there was a need for further developments of the case law.[34] In respect of the case law developments, the Grand Chamber of the Court took comparative law considerations as its starting point. The Court observed that that there was 'widespread consensus amongst Council of Europe member States, which either implicitly or explicitly provide for applicability of Article 6 guarantees to interim measures'.[35] The Court's expression

[30] Harris et al, *Law of the European Convention on Human Rights* (n 9) 221. *Cf* also R White and C Ovey, *Jacobs, White and Ovey: The European Convention on Human Rights* (Oxford, Oxford University Press, 2010) 252 highlighting the fact that the application of the rule in *Pellegrin* was capable of bringing 'anomalous results'.

[31] *Micallef v Malta* (n 18), paras 6–7.

[32] ibid, para 65 (invoking *Eskelinen*) and para 63 (no right to be heard in injunction proceedings under Maltese law).

[33] The government's stance, as reproduced by the Court in (ibid), para 75 of the judgment.

[34] ibid, paras 74–77.

[35] ibid, para 78 (the position taken on the issue by the European Court of Justice was also referred to in support of the Grand Chamber's stance).

calls for two short comments. First, the consensus was labelled as widespread, which gives the impression that there was indeed no proper consensus within the exact meaning of the term. If something is widespread it is not universally accepted among the Member States and if so, there is no consensus. Second, the word 'implicitly' comes before the word 'explicitly', so as to create the impression that the former is more often the case among Member States than the latter. The relevant paragraph of the judgment, consecrated to comparative and European Union law and practice, mentions more than 20 Member States of the Council of Europe and remains incomplete to some extent. Its wording shows that it was drafted 'on the basis of the material available to the Court'.[36]

The Court thus found it necessary to develop its own case law. It opposed the idea that interim measures were insufficiently important for deciding on the merits of a case. On the contrary, those measures in the Court's view may result in 'long lasting and permanent effects'. That is why the Court did not find it justified 'to automatically characterise injunction proceedings as not determinative of civil rights and obligations'.[37] The Court went on to introduce a new approach to the issue as well as a new rule. The Court's stance was that not all interim measures determine civil rights and obligations within the meaning of Article 6 of the Convention. The applicability of the provision should therefore be subject to certain requirements and conditions. The first condition was that the 'right at stake in both the main and the injunction proceedings should be "civil" within the autonomous meaning of that notion under Art 6'. Second, the Court stated it would find Article 6 applicable when 'an interim measure can be considered effectively to determine the civil right or obligation at stake'. The Court nevertheless accepted in this regard that in exceptional cases 'other procedural safeguards may apply'. The latter should be the case when 'the independence and impartiality of the tribunal or the judge concerned is an indispensable and inalienable safeguard' in certain proceedings. The Court's ruling was therefore that Article 6 was applicable to the case.[38]

The substantive issue raised under Article 6 of the Convention in *Micallef* concerned impartiality of the tribunal. The complaint was that the Court of Appeal at domestic level 'had lacked impartiality'. The applicant also complained of having been denied opportunity to make submissions.[39] The impartiality issue was complained of on the grounds that under Maltese law 'it was not possible to challenge judges on the basis of a relationship with a party's advocate unless it was a first degree relationship of consanguinity or affinity'. In the present case the applicant's sister, while pursuing her case, 'was faced with a panel of three

[36] ibid, para 31 of the judgment. The criticism expressed here may seem awkward, because the author of this chapter was in the formation on the bench, which gave the judgment and voted in favour of its operative part. However, the changing of the position and perspective, while making a scholarly analysis of the text of the judgment rendered the remark indispensable.

[37] ibid, paras 79–80.

[38] ibid, paras 83–86 and 89.

[39] Para 21 of the chamber judgment in this case, given on 15 January 2008.

judges, one of whom was the brother and at a later stage the uncle of the opposing parties' advocate'. The chamber that gave judgment expressed the view that the family ties were such 'to justify objectively the applicant's fears that the presiding judge lacked impartiality'.[40]

The lack of impartiality was reiterated at the Grand Chamber level. The Grand Chamber judgment contains a lengthy exposal of general principles in respect of impartiality of a tribunal, considered both from the subjective and objective standpoints.[41] Applying the principles to the case the Grand Chamber found a violation of Article 6.1, rejecting the complaint under the subjective test, while at the same time confirming the chamber conclusion on the objective test. Family ties sufficed to objectively justify fears that the presiding judge on the bench lacked impartiality.[42]

Giving a judgment in the applicant's favour and finding a violation of Article 6.1 in this case the Grand Chamber of the Court introduced a new approach to the requirements of applicability of Article 6 and confirmed the rule in *Eskelinen*.[43] The Court indeed overruled its previous doctrine of non-applicability of Article 6 to injunction proceedings. This had already been announced in the national judge's concurring separate opinion, attached to the chamber judgment in this case. The national judge was of the opinion that, to borrow his expression, the *Vilho Eskelinen* doctrine 'should never be seen to afford lesser protection to human rights than the domestic courts do'. He added that 'when the domestic courts deem Art 6 applicable to a judicial controversy, Strasbourg would do ill to act differently'.[44]

D. Common Features

Despite notorious differences there are features in common between the cases of *Eskelinen* and *Micallef*. In both judgments the Grand Chamber overruled its previous jurisprudence. Moreover, and that is important for this text, the Grand Chamber showed a trend to enlarge the scope of application of Article 6 of the Convention, while it basically ruled on the requirements of its application. The same trend has also been evident on some other occasions, namely in certain cases in which the Grand Chamber was driven by the facts to rule directly, irrespective of the requirements issue, on the scope of application of that provision.

[40] ibid, para 79 of the Chamber judgment.

[41] *Micallef v Malta* (n 18), paras 93–99.

[42] ibid, paras 100–04.

[43] For some more comments on the case, as well as the scope and conditions of application of its rule, see A Peters and T Altwicker, *Europäische Menschenrechtskonvention* (Munich, CH Beck, 2012) 141; *cf* also Sudre, *Droit européen et international des droits de l'homme* (n 29) 387.

[44] *Cf Micallef v Malta*, chamber judgment of 15 January 2008, given in the case; the national judge, Bonello, concurring, para 15.

III. EXPANDING THE SCOPE OF APPLICATION

A. The Origin

Expansion of the scope of application of Article 6 of the Convention in respect of access to justice occurred in the Grand Chamber rulings in prisoners' cases as well as in cases concerning State immunity under international law.

The whole pattern of access to justice, as developed in the Convention system of protection of human rights, finds its origin in a prisoner's case. It was in *Golder*, the case in which a prisoner was deprived of the possibility of suing a prison officer that the Court for the first time spelt out the right of access to justice as guaranteed by the European human rights law.[45]

The facts in *Golder* concerned a convict who allegedly had taken part in a serious disturbance in a recreation area of the prison in which he was serving his sentence. A prison officer made a statement mentioning the convict's participation in the events. When Golder asked for permission to consult with a solicitor with a view to taking a civil action for libel against the prison officer he was refused by the Home Secretary.[46]

The Court stated in the judgment that it was called upon to decide whether 'Art 6 [was] limited to guaranteeing in substance the right to a fair trial in legal proceedings which are already pending, or whether it in addition secured a right of access to courts for every person wishing to commence an action'? Another question was, in case the first were to be answered in the affirmative, whether there were implied limitations on the right of access to justice?[47]

The Court found first that the right which Golder wished to invoke was a civil right. It further concluded that although Article 6 did not state there was a right of access to courts or tribunals in express terms, the latter stemmed from the same basic idea put forward by the provision text. Therefore it should be taken together with the rest of the provision, despite the fact that it was not specifically defined in the narrower sense of the term. The Court formulated its principal stance in the following words:

> It is the duty of the Court to ascertain, by means of interpretation, whether access to courts constitutes one factor or aspect of this right.[48]

Taking such a starting point the Court concluded in the judgment that the terms of Article 6 provided reason to think that the right of access to court is included

[45] *Golder v the United Kingdom* App no 4451/70 (ECtHR, 21 February 1975), para 32. For a bibliography on the *Golder* case, *cf* Berger, *Jurisprudence de la Cour européenne des droits de l'homme* (n 6) 195–96. For a brief account of the *Golder* case and the Court's jurisprudence following it, *cf* Shelton, *Remedies in International Human Rights Law* (n 4) 125–30.

[46] *Golder v the United Kingdom* (ibid), paras 9–18.

[47] ibid, para 25.

[48] ibid, para 28.

among the guarantees set forth by that provision. The Court expressed it in the following way:

> The terms of Art 6.1 of the Convention, taken in their context, provide reason to think that this right is included among the guarantees set forth.[49]

Ruling on the second issue mentioned above as one of the Court's tasks in this case, the Court stated that the right of access to justice was not absolute, but could be subject to restrictions.[50] Eventually, the Court ruled for the applicant, on the grounds of its finding that 'Golder could justifiably wish to consult a solicitor with a view to instituting legal proceedings'.[51]

The dissenters in this case, judges Verdross, Zekia and Fitzmaurice were against the idea that, to borrow the expression from judge Zekia, 'a right of access to the courts ought to be read into Art 6.1'. Destiny did not take their part. Despite Fitzmaurice's lengthy dissent, matching the judgment itself in number of paragraphs, the evolution of the Court's jurisprudence went into the direction traced by the majority of the sitting judges in this case. *Golder* provided a landmark ruling and represents a milestone in the evolution of the Court's jurisprudence.[52] It is worth noting today, after decades of development of the Court's case law, that the learned commentators and scholars are practically unanimous in their conclusions in this regard. They comment on the right of access to justice as if it had been provided for by the Convention text itself.[53]

It could be noted that the *Golder* case included in essence an aspect which has been a matter of discussion and controversy to this day. The applicant in *Golder* technically sought access to legal advice. The latter has been subject to judicial decisions in the United Kingdom in respect of suspected terrorists held in custody.[54] The Court's stance in *Golder* was that the interpretation given to Article 6 '*a fortiori* included access to legal counsel to prepare a defence in order to permit the realization of effective legal remedies'.[55] Therefore the subordinate issue of access to counsel did not arise at all.

The right to legal assistance was also raised before the Court in the *Salduz* case.[56] The applicant complained under Article 6 of the Convention that he had

[49] ibid, para 31.
[50] ibid, para 38.
[51] ibid, para 40.
[52] For the case law following *Golder* in the same pattern of cases concerning prisoners in the United Kingdom, *cf* Harris et al, *Law of the European Convention on Human Rights* (n 10) 236.
[53] Popović, *The Emergence of the European Human Rights Law* (n 29) 127–28 (see references to authors and their works cited).
[54] A McColgan, 'Lessons from the Past? Northern Ireland, Terrorism Now and Then, and the Human Rights Act' in T Campbell, KD Ewing, and A Tomkins (eds), *The Legal Protection of Human Rights—Sceptical Essays* (Oxford, Oxford University Press, 2011) 196.
[55] Francioni in Francioni, *Access to Justice as a Human Right* (n 4) 35.
[56] *Salduz v Turkey* App no 36391/02 (ECtHR, 27 November 2008).

not been assisted by a lawyer while in police custody. The Grand Chamber ruled for the applicant and spelt out a rule, guaranteeing the right to counsel:

> This right indeed presupposes that the prosecution in a criminal case seek to prove their case against the accused without resort to evidence obtained through methods of coercion or oppression in defiance of the will of the accused.[57]

The *Salduz* case however concerned the criminal limb of Article 6 of the Convention, which remains outside the scope of our interest in this chapter. The civil limb of the provision was at stake in prisoner cases recently dealt with.

B. Prisoners' Cases

The prisoners' cases that the Grand Chamber has recently dealt with were different from *Golder*. In *Enea v Italy* a person convicted for crime committed while participating in a mafia type organisation was imprisoned after conviction and put under the regime of high supervision. He was detained in several Italian prisons and was subject to the regime provided for by section 41 *bis* of the Prison Administration Act of 1975, as amended in 2002.[58] The prisoner was indeed in such a state of health that he had to use a wheelchair.[59]

The question before the Court was whether Article 6 of the Convention could apply to the case? Serving a sentence for a criminal offence was in principle not susceptible to the protection of Article 6. The reason was quite simple—in terms of the provision it did not concern a criminal charge against an individual appearing before a court of law. Therefore the real issue was if the civil limb of the provision mentioned was applicable to the case?

The Court's finding was that a dispute over a civil right existed in *Enea*.[60] The Court made reference to *Golder* in support of its stance that the case related to Article 6 of the Convention under its civil head. The high supervision regime, in the Court's view, affected the applicant's civil rights, such as for instance those to receive visits in prison and maintain correspondence.[61] Those were the grounds guiding the Grand Chamber to rule for the applicant, finding a violation of Article 6.1 of the Convention.

The innovation in *Enea* was the Court's approach to the issue of applicability of Article 6. The civil limb of that provision was considered to be applicable to the regime of serving criminal sentences, because of its connection to the enjoyment of civil rights that may have been and indeed were in dispute between the applicant and the prison administration. Scholarly comments pointed out above

[57] ibid, para 54. For a brief account of the judgment and the Court's subsequent jurisprudence, *cf* Popović, *The Emergence of the European Human Rights Law* (n 29) 84–87.

[58] App no 74912/01 (ECtHR, 17 September 2009), paras 10–16.

[59] ibid, para 17.

[60] ibid, paras 102 and 103.

[61] ibid, paras 104 (reference to *Golder*), 107 and 119.

all that the Court's interpretation of Article 6.1 in *Enea*, by applying the civil limb of Article 6 of the Convention made 'the legally non-regulated zones of the penitentiary world step back'.[62] Others insisted on the fact that it overruled the previous Court's jurisprudence, which had taken the stand that 'the organisation of life in prison was inherent to prison administration discretion, so that it was not subject to judicial control'.[63]

The same topic re-emerged in a case against Luxembourg, in which the facts were as follows. The applicant, who was serving a long-term prison sentence, requested prison leave in order to follow a course in psychotherapy, which he had begun before starting to serve the sentence. He also requested leave to spend a weekend with his three children, all of them minors, following a divorce from their mother.[64]

The Chamber of the Court ruled for the applicant and found a violation of Article 6 in the case.[65] It was subsequently presented to the Grand Chamber. The respondent government submitted before the Grand Chamber that the case was distinguishable from *Enea*, whereas the applicant invoked the same precedent inviting the Court to apply its rule to his case.[66] The Grand Chamber was of opinion that the issue of applicability of Article 6 to the case was closely linked to its merits and therefore decided to rule on the applicability considering the merits of the case.[67]

Following such a method the Grand Chamber distinguished the case from *Enea*. Although the Court admitted that in both cases family visits to prisoners were at stake, the Grand Chamber made the distinction on the grounds that 'the line of case-law [followed in *Enea*, DP] did not concern the situation under consideration' in *Boulois*.[68] The Grand Chamber's reasoning appears to be clearer in its statement that the applicant had no right under Luxembourg law, the fact that eventually rendered Article 6 inapplicable to the case.[69] Assessing whether the applicant had a right in terms of Article 6 of the Convention the Grand Chamber referred both to *Micallef* and *Eskelinen*.[70] The conclusion that the applicant had not been entitled to enjoy any right under domestic law was made by the Court on the grounds of distinguishing the case from *Enea*, as well as from *Eskelinen*. The requirements to apply the rule of the latter precedent were not fulfilled.[71]

[62] F Sudre, 'La réécriture de la Convention par la Cour européenne des droits de l'homme' in P Titiun, *La conscience des droits—Mélanges en l'honneur de Jean-Paul Costa* (Paris, Dalloz-Sirey, 2011) 603: 'faisant reculer un peu plus les zones de non-droit au sein du monde pénitentiaire'.

[63] Casadevall, *El Convenio europeo de Derechos humanos* (n 26) 278.

[64] *Boulois v Luxembourg* App no 37575/04 (ECtHR, 3 April 2012), paras 15–34.

[65] ibid, para 64.

[66] ibid, paras 73 and 78.

[67] ibid, para 81.

[68] ibid, para 88.

[69] ibid, para 104.

[70] ibid, paras 90 and 94.

[71] ibid, paras 98 and 100.

Although the Grand Chamber failed to follow in *Boulois* its own rule in *Enea*, the reasoning given for such a stance does not leave room for doubt as regards the applicability of the civil limb of Article 6.1 to prisoners' cases. The rule in *Enea* remains valid and a deviation from it, which the Court made in *Boulois* represents an exception. It was introduced on the grounds of distinguishing the two cases. The Court expanded the field of application of the civil head of Article 6.1 to the class of cases concerning prisoners serving their sentences. That was done insofar as there was a connection to a dispute over civil rights and obligations in terms of the said provision. However, as one can learn from the rule in *Boulois*, to attract protection of Article 6.1 the applicant must have had an arguable claim at domestic level.

C. State Immunity Cases

The other direction of expanding the scope of application of Article 6 of the Convention has occurred in State immunity cases. Two judgments are of interest to this chapter. They were given in the cases of *Čudak v Lithuania* and *Sabeh el Leil v France.*[72]

The line of developments to follow in the analysis begins with the *Fogarty* case.[73] In that case, the applicant, who was an Irish national, was dismissed from her post in the United States embassy in London, where she had worked as an administrative assistant. She brought proceedings at domestic level following the dismissal, claiming the latter had been the result of sex discrimination. She won the case at the industrial tribunal, receiving compensation of £12,000. The United States did not invoke immunity in those proceedings. Later on the applicant obtained another 12-month contract of employment with the same employer. As the term of the contract had expired the embassy had refused to re-employ her and she brought another set of proceedings before the competent industrial tribunal. The applicant claimed that the refusal to re-employ her was the result of her previous successful sex discrimination claim. As her second attempt to bring proceedings at domestic level turned out to be unsuccessful because the United States claimed immunity before the industrial tribunal in England, the applicant lodged a complaint with the Court in Strasbourg.[74] The Court found no violation of Article 6 in the case, on the grounds that 'in conferring immunity to the United States by virtue of the State Immunity Act 1978 the United Kingdom [could] not be said to have exceeded the margin of appreciation allowed to States in limiting an individual's access to a court'.[75]

[72] *Čudak v Lithuania* App no 15869/02 (ECtHR, 23 March 2010); *Sabeh el Leil v France* App no 34869/05 (ECtHR, 29 June 2011).

[73] *Fogarty v the United Kingdom* App no 37112/97 (ECtHR, 21 November 2001).

[74] ibid, paras 10–14 of the judgment.

[75] ibid, para 39.

The only dissenter in the Grand Chamber in this case was judge Loucaides. His stance was that the rule in *Pellegrin* was not applicable to the case because 'the duties involved in the posts to which the applicant was seeking employment did not fall within the criterion of 'exercise of powers'. Subsequently there was no special bond of trust and loyalty, which represented the fundamental feature of the criterion applied in *Pellegrin*.[76] The dissenting judge opposed the majority opinion to allow the respondent State to grant immunity for several reasons. In his view the facts of the case did not concern 'employment of a member of a mission', but rather the 'sex discrimination'. Further on, he stated that restrictions to the rights guaranteed under Article 6 of the Convention 'should be interpreted strictly and narrowly'.[77]

The applicant in *Čudak* was an employee of the Polish embassy in Lithuania who had alleged sexual harassment and was subsequently dismissed from her post of secretary and switchboard operator in the embassy. She instituted proceedings in domestic courts, but lost the case eventually before the Supreme Court of Lithuania that applied jurisdictional immunity of the Republic of Poland.[78]

The question of applicability of Article 6.1 of the Convention was raised before the Court in Strasbourg. To resolve the issue the Grand Chamber was first tempted to apply the rule in *Eskelinen*. Its finding was that the two cases were distinguishable, because the issue in *Čudak* did not concern a dispute between a State and its own civil servant. Besides the second requirement of the test in *Eskelinen* was not fulfilled, for in the Court's view the duties performed by the applicant could 'hardly give rise to objective grounds for exclusion [of the applicant's claim] in the State interest within the meaning of the rule in *Eskelinen*'.[79]

The Grand Chamber then turned to the question that has already been dealt with in prisoners' cases and especially in *Enea*, namely whether there was a dispute over rights on arguable grounds under domestic law. By using this approach to the topic the Court found Article 6.1 of the Convention applicable to the case.[80]

At this point the respondent government claimed State immunity under international law. It did so with reference to the rule in *Fogarty*. The latter stemmed from a Grand Chamber judgment given in 2001 in a case against the United Kingdom. The case was, as already mentioned above, about sex discrimination performed by the United States embassy in London, while recruiting staff.[81] The Court distinguished the case from *Fogarty* on the ground that the latter concerned recruitment of staff, which was not in dispute in *Čudak*. To support the distinction and indeed making a move towards overruling the previous stance, which

[76] ibid, judge Loucaides dissenting.

[77] *Eodem loco*.

[78] *Čudak v Lithuania* (n 73), paras 10–18.

[79] ibid, paras 42–44.

[80] ibid, paras 45–47. As regards the attitude that both judgments in *Enea* and in *Čudak* served the purpose of widening the scope of application of Art 6 of the Convention, *cf* Casadevall, *El Convenio europeo de Derechos humanos* (n 26) 278.

[81] ibid, paras 49–53 (government submissions) and para 55 (the Court's reference to *Fogarty*).

the Grand Chamber did not do in express terms, the Court referred to a trend of limiting State immunity in international law.[82]

On the grounds of such analysis the Grand Chamber concluded that the respondent State, by declining jurisdiction to hear the applicant's claim, overstepped the margin of appreciation and impaired the very essence of the applicant's right to a court.[83] Article 6 of the Convention was therefore violated in this case.

A quotation from *Čudak* that makes clear the role of the State immunity as regards the Convention provisions could serve the purpose of summing up the Court's attitude. The Court put it in the following words:

> Generally recognized rules of public international law on State immunity cannot in principle be regarded as imposing a disproportionate restriction on the right of access to a court as embodied in Art 6.1.[84]

The State immunity of jurisdiction, although admitted under international law, could not in the Court's view hinder the access to justice at any cost. It could only do so if it did not put an excessive burden to an individual seeking protection of his or her rights under the Convention.

The case of *Sabeh el Leil v France* raised the same issue as earlier, although the facts were different. The applicant had been appointed by the State of Kuwait as an accountant in the Kuwaiti embassy in Paris and became head accountant in 1985. More than a decade later his contract was unilaterally terminated by his employer. The applicant brought proceedings in France and won the case at first instance. He nevertheless appealed, being dissatisfied with the amount awarded by the first instance court. The Court of Appeal applied the State immunity rule and consequently found the case inadmissible 'by virtue of the principle of jurisdictional immunity of foreign States'. The Court of Cassation found the appeal in cassation to be 'not such as to warrant admitting the appeal on points of law'.[85]

Ruling on the admissibility of Article 6 of the Convention the Court applied the same approach as in *Čudak*. The Grand Chamber did not find the rule in *Eskelinen* applicable to the case. The rule, which emerged in the case against Finland, concerned relations between the State and its own civil servants, the fact that made it different from the case against France.[86]

The Court went further to find that the case concerned unfair dismissal, which resulted in a dispute over a civil right within the meaning of Article 6.1 of the Convention. For that reason the Court ruled that Article 6.1 was applicable to the case.[87]

[82] ibid, paras 62 (distinguishing) and 63 (invoking the limiting trend).
[83] ibid, para 74.
[84] ibid, para 57. For more data on this principle, accompanied by a reference to the relevant Court's case law, *cf* K Reid, *A Practitioner's Guide to the European Convention on Human Rights* (London, Sweet and Maxwell, 2008) 93.
[85] *Sabeh el Leil v France* (n 73), paras 7–17.
[86] ibid, para 38.
[87] ibid, paras 40–42. This makes the Court's reasoning nevertheless close to the *Eskelinen* rule.

To introduce the issue of State immunity in favour of its thesis the respondent government first invoked both *Fogarty* and *Čudak.*[88] However, the government went on to invite the Court to distinguish the case from *Čudak,* for in the government's view there was 'no reprehensible conduct on the part of an embassy staff member directed against the applicant'. By contrast, there was harassment in *Čudak.*[89]

The Court reiterated the rule in *Čudak* according to which the State immunity in international law could not in principle impose too heavy a burden and therefore a disproportionate restriction on the right of access to justice as embodied in Article 6.1 of the Convention.[90] Applying the same line of reasoning as followed in the Lithuanian case mentioned, the Grand Chamber found a violation of Article 6.1 on proportionality grounds. The Court stated that 'by upholding an objection based on State immunity and dismissing the applicant's claim without giving relevant and sufficient reasons the French courts failed to preserve a reasonable relationship of proportionality. They thus impaired the very essence of the applicant's right to access to a court'.[91]

In both cases concerning State immunity of jurisdiction referred to in this chapter the Grand Chamber of the Court maintained its principal position of following the respective rule of international law providing for immunity, but it was nevertheless inclined to put limits to its implementation. By doing so, the Grand Chamber widened the scope of application of Article 6 of the Convention.[92]

IV. CONCLUSIONS

Two trends have emerged from this survey of some of the Court's recent jurisprudence regarding access to justice in the Convention system. The first consists of the Grand Chamber's effort to render precise requirements of the application of Article 6.1 of the Convention in general. In doing so, the Court has fundamentally expanded the scope of application of the provision in question. The Court gave up the use of the functional criterion, which excluded from the protection of Article 6 the persons owing special loyalty to the State. The Court also ruled that Article 6 was to apply to injunction proceedings.

88 ibid, para 44.

89 ibid, para 45.

90 ibid, para 49.

91 ibid, para 67.

92 It is worth contrasting such developments to the position taken by the International Court of Justice in one of its most recent rulings; see G Cataldi, 'The Implementation of the ICJ's Decision in the *Jurisdictional Immunities of the State* Case in the Italian Domestic Order: What Balance should be made between Fundamental Human Rights and International Obligations?' (2013) 2 *ESIL Reflections*, available at http://www.esil-sedi.eu/sites/default/files/Cataldi%20Reflections.pdf.

The second trend was clearly an extension of the provision of Article 6 to certain classes of cases to which it had not been applicable before the Court rendered judgments discussed in this chapter. Such classes of cases were those of prisoners serving their sentences, as well as those concerning State immunity of jurisdiction. In prisoners' cases the Court was guided by the idea of applying the civil limb of Article 6 of the Convention, whereas in the State immunity cases it tended to put restrictions to the rule of jurisdictional immunity of foreign States under international law.

12

Fundamental Rights and Judicial Cooperation in the Decisions of the Court of Justice on the Brussels I Regulation 2009–2014

The Story So Far

LORNA GILLIES*

I. INTRODUCTION

> … as from the date of entry into force of the Treaty of Lisbon, 1 December 2009, the fundamental principles of EU law and the EU system of judicial protection such as primacy, direct application, direct effect and interpretation in conformity, have become of full application in the whole domain of the AFSJ.[1]

Ever since the enactment of the European Convention on Human Rights (ECHR), fundamental rights have operated at and between national and EU law.[2] With the enactment of the Charter of Fundamental Rights (the Charter) via, inter alia, Article 67, Title V of the Treaty on the Functioning of the European Union (TFEU), a further layer of fundamental rights has emerged. The Charter addresses the protection of six key rights, one of which is justice. As justice is a broad concept, for present purposes it is useful to identify those particular aspects of the Charter aligned with justice in a specific context. The relevant aspects of the Charter are Articles 6, on the preservation of individual liberty and security of person and Article 47 on the right to an effective remedy and a fair trial. The emergence of the Charter as a source of fundamental rights law provides an opportunity to consider

* Senior Lecturer in Law, School of Law, University of Leicester.

[1] J de Zwaan, 'The New Governance of Justice and Home Affairs: Towards Further Supranationalism' in S Wolff, FANJ Goudappel and JW de Zwaan (eds), *Freedom, Security and Justice After Lisbon and Stockholm*, (The Hague, TMC Asser Press, 2011) 25.

[2] HS Raulus, 'Fundamental Rights in the Area of Freedom, Security and Justice' in S Wolff et al, *Freedom, Security and Justice After Lisbon and Stockholm* (ibid).

and determine the tripartite[3] relationship between national human rights law, EU law (including human rights law) and the Charter. This chapter is focused on the extent to which the Court of Justice of the European Union (CJEU) is increasingly having regard to the Charter when interpreting secondary EU laws[4] in the field of judicial cooperation in civil matters. The extent to which such EU laws are interpreted in accordance with the Charter demonstrates a particular aspect of the EU's 'role [...] in setting fundamental right policies'.[5] In essence, the introduction of the Treaty of Lisbon and the policy objectives it seeks to achieve necessitate a coherent approach to embedding the Charter across the 'EU constitutional legal order'.[6] Raulus recently concluded that due regard to the Charter required to be demonstrated through a combination of 'the legislative process [...] judicial review of EU law [and] the accession of the EU to the ECHR'.[7] With regard to the last point, the recent Opinion 2/13 of the Court of Justice confirms that the European Convention on Human Rights and Fundamental Freedoms is not compatible with Article 6(2) TFEU and the Protocol on accession. Nevertheless, the focus of this chapter is on the second point, ie, judicial review of EU law. In particular, this chapter will consider how the CJEU's recent jurisprudence[8] on the interpretation of secondary EU laws for judical protection in civil and commercial matters in the field of Justice and Home Affairs are increasingly taking account of fundamental rights in the Charter.

In December 2014, five years will have passed since the enactment of both the Treaty of Lisbon and the Charter. During that time, attention has focused on the role of the CJEU and its role in supporting a particular policy objective of the Treaty of Lisbon, namely the establishment of an Area of Freedom, Security and Justice for the protection of EU citizens. In accordance with Article 81 of the Treaty of Lisbon, a key aspect of that policy is the establishment of judicial cooperation in civil and commercial matters between the Member States through the approximation of laws and rules of jurisdiction. This policy is related to particular objectives in the Charter related to justice in the context of the right to access a court and an appropriate remedy (Articles 6 and 47). Prior to the Treaty of Amsterdam, the key measures taken in the related field of Justice and Home Affairs were the Brussels

[3] Case C-7/98 *Dieter Krombach v André Bamberski* [2000] ECR I-01935 at para 25; B Juratowitch, 'The European Convention on Human Rights and English Private International Law' (2007) 3 *Journal of Private International Law* 173 at 188.

[4] Case C-483/11 *Boncea and Others*, Order of the Court (Sixth Chamber), 14 December 2011, [2011] ECR I-00198 and Case C-617/10 REC *Åkerberg Fransson*, Order of the Court (Grand Chamber), 7 May 2013 (unreported).

[5] Raulus, 'Fundamental Rights in the Area of Freedom, Security and Justice' (n 2) at 214.

[6] G Sanna, 'Article 47 of the EU Charter of Fundamental Rights and its Impact on Judicial Cooperation in Civil and Commercial Matters' in G Di Federico (ed), *The EU Charter of Fundamental Rights From Declaration to Binding Instrument* (Dordrecht, Springer, 2011) 161.

[7] Raulus, 'Fundamental Rights in the Area of Freedom, Security and Justice' (n 2) at 240. On the accession of the EU to the ECHR, see the recent Opinion 2/13 of the Court (Full Court), 18 December 2014, Opinion pursuant to Article 218(11) TFEU.

[8] V Trstenjak and E Beysen, 'The Growing Overlap of Fundamental Freedoms and Fundamental Rights in the Case-Law of the CJEU' (2013) 38 *EL Rev* 293 where the authors consider the 'overlap of fundamental freedoms and fundamental rights' in the 'application and *observance*' of fundamental rights, at p 293, word italicised for emphasis.

Convention on Jurisdiction in Civil and Commercial Matters 1968 and the Rome Convention on the Law Applicable to Contractual Obligations 1980. Whilst both instruments were enacted and regarded as 'international instruments',[9] the justification for their introduction[10] was to support the objectives of the EC at the time.[11] Therefore, the interpretation of both instruments was not strictly focused on ensuring compatibility with human or fundamental rights per se. Given the transference of judicial cooperation in civil and commercial matters from the third to the first pillar by the Treaty of Amsterdam, the EU has had competence to conclude secondary EU legislation operating between the Member States.[12] The notion of competence remains significant from the perspective of accession to the ECHR. As the Opinion 2/13 confirms '[s]uch accession shall not affect the Union's competences as defined in the Treaties.'[13] Article 81 of the Treaty confirms that judicial cooperation in civil and commercial matters between the Member States is required 'in so far as necessary for the proper functioning of the internal market'. Whilst the requirement for necessity is regarded by Peers as less debatable in terms of satisfying the internal market requirement,[14] it must still nevertheless be established that measures are more appropriately taken at EU than national level. What this means is that the EU Commission must demonstrate two things. First, it must be demonstrated that continued divergences between Member States' private international laws affect one of the four freedoms. Second, action by the EU to reduce divergences through the introduction of approximated EU laws must be proportionate. Since 2002, in order to address continued divergences between Member States' laws as regards jurisdiction and the recognition of judgments, the EU has enacted a number of Regulations in EU private international law. The most prominent measures in the field of EU private international law are the Brussels I Regulation for Jurisdiction in Civil and Commercial Matters,[15]

[9] Some Member States enacted and regarded these measures as equivalent to 'international instruments'; S Peers, *EU Justice and Home Affairs Law*, 3rd edn (Oxford, University Press, 2011) at 9–10; PM North, 'The E.E.C Convention on the Law Applicable to Contractual Obligations (1980): Its History and Main Features' in PM North (ed), *Contract Conflicts The EEC Convention on the Law Applicable to Contractual Obligations: A Comparative Study* (Amsterdam, North Holland Publishing Company, 1982) at 11–12.

[10] Report by Mr. P. Jenard on the Convention of 27 September 1968 on jurisdiction and the enforcement of judgments in civil and commercial matters, 3 June 1971 [1979] OJ C59/1; Council Report on the Convention on the law applicable to contractual obligations, by Professors Mario Giuliano and Paul Lagarde' [1980] OJ C282/1.

[11] P Craig, 'The Charter, the ECJ and National Courts' in D Ashiagbor, N Countouris and I Lianos (eds), *The European Union After the Treaty of Lisbon* (Cambridge, Cambridge University Press, 2012) at 79.

[12] The Lugano Opinion also equips the EU with external competence to enter into agreements with non-EU Member States, on behalf of the Member States; Opinion 1/03 of the Court on the competence of the Community to conclude the new Lugano Convention on jurisdiction and the recognition and enforcement of judgments in civil and commercial matters [2006] ECR I-1145.

[13] Opinion 2/13, fn 7 at para 160.

[14] Peers, *EU Justice and Home Affairs Law* (n 9) at 605.

[15] Council Regulation (EU) No 44/2001 [2001] OJ L12/1; to be replaced by Council Regulation (EU) No 1215/2012 [2012] OJ L351/1, effective from 10 January 2015.

the Brussels IIa Regulation for Jurisdiction in Matrimonial Matters and Child Custody[16] and the Rome I[17] and Rome II[18] Regulations on the Law Applicable to Contractual and Non-Contractual Obligations respectively. In particular the Brussels I Regulation seeks to provide a coherent set of general, exclusive and special jurisdiction rules for civil and commercial disputes. A hierarchy of jurisdiction rules (exclusive, general and special) in the Brussels I Regulation determines whether a defendant domiciled in one Member State may be sued in the courts of another Member State. In addition, the Brussels I Regulation contains rules on when recognition and enforcement of foreign judgments can be automatically permitted or refused. The Brussels IIa Regulation also seeks to provide a set of coherent jurisdiction rules for matrimonial matters and for disputes relating to parental responsibility. The Rome I and II Regulations contain rules which determine what law applies to a contractual or non-contractual obligation respectively and when the *lex fori's* public policy or mandatory rules may be enforced to restrict the applicable law.[19] It is worth noting of these four Regulations, it is only (*currently*) the Brussels IIa Regulation which seeks to 'recognise the fundamental rights and observe the principles of the Charter [...] In particular [...] to ensure respect for the fundamental rights of the child as set out in Article 24 of the Charter...'.[20]

The CJEU has continued to provide autonomous and independent interpretations to ensure consistency with the objectives of these secondary EU instruments. However, the introduction of the Treaty, the enactment of the Charter in 2009 and the advancement towards accession of the ECHR by the EU[21] reinforces De Burca's recent thesis that due reference to and application of the Charter should be demonstrated in the CJEU's interpretation and decisions through (inter alia) greater regard for the reasoning offered in Advocate Generals' Opinions.[22] The opinions of the Advocate Generals often offer a significant insight into the Court's *general* 'supervisory role'.[23] More specifically, the decisions of the CJEU on the Brussels I Regulation continue to march towards an increasingly particularised

[16] Council Regulation (EU) No 2201/2003 [2003] OJ L338/1.

[17] Council Regulation (EU) No 593/2008 [2008] OJ L177/6.

[18] Council Regulation (EU) No 864/2007 [2007] OJ L199/40.

[19] *Cf* Juratowitch, 'The European Convention on Human Rights and English Private International Law' (n 3) at 193 on the application of foreign law and compliance with the ECHR.

[20] Recital 33 Brussels IIa Regulation (n 16); Case C-491/10 PPU *Aguirre Zarragav Simone Pelz* [2010] ECR-14247, paras 59 et seq; Case C-400/10 *J Mc B v LE* [2010] ECR I-08965; Case C-4/14 *Bohez v Wiertz*, 6 January 2014 (Request for Preliminary Ruling). On January 2015, the Brussels I Regulation was replaced by Council Regulation (EU) No 1215/2012, the Brussels I Recast Regulation. Recital 38 of that Regulation also acknowledges 'respect' for the Charter, specifically Article 47; Recital 38 Council Regulation (EU) No 1215/2012 [2012] OJ L351/1 at 5; Opinion 2/13, n 7 at para 171.

[21] Art 6 Treaty on European Union (TEU); P Craig, 'EU Accession to the EUHR: Competence, Procedure and Substance' (2013) 36 *Fordham International Law Journal* 1115; Oxford Legal Studies Research Paper No 4/2014, available at http://papers.ssrn.com/sol3/papers.cfm?abstract_id=2354975 (accessed September 2014) at 1114–18; Opinion 2/13, n 7 at para 158.

[22] G de Búrca', After the EU Charter of Fundamental Rights: The Court of Justice as a Human Rights Adjudicator?' (2013) 20 *Maastricht Journal of European and Comparative Law* 168 at 169.

[23] A Kaczorowska, *European Union Law*, 3rd edn (Oxford, Routledge, 2013) at 40.

jurisprudential framework for the autonomous interpretation of EU private international laws. As Trstenjkak and Beysen's recent contribution to the debate concludes, the key developments lie in the broadening or 'gradual expansion'[24] of fundamental rights but crucially also '*adjustments* [...] on the grounds of justification for restrictions of those rights ...'.[25] Accordingly, this chapter seeks to review a number of key CJEU cases on the Brussels I Regulation issued by the court in the period 2009–2014. It will be considered first, to what extent those recent decisions are first illustrative of that 'gradual expansion'[26] towards a *lex specialis* in field of judicial cooperation generally and second how justice is taken account as a fundamental right in the Court's decisions.[27] As part of that continued 'dialogue'[28] between the Court of Justice and the European Court of Human Rights, the Opinions of the Advocates General should continue to shed light on the future influence of the Charter through the Court of Justice's objective to provide autonomous, independent interpretations of the emerging set of EU private international laws.

II. THE AREA OF FREEDOM, SECURITY AND JUSTICE IN TITLE IV OF THE LISBON TREATY AND THE CHARTER OF FUNDAMENTAL RIGHTS

Private international law rules are a set of 'secondary rules'[29] which determine what court is competent to hear a dispute (jurisdiction) and which country's laws apply (*lex fori*, *lex loci*). These rules have been developed and interpreted by and between sovereign jurisdictions in pursuit of Kegelian notions of 'conflicts justice';[30] namely certainty and predictability with due regard to the mutual principles of comity and reciprocity (trust[31] and confidence) when recognising and enforcing judgments from other sovereign States. Since its inception, the EU moved forward with the 'Europeanisation'[32] of jurisdiction rules and the reciprocal enforcement of judgments between the Member States. This has continued apace with a more far reaching programme of approximation of Member States'

[24] Trstenjkak and Beysen, 'The Growing Overlap of Fundamental Freedoms and Fundamental Rights' (n 8) at 294.

[25] ibid.

[26] ibid.

[27] Opinion 2/13, n 7 at para 168.

[28] Opinion 2/13 of the Court (Full Court), 18 December 2014, Opinion pursuant to Article 218(11) TFEU, n 7 at 43 referring to the 'Declaration on Article 6(2) of the Treaty on European Union.'

[29] A Mills, *The Confluence of Public and Private International Law, Justice, Pluarlism and Subsidiarity in the International Constitutional Ordering of Private Law* (Cambridge, Cambridge University Press, 2010) at 19–20.

[30] G Kegel, 'Fundamental Approaches' in K Lipstein (ed), *International Encyclopedia of International Law, Volume III/1, Private International Law* (Leiden, Boston, Mohr Siebeck, Martinus Nijhoff Publishers, 2011).

[31] 'Mutual Trust'; Opinion 2/13, n 7 at para 151.

[32] P Graziano and MP Vink, *Europeanization New Research Agendas* (Basingstoke, Palgrave MacMillan, 2007).

rules of private international laws via (inter alia) the secondary EU instruments mentioned earlier, in furtherance of the policy to establish an 'Area of Freedom, Security and Justice' (AFSJ).

Raulus has confirmed that there is a 'close connection between the AFSJ policies and fundamental rights…'.[33] Since the Tampere Council in 1999,[34] the establishment of an AFSJ was affirmed as a 'most important specific objective'[35] of the EU. The AFSJ is an explicit objective of the Treaty of Lisbon, the TFEU and the Charter. Article 2 of the Treaty of Lisbon provides, inter alia, that the 'Union shall offer its citizens an area of freedom, security and justice without internal frontiers, in which the free movement of persons is ensured…'. Article 4 of the TFEU confirms that the AFSJ is an area of 'shared competence between the Union and the Member States…'. The Preamble of the Charter states that the 'creation of an area of freedom, security and justice' is necessary to protect EU citizen's fundamental rights. Measures taken by the EU in the field of AFSJ must be within the realms of the Union's competence. In its desire to approximate jurisdiction rules in civil and commercial matters, the EU has taken action to update existing secondary EU laws and introduce new measures. Since (inter alia) the Treaty of Amsterdam in 1997 and more recently Articles 81 and 114 of the TFEU, the CJEU's role in delivering autonomous, independent and arguably more particularised interpretations of these Regulations has continued to exert considerable influence on the evolution and interpretation of private international laws—on the one hand, pragmatically viewed as the remit of sovereign states, but on the other hand, regarded as an emerging branch of EU private law.[36]

The cornerstone of AFSJ is the principle of mutual recognition of Member States' laws and procedures. The principle of mutual recognition, derived from the CJEU in *Cassis de Dijon*,[37] has ensured that Member States respect and recognise the rules and procedures of other Member States. This principle must be balanced with the general objective of the AFSJ where there is a 'presumption of compliance, by other Member States, with European Union law, and, in particular, human rights'.[38] The discrete question that has arisen from a number of CJEU decisions on judicial cooperation is whether mutual recognition is 'problematic from the fundamental rights protection point of view'?[39] In the field of judicial

[33] Raulus, 'Fundamental Rights in the Area of Freedom, Security and Justice' (n 2) at 229.

[34] Kazcarowska, *European Union Law* (n 23) at 44.

[35] Kaczarowska, *European Union Law* (n 23) at 41.

[36] P Letto-Vanamo and J Smits (eds), *Coherence and Fragmentation in European Private Law* (Munich, Sellier: European Law Publishers, 2012).

[37] Case C-120/78 *Rewe-Zentral AG v Bundesmonopolverwaltung fur Branntwein (Cassis de Dijon)* [1979] ECR 649.

[38] J Polakiewicz, 'The EU Law and the ECHR: Will the European Union's Accession Square the Circle?' (2013) 6 *European Human Rights Law Review* 592 at 602 quoting AG Trstenjak's Opinion in the Joined Cases C-411/10 and C-493/10 *NS* and *ME*, 5 October 2010 (nyr) at paras 38, 41.

[39] Raulus, 'Fundamental Rights in the Area of Freedom, Security and Justice' (n 2) at 229.

cooperation, the two broad areas where the tension between mutual recognition and fundamental rights has arisen have been either when applying the Regulations for the purposes of establishing jurisdiction in the courts of a Member State or in determining in what circumstances recognition and enforcement of another Member State's judgment can legitimately be refused. More specifically, the cases on the Brussels I Regulation to be considered later in this chapter, reflect the need for greater coherence between the potentially competing notions of mutual recognition, effective judicial cooperation and rights enshrined under the ECHR and the Charter. This has also been reflected in cases on the analogous Brussels IIa Regulation on jurisdiction, recognition and enforcement in matrimonial matters and parental responsibility. For example, in Case C-400/10 PPU *McB*, the CJEU confirmed that it was able to take account of the Charter when interpreting the Brussels II Regulation.[40] The CJEU confirmed that the Charter should apply if *mutatis mundandis* with the ECHR.

In the context of judicial cooperation for civil and commercial matters, the challenge of reconciling mutual recognition with fundamental rights protection persists. Therefore, considering the decisions of the CJEU's approach and rationale in its interpretation of EU private international laws provides an opportunity to reflect on how the objectives of mutual recognition correlate with first the increasing expectations of fundamental rights protection via the application of Article 6 and 47 of the Charter and Article 67(1) of the TFEU. In a series of judgments prior to and since the introduction of the Charter, the CJEU has affirmed that the principle of mutual recognition cannot be applied at the expense of fundamental rights derived either from the ECHR or the Charter. Rodgerson identifies that the use of Article 6 of the ECHR in particular will operate 'to prevent the enforcement of foreign judgments which have been obtained in breach of Article 6 ECHR'.[41] In the AFJS, a more far reaching question posed by Polakiewicz is whether 'human rights standards, based on either national, ECHR or EU law, may be invoked to *refuse* mutual recognition in cases where the relevant EU legislation does not provide for such a refusal ground'.[42] The next section of this chapter will consider how particular decisions on the Brussels I Regulation by the CJEU during the period 2009–2014 demonstrate the emergence of De Burca's second and third points on the metamorphosis of the Charter, beyond its 'adoption … [to its] cit[ation] or argu[ment] before the Court … [and] the Court's engag[ment] … and … prominence …'.[43]

[40] Case C-400/10 PPU *J McB v LE* (n 20); S Barriati, *Cases and Materials on EU Private International Law* (Oxford, Hart Publishing, 2011) at 193–94.

[41] P Rogerson, *Collier's Conflict of Laws*, 4th edn (Cambridge, Cambridge University Press) at 431.

[42] J Polakiewicz, 'The EU Law and the ECHR: Will the European Union's Accession Square the Circle?' (2013) 6 *European Human Rights Law Review* 592 at 603. Word italicised for emphasis.

[43] de Búrca, 'After the EU Charter of Fundamental Rights' (n 22) at 168.

III. A GRADUAL EXPANSION: DECISIONS OF THE CJEU ON THE BRUSSELS I REGULATION AND THE CHARTER

Before turning to the approach in recent CJEU cases, it is instructive to briefly consider the extent to which the pre-Lisbon and Charter case law from the CJEU considered the notion of fundamental rights, derived from interpretation of the ECHR, in its interpretation of both the Brussels Convention 1968 and the Brussels I Regulation. At this juncture, the distinction must be made between those cases which fall under the scope of the EU rules and those which remain subject to Member States' residual jurisdiction and procedural mechanisms. Not only does this distinction define the temporal scope of the Regulations between the Member States, it also serves to highlight that the Charter's influence is restricted to the 'EU legal order'.[44] The key cases in which the provisions of the ECHR have arisen under the Brussels Convention and Regulation are in relation to the restrictive review of the Court's jurisdiction, the compatibility of provisional and protective measures and the extent to which a foreign judgment may be refused recognition and enforcement. These will now be considered in turn.

A. Case C-7/98 *Dieter Krombach v Andre Bamberski*: Does Enforcement of a Foreign Judgment Infringe a Fundamental Right?

Case C-7/98 *Dieter Krombachv Andre Bamberski*[45] illustrates the role of the Court in the tripartite relationship between national law, the Brussels Convention 1968 and fundamental rights under the ECHR. The core issue was whether a judgment from one Member State could, under Article 27 of the Convention, be refused recognition in another Member State. In this case, the defendant was not present to be able to defend (inter alia) civil proceedings which took place in France. A judgment was issued against him which required him to pay compensation. The French judgment was sought to be enforced in Germany. In response, refusal to enforce the judgment was sought because the defendant claimed he was 'unable effectively to defend himself'.[46] Article 27 provided that refusal to enforce could only be permitted if enforcement was contrary to public policy. The CJEU held that whilst it was not possible to review the court of origin's jurisdiction,[47] it would be for the national court to determine whether there had been a breach of Article 27 on the basis that enforcement of the judgment would be 'at variance to an unacceptable degree with the legal order of the State in which enforcement is

[44] See, for example, LFM Besselink's recent comments on Case C-399/11 *Melloni v Ministerio Fiscal* [2013] QB 1067 in 'The Parameters of Constitutional Conflict After Melloni' (2014) *EL Rev* 531 at 537, 539, 541. On national approaches, with English private international law as an exemplar, see Juratowitch, 'The European Convention on Human Rights and English Private International Law' (n 3).

[45] [2000] OJ C163/1.

[46] ibid at para 16.

[47] ibid at para 31.

sought in as much as it infringes a fundamental right [...] *within that legal order*'.[48] In referring to the earlier Opinion 2/94, the CJEU confirmed that its role was to interpret the 'limits'[49] of public policy under Article 27 of the Brussels Convention whilst at the same time ensuring that the 'right to a fair hearing is [maintained as a] fundamental principle of Community law which must be guaranteed...'.[50] The Court confirmed that the public policy exception in the Brussels Convention could operate only in those 'exceptional cases'[51] where the 'opportunity to hear the defence of an accused person who is not present at the hearing...'.[52] In conclusion, the CJEU affirmed that the aim of mutual recognition of judgments was not to 'undermin[e] the right to a fair hearing...'.[53] Therefore whilst it would appear that fundamental rights trump mutual recognition, the Court was affirming its previous position in Case C-49/84 *Debaecker and Plouvier v Bouwman*.[54] In essence, a check and balance approach operates in that refusal to recognise the judgment of another Member State under the public policy exception takes effect only in such situations where breach of an essential fundamental right as provided for by the *national* court of enforcement can be established.

B. Case C-394/07 *Marco Gambazzi v Daimler Chrysler*: Restrictions must not be 'Manifestly Disproportionate'

The second key case brought under the Brussels I Regulation before the introduction of the Charter was Case C-394/07 *Marco Gambazzi v Daimler Chrysler*.[55] The dispute in *Gambazzi* was concerned with the compatibility of a freezing order, or Mareva injunction, with the Brussels I Regulation. This freezing order was intended to prevent Mr Gambazzi from participating in court proceedings in which he was a defendant. The Advocate General in *Gambazzi* took the view that such an order was the 'most serious restriction possible on the rights of the defence'.[56] In *Gambazzi*, the Court affirmed that the balance to be struck between fundamental rights and public policy was to ensure that the 'objectives [...] corresponded [with the] public interest pursued [and were not] disproportionate ...'.[57] In essence, the CJEU's approach has been to offer 'general criteria'[58] to be used by

[48] ibid at para 37; words removed and italicised for emphasis.
[49] ibid at paras 1, 22, 23; Opinion of the Court of 28 March 1996 on the Accession by the Community to the European Convention for the Protection of Human Rights and Fundamental Freedoms 1996 ECR I-01759.
[50] ibid at para 42, words removed and added for syntax.
[51] ibid at para 44.
[52] ibid at para 44.
[53] ibid at para 43.
[54] ibid at para 43; Case C-49/84 *Debaecker and Plouvier v Bouwman* [1985] ECR 1779.
[55] [2009] ECR I-02563.
[56] ibid at para 33.
[57] ibid at para 29.
[58] ibid at para 39.

national courts in determining whether the objectives are proportionate relative to the defendant's remedies and his right to be heard.

IV. TAKING ACCOUNT OF THE CHARTER IN THE CASE LAW OF THE CJEU ON THE BRUSSELS I REGULATION 2009–2014

A. Prorogation of Jurisdiction and Coherence with Article 47: Case C-112/13 *A v B*

In Case C-112/13 *A v B*,[59] the Oberster Gerichtshof, Austria referred three questions to the CJEU which were concerned with the interaction between Articles 24 of the Brussels I Regulation and Article 47 of the Charter. The facts were as follows. A number of claimants sued 'A' for damages based on the allegation that A was responsible for the abduction of B's family members in a non-Member State. The claimants argued that 'A' was domiciled in Austria and that the Austrian courts had jurisdiction. The first question asked by the Austrian court was whether in a situation where national law is not compliant with the Charter, it should not be applied and referred for further, national assessment. The second and third questions put to the Court was whether in circumstances where the defendant is absent and a representative is appointed to appear, this constitutes 'appearance'—and thereby 'tacit prorogation'[60] of jurisdiction—for the purposes of Article 24 of the Brussels I Regulation. The third related question was whether such an interpretation of Article 24 of the Brussels I Regulation was in accord with Article 47 of the Charter. The defendant argued that if appearance in this manner was established under Article 24, this would constitute a failure to take account of Article 6 of the ECHR and Article 47 of the Charter. In response, the claimants argued that if appearance was not established then this would be at odds with their right to an effective remedy under Article 47. With regard to the first question, Advocate General Bot observed that whilst there was a lack of definition of appearance under Article 24,[61] Article 24 was to be interpreted in support of the Regulation's objectives.[62] Advocate General Bot was of the opinion that to ensure an 'autonomous definition'[63] of the Article and a 'high level of predictability'[64] in relation to its potential effects on special jurisdiction rules,[65] Article 24 *in particular* should be 'narrowly construed'.[66] Advocate General Bot was also of the opinion that in such cases, jurisdiction did not constitute the entry of an appearance by the defendant such as required by Article 24 of the Brussels I Regulation and that

[59] Judgment of the Court (Fifth Chamber), 11 September 2014 (nyr).
[60] Case C-112/13 *A v B* (ibid), Opinion of AG Bot, 2 April 2014, at paras 36, 39, 40, 41, 42.
[61] Opinion of AG Bot (ibid) at para 35.
[62] ibid at para 35.
[63] ibid at para 35.
[64] ibid at para 37; affirmed in judgment of the Court at para 57.
[65] ibid at para 39.
[66] ibid at para 38.

tacit prorogation may operate only if 'all the parties to the dispute—and above all, the defendant—have deliberately chosen that jurisdiction'.[67] In relation to the third question, the Advocate General reaffirmed the need for deliberate choice, a point confirmed by the CJEU in its decision.[68] The Judgment of the Court also distinguished the earlier Case C-327/10 *Hypotecní banka a.s*[69] with the facts of the present case since '... the effect under national law that A must be regarded as having entered an appearance before the court seised'.[70]

B. Exclusive Jurisdiction: Case C-483/12 *Irmengard Weber v Mechthilde Weber*

In the recent Case C-438/12 *Irmengard Weber v Mechthilde Weber*,[71] the CJEU was requested by the Oberlandesgericht Munchen, Germany to consider which court could assert jurisdiction under Article 22 of the Brussels I Regulation. Article 22 provides exclusive jurisdiction for rights *in rem* over immovable property. The related question was that if the court first seised did not have exclusive jurisdiction by virtue of Article 22, could the continuation of proceedings there potentially restrict recognition of a subsequent judgment under Article 35(1) of the same Regulation? The Court was also asked whether, in accordance with the Regulation the court second seised—having exclusive *in rem* jurisdiction as the place where the object was situated—should stay proceedings in favour of the court first seised (*lis pendens*). Advocate General Jääskinen re-aligned the questions in the Preliminary Reference to follow the structure of the Regulation. In respect of the first question, he confirmed that the Italian courts as the courts first seised had already made a declaration declining jurisdiction over the subject matter of the dispute in favour of the German courts.[72] Since the 'jurisdiction of the court first seised [could not be] be formally established'[73] the Advocate General confirmed that there was no *lis pendens* in operation in this case and proceedings in the court second seised need not be stayed. He relied on dicta in *Overseas Union Insurance*[74] to justify that it was 'inappropriate for it to stay proceedings pending before it...'.[75] The justification for the 'reliable assessment'[76] was premised on the fact that the court first seised did not have jurisdiction and could not therefore either determine the question of *lis pendens* nor issue a judgment capable of recognition under Articles 35(1) and 45(1). Furthermore, since the court second seised may very well have exclusive jurisdiction by virtue of Article 22, it would be unnecessary to require that court

[67] ibid at para 42.
[68] Case C-112/13 *A v B* (n 60), judgment of the Court at paras 53–54 et seq.
[69] C-327/10 *Hypotecní banka a.s v Udo Mike Linder* [2011] ECR I-11543.
[70] Case C-112/13 *A v B* (n 60), judgment of the Court at para 60.
[71] [2014] OJ C/159/6.
[72] ibid at para 17 of AG Opinion.
[73] ibid at para 37 of AG Opinion.
[74] Case C-351/89 *Overseas Union Insurance and Others* [1991] ECR I-3317.
[75] Case C-438/12 *Irmengard Weber v Mechthilde Weber* (n 71) at para 40 of AG Opinion.
[76] ibid at para 42 of AG Opinion.

to stay proceedings. The Advocate General also provided an interpretation of Article 27 of the Brussels I Regulation as to whether *lis pendens* required to operate 'between the same parties'.[77] In line with earlier jurisprudence, the Advocate General confirmed that it was possible for parties to have different procedural titles in each case and be at least one of the parties in both sets of proceedings. Both situations arose in this case: with the former criteria, one of the parties (Ms I Weber) was a defendant to the first set of proceedings in Italy, whereas she was a claimant in proceedings brought against her sister (Ms M Weber) in Germany. The Advocate General confirmed that in a situation where the parties were 'not strictly identical',[78] the court second seised still had to be satisfied that the 'parties' interests are the same and inseparable'.[79] Crucially, for the purposes of this analysis, the Advocate General took the view that if the court second seised was not limited to determining the 'identity and indivisibility between the parties'[80] for the purposes of Article 27, a 'denial of justice'[81] in breach of the parties' fundamental rights may occur. The Advocate General confirmed that Articles 6 and 13 of the ECHR and Article 47 of the Charter are:

> [I]ndividual rights which exist regardless of whether or not the natural or legal person concerned has interests inseparable from or identical to those of another person [...] An individual cannot be legitimately deprived of the opportunity of having his action examined without delay because another individual is the defendant in a dispute brought before the courts of another Member State.[82]

In sum, the Advocate General concluded that in the present case the requirement to stay proceedings in the court second seised (which had exclusive jurisdiction) would 'jeopardise the effective judicial protection of the parties'[83] and that the proceedings in both the Italian courts and the German courts were not *lis pendens* and therefore not subject to Article 27. The Advocate General also confirmed that the 'right of the applicant to have access to justice [was] consistent with the right to effective juridical protection guaranteed by Articles 6 and 13 of the ECHR and the first and second paragraphs of Article 47 of the Charter'.[84] The Advocate General also remarked that in their opinion the application of Article 27 would not render a breach of Article 47 since it was plainly evident in this case that all parties had been able to access justice in their chosen courts.

In response, the CJEU itself re-aligned the order of the questions referred to but nevertheless still ruled that a judgment granted by a Member State court that did not take account of the exclusive jurisdiction rule in Article 22 'will not

[77] ibid at para 17 of AG Opinion.
[78] ibid at para 53 of AG Opinion.
[79] ibid at para 54 of AG Opinion.
[80] ibid at para 53 of AG Opinion.
[81] ibid at para 55 of AG Opinion.
[82] ibid at para 55 of AG's Opinion. Words in brackets removed for syntax.
[83] ibid at para 58 of AG's Opinion.
[84] ibid at para 87 of AG's Opinion.

be recognised in the other Member States, in accordance with Article 35(1) of that regulation'.[85] The Court also agreed that in the circumstances of the present case—the court second seised having exclusive jurisdiction—the issue of *lis pendens* did not arise.[86]

V. COMPATIBILITY OF SERVICE VIA PUBLIC NOTICE WITH ARTICLE 6 ECHR/ ARTICLE 47 CHARTER: CASE C-292/10 *G v CORNELIUS DE VISSER*

In Case C-292/10 *G v Cornelius De Visser*,[87] Ms G raised proceedings in the German Landgericht Regensburg court in which she sought to establish Mr De Visser's liability for infringement of her personality rights. Mr Visser was alleged to have posted partly naked photographs of Ms G without Ms G's consent on a website with a German top level domain address (.de) both of which were owned by him. The difficulty in this case was that, despite investigations in Germany and the Netherlands, it was not possible to establish where Mr De Visser was domiciled (ie Germany, the Netherlands or somewhere else) and whether an eventual default judgment could be issued against him. Ms G initiated proceedings via public notice in Germany. There were a number of questions referred to the CJEU, a number of which were on the how Article 5(3) of the Brussels I Regulation could be applied to such infringement claims. For the purposes of this chapter, the two key, competing issues were the compatibility of serving proceedings in this manner with the Brussels I Regulation and, in the absence of being able to definitively establish the defendant's domicile, the claimant's right to an effective remedy under Article 47 of the Charter. The Court referred to Case C327/10 *Hypotecní banka*[88] and confirmed that where there was no evidence that an EU citizen was domiciled in a non-Member State, the 'international jurisdiction of a court of a Member State is established [...] when the conditions for application of one of the rules of jurisdiction [...] are met'.[89] On the question of compatibility of the national procedural rules for public service of proceedings, the Court also confirmed that such rules were permitted provided they did not 'infringe European Union law'[90] and—in accordance with earlier CJEU authority from *Denilauler*[91] and *Gambazzi*[92]—that the 'rights of the defence are observed'.[93] With regard to the effective application of Article 47 of the Charter, the Court was

[85] ibid, judgment of the Court at paras 48, 55.
[86] ibid, judgment of the Court at paras 62–64.
[87] [2012] OJ C133/5.
[88] Case C-327/10 *Hypotecní banka a.s* (n 69).
[89] Case C-292/10 *G v Cornelius De Visser* (n 87), judgment of the Court at para 41. Words removed for syntax.
[90] ibid at para 45.
[91] C-125/79 *Bernard Denilauler v SNC Couchet Frères* [1980] ECR 1153 at para 13.
[92] Case C-292/10 *G v Cornelius De Visser* (n 87) at para 23.
[93] ibid at para 47.

also at pains to observe that that latter requirement—rights of the defence—had to be balanced with the 'applicant's right to bring an action'.[94]

The CJEU offered a three-point response. First, it reinforced *Gambazzi* that there could be occasions where the rights of the defence 'may be subject to restrictions'.[95] Second, in reinforced *Hypotecní* in stating that such restrictions had to 'correspond [...] to the objectives of public interest'.[96] Third, in determining that such a restriction did not constitute 'a disproportionate breach of those rights',[97] it referred to Article 26(2) of the Brussels I Regulation which requires proceedings to be stayed where the defendant has not had 'sufficient time [...] to arrange [a] defence or [take] all necessary steps'.[98] Having considered the earlier CJEU case law, the Court then turned to the European Court of Human Rights case of *Nunes Dias v Portugal*[99] to reinforce the point that service by public notice could be effected provided corresponding rights under Article 6 ECHR were 'properly protected'.[100] This enabled the CJEU to conclude affirmatively that subject to 'all investigations required by the principles of diligence and good faith are undertaken',[101] such service was compatible with Article 6 ECHR and Article 47 of the Charter.

A. Protective Measures under the Brussels I Regulation: Case C-350/13 *Antonio Gramsci Shipping Corp v Aivars Lembergs*

In Case C-350/13 *Antonio Gramsci Shipping Corp v Aivars Lembergs*,[102] the question referred to the CJEU by the Latvian court was whether it was compatible with the Brussels I Regulation for a Mareva injunction[103] to be enforced in the courts of another Member State when damage to *third parties* may occur as a result of such enforcement. The Latvian court asked two related questions. The first question was related to Article 34(1) of the Brussels I Regulation which provides that a judgment will not be recognised if it is 'manifestly contrary to public policy in the Member State in which recognition is sought'. The first question was whether the circumstances permitted the refusal to enforce a judgment in accordance with Article 34(1)? If so, the second and related question asked by the Latvian court was whether Article 47 of the Charter extended to provisional measures that 'limit

[94] ibid at para 48.
[95] ibid at para 49.
[96] ibid at paras 49–50, words removed for syntax.
[97] ibid at paras 49 and 51.
[98] ibid at para 51 words removed and added for syntax.
[99] App nos 69829/01 2672/03 (ECtHR, 10 April 2003).
[100] Case C-292/10 *G v Cornelius De Visser* (n 87) at para 58.
[101] ibid at para 59.
[102] Order of the Court (Eighth Chamber) [2014] OJ C261/7; L Collins, A Briggs, J Harris, JD McClean, C McLachlan and CGJ Morse (eds), *Dicey, Morris and Collins, The Conflict of Laws*, 15th edn (London, Sweet and Maxwell, 2012) at para 14-160.
[103] An order of the English court granted against an *individual*, having extraterritorial effect.

the economic rights of a person who has not been a party to the proceedings'[104] if that person can apply for those proceedings to be 'varied or discharged'?[105] In the intervening time, the Mareva injunction had been withdrawn. This plainly had the effect of negating the status of the case as one pending before the courts of a Member State in accordance with Article 267 TFEU.[106] Whist the Court recognised that 'in exceptional circumstances, it can examine the conditions [to determine] jurisdiction',[107] in accordance with *Di Donna*,[108] the Court plainly refused to give a ruling on the matter. The question therefore remains as to whether a Mareva injunction or similar procedural mechanism granted by the courts of a Member State, could legitimately constitute an infringement of the rights of third parties in breach of Article 47 of the Charter.

B. Refusal to Recognise a Foreign Judgment and Article 47 of the Charter: Case C-619/10 *Trade Agency Ltd v Seramico Investments Ltd*

In Case C-619/10 *Trade Agency Ltd v Seramico Investments Ltd*,[109] the issue of whether there was a 'manifest and disproportionate breach of the defendant's rights' contrary to Article 47 of the Charter was raised for the CJEU to consider. In essence, this case raised a question about the competing priorities of mutual trust (a cornerstone of the Brussels I Regulation), on the one hand, and the 'right to a fair trial under Article 47 of the Charter',[110] on the other. In this case a claim form was raised and served by the claimants for payment by the defendant. In the absence of the defendant lodging a defence, the English High Court granted a default judgment. The claimants thereafter sought to have the judgment recognised and enforced in the District Court North Riga, Latvia. Article 54 of the Brussels I Regulation (currently) provides that a person seeking enforcement of a judgment is required to present (in addition to a copy of the judgment) a certificate of enforceability from the court of a Member States where the judgment was issued. The claimant submitted a certificate in accordance with Article 54. The relevant provisions of the Brussels I Regulation in this case are Articles 34, which provides limited grounds to refuse the recognition of a foreign judgment and Article 35, which confirms (inter alia) that the test of public policy does not apply to rules of jurisdiction, and Article 36 which confirms (inter alia) that the substance of a judgment cannot be reviewed. The Latvian court duly granted the application for recognition and enforcement and the defendant lodged an appeal. A further appeal was raised to the Senate of the Supreme Court, on the basis that

[104] Case C-350/13 *Antonio Gramsci Shipping Corp* (n 102) at para 4(2).
[105] ibid at para 4(2).
[106] ibid at para 11.
[107] ibid at para 9.
[108] Case C-492/11 *Ciro Di Donna v Societa Imballaggi Metallic Salerno (SISMA)*, 27 June 2013 (nyr).
[109] [2012] OJ C331/3.
[110] ibid at para 47.

recognition and enforcement should be refused due to first, breach of 'rights of defence'; second, the defendant's lack of notice of English legal proceedings and, third, that the absence of reasons in the English default judgment was 'manifestly contrary to Latvian public policy'.[111]

There were two questions referred by the Latvian Senate of the Supreme Court to the CJEU. The first question, in the case of a request for enforcement of a judgment from another Member State under Article 34 of the Brussels I Regulation, was whether an enforcing court could consider evidence from the certificate as grounds to refuse recognition of a judgment granted in default of appearance and the compatibility of the need for mutual trust. The Latvian Supreme Court started by looking at Article 54 and confirmed that whilst there was no requirement for the enforcing court to go beyond the information provided in the certificate, the (pre-Charter) Case C-283/05 *ASML*[112] confirmed that the 'observance of the rights of the defence of a defendant in default of appearance is ensured by a double review, also carried out by the court hearing the application for recognition or enforcement of the foreign judgment'.[113] Interestingly, the Latvian Supreme Court also regarded there to be a connection between the infringement of Latvian public policy, on the one hand, and both the ECHR and the Charter, on the other hand. It observed that both of the latter instruments necessitate that 'national courts [have an] obligation to set out in their judgments the grounds on which they were adopted…'.[114]

In answering that question, the CJEU's methodology was to consider both the 'wording of the provision [and the] system established by the Regulation…'.[115] In the earlier decision Case C-420/07 *Apostolides v Orams*,[116] the CJEU confirmed that a defendant 'should, where necessary, be able to appeal in an adversarial procedure against [a] declaration of enforceability if he considers one of the grounds for non-enforcement to be present'.[117] The Court confirmed that in line with the spirit of Recital 17 of the Brussels I Regulation and the earlier Case C-139/10 *Prism Investments*[118] that the practical consequence of Recital 17 when the request for enforcement is made 'may involve only a purely formal check of the documents…'.[119] The Court pointed out that when the enforcing court issues a declaration in accordance with Article 42(2), Article 43 may then raise the issue of enforceability in the enforcing court. The CJEU confirmed the earlier decision of *ASML* that Article 34(2) 'aims to ensure that the rights of defence of a defendant

[111] ibid at para 20.
[112] [2006] ECR I-12041 .
[113] Case C-619/10 *Trade Agency Ltd* (n 105) at para 22.
[114] ibid at para 24.
[115] ibid at para 27.
[116] Case C-420/07 *Meletis Apostolides v DC Orams and LE Orams* [2009] ECR I-03571.
[117] ibid at para 43.
[118] Case C-139/10 *Prism Investments BV v Jaap Anne van der Meer* [2011] ECR I-09511.
[119] Case C-619/10 *Trade Agency Ltd* (n 109) at paras 28–29.

in default of appearance delivered in the Member State of origin are observable by a double review'.[120] It is at this stage that the Court, where enforcement is sought, can in accordance with Case C-166/80 *Klomps v Michel*[121] undertake an 'overall',[122] 'independent assessment'[123] of the facts, including whether the defendant was served with proceedings. The Court referred to the Advocate General Opinion where it was remarked that the certificate has 'prima facie value'[124] in so far as there are—inevitably—different courts involved in issuing and enforcing a given judgment.

The second question was whether a decision in default of appearance that does contain reasoning is compatible with the defendant's right to a fair hearing in accordance with Article 47 of the Charter. Here, the CJEU made three significant points. The first reinforced the view from *Apostolides v Orams* that Article 34(1) 'may be relied on only in exceptional cases'.[125] In asserting that Member States determine their own public policy objectives as a starting point, the CJEU's role—affirmed in a series of earlier cases[126]—is to 'review the limits within which the courts of a Member State may have recourse to that concept *for the purposes of refusing recognition…*'.[127] Second, there would require to be 'breach of a fundamental principle […] regarded as essential in the legal order of the State in which enforcement is sought…'.[128] The third, connected and concluding point was that the right to a fair trial under Article 47 is a *coalescing* right in the sense that it '*results* from the constitutional traditions *common* to the Member States …'.[129] On that basis, the enforcing court may, as a starting point, regard a judgment lacking in 'assessment of subject-matter, basis and merits of the action, is a restriction on a fundamental right within the legal order of that Member State'.[130] The Court confirmed that a range of factors that required to be taken into account (such as 'nature of decision […] procedural guarantees … [availability of] an appropriate and effective appeal')[131] when determining whether the default judgment was *manifestly disproportiate* to the defendant's right of a fair trial. In line with the defences to recognition and enforcement and mutual recognition of judgments, a high threshold test would appear to be required.

[120] ibid at para 32.
[121] [1981] ECR 1593.
[122] Case C-619/10 *Trade Agency Ltd* (n 109) at para 33.
[123] ibid at para 38.
[124] ibid at para 36.
[125] ibid at para 48.
[126] Case C-7/98 *Krombach* (n 45), Case C-38/98 *Renault* [2000] ECR 1-2973 and Case C-420/07 *Apostolides* (n 116).
[127] Case C-619/10 *Trade Agency Ltd* (n 109) at paras 49–50, words italicised for emphasis.
[128] ibid at para 51.
[129] ibid at para 52. Words italicised for emphasis.
[130] ibid at para 54.
[131] ibid at para 60. Words removed and added for syntax.

C. Enforcement of Judgments under the Brussels I Regulation and Article 47 of the Charter

(i) Case C-156/12 GREP GmbH v Freistaat Bayern

The question in Case C-156/12 *GREP GmbH v Freistaat Bayern*[132] was, in matters concerned with declarations of enforceability of a judgment under Article 43 of the Brussels I Regulation, does the 'right to legal aid'[133] form part of a party's right to a fair trial under Article 47 of the Charter and/or Article 6 ECHR? The CJEU confirmed the approach in Case C283/05 *ASML*[134] that a balance must be struck under the Brussels I Regulation to prevent 'undermin[ing] … the rights of the defence…'.[135] Once again, the rhetoric from the Court was clear; this balance must reflect effective judicial protection, itself to be achieved in fulfilment of 'the common constitutional traditions of the Member States…'[136] and thereby the ECHR. In short, the CJEU held that there was a requirement to include legal aid within the criteria for assessing how a party could effectively bring a declaratory request under Article 43. Nevertheless, such a requirement could be subject to a restriction imposed by the court of enforcement, provided that such a restriction on the rules granting legal aid in that jurisdiction are not 'manifest and disproportionate'.[137] Again, for the purposes of reviewing proportionality, the CJEU provided an instructive set of indicators of what connecting factors would be necessary for the national court of enforcement to review. These included the nature, gravity and legal basis of the proceedings, success rate and the procedural rules and costs applicable.[138]

(ii) Preliminary Reference in Case C-4/14 Bohez v Wiertz

In the recent Case C-4/14 *Christophe Bohez v Ingrid Wiertz*[139] (6 January 2014), the Korkein oikes court in Finland made a Preliminary Reference on a number of key questions, two of which are most relevant for this analysis. The first, and general question, the Court was asked, was whether an order to enforce and payment of a principal obligations in a child custody or access case was outside the scope of the Brussels I Regulation. The second, and more particular question

[132] Order of the Sixth Court, 13 June 2012 (unpublished decision).
[133] ibid at para 23.
[134] Case C-283/05 *ASML* (n 112).
[135] Case C-156/12 *GREP GmbH* (n 132) at para 32.
[136] ibid at para 35; the court also referred to Case C-409/06 *Winner Wetten GmhB v Mayor of Bergheim* [2010] OJ C288/6 in support of this general principle.
[137] Case C-156/12 *GREP GmbH* (n 132) at para 39.
[138] ibid at para 41; on costs the CJEU referred to Case C-279/09 *DEB Deutsche Energiehandels-under Beratungsgesellscahr mbH c Bundesrepublik Deutschland* [2010] ECR I-13849.
[139] [2014] OJ C71/21.

vis-à-vis fundamental rights—relative to Recital 33 of the Brussels IIa Regulation and the right of access—asked the CJEU to confirm first, which court has jurisdiction to examine the issue of enforcement of a periodic penalty payment and second whether the court of enforcement's role is limited to enforcement or whether it is permitted to enter into an examination of the reasons for failure to comply with rights of access. In some respects, an analogy could be made with the *Trade Investments* case above, where the CJEU provided criteria as to how restrictions on defending the enforcement of a foreign judgment may be compliant with Article 47 of the Charter. At the time of writing this chapter a decision is awaited. It therefore remains to be seen to what extent the CJEU will consider this case in the context of a right of access case under the Brussels IIa Regulation. This case may also provide the CJEU with an opportunity to clarify a particularised set of criteria as to whether restrictions on the Court's powers to review a foreign judgment are not 'manifestly disproportionate' to Article 24 of the Charter in the particular context of the Brussels IIa Regulation.

VI. CONCLUSIONS

It was the purpose of this chapter seeks to review a number of key Preliminary Rulings from the CJEU on the Brussels I Regulation during the period 2009–present. It has been considered first, to what extent those decisions are illustrative of *lex specialis* generally in the field of judicial cooperation and specifically on fundamental rights. Second, where available, this chapter has sought to consider how the Advocate General's Opinion in these cases may shed light on the future influence of the Charter in seeking to derive autonomous, independent interpretations of secondary EU private international laws. It is clear that Articles 6 and 47 of the Charter is beginning to emerge as a distinct influence on the CJEU's interpretation of secondary EU measures for judicial cooperation in civil matters designed to advance the Lisbon Treaty's objective of an AFSJ. The role of the national court is clearly significant; both in terms of the continued referral of questions in Preliminary Rulings which seek clarification on the influence of the Charter and in its eventual interpretation of those Rulings. The CJEU has responded by integrating the influence of the Charter into its interpretation of articles of the Brussels I Regulation. Whilst a 'gradual expansion'[140] is occurring, two wider issues persist. The first issue is how the ideology of the Charter within

[140] Trjstenjak and Baysen, n 8.

the EU legal order will continue to restrict the mutual recognition of jurisdiction and judgments in civil and commercial matters. The second, related matter is that of effective interpretation. Whilst not all the cases referred to contained an Opinion from the Advocate General, if the objective of the CJEU is to 'improve the quality and fairness of its judgments and strengthen its legitimacy…'[141] then, as de Burca attests, a more nuanced assessment of the 'rulings of other courts or on the relevant jurisprudence of regional and international bodies when interpreting and establishing human rights standards under the EU Charter of Rights'[142] is necessary to ensure the tripartite relationship between national law, EU law and the Charter is firmly and expressly grounded in the CJEU's interpretative approach.

[141] De Burca, n 22 at p.184.
[142] De Burca, n 22 at p.185.

13

Concluding Remarks

SONIA MORANO-FOADI AND LUCY VICKERS

THE AIM OF this volume was to analyse the new architecture of Europe after the Lisbon Treaty including some reflections on the accession of the European Union (EU) to the European Convention on Human Rights (ECHR). The contributors have considered both the legal and political complexities of the whole accession process, in terms of the internal rules relating to accession and the urgent need for certainty and coherence of approach when it comes to protecting fundamental rights of EU citizens and individuals legally residing in Europe. The approach adopted has been to explore these issues from the point of view of practitioners, judges, and European policy makers as well as members of the scholarly community. This has enabled a wide range of perspectives to be drawn upon, and has facilitated an interdisciplinary approach to be taken to exploring the political and legal dynamics of accession.

In addition to a review of the accession process, including the final rejection of the accession agreement in December 2014, from both practitioner and academic viewpoints, the volume has undertaken a contextual analysis of areas of law which are likely to be affected by interaction of the jurisprudence of the Court of Justice of the European Union (CJEU) and the European Court of Human Rights (ECtHR) in protecting fundamental rights when accession eventually occurs. The areas covered are equality rights in employment law, citizenship and migration, internet law, access to justice and judicial cooperation in civil and commercial matters.

The chapters in this volume have raised a number of recurring questions relating to the future relationship between the two Courts. What has been seen is broadly a shift by the CJEU from a more conservative approach to the protection of rights towards something more progressive. What remains to be seen is how precisely the future interaction of the Courts will occur, following any eventual accession, with a number of questions being raised regarding which Court will take precedence when it comes to resolving any conflicts between their respective approaches to overlapping areas of competence.

The chapters have also debated the relative benefits of precedence being given to the approach of either one of the two Courts. Thus, Loenen and Vickers warned of the danger that strong EU protection for fundamental rights relating to gender might be diluted as a result of the process of legal integration with the narrower human rights protection for religious freedom. In contrast, Wintemute welcomed the integration of the two systems as a way in which the EU may be encouraged to be bolder in its protection for fundamental rights. Pollicino also suggested that dialogue between the two Courts has constituted a valuable way to develop the case law on freedom of expression as it relates to the internet. Morano-Foadi found that the 'dialogue' works well in the specific field of migration and human rights as suggested by empirical research and the two Courts' case law

As shown in the chapters, even without accession the Courts already enjoy a significant amount of interaction and with mixed results as far as the improvement of fundamental rights protection was concerned. In these cases, the relationship between the two Courts could be understood as one based on reciprocal balancing between social and economic rights, where neither set of interests take precedence. After any future accession, this process will need to be further developed, in order to achieve consistency and coherence of approach, as well as to achieve procedural certainty. Thus, the two European legal systems will have to develop a parallel form of dialogue to that which already exists between member states and the EU and ECHR respectively.[1] The process by which this may occur is discussed by Velluti and Morano-Foadi in their respective chapters.

In addition to exploring the interaction of the jurisprudence of the two Courts, this volume has considered a number of questions relating to the practical and procedural workings of the deliberative process that has been suggested as the way forward. Evidence from an empirical survey of judges from both Courts, as illustrated by Andreadakis in his chapter, suggests that there is no clear consensus on how the two Courts are likely to work together in practice to develop a coherent system of protection across the two jurisdictions following any future accession. Examples can be found of how the ECtHR is already acting as an enforcer within the realm of EU law.[2] However, the discussions in the chapters of this volume have shown that much work will need to be done to finalise procedural arrangements if accession is to occur.

In terms of ways forward, two options have been identified in the volume. One is for a pluralistic vision of Europe where the two complex and multifaceted European entities grow alongside each other without paying particular attention to each other, having a separate scope and adopting diverging tools. The danger of such an approach is that it will slow down the integration process moving towards a more intergovernmentalist view of Europe. This seems to be the approach that has to be taken following the decision of the CJEU to reject the current accession agreement.

An alternative option might be possible following accession, a model which would be a monist (quasi) federal model based on an umbrella of judicial, institutional and informal dialogues between the two Courts in the field of human

[1] Discussed in C Sabel and O Gerstenberg, 'Constitutionalising an Overlapping Consensus: The ECJ and the Emergence of a Coordinate Constitutional Order' (2010) 16 *European Law Journal* 511.

[2] *Dhahbi* v *Italy* App no 17120/90 (ECtHR, 8 April 2014).

rights by placing the ECtHR at the apex of the hierarchy.[3] Such an approach would ensure the smoothest functioning of the two systems post-accession, and would avoid conflicts and different interpretations by placing fundamental rights on a single consistent foundation throughout the EU. Such a theory is reinforced by the mechanisms contained within the Accession Agreement, discussed in the chapters of this volume, to allow for an internal review by the CJEU and an external review by ECtHR. However, although contributors to the volume may well have preferred this option, the rejection of the Accession Agreement by the CJEU in December 2014 means that achievement of this goal has been put on hold for the time being.

Questions on the future of fundamental rights in Europe have been recurring throughout the chapters in this collection. The answers to most of them will depend on the role taken by the Courts and in particular the CJEU following the decision to continue for now without accession. Integration may still be advanced if the CJEU shifts towards a more progressive and creative jurisprudence in enhancing fundamental rights.

Although, it is currently too early to be able to conclude that the legal and judicial frameworks of the EU and the Council of Europe equally and comprehensively address fundamental rights in a conceptually robust and integrated fashion, the prospect for the future does still hold some promise. Yet, as a whole this promise remains vulnerable, unless all actors involved in the process, EU and Council of Europe's officials, the European judiciary and member states persevere in their commitment to the overarching human rights project. We hope that the chapters in this collection can contribute to this process.

[3] For further discussion, see S Morano-Foadi and S Andreadakis, Report on the Protection of Fundamental Rights in Europe—A Reflection on the Relationship between the Court of Justice of the European Union and the European Court of Human Rights post Lisbon, July 2014, available at http://www.coe.int/en/web/dlapil/news-dlapil; S Morano-Foadi 'Fundamental Rights in Europe: "Constitutional" Dialogue between the Court of Justice of the EU and the European Court of Human Rights' (2013) 5 *Oñati Journal of Emergent Socio-legal Studies* 64–88.

Index

*NB—page numbers in **bold** indicate references to tables.*

www.ingramcontent.com/pod-product-compliance
Ingram Content Group UK Ltd.
Pitfield, Milton Keynes, MK11 3LW, UK
UKHW020136290926
15471UKWH00003B/524

9 781509 915477